方显廷文集

第 4 卷

方显廷 著

商务印书馆
2015 年·北京

《方显廷文集》编辑委员会委员

主　编：厉以宁　熊性美

副主编：方惟琳

编　委：穆家修　常绍民　叶　坦　纪　辛
　　　　张世荣　方露茜　方菊龄(Julie Thomas)
　　　　方　郁　魏　玥　关永强

方显廷

(1903—1985)

1929—1937年在经济研究所任教时所摄

1937年方显廷先生全家福
左起：方显廷、方素芬、方惟琳、夏菊美、方菊龄、王静英、方露茜

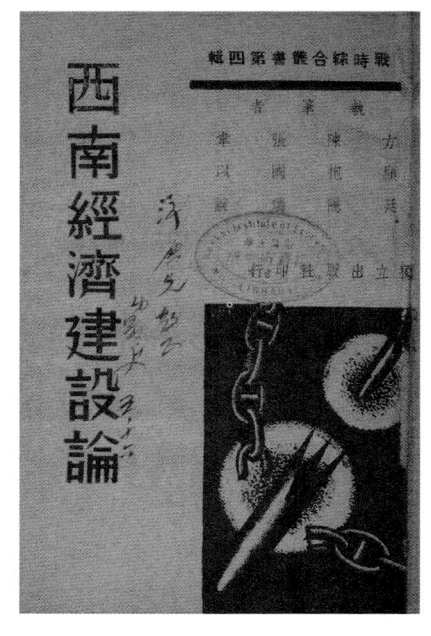

本卷所收录的方显廷先生
部分著述文章书影之一（南开大学图书馆藏）

本卷所收录的方显廷先生
部分著述文章书影之二（南开大学图书馆藏）

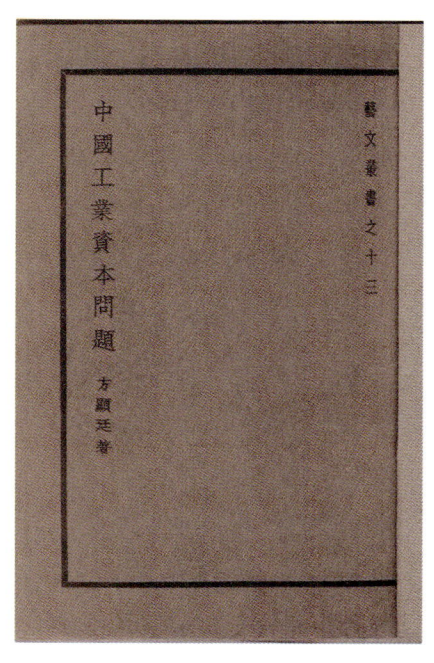

本卷所收录的方显廷先生
部分著述文章书影之三（南开大学图书馆藏）

本卷所收录的方显廷先生
部分著述文章书影之四（南开大学图书馆藏）

本卷所收录的方显廷先生
部分著述文章书影之五（南开大学图书馆藏）

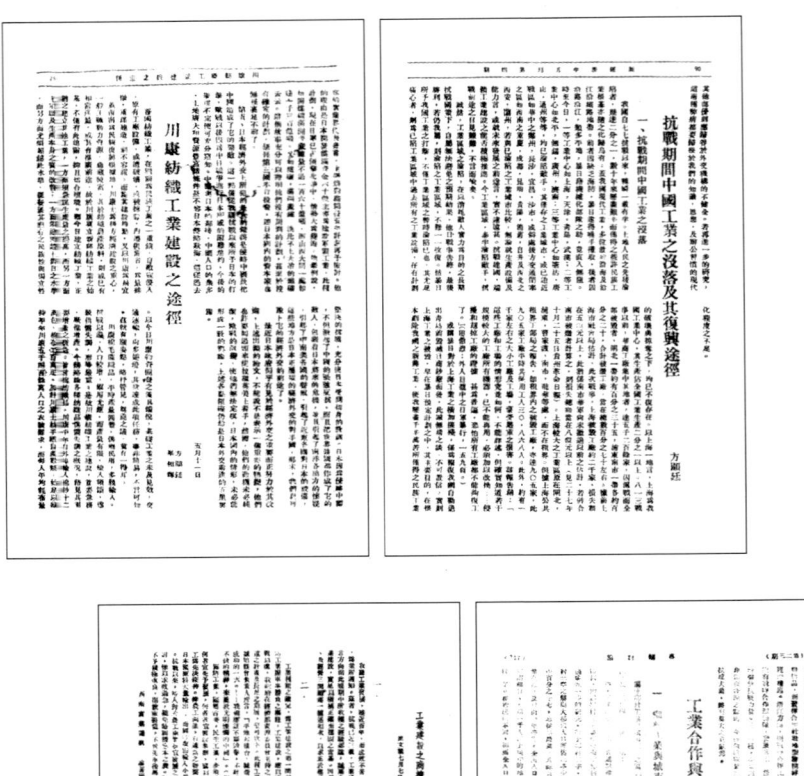

本卷所收录的方显廷先生
部分著述文章书影之六（南开大学图书馆藏）

总　　序

厉以宁

我是1951年9月进入北京大学经济系的,1955年毕业,毕业后留校工作至今。陈振汉先生是我的老师,也是我研究经济史的领路人。从1951年我进入北大到2008年陈振汉先生逝世,我们作为师生和同事相处了58年之久。陈振汉先生毕业于南开大学经济系,方显廷先生长期执教于南开大学,是陈振汉先生的老师。

我没有见过方显廷先生,但我不仅从陈振汉先生那里了解到南开大学经济研究所和方显廷先生的学术成就,而且也了解到方显廷先生的人品和治学态度,使我很早就对方显廷先生十分仰慕。商务印书馆在2006年出版《方显廷回忆录》之后,立即准备出版6卷本的《方显廷文集》,原来是请陈振汉先生撰写序言的,但陈振汉先生这时已卧病在家(2006年他94岁高龄了),他嘱咐我代为执笔,我应允了。这篇序言,既可表达我对方显廷先生这样一位学术界前辈的崇敬与仰慕,又可作为我对我的老师陈振汉先生的纪念与追思。

方显廷先生的早年生活是很艰苦的。据他在回忆录(商务印书馆2006年出版)中的记述,他原籍浙江宁波,1906年他3岁时家里遭了一场大火,一切尽化为灰烬。1910年他7岁时,父亲病故,家业衰败。他在家乡只受过初等教育。14岁那年(1917年)经亲戚介绍来到上海厚生纱厂当了学徒。厚生纱厂的经理是著名民族企业家穆藕初先生,他同时也是学徒们的师傅。由于方显廷先生刻苦学习英语,英语程度较高,所以只做了半年学徒,就被调到办公室工作。他工作出色,得到穆藕初先生赏识。1921年,方显廷先生18岁,在穆藕初先生资助下,赴美国继续学习,先后在美国威斯康辛大学读预科,在纽约大学读完本科,获学士学位,再进入耶鲁大学攻读经济学,1928年获哲学博士学位。这一年他25岁。第二年(1929年)他回国任教于南开大学。陈振汉先生是1931年考进南开大学经济系,1935年毕业的,在这段时间内受业于方显廷先生。

  陈振汉先生多次和我谈起,方显廷先生的治学方法有着明显的特点,可以归结为经济理论、经济史研究、统计学三者并重和交融。经济理论被认为是经济研究的基础,如果经济理论缺乏深厚的功底,研究难以深入,更难以有新的见解。经济史研究,是指研究者应当具备广博的经济史知识,因为现实经济中的重大问题绝不是凭空出现的,总有其历史的渊源以及其产生、发展、演变的过程。脱离历史背景去进行研究,往往难以认清规律,难以作出清晰的判断。而统计学,则被认为是一种必不可少的方法论基础,如果不能运用科学的统计方法,结论通常是缺乏依据的,或者会误导研究者得出错误的结论。陈振汉先生自称他在治学方法上受到了方显廷先生的影响,所以多年来一直强调把经济理论、经济史研究和统计学三者结合在一起的必要性。陈振汉先生还说,这也是南开大学经济系和南开大学经济研究所多年坚持的治学方法。从方显廷先生的著作中,我们可以处处看到经济理论、经济史研究和统计学三者的融合。

方显廷在纽约大学和耶鲁大学学习期间,受过严格的西方经济学训练,功底十分深厚。他在耶鲁大学的博士论文,题为《英格兰工厂制度之胜利》,赢得了国外学术界的好评。据方显廷先生在回忆录中所述,十九世纪中期前后的英国工厂组织,传统的分类方法是按照个体手工工匠、家庭作坊制和工厂制度来划分的,而方显廷先生在博士论文中则按照另一种划分方法,即按照手工艺人、商人雇主和工厂制度分类,这种分类主要突出了商人雇主在工业化初期的作用,工厂制度的胜利实际上也就是工厂组织取代商人雇主制度的胜利。① 这篇博士论文不仅可以看成是工业经济史研究的成果,而且也可以看成是企业组织理论的一项突破。

方显廷先生回国以后,除了对欧洲经济史继续进行研究以外,他的主要研究领域转入了中国近代工业史和中国近代地区经济发展史。在这次出版的6卷本的《方显廷文集》中,至少有一半以上的内容是中国近代工业史和中国近代地区经济发展史方面的著作。1934年由国立编译馆出版的《中国之棉纺织业》,是方显廷先生的力作,也是第一本对中国棉纺织业进行系统研究的学术著作,资料翔实,分析透彻,尤其是在该书中专门论及中国棉纺织业发展中所遇到的阻力以及今后的发展前途等章节,反映了方显廷先生对国民经济中这一重要产业的远见卓识。

在有关中国近代地区发展史方面,方显廷先生由于长期执教于南开大学,所以把华北地区的经济发展作为研究重点。他所撰

---

① 参看方显廷著,方露茜译:《方显廷回忆录》,商务印书馆2006年版,第47、135页。

写的《天津地毯工业》、《天津织布工业》、《天津针织工业》、《天津棉花运销概况》、《华北乡村织布工业与商人雇主制度》等，都是在广泛社会经济调查的基础上完成的。方显廷先生在回忆录中写道："我发现为三、四年级学生讲授好3小时的经济史课程不难，但是要充分准备一份关于天津地毯工业的报告却需要投入大量的时间。"①尽管这项研究在方显廷先生从事之前已由南开大学的其他研究人员做过，方显廷先生认为："但是所收集到的情况完全不够充分。我不得不多少重新开始这一工作。首先，对这一工业进行概括的了解；然后，到天津不同地区亲自去参观那些用手工编织地毯的作坊。"②正因为有了详细而认真的调查，才完成了《天津地毯工业》这样一本专著（1929年出版）。

对于华北的乡村工业发展，方显廷先生选择了河北省高阳的织布业作为研究对象，题目定为《华北乡村织布工业与商人雇主制度》。这是同方显廷先生的博士论文《英格兰工厂制度之胜利》有相当密切的联系的，因为正如前面已经提到的，在那篇博士论文中，方显廷先生用商人雇主制度作为工业化初期的分类形式之一代替了传统的分类方法中的家庭作坊制。商人雇主制度使工业化初期的商人雇主的作用更加突出，反映了商人资本在活跃城乡经济和以供给工具和原料、订货和包销等手段成为乡村工业的实际控制者，从而说明了华北地区的乡村工业距工厂制度的建立还存在一定的差距。

在方显廷先生的经济研究中还有一个重要领域，这就是对抗

---

① 方显廷著，方露茜译：《方显廷回忆录》，第71页。
② 同上。

日战争胜利之后中国经济建设途径的探讨。方显廷先生早就认为日本必败,中国必胜,对前途充满信心。1941年至1943年,他受美国洛克菲勒基金会的邀请,到美国进行访问,访问期间先在哈佛进行研究,半年后去华盛顿的战时经济委员会(后改称国外经济管理局,以后又改称国外开发总署)做研究工作。据方显廷先生在回忆录中所述,这是一个庞大的组织,拥有好几百名雇员,其中包括一些专家,调查分析研究亚洲国家经济状况。战后中国经济如何重建,是该组织研究项目之一。① 在这期间,即1943年12月4日至14日,方显廷先生由美国去加拿大魁北克参加太平洋国际学会第八届会议。与会者有来自美国、英国、苏联、荷兰、加拿大、澳大利亚、中国、印度和泰国的150位代表。② 这次会议对中国在过去六年来(1937—1943)抵抗日寇侵略战争之举表达敬佩之意,会议一致同意有必要废除自鸦片战争以来中国同西方列强签署的不平等条约,一致赞成将台湾归还中国,允许朝鲜独立,惩罚日本战争罪犯,解除日本武装并支付战争赔款等。③

关于抗日战争结束后中国的经济重建问题,方显廷的经济观点和政策建议,见于文集的第3卷(《中国战后经济问题研究》等)、第5卷(《现代中国的经济研究》、《中国经济危机及其挽救途径》、《胜利后的中国经济》等)。他的基本思路依然是中国必须早日实现工业化。20世纪30年代他是这样主张的,20世纪40年代后半期他仍坚持这一观点。

---

① 参看方显廷著,方露茜译:《方显廷回忆录》,第138—139页。
② 同上书,第141页。
③ 同上。

把凯恩斯经济学介绍给中国学术界，是方显廷先生20世纪40年代的贡献之一。这同他自1939年起在南开大学经济研究所主持工作和1941年在哈佛大学进行访问、研究有关。凯恩斯的代表作《就业、利息和货币通论》出版于1936年2月。凯恩斯在这部著作中系统阐述了自己的宏观经济学理论，对西方国家的经济政策的制定有着深远的影响。西方经济学界普遍认为这是一场"凯恩斯革命"，但又是双重意义上的"凯恩斯革命"，即一方面是经济理论的革命（以有效需求不足理论代替了新古典经济学的均衡论），另一方面是政策意义上的革命（以国家对经济调节的政策代替传统的政府不干预经济的政策）。① 方显廷先生抗战期间在重庆南开大学经济研究所主持工作，他在回忆录中写道："研究所之所以将培训研究生的方向选定为经济理论和货币问题，是受到1936年2月英国经济学家凯恩斯议员出版《货币通论》之后兴起的'凯恩斯革命'的影响。"② 稍后，方显廷先生到了美国，他在哈佛大学进行访问和研究时，同一些美国经济学家接触，更深入地了解到"凯恩斯革命"的影响。他在美国设法为研究所通过海运，并通过滇缅通道运来一批关于"凯恩斯革命"的最新书籍。20世纪40至50年代，南开大学能成为国内在研究当代西方经济学方面处于前列的高等学府之一，同方显廷先生的功绩是分不开的。

1947年，方显廷先生应联合国的聘请，在联合国及亚洲远东经济委员会（ECAFE）工作，任调查研究室主任，具体任务是研究亚洲及远

---

① 参看厉以宁：《宏观经济学的产生和发展》，湖南出版社1977年版，第109—119页。

② 方显廷著，方露茜译：《方显廷回忆录》，商务印书馆2006年版，第111页。

东地区各国的经济状况和发展趋势,编辑《亚洲及远东经济年鉴》。该委员会原在上海,1949年1月迁往曼谷,那年方显廷先生46岁。1964年他61岁时从联合国机构退休。但紧接着又担任了亚洲经济发展及计划研究院副院长。这是一个由联合国开发计划署主要提供资金的、以研究亚洲经济发展和培训亚洲及远东地区各国企业家、银行家和政府官员为宗旨的机构。方显廷先生在这里工作一年后便离去,过着自己向往的清闲退休生活。但不久他又被聘为新加坡南洋大学客座教授,1971年再度退休,从此去瑞士定居,安度晚年。

从1947年进入联合国机构工作起,到1971年自新加坡南洋大学退休为止,将近25年的国外生活,使方显廷先生的研究方向发生了一个转折,即从专心致志研究中国工业化转而关注东南亚经济发展。在这些年内,他撰写了一些有关东南亚国家的经济发展的文章,收集到这部文集的有:《太平洋各国经济问题》、《新加坡的小型工业》、《新加坡经济发展的策略》、《亚洲及远东地区工业品出口的发展》等。但他更多的精力和时间放在编辑历年的《亚洲及远东经济年鉴》之上。这套年鉴很有价值,它见证了这一地区的发展中国家在第二次世界大战结束后是如何一步步从衰退趋于复苏,再迈向成长和繁荣的。

方显廷先生是一位爱国者。即使他在联合国机构中工作多年,后来又在新加坡南洋大学任教,但他始终忘不了祖国的工业化,忘不了祖国大陆的经济建设。据方显廷先生在回忆录中所述,《亚洲及远东经济年鉴》的内容自1953年起有所改动,即"《年鉴》对于中国大陆的发展给予更为透彻的报导"。[①] 此外,1953年11月出版的《亚洲

[①] 方显廷著,方露茜译:《方显廷回忆录》,商务印书馆2006年版,第175页。

及远东经济季刊》(这是联合国亚洲及远东经济委员会下设的刊物,创刊于1950年)上,发表了方显廷先生撰写的《1949—1953年中国大陆的经济发展》一文,引起了国外经济界的注意。方显廷先生在这篇文章中引用了中国政府公布的许多数字,他用这些数字说明中国经济恢复的速度是惊人的。文章中写道:"生产的恢复受益于多种因素,而其中最为重要的一个,无疑是和平与秩序的恢复。"①文章还肯定了中华人民共和国成立初期制度变革的积极作用:"毋庸置疑,制度的改变对于自1949年以来经济的恢复也是一个重要方面,因而关于在过去几年过程中,中国经济框架的改变对生产的恢复起到了一定作用这一判断应当是中肯的。"②

6卷本的《方显廷文集》出版了。这里记录下方显廷先生一生的主要论著。国内人士尽管过去对方显廷先生的学术贡献了解得不多,但我深信,历史是公平的、公正的,只要认真阅读了《方显廷文集》中各个时期的著述,就一定会了解方显廷先生为人处世的原则、他的治学方法、他的学术成就,以及他在经济学和经济史领域所作出的贡献。

2009年6月2日于北京大学光华管理学院

---

① 方显廷:《1949—1953年中国大陆的经济发展》,"引言",载联合国《亚洲及远东经济季刊》,1953年11月;另见方显廷著,方露茜译:《方显廷回忆录》,第286页。

② 方显廷著,方露茜译:《方显廷回忆录》,第286页。

本卷序言
——方显廷乡村工业化思想浅析

熊性美 关永强

在第二卷序言中,我们曾经对方显廷先生的乡村工业化研究进行过简要介绍;而第三和第四卷集中选取了他在这一领域的多篇重要论著,因此,我们这里再作几点补充说明,以期抛砖引玉,引起学界对这一问题更多的关注与思考。

在近现代中国,关注和研究乡村工业的学者很多,而方显廷与其他学者的一个主要的不同之处在于,他不仅是从救济农村出发而关注乡村工业,而且还以经济学家的视角,从实现中国工业化的途径这一角度来强调乡村工业的意义。

早在1928年研究英格兰工业化进程的博士论文中,方显廷就曾经提出用"商人雇主制"取代学界原来使用的"家庭生产制"来描述英国乡村工业,并被学术界所广泛接受。他在1930年代对中国乡村工业组织制度的深入研究,就体现了这一思想的进一步发展与中国化;而后来在1970年代曾盛行于西方经济史学界的原工业化理论①可能与此也有着某种渊源关系。

作为一位深受历史（制度）学派影响的经济学家，方显廷清晰地认识到，中国的经济发展水平和政治、社会、文化背景都与西方有着巨大的差异，因此也就不能简单地模仿西方的工业化过程，而应从自身的经济社会条件出发，寻求一条更适合本国国情的发展道路。他对近代中国的要素条件、制度环境和市场情况都进行了详细地考察，认为发展重工业所需要的各种原材料、巨额资本和熟练劳动者，在当时的中国都不具备，传统社会文化也不利于大机器工业的发展，而乡村工业的发展却并不依赖于这些要素条件，也更加适应中国的传统社会结构；与此同时，国际市场已经被发达国家的大企业所掌控，而以小农为主体、占全国人口四分之三以上的内地地方性市场（特别是基层市场），却由于交通闭塞、运费高昂和农民收入水平低下，不易被机制工业品占领，也正适合乡村工业去争取。

方显廷还结合欧洲与美国的工业发展史，指出工业化并不一定必须经历大工厂的集中化阶段才能实现，而机器大工业的过度发展会给传统社会带来很多危害，20世纪初的欧美国家就已经出现很多有关工业分散化的主张，因此中国无须再走欧美工业那种先集中于

---

① 原工业化(proto-industrialization)理论认为16—18世纪欧洲的乡村工业是一种经由商人雇主为外地市场生产而非服务于本地消费的工业模式，它不仅推动了市场经济的发展，而且改变了欧洲的家庭结构和生育机制，推动了新型商业市镇的兴起，从而为工业革命提供了重要的准备，因而将其视为工业革命的先导或工业化进程的早期阶段，称之为"原工业"。这种观点存在着很多问题和不足，也不足以解释工业革命的渊源，但对于理解欧洲经济发展史具有重要的启发意义，在1970-1980年代引起了很多学者的重视。这里只是指出，该理论与方显廷关于乡村工业的商人雇主制等思想之间存在着很多相通之处。关于原工业化理论的一个较好的综述，可参见 L. A. Clarkson, Proto-industrialization: *the First Phase of Industrialization*? MacMillan, 1985.

城市、再分散到乡村的路径,而可以直接以乡村工业为基础来实现中国的工业化,乡村工业以家庭为生产单位和兼业的生产方式,还有助于舒缓经济波动的冲击,减少工业化对传统社会生活带来的负面影响。美国学者曾玛莉(Margherita Zanasi)甚至认为,这些主张体现了方显廷希望通过发展乡村工业来阻止经济全球化浪潮对中国经济和社会肌体侵蚀的民族主义者的一面,以及他对个体自由主义经济的不信任和经济统制论者的倾向①。

为了找到适合中国乡村工业发展的具体道路和方式,方显廷在1930年代领导南开大学经济研究所的师生对华北和浙江等地进行了大量实地调查,并对全国各地的各类乡村工业研究资料进行了全面的疏理,详细地分析了中国乡村工业的组织制度、经营状况和所面临的外部挑战与内部问题。

他清楚地意识到,在外国大机器工业的竞争下,中国乡村工业正处于急剧衰落之中,而乡村工业在规模上的劣势也无法得以根本克服。但他从技术和组织两方面为中国的乡村工业找到了发展的方向和成功的希望:在技术方面,以高阳铁轮机为代表的这种人与机器结合的机械发明,有利于工业分散化的发展和吸纳乡村就业,因此可以

---

① 曾玛莉认为,方显廷认识到机器大工业带来的集中化和专业化会导致劳动者与产品和价值之间的疏离,割裂劳动者与传统社会群体之间的关系,而乡村工业则可以让劳动者明了商品制造与应用中的全部关系,"使一个人的工作,不但与他一人的生命有关系,同时与他所处的社会也发生关系",发展乡村工业可以避免大量人口向城市集中,从而抑制经济全球化浪潮对中国传统经济与社会肌体的侵蚀。此外,方显廷还在论著中表达了对自由放任的个体主义经济发展模式的不信任,积极主张由政府推行统制经济政策,主导合作运动以取代乡村工业中的商人雇主制,曾玛莉将其归纳为方显廷的经济统制论(或国家主义,Statist)倾向,详见 Margherita Zanasi, Far from the Treaty Ports: "Fang Xianting and the Idea of Rural Modernity in 1930s China", *Modern China*, Vol. 30, No. 1 (Jan., 2004), pp. 113-146.

通过加强调查和聘请工程师、成立工业试验所的方法,大力推进这类技术的发明和传播①;在组织方面,方显廷主张以政府主导的合作组织取代商人雇主制度,通过各类合作组织来保护劳工,同时促进手工业者加强在资金、原材料采购和产品销售上的相互扶持,提高市场议价和抵御市场波动的能力。

最后,我们需要再次指出,乡村工业化思想作为方显廷基于当时中国客观条件而做出的判断,是他工业化思想体系的一个重要组成部分,但并非全部。方显廷领导南开大学经济研究所开展中国工业化调查研究之际,正值日本帝国主义势力对华北虎视眈眈之时,他深知发展重工业特别是国防工业的重要性,并曾在抗战爆发前撰文指出,中国过去的工业资本投资忽视了国防工业的建立,今后应由政府大力筹集资金、外汇,通过统制经济的方式创办和发展国防军事工业。

而且,我们在文集中还会看到,方显廷对钢铁、水泥等重工业和机器纺织工业也都进行过深入研究,在后来为战后中国制订的工业化方案中,他也主张大力引进外国资金和技术来发展中国的矿冶、制造和交通、通讯等现代工业。这些我们曾在第二卷序言中进行过介绍,这里就不赘述了。

---

① 值得一提的是,近年来,以杉原薰为代表的一些日本经济史学者正在强调这种东亚劳动力密集型发展模式的重要意义及其与西方的差异,认为东亚国家在工业化的过程中混合了传统的劳动力密集型技术和西方的机器动力技术,走出了一条人与机器相结合的发展道路,与西方的资本密集型发展模式相比,这种劳动力密集型发展模式较少使用机器和资本、而更多注重劳动力和人力资源,更有助于节约资源和缩小收入差距。感兴趣的读者可以参见乔万尼·阿里吉、滨下武志、马克·塞尔登主编,马援译,《东亚的复兴:以500年、150年和50年为视角》,社科文献出版社,2006年,第96—152页;Gareth Austin, Kaoru Sugihara (eds.), *Labour-intensive Industrialization in Global History*, Routledge, 2013.

本卷说明

本卷收录了方显廷先生著述 19 种,分为五编。

第一编中国工业概论:《中国工业化之程度及其影响》,何廉、方显廷著,实业部工商访问局 1929 年出版;《中国工业化之统计的分析》,刊载于南开大学《经济统计季刊》第 1 卷第 1 期,1932 年;《吾人对于工业化应有之认识》,刊载于方显廷编《中国经济研究》下册,商务印书馆 1938 年版;"Industrial Organization in China",刊载于 Nankai Social and Economic Quarterly, Vol. IX, No. 4., January, 1937,无中文版;《中国工业资本问题》,商务印书馆 1939 年版。

第二编中国工业化与乡村工业:《中国之乡村工业》,方显廷、吴知著,刊载于《经济统计季刊》第 2 卷第 3 期,1933 年;《乡村工业与中国经济建设》,刊载于《南大半月刊》1934 年第 13—14 期;《中国之工业化与乡村工业》,原载《大公报·经济周刊》,1936 年 5 月 20 日,后转载于方显廷编《中国经济研究》下册,商务印书馆 1938 年版。

第三编部门工业概览:《我国钢铁工业之鸟瞰》,方显廷、谷源田著;《中国水泥工业之鸟瞰》,方显廷、谷源田著,两文均刊载于方显廷编《中国经济研究》下册,商务印书馆 1938 年版。

第四编中国区域与战时工业论丛:《西南经济建设与工业化》,刊载于《新经济》半月刊,1938 年第 1 卷第 2 期;《抗战期间中国工业之没落及其复兴途径》,刊载于《新经济》半月刊,1939 年第 1 卷第 4 期;《中国小工业之衰落及其复兴途径》,刊载于《经济动员》1939 年第 2 卷第 3 期;《川康纺织工业建设之途径》,方显廷、毕相辉著,刊载于《新经济》半月刊,1940 年第 3 卷第 11 期;《论农业与工业之关系》,刊载于《西南实业通讯》1940 年第 1 卷第 3 期;《论工业建设》,刊载于方显廷编《战时中国经济研究》,商务印书馆 1941 年版;《工业建设之商榷》,刊载于《西南实业通讯》1940 年第 2 卷第 2 期;《中国工业上的几个问题》,方显廷讲,顾浚泉记,刊载于《西南实业通讯》1941 年第 4 卷第 5—6 期。

第五编工业文献及述评:《中国之工业讲义大纲》,方显廷、谷源田合编,南开大学经济学院 1934 年 1 月印行。

本卷收录的方显廷中英文版著作,均经方显廷先生手订,本次出版,除将繁体字转为简体,并修订明显讹误外,译名(人名、地名)、术语、数字用法与今不一致者,均一仍如旧。个别因原件不清无法辨识的字用"□"代替。

深切怀念主编熊性美教授和编委张世荣先生。他们为《方显廷文集》耗尽了自己最后一丝精力。

《方显廷文集》编辑委员会

目 录

第一编 中国工业概论

中国工业化之程度及其影响 ·················· 何　廉　方显廷　3
中国工业化之统计的分析 ································ 51
吾人对于工业化应有之认识 ······························· 99
INDUSTRIAL ORGANIZATION IN CHINA ····················· 109
中国工业资本问题 ····································· 233

第二编 中国工业化与乡村工业

中国之乡村工业 ······················· 方显廷　吴　知　293
乡村工业与中国经济建设 ································ 359
中国之工业化与乡村工业 ································ 371

第三编 部门工业概览

我国钢铁工业之鸟瞰 ··················· 方显廷　谷源田　393
中国水泥工业之鸟瞰 ··················· 方显廷　谷源田　413

第四编　中国区域与战时工业论丛

西南经济建设与工业化 ··· 429
抗战期间中国工业之没落及其复兴途径 ································ 443
中匡小工业之衰落及其复兴途径 ······································· 459
川康纺织工业建设之途径 ····················· 方显廷　毕相辉　473
论农业与工业之关系 ··· 481
论工业建设 ··· 487
工业建设之商榷 ·· 495
中匡工业上的几个问题 ··················· 方显廷 讲　顾浚泉 记　503

第五编　工业文献及述评

中匡之工业讲义大纲 ····················· 方显廷 谷源田　合编　513

第一编
中国工业概论

中国工业化之程度及其影响

何 廉　方显廷

---

① 何廉、方显廷：《中国工业化之程度及影响》，实业部工商访问局，1929年。

（一）绪论。—A 工业化之定义—B 工业化与其他经济蜕变之关系。一、国外贸易之增进。二、运输业之发展。三、银行与公司之兴起。四、工商业中心城镇之拓张。

（二）中国工业化之程度。—A 工厂（一九一二至一九二〇年）一、工厂统计。二、工厂工人。—B 各业工人之分配。—C 工厂规模之比较。—D 实例择要。一、棉纺织工业。二、缫丝工业。三、面粉工业。四、榨油工业。五、火柴工业。六、电气工业。

（三）中国工业化之影响。—A 工厂制度之发达。—B 劳动问题之兴起。—C 罢工之骤增。—D 童工与女工之引用。—E 国外贸易与贸易政策之改变。—F 技术专家之亟需。—G 天然富源之开采。

（四）结论。

（一）绪论

中国之近代工业化，久已引起中外经济学者之注意，尤以欧战后为甚。其论述之者，往往引用工业化一词以指中国受西方文明之影响，因而突起之经济蜕变。依此而论，工业化一词，与工业革命一词有同一之含意。西人用此词，率有广狭二义之分。在"英国工业革命一语中"，工业化之意，系包括制造业、农业、商业、运输业之革命言，所谓广义是也。今之经济学者，尚有沿用之者。然普通一般经济学者用此词时，仅指制造业之革命，所谓狭义是也。本文即采用该词之狭义。所谓工业化者，专指因机器之助，用雄厚之资本，以实行大规模生产之制造业而言者也，至于农业、商业、运输业，以及其他一切之经济蜕变，悉不在该词定义之内。虽间有论及，亦不过为阐明本题之便利计耳。

工业化与其他经济蜕变之关系——工业化之定义既如上述，则其为中国各种经济蜕变中之一种，自不待言；中国之经济蜕变，不仅限于制造业一业之变化，其余如商业、交通、以及金融财政，莫不有同一现象；不徒其变化同时俱来，即彼此变化之程度，亦有一定之关系。一业之蜕变，与其他各业，莫不有直接间接之重大影响。换言之,每一业变化之程度,即可视为其他各业变化之指数。兹为研究工业化之程度计,特先说明商业、交通、以及金融财政发达之情况。近年来中国商业之进步,亦甚可惊,惜国内贸易每年之额数,迄今尚无统计;惟国外贸易之额数,有海关所制之统计,可供研究之用。海关之贸易统计,起于一八六四年。自此年始而至现在,每年均有统计。从下列之表中,可以看出自一八六四年至一八九〇年之期间,国外贸易总额增加二倍有半;从一八九〇年至一九一五年之期间,增加四倍;从一九一五年至一九二七年之期间,又增加二倍;从一八九〇年至一九一五年二十五年间之四倍增加,与中国棉纺绩业、缫丝业,以及钢铁等工业之进步,正彼此相应。自一九一五年至一九二七年十二年间之二倍增加,一方面既可证明中国因受之激动,与外来制成品短缺之故,工业上致有急剧之进步,他方面亦可证明此次国外贸易额之增加,与自一八九〇年至一九一五年之增加为相似之事实。

第一表　中国国外贸易(1864—1927)

年	进口货(海关两)	出口货(海关两)	贸易总额(海关两)
1864	51,293,578	54,006,509	105,300,087
1865	61,844,158	60,054,634	121,898,792
1870	69,290,722	61,682,121	130,972,843
1875	67,803,247	68,912,929	136,716,176
1880	97,293,452	77,883,587	157,177,039
1885	88,200,018	65,005,711	153,205,729
1890	127,093,481	87,144,480	214,237,961
1895	171,696,715	143,293,211	314,989,926
1900	211,070,422	158,996,752	370,067,174
1905	447,100,791	227,888,197	674,988,988
1910	462,964,894	380,333,328	843,798,222

(续表)

年	进口货(海关两)	出口货(海关两)	贸易总额(海关两)
1915	454,475,719	418,861,164	873,336,883
1920	762,250,230	541,631,300	1,303,881,530
1921	906,122,439	601,255,531	1,507,377,970
1922	945,049,650	654,891,933	1,599,941,583
1923	923,402,887	752,917,416	1,676,320,303
1924	1,018,210,677	771,784,468	1,789,995,145
1925	947,864,944	776,352,937	1,724,217,881
1926	1,124,221,253	864,294,771	1,988,516,024
1927	1,012,931,624	918,619,662	1,931,551,286

交通之进步,亦为中国工业化之一象征。铁路之修筑及船舶之制造,莫不与日俱进。自铁路建筑之始,至一九二四年止,中国已筑之铁路共有一万五千三百又百分之十三基罗米突。其中七千七百零七又百分之六十五基罗米突为政府所有,一千五百十三又百分之六十六基罗米突为民有,六千零七十八又百分之八十二基罗米突为外人所办。此一万五千三百又百分之十三基罗米突铁路各省之分配见下表:

第二表　中国铁路各省之分配(1924)(基罗米突)

省名	铁路之类别			总长
	国有	民有	外人建筑	
黑龙江	—	28.73	930.00	958.73
吉林	123.61	64.00	2,362.13	2,549.74
辽宁	934.57	109.32	2,276.03	3,319.92
河北	1,669.25	260.68	—	1,929.93
察哈尔	194.74	—	—	194.74
绥远	200.86	—	—	200.86
山东	946.37	78.05	—	1,024.42
山西	342.98	—	—	342.98
江苏	677.09	22.98	—	700.07

（续表）

省名	铁路之类别			总长
	国有	民有	外人建筑	
安徽	280.62	38.61	—	319.23
河南	1,224.65	7.00	—	1,231.65
湖北	338.70	24.43	—	363.13
浙江	208.75	—	—	208.75
江西	34.20	128.14	—	162.34
湖南	311.04	—	—	311.04
福建	28.00	—	—	28.00
广东	192.22	583.09	46.66	821.97
云南	—	73.00	464.00	537.00
四川	—	95.63	—	95.63
干路与支路之总长	7,707.65	1,513.66	6,078.82	15,300.13

船舶运输上之功用虽较铁路为次，然在中国运输业中，亦居重要地位。自一八六四年起，各海口轮船帆船出入口之吨数，海关每年均有统计。在过去六十年中各海口轮船帆船出入口之总吨数，有十八倍之增加。海关起始编制船舶吨数统计在一八六四年，是年出入各海口之船舶总数为一万七千九百七十六只，其总吨数为六百六十三万五千五百零五吨。至一九二七年出入各海口之船舶总数增至十五万四千二百七十五只，其总吨数增至一亿一千六百二十一万零七百八十五吨。船舶总数及其吨数之大增，固足引吾人之注意，然轮船数目之逐渐增加，与帆船数目之日见减少，亦颇有研究之必要。在一八七五年时，轮船之吨数居总吨数百分之八十五，至一九二七年轮船之吨数增至总吨数百分之九十七。轮船营业果如是发达不已，数年或十数年之后，帆船在航业上之地位将完全为轮船替代矣。自一八六四年至一九二七年中国船舶吨数增加之详细情形，请看下表：

第三表 中国航业之吨量（1864—1927）

年	出入之轮船			出入之帆船			总数	
	只数	吨数	百分比	只数	吨数	百分比	只数	吨数
1864							17,976	6,635,505
1865							16,628	7,136,301
1870							14,136	6,907,828
1875	11,406	8,364,481	85	5,588	1,503,160	15	16,994	9,867,641
1880	17,300	14,572,718	92	5,670	1,301,634	8	22,970	15,874,352
1885	18,691	17,012,930	94	4,749	1,055,274	6	23,440	18,068,177
1890	25,838	23,928,557	96	5,295	947,902	4	31,133	24,876,459
1895	28,176	28,683,408	96	8,956	1,053,670	4	37,132	29,737,078
1900	57,576	39,555,768	97	11,654	1,251,474	3	69,230	40,807,242
1905	88,362	66,372,624	91	135,597	6,382,923	9	293,919	72,755,547
1910	96,196	82,337,331	93	123,614	6,439,358	7	219,810	88,776,689
1915	103,963	84,641,227	93	102,924	6,021,778	7	206,887	90,663,005
1920	121,338	99,642,210	96	89,271	4,624,485	4	210,609	104,266,695
1921	125,432	109,319,714	95	89,134	5,299,830	5	214,566	114,619,544
1922	123,401	119,354,968	96	63,027	4,776,393	4	186,428	124,131,361
1923	122,373	127,279,000	97	60,349	4,025,556	3	182,722	131,304,556
1924	132,213	136,829,598	97	54,169	4,603,229	3	186,382	141,432,827
1925	120,092	124,516,464	97	47,654	3,686,161	3	167,746	128,202,625
1926	117,319	132,249,431	98	41,677	2,410,175	2	158,996	134,659,606
1927	106,588	112,048,073	97	47,687	4,162,712	3	154,275	116,210,785

就中国之金融财政言,受工业化之影响而起显著之变化者,为银行之成立及各种公司之兴起。握中国昔日金融界之中枢者为钱庄银号,自工业化起始之后,其资既微,不足与银行竞争,信用制度亦远不如银行之便利,故其地位率为银行所取代,自一九一二至一九二○之九年间,前北京政府农商部曾编制钱业统计,但自一九二○年后即行停止;即农商部之统计。仅有前四年所编制者较为可靠,盖自一九一五年以后,中国内乱频仍。交通梗阻,许多省分不能以可靠之材料,供给农商部,故一九一六年至一九二○年五年间之钱业统计,殊欠详备。不徒钱业统计如是,即其他一切经济问题之统计材料,莫不陷于同一难境。然从农商部之统计中,可以探知一九一二至一九二○年间银行钱庄二者已投资数量之变迁。兹列表于下:

第四表　中国之银钱业投资（1912—1920）

年	钱庄(元)	百分比	银行(元)	百分比	总数(元)
1912	75,098,313	68	36,254,919	32	111,353,232
1913	86,628,664	76	27,301,526	24	113,930,190
1914	53,110,635	73	19,726,716	27	72,837,351
1915	64,463,021	82	14,136,426	18	78,599,447
1916	246,229,262	87	37,803,690	13	284,032,952
1917	171,457,373	78	46,072,611	22	217,529,984
1918	169,329,736	83	34,685,195	17	204,014,931
1919	37,448,536	41	54,247,711	59	91,696,247
1920	31,314,932	37	51,987,077	63	83,302,009

上表殊不完备。由此表所得,吾人对银行之发展,不能下一定之断语。但钱庄与银行投资数量比例之变化,则表现甚为明了。自一九一二至一九一六年间钱庄投资之数量,均远较银行投资为大;然自一九一六年以后,银行之投资渐增,钱庄之投资渐减,与以前变化之方向适相反对。至一九二〇年时,银行投资竟增至钱业投资总数百分之六十三。然银行资本数量之骤增或非由银行特别发达原因之所致。盖自一九一六年至一九二〇年间,国内发生内乱,十余省对中央无报告。有报告者或许为银行特别发达之省分,无报告者或许为银行不发达之省分。银行投资与钱庄投资比例骤增之现象,或亦由受内乱之间接影响。

新式公司之兴起,亦为中国经济蜕变中之一重要现象。近世工商业规模之繁巨,绝非旧式小规模之个人营业或合伙营业所能胜任。资本之数量既巨,投资之人数复增,必须更完更见复杂之组织以为经营之工具。依前农商部之调查,一九一二年时共有公司九百七十七家,其资本总额有一亿一千一百万元。无论商业、农业、制造业以及运输业,无不有新式公司之成立。一九一二至一九二〇年间,各业之资本数量莫不有一定比例之增进,其中制造业几占百分之六十至七十,运输业及商业则上下于百分之十至十五之间,农业亦在百分之五至十之间。

各公司之资本,大小不同,但资本在一万元以下者,为数最多。自一九一二至一九二〇年,此等公司居公司总数百分之三十五至五十,公司资本之自一万元至五万元者,占公司总数百分之二十五至三十,公司资本在五万元至十万元者,约居百分之十。从下列之表中,可见各业公司投资之数量。

第五表 中国各种公司之投资（1912—1920）

年	农业 以千元为单位	百分比	工业 以千元为单位	百分比	商业 以千元为单位	百分比	运输业 以千元为单位	百分比
1912	6,352	5	54,808	50	13,427	12	36,309	33
1913	6,010	7	49,875	58	7,696	9	22,783	26
1914	4,960	6	62,108	68	11,689	13	11,765	13
1915	6,241	4	106,901	67	17,958	11	30,390	18
1916	9,791	5	132,780	72	20,579	11	23,319	12
1917	10,663	6	128,244	67	22,347	11	30,341	16
1918	9,498	6	108,903	67	22,044	14	21,688	13
1919	12,469	6	129,221	67	24,092	13	21,723	12
1920	41,145	16	155,221	61	35,209	14	21,213	9

第六表 中国公司资本之比较（1912—1920）

资本 年	万元以下		万元至 五万元		五万至 十万元		十万元至 二十万元		二十万元至 五十万元		五十万元至 百万元		百万元 以上		总数
	数目	百分比	数目	百分比	数目	百分比	数目	百分比	数目	百分比	数目	百分比	数目	百分比	数目
1912	522	53	241	25	68	7	60	6	49	5	12	1	25	3	977
1913	501	50	294	29	68	7	55	6	42	4	17	2	16	2	993
1914	551	48	305	26	85	7	73	6	95	9	19	2	22	2	1,150
1915	476	42	359	32	86	8	90	8	67	6	23	2	26	2	1,127
1916	445	42	302	29	111	13	88	8	34	3	21	2	38	3	1,039
1917	387	37	305	29	112	13	79	8	76	7	29	3	36	3	1,024
1918	378	40	275	29	86	9	79	8	78	8	27	3	33	3	956
1919	244	32	224	30	73	10	71	9	76	10	21	3	43	6	752
1920	204	31	161	24	66	10	57	9	82	12	33	5	57	9	660

工业与商业中心之兴起,亦为经济蜕变中一重要现象。上海、无锡、通崇海、武汉、天津、唐山、青岛、济南、大连、辽宁、广州,近来均变为工商业中心城镇,中国人民之城市生活,因之亦日进千里。城市化已成为重要问题。各城之工业均渐行地方化,如上海、无锡。通崇海、武汉、天津、青岛之为棉纺织业中心,上海、无锡、天津之为面粉业中心,缫丝业则集中于上海、无锡与广州,大连则榨油业独盛;唐山为产煤要地,武汉则以钢铁著称,余如天津北平之地毯,上海天津之提花布,天津、北平、武汉、平湖等处之针织业,以及杭州绍兴之锡箔,均渐成该地方之重要工业、工业中心若在沿海或处陆地交通便利之地位,亦往往同时为商业上之中心,如上海为中国工业中心,同时亦为中国商业中心,其余如天津、大连、广州、武汉等埠亦莫不然。各商业中心之重要,从各埠每年之贸易额及其与外国直接之贸易额可以见之。下表乃海关所制各要埠每年贸易额之详确统计。

第七表　中国十大商埠之贸易总额及其直接国外贸易额之比较(1927)

埠　名	总贸易额		直接国外贸易额	
	海关两	百分比	海关两	百分比
上　海	868,978,484	27	785,823,191	40
大　连	336,372,493	13	258,935,931	13
天　津	325,339,223	11	189,801,157	10
汉　口	200,959,244	6	30,917,424	2
广　州	172,482,412	5	113,455,899	6
胶　州	149,499,859	5	78,324,016	4
安　东	105,530,916	3	90,503,675	5
哈尔滨	90,044,789	3	90,380,793	5
汕　头	87,786,646	3	41,546,367	2
牛　庄	71,175,375	2	17,125,622	1

（续表）

埠 名	总贸易额		直接国外贸易额	
	海关两	百分比	海关两	百分比
其余三十六埠	711,649,474	22	234,737,211	12
总 数	3,119,819,615	100	1,931,551,286	100

各工商业中心重要之比较，亦可从各埠人口之多寡见之。但各埠精详之人口统计，尚未编制；各商埠之海关虽有租界之估计，然非将来有精确之调查与之对核，不能即视为最可靠之材料。但为读者明了各埠之相对的重要计，故取一九二七年海关之估计列表于下。

第八表　中国二十万人口以上之城镇（1927）

城名	人 口	城名	人 口	城名	人 口
武汉	1,583,900	上海	1,500,000	天津	800,000
广州	746,300	重庆	623,030	长沙	535,800
苏州	500,000	杭州	380,000	南京	360,500
福州	314,900	青岛	308,200	厦门	300,000
宁波	284,300	大连	222,400	温州	202,700

（二）中国工业化之程度

中国工业化之正在进行中，已为事实。但现在已至何程度，则除少数人之臆测外，尚无确切之调查。各种工业之普遍的采用工厂制度，固可视为工业化之明证。然一加精密之研究，则知中国所采用之工厂制度与世人普通之所谓工厂制度，尽有不同之处。严格论之，工厂制度有三种要素，曰工作集中，曰实行监督，曰固定资本：如原动力是，三者缺一，不可谓之工厂。现在中国之所谓工厂，竟将三数手艺人所成之作坊，亦包括在内，殊有名不符实之弊。名之者非出于无识之徒根本昧于作坊与工厂之分别，即舍旧趋新之辈，故藉此名以惑众。现在无论私人与政府，对工业之实况，均无精详之调查。前农商部所制九年间（一九一二至一九二〇）农商统计，其详备之程度如何，可置不论，然其全国工厂统计之不能使人满意，为显明之事实。其所得之统计所以不能使人满意者，约有数点：第一，从普及全国各省之一点言，农商部之统计，仅自一九一二至一九一五年四年之统计为可靠。自一九一五年以后，内战频仍，各省向农商部作工厂统计报告以及其他经济的统计报告者，年减一年，及至一九二〇年，仅有十省而已。第二，农商部定凡任用七人以上之制造场所即为工厂，未将固定资本之要素，加入规定之中。依农商部之规定，在一九一二年时，有九百八十七家成衣工厂，任用工人一万四千八百八十六人。第三，其所制之统计，既不完备，复欠精确。即在比较最可靠之四年中，各省均向该部作报告之时，尚常因经验缺乏，或执事者疏忽之故，错误甚多。其他统计之更不可依据，不待论矣。不徒各种工业每年总数时有不符，即同一工业每年之总数，亦记载不同，如一九一五及一九一六两年所得之报告，与一九二〇年之报告，相去甚远。其他错误，更难枚举。由于计算不慎者有之，由于印刷错误者亦有之。一九一八年纺织工业工人之总数，本为二七〇、八一五，错印为二〇七、八一五。此等大错，一九一九年与一九二〇年两次报告，竟未加改正，其粗略可想而知。农商部之报告，缺点固多，然除此而外，欲得一较为可靠，足以表示中国采用工厂制之进行，及中国工业化已至之程度者，竟不可复得。下列之表，即取自农商部自一九一二年至一九二〇年之报告中。

第九表 中国工厂工人之数目（1912—1920）

业别 年	织染业 人数	百分比	机械器具业 人数	百分比	化学业 人数	百分比	饮食业 人数	百分比	杂业 人数	百分比	特别业 人数	百分比	总数 人数	百分比
1912	228,497	34	33,267	5	154,421	23	208,900	32	30,926	5	5,773	1	661,784	100
1913	249,324	39	36,697	6	94,745	15	181,732	29	64,352	10	4,040	1	630,890	100
1914	288,212	46	37,515	6	118,016	19	141,566	23	30,004	5	9,161	1	624,524	100
1915	294,935	48	25,183	4	113,115	18	139,117	22	34,328	6	13,051	2	619,729	100
1916	277,309	49	26,096	5	110,505	20	122,408	21	27,780	5	1,157	—	565,255	100
1917	293,366	53	22,333	4	99,426	18	103,931	19	29,111	5	4,425	1	552,592	100
1918	270,815	51	24,814	5	92,754	18	103,010	20	30,006	6	1,559	—	522,958	100
1919	241,229	59	17,887	4	66,138	16	56,073	14	27,006	7	946	—	410,279	100
1920	301,544	73	17,951	4	42,002	11	36,762	9	13,866	3	915	—	413,040	100

依上表所示,则织染工业任用工人之数目为最多,其次则为饮食工业、化学工业、机械器具工业、杂工业及特别工业。织染工业系包括缫丝业、制棉业、纺织业、制线业、织物业、刺绣业、成衣业、染色业及编物业而言,其中织布业、棉纺织业及缫丝业用人最多;饮食工业系包括酿造业、制糖业、烟草业、制茶业、盐业、汽水及冰业、糕点业、罐头业、碾米制粉业、畜产水产业等而言,其中以制茶业、酿造业、碾米制粉业及烟草业,任用工人最多;化学工业系包括窑磁业、造纸业、油蜡业漆业、火柴火药业、制药业、造胰业、化妆品业、染料业、香烛业、熟皮业以及其他而言,其中以窑磁业、火柴火药业、造纸业所用之工人为最多,至于其他工业,如机械器具业、杂业及特别业等,其所用工人总数之百分比,尚不及十五,势力微弱,故不复再加论列。由下表中可以看出各业工人分配之数量。

第十表　中国工厂工人之分配(1912—1920)(以一千为单位)

1. 织染业	1912	1913	1914	1915	1916	1917	1918	1919	1920
缫丝业	90.5	131.3	113.4	11.80	69.2	114.3	88.0	71.7	54.4
制棉业	1.8	26.0	6.7	1.3	2.5	2.1	2.0	2.4	2.7
纺织业	18.0	19.0	34.4	43.0	36.5	43.0	43.8	39.8	141.3
制线业	3.3	0.6	0.8	0.7	1.1	8.1	0.2	0.8	0.3
织物业	87.8	59.6	97.2	108.2	145.0	99.8	110.8	98.7	80.1
刺绣业	1.4	1.2	0.4	2.4	0.2	0.3		0.3	2.1
成衣业	14.9	7.8	11.5	7.6	9.4	8.7	7.5	4.4	3.1
染色业	3.6	3.4	15.8	8.2	8.0	7.0	7.1	3.0	3.1
编物业	7.2	0.3	8.1	5.6	4.5	10.1	11.1	20.0	14.7
总数	228.5	249.2	288.3	295.0	276.4	293.4	270.7	241.1	201.8
2. 机械器具业									
机器业	0.9	0.7	9.4	5.2	3.3	3.9	2.7	2.4	2.1
船车业	2.7	2.8	1.9	1.8	4.7	1.6	3.5	3.0	3.3

(续表)

器具业	3.4	8.0	8.6	2.5	1.7	1.7	1.9	1.2	0.4
金属品业	26.2	25.2	17.7	15.7	16.4	14.7	16.7	11.4	12.2
总数	33.2	36.7	37.6	25.2	26.1	21.9	24.6	18.0	18.0
3. 化学业									
窑磁业	67.7	31.6	38.3	40.1	37.3	31.3	28.6	13.0	13.4
造纸业	38.3	36.2	34.3	30.3	24.5	25.7	24.8	24.1	3.3
油蜡业	20.7	11.8	19.2	28.7	18.8	18.1	16.2	9.1	6.6
漆业	0.2	0.7	1.1	1.0	0.6	0.2	0.3	0.1	0.2
火柴火药业	10.5	6.3	15.5	11.3	16.8	11.4	11.0	8.8	9.6
制药业	1.7	0.8	0.9	1.9	1.8	1.3	1.9	1.5	0.9
造胰业造烛业	1.5	0.5	0.6	2.1	3.5	3.2	2.4	3.0	2.5
化妆品业	0.2	0.4	0.4	0.7	0.3	0.2	0.9	1.9	1.2
染料业	0.7	0.5	0.9	0.8	0.3	0.8	0.4	0.1	0.1
香烛等业	9.5	1.0	2.2						
熟皮业			1.2	4.4	4.3	4.9	5.0	3.9	3.9
杂业	3.5	4.9	3.6	1.6	2.3	2.4	1.3	0.6	0.4
总数	154.5	94.7	118.2	122.9	110.5	99.5	92.8	66.1	42.1
4. 饮食业									
酿造业	19.5	30.1	20.3	20.3	19.5	22.2	25.6	15.2	7.5
糖业	9.4	13.7	16.2	7.1	3.5	3.1	1.0	0.3	0.2
烟业	18.0	14.0	13.5	12.4	13.5	15.5	15.3	10.3	6.7
茶业	145.7	100.3	69.5	85.0	74.4	54.9	47.1	20.7	15.4
盐业	2.5	14.3							
汽水及冰业	0.1	0.2	0.1	0.2	0.2	0.1	0.1	0.1	0.1
糕点业	2.3	2.3	2.8	2.5	2.4	1.8	2.0	1.4	0.9
罐头业	1.5	0.7	0.5	0.2	0.4	0.1	0.1	0.1	0.4
碾米制粉业	5.9	3.4	4.6	5.3	5.9	1.6	8.0	6.2	4.0
畜产水产业	0.1	0.5		0.1	0.1	0.1	1.9	0.1	
杂业	3.8	2.3	13.6	6.0	2.5	3.4	1.8	2.5	1.6

（续表）

总数	208.8	181.8	141.1	139.1	122.4	102.8	102.9	56.9	36.8
5.杂业									
草帽及草帽辫业				1.1	0.7	0.7	0.7	0.7	0.2
印刷业	2.0	4.6	6.2	4.3	3.0	5.4	4.5	4.1	4.4
文具业	3.5	7.2	3.1	4.5	3.7	2.6	3.9	4.1	0.1
木竹制品业	8.0	10.4	3.5	10.0	9.7	9.7	7.6	5.5	4.7
革皮业	7.7	9.8	7.0	3.2	3.4	4.0	4.6	3.5	2.6
玉石骨角业	0.6	1.0	0.8	0.5	0.9	0.9	2.3	0.1	0.2
杂业	9.1	31.3	9.3	10.8	6.5	4.9	6.4	8.9	7.5
总数	30.9	64.3	29.9	34.4	27.9	28.2	30.0	26.9	19.7
6.特别业									
电汽业	0.1	0.4	0.3	0.5	0.6	0.7	1.4	0.5	0.5
金属精炼业	5.6	3.6	8.8	12.5	0.3	3.4		0.3	0.3
瓦斯业									
自来水业					0.2	0.3	0.2	0.1	0.1
总数	5.7	4.0	9.1	13.0	1.1	4.4	1.6	0.9	0.9

织染业、饮食业、化学业、机械器具业、杂业及特别业六业中之工厂，规模颇小，所用之工人，多半均在十人至五十人之间。至于棉纺织业、缫丝业、火柴火药业、制茶业、机器业、印刷业、电汽业八业中，其工厂之规模则较大。下表为前列六种工业工厂人数之调查表。

第十一表　中国工厂工人之平均数目（1912—1920）

1.织染业	1912	1913	1914	1915	1916	1917	1918	1919	1920
缫丝业	286	112	248	200	200	273	268	531	671
制棉业	16	27	28	16	35	28	31	48	35
纺绩业	1,122	60	340	1,227	1,257	1,264	1,217	1,136	4,155
制线业	14	16	13	15	25	173	8	46	26

（续表）

织物业	41	46	40	31	47	44	46	45	54
刺绣业	169	47	15	134	33	23	19	27	295
成衣业	15	14	18	16	22	23	21	27	19
染色业	14	13	56	33	32	35	35	19	30
编物业	103	14	121	65	52	83	87	73	105
2.机械器具业									
机器业	69	29	156	47	52	67	52	59	61
船车业	13	15	12	13	28	13	30	36	41
器具业	11	21	15	14	13	15	31	16	17
金属品业	14	13	13	13	12	13	14	14	16
3.化学业									
窑磁业	31	17	23	18	22	19	21	17	23
造纸业	14	14	12	13	13	14	14	18	15
油蜡业	12	12	12	19	14	14	15	12	14
漆业	11	23	12	12	15	9	17	20	39
火柴火药业	131	191	282	122	76	59	143	156	205
制药业	14	10	11	22	23	26	35	29	31
造胰业造烛业	19	19	16	10	17	20	17	21	23
化妆品业	9	13	12	28	18	15	67	121	150
染料业	10	9	13	16	11	11	9	9	30
香烛等业	36	10	11						
熟皮业			17	19	17	17	19	20	19
杂业	18	28	21	25	64	100	23	18	17
4.饮食业									
酿造业	14	12	12	12	13	15	16	15	12
糖业	13	14	18	14	12	11	12	11	22

(续表)

烟业	18	18	16	19	22	26	28	39	38
茶业	236	143	138	172	169	137	153	190	314
盐业	17	26							
汽水及冰业	23	19	15	18	26	20	19	16	15
糕点业	9	11	11	11	12	12	13	11	12
罐头业	15	15	21	36	29	25	27	130	44
碾米制粉业	20	12	18	17	19	19	25	22	18
畜产水产业	6	10	8	14	10	13	84	12	
杂业	16	17	18	15	19	18	12	21	22
5 杂业									
草帽及草帽辫业				16	11	10	11	11	13
印刷业	39	82	133	134	131	186	140	132	260
文具业	30	24	17	22	24	17	23	34	37
木竹制品业	13	17	14	16	15	17	14	15	16
羽支业	18	18	17	13	11	15	18	20	22
玉石骨角业	11	14	14	11	12	12	24	11	27
杂业	19	52	24	40	28	17	32	24	74
6. 特别业									
电气业	73	44	28	65	53	61	126	52	70
金属精炼业	63	24	26	37	25	12	8	29	29
瓦斯业				8					
自来水业					38	240	168	160	106	106

总之,中国之工厂规模均颇小,七人至二十九人之工厂,居工厂全数百分之八十至八十五,三十人至九十九人之工厂居全数百分之十,其余百分之十工厂用人均在百人以上。从下列之表中,自一九一二至一九二〇年中国各工厂用人之数目,可以窥知。

第十二表 中国各工厂工人之分配(1912—1920)

年	7—29		30—49		50—99		100—499		500—999		1000—		总数	
	人数	百分比	人数	百分比	人数	百分比	人数	百分比	人数	百分比	人数	百分比	人数	百分比
1912	18,212	88.0	990	4.8	798	3.7	514	2.4	181	0.9	54	0.2	20,749	100
1913	18,830	86.9	1,146	5.3	833	3.7	726	3.3	145	0.7	33	0.1	21,713	100
1914	17,447	86.1	1,193	5.9	873	4.3	549	2.7	161	0.8	47	0.2	20,770	100
1915	16,618	86.0	1,068	5.5	819	4.1	602	3.1	174	1.0	40	0.3	19,321	100
1916	16,309	86.0	1,034	5.8	762	4.0	591	3.2	157	0.8	44	0.2	18,957	100
1917	13,076	83.2	1,176	7.5	667	4.2	589	3.5	179	1.1	49	0.5	15,736	100
1918	11,945	83.0	1,047	7.0	720	5.0	491	3.5	122	0.9	49	0.6	14,374	100
1919	8,813	84.5	561	5.4	464	4.5	443	4.2	115	1.1	29	0.3	10,425	100
1920	5,212	80.0	446	6.8	367	5.6	376	5.6	98	1.5	25	0.5	6,514	100

中国现时工业化之程度,其大概已如上述,为切实计。可择其中于工业化有比较重要关系之工业,以为分析研究之用。如棉纺织工业、缫丝业、面粉工业、榨油工业、火柴工业及电气工业是也。在此等工业中,不徒工厂制度之引用,比较完整,即工厂制度之性质,亦表现特别显明。棉纺织业采用工厂制度,虽在钢铁业采用之后,然实为今日中国最大之工厂工业。棉纺织业之采用工厂制度,始于一八九〇年。李鸿章氏曾设厂于上海,该厂有六万五千只纺锤,六百架织机,未几该厂遭火。中国政府不欲再行投资,于是转售之于一私人所组织之纺织公司,改名华盛。自一八九六年中日条约成立后,外人得在中国商埠设立工厂之权。英人所办之怡和老公茂,及德人所办之瑞记各纱厂,遂相继设立。在一八九六年,在上海、无锡二处先后设立九厂,其中为国人所设而比较重要者为华盛、大纯、裕源及业勤四厂,相继设立于苏州者有苏伦,设于南通者有大生。上海之大纯,因营业不振,旋即售与日人,改名为上海纺织公司第一厂,是为外人购买国人工厂之始。日俄战争之后,满洲一变而为一棉织品之市场,纱厂逐渐设立,织机亦日见增加,以应需求。于是利用其自制纱之方法亦日精。一九〇八年江苏一省,即有二十三纱厂,所用之纺锤,为数有五十八万七千六百四十六只之多,织机亦有三千〇六十六架;至一九一八年,纱厂之数增至三十四家,纺锤增至九十九万七千二百三十八只,织机增至五千四百三十八架,投资总额增至三千五百万元之巨。从下列之表中,棉纺织业进步之情况,可以一目了然。

第十三表　中国纱厂(1891—1928)

年	1891	1896	1902	1911
厂数	11	12	17	32
纺锤数	65,000	417,000	565,000	831,000

（续表）

年	1916	1918	1919	1923	1928
厂数	42	49	54	120	120
纺锤数	1,145,000	1,478,000	1,650,000	3,550,000	3,850,000

纱厂自一九一六至一九二三，八年间，由四十二厂激增至一百二十厂之现象，甚堪注意。此次激增之主因，为受欧战之影响，外国棉纱供给缺乏，外国供给缺乏，结果竞争者少，予中国操纱厂业者以兴隆获利之机会。不徒中国纱厂业有空前之进步，东方各国，莫不如是。因生意畅茂之故，投资于此业者极其踊跃，各处纱厂，莫不如雨后春笋，蒸蒸日上。激进期约在自一九一五至一九二四年之十年间，新立之工厂，共有八十所。

第十四表　中国各期成立之纱厂（1928）

成立时间	1914	1915—1924	1915	1916	1917
厂数	31	80	1	3	1
成立时间	1918	1919	1920	1921	1922
厂数	8	5	6	21	20
成立时间	1923	1924	1925—1928	成立期未知	总数
厂数	6	9	7	2	120

据最近华商纱厂联合会之统计，一八二八年中国共有一百二十纱厂，共用三百八十五万零十六只纺锤。各省纱厂及其纺锤数目之分配如下表。

第十五表　中国各省纱厂之分配（1928）

省　　名	工厂数目	纺　　锤	
		数目	百分比
江苏	78	2,540,176	66.0
山东	10	323,780	8.0
湖北	6	290,152	7.5
河北	9	289,756	7.5
辽宁	4	125,544	3.0
河南	4	107,280	3.0
其余各省（浙江、湖南、江西、山西、安徽、陕西）	9	173,328	5.0
总数	120	3,850,016	100.0

第十六表　中国各城纱厂之分配（1928）

城　　名	数　　目	纺　　锤	
		数目	百分比
上　海	59	2,100,360	54
青　岛	9	296,780	8
武　汉	6	290,152	7
天　津	6	226,808	6
通崇海	5	177,564	5
无　锡	6	150,800	4
其　他	29	607,552	16
总　数	120	3,850,016	100

如上表之所示，十二省中共有六城为纱厂业之中心，即上海、青岛、武汉、天津、通崇海及无锡。在此六城中，有九十一纱厂，其纺锤数目居全数百分之八十四。

在此一百二十所之纱厂中,其任用工人之数目,及使用纺锤之数目,自有多少之别。若以工人数目之多寡,以定工厂规模之大小,则此一百二十纱厂中,任用工人自一百一十至九千五百五十六者均有。其中任用工人自五百至二千四百九十九者,共有八十二厂。从下列之表中,可立知中国各级纱厂任用工人多寡之数目。

第十七表　中国各纱厂工人之分配(1928)

每厂工人之数目	工厂数目	每厂工人之数目	工厂数目
500 以下	3	500—999	16
1,000—1,499	29	1,500—1,999	15
2,000—2,499	22	2,500—2,999	3
3,000—3,499	10	3,500—3,999	5
4,000—4,499	5	4,500—4,999	1
5,000—9,999	5	未知	6
总　　数	120		

若以纺锤之数目定各厂规模之大小,则自最低用二千八百八十只至最高用九万只者不等,厂数共有一百一十九所。其中每厂使用纺锤自一万只至三万九千九百九十九只者有七十九厂。从下表中即可得知各纱厂所用纺锤数目之多寡。

第十八表　中国各纱厂纺锤之分配(1928)

每厂之纺锤数	厂数	每厂之纺锤数	厂数
2,000—4,999	3	5,000—9,999	5
10,000—14,999	9	15,000—19,999	13
20,000—24,999	19	25,000—29,999	21
30,000—34,999	9	35,000—39,999	8

（续表）

每厂之纺锤数	厂数	每厂之纺锤数	厂数
40,000—44,999	4	45,000—49,999	4
50,000—54,999	6	55,000—59,999	4
60,000—64,999	6	65,000—90,999	8
总　　数	119		

一百二十所纱厂，非皆是独立营业。其中有五十八厂为十四棉业组织所有。十四组织之中，日人所设者八，国人所设者五，英人所设者一。下表即将此十四组织之纱厂数目、资本额数、纺锤数、织机数、工人数，以及其所用原动力之大小，一一示明。在下表中各组织排列之次序，以其所用纺锤之数目而定。

此十四棉业组织中，共有二百一十万零二千一百一十只纺锤，与中国纺锤总数三百八十五万零十六只比，为百分之五十五。内外棉业组织为日人所设之最大者，有四十四万六千零五十六只纺锤，占全国总数百分之十二，将其所有之纺锤分用于其经营之十五纱厂中。大生棉业组织，为吾国设立之最大者，有纺锤十六万三千五百六十四只，分用于其经营下之南通四厂中。该组织之纺织数目与全国总数比，居百分之四。

中国之纱厂业，不全操于国人之手。以纺锤之数目论，国人所有者占全国总数百分之五十七，日人所有者百分之三十九，英人所有者百分之四。但以投资之数额论，则国人之棉纺织业投资，仅居投资总额百分之二十八，日人之投资为百分之七十，比较言之，中国纱厂中每一纺锤仅有资本三十九两，在日本人所设之工厂中，每一纺锤，竟有资本一百三十七两。易词言之，日人所设纱厂之财力，

第十九表 中国之棉业组织(1928)

组织名称	厂数	资本		纺锤	织机	工人	原动力	
							基罗瓦特	马力
1 中外	15	18,500,000	日元	446,056	1,600	15,505	14,850	800
2 申新	6	300,000 6,000,000	两 元	232,772	3,573	18,423	9,488	5,200
3 日华	6	11,000,000	日元	231,232	500	12,603	42,200	
4 大生	4	6,916,390	两	163,564	1,342	14,079	550	4,500
5 永安	3	6,000,000	元	169,750	1,526	8,800	4,500	
6 怡和	3	25,400,000	两	153,320	1,900	13,000		
7 上海	4	6,000,000	两	131,752	2,352	7,066	3,252	1,900
8 大康	2	5,200,000	日元	123,680	726	6,730	8,000	
9 华新	4	9,600,000	元	113,600	250	9,073	3,295	2,200
10 公大	2	10,000,000	两	99,288	1,904	5,605	2,700	1,000
11 同兴	2	15,000,000	日元	89,360	1,040	4,010	2,500	
12 溥益	2	2,500,000	两	52,120	500	2,409	1,550	
13 满洲	2	8,000,000	日元	50,176	504	21,976	1,700	
14 东华	3	6,000,000	日元	45,440		1,785	1,600	
总数	58	31,116,390 63,700,000 21,600,000	两 日元 元	2,102,110	17,717	141,064	96,185	15,600

较国人所设者大三倍有半。国人所设之纱厂,因资本短缺之故,大部资本均用之于购地建屋买机器等固定资本中,用于购原料付工资以及其他经营成本之流动资本者,为数则殊少。故一遇经济恐慌之时,因流动资本短少而遭失败者,时有所闻。而日人或英人之纱厂,无不平稳而过。除此资本不足一弱点之外,国人所办纱厂之地位,均较日人所办者为优。国人纱厂之纺锤数目,占全国总数百分之五十七,日人之纱厂则仅占百分之三十九;国人纱厂所用之工人,居总数百分之六十五,购用全国棉量百分之六十,所出之棉纱,居总数百分之六十三,而日人纱厂所用之工人。占工人总数百分之三十,购用之棉量为总数百分之三十六,所产之棉纱占总数百分之三十二。下表为一九二八年中国纱厂之统计。

第二十表　中国纱厂统计(1928)

	中国		日本		英国		总数	
	数目或数量	百分比	数目或数量	百分比	数目或数量	百分比	数目或数量	百分比
纱厂	73	60	44	37	3	3	120	100
资本(两)	84,000,000	28	208,000,000	70	5,400,000	2	297,400,000	100
纺锤	2,181,880	57	1,514,816	39	153,320	4	3,850,016	100
工人	156,298	65	72,261	30	13,000	5	241,559	100
消棉量(担)	4,946,495	60	2,927,527	36	300,000	4	8,174,022	100
产纱量(包)	1,377,788	63	695,656	32	129,522	5	2,202,966	100
织机	16,787	57	10,896	37	1,900	6	29,583	100
产布量(疋)	6,900,038	64	3,758,750	36			10,658,788	100

缫丝业工业化之进步亦甚速。在纺织工业中仅次于纱厂业。中国之采用蒸汽缫机,约在六十年之前。但因缺乏详细统计,故现已发达至何程度,甚难断定。据已得之统计,缫丝工业大概集中于江苏、浙江、广东、四川四省。较次者为湖北与山东二省。现在江

苏一省有缫丝工厂一百四十六所,上海一城有一百零四厂,无锡有三十七厂,苏州有三厂,浙江一省有十六厂。江苏共有缫丝机三万三千架,浙江有三千架。在一九二七年,四川有二十五家缫丝厂,其中二十家有缫丝机二千三百十八架。依一九一一年之报告,广东有缫丝厂二百九十九家,共有缫丝机十三万一千二百六十架。上海一处,缫丝业自一八九○年至一九二九年之进步程度,从下表中可以看出。全国缫丝业之进步,亦可窥见一斑。

第二十一表　上海缫丝业之发展（1890—1929）

成立时期	缫丝厂数	缫丝机数	成立时期	缫丝厂数	缫丝机数
1890	5		1906	23	8,026
1891	5		1907	28	9,686
1892	8		1908	29	10,006
1893	9		1909	35	11,058
1894	10		1910	46	13,298
1895	12		1911	48	13,737
1896	17		1912	48	13,292
1897	25	7,500	1913	49	13,392
1898	24	7,700	1914	56	14,424
1899	17	5,800	1915	56	14,424
1900	18	5,900	1916	61	16,192
1901	23	7,830	1917	71	18,800
1902	21	7,306	1918	71	19,200
1903	24	8,526	1927	93	22,168
1904	22	7,826	1929	104	23,582
1905	22	7,610			

上海有缫线厂一百零四家,共缫丝机二万三千五百八十二架,任用男工五千,女工五万八千九百。各厂用缫丝机自七十架至六百架不等,然一百零四厂中用二百架至二百九十九架者有六十家

之多。每厂通常用女工自五百至六百九十九人者共有五十九家。上海各缫丝厂缫丝机之分配见下表。

第二十二表　上海缫丝厂缫丝机之分配（1929）

每厂缫丝机之数目	缫丝厂之数目
100 以下	1
100—199	30
200—299	60
300—399	6
400—499	5
500—599	1
600	1
总数	104

第二十三表　上海缫丝厂女工之分配（1929）

每厂之女工数目	缫丝厂之数目
200 以下	1
200—299	4
300—399	8
400—499	18
500—599	39
600—699	20
700—799	3
800—899	4
900—999	—
1,000—1,599	7
总数	104

广东之缫丝厂普通较上海各厂之规模均为宏大。在一九一八年，该省缫丝厂用四百架至四百九十九架缫丝机者，二百九十九厂中有一百五十五厂之多。广东各厂规模之大小，从下表可以窥知。

第二十四表　广东缫丝厂缫丝机之分配（1918）

每厂缫丝机之数目	缫丝厂之数目
300 以下	1
300—399	55
400—499	155
500—599	44
600—699	27
700—799	9
800—899	4
900—1,299	4
总数	299

广东各厂设立于一九〇一年以后者为最多。其详情见下表。

第二十五表　广东各期成立缫丝厂之数目（1918）

成立时期	工厂数目
1872—1880	1
1881—1890	11
1891—1900	36
1901—1910	187
（1901）	（2）
（1902）	（24）
（1903）	（8）
（1904）	（13）
（1905）	（18）
（1906）	（21）
（1907）	（28）
（1908）	（21）
（1909）	（26）
（1910）	（26）
1911	31
日期未知者	33
总数	299

设立缫丝工厂所需之资本不必甚巨,因地基房舍及缫丝机等,均可以赁租之法得之。据估计所得,每缫丝机所需之资本为二百六十两,包括该机之成本、原动力、地基、房舍等在内。每机所需之流动资本,规银一百六十两即足应用。有三百缫丝机之工厂,需资本十二万六千两。然若所有之固定资本均由租赁而得,则有银四万八千两已足应用。据一九二六年丝茧公会之报告,是年上海有八十二家缫丝厂,其中五十七厂共用资本一百七十九万一千两,每厂平均之资本数为三万一千四百两。从下列之表中,即可看出三万两资本之丝厂为数最多。

第二十六表　上海各缫丝厂资本之分配(1926)

每厂之资本(两)	厂数
7,000	1
10,000	5
20,000	14
30,000	19
40,000	8
50,000	8
60,000	1
100,000	1
总数	57

中国旧有之磨粉工业,各地虽仍然存在,然机器面粉工业之日益发达,亦为显明之事实。依一九二八年六月前经济讨论处之报告,全国共有机器面粉工厂一百九十三所。一八九六年上海已有面粉工厂之设立,该厂为日人所办,名增裕(译音)面粉工厂。就有开办年份统计之一百七十六面粉工厂中,有六分之五皆建筑于一九一○年之后。

第二十七表　中国各期面粉工厂成立之分配（1928）

成立时间	厂数
1896—1900	3
1901—1905	11
1906—1910	17
1911—1915	52
（1911）	（6）
（1912）	（8）
（1913）	（12）
（1914）	（16）
（1915）	（10）
1916—1920	58
（1916）	（5）
（1917）	（12）
（1918）	（13）
（1919）	（8）
（1920）	（20）
1921—1925	35
（1921）	（13）
（1922）	（11）
（1923）	（6）
（1924）	（2）
（1925）	（3）
总数	176

中国面粉工厂各省之分配，以东三省、江苏、山东、河北及湖北各省为最多，他省亦间有之。下表即为前"经济讨论处"所编制之《一九二八年中国面粉工厂各地分配之统计》。

第二十八表　中国面粉工厂各地之分配（1928）

地名	厂数
北满	12
长春	7
南满	25
哈尔滨	29
济南	12
山东（济南在外）、山西、河南及江苏之一部	14
天津	14
河北及绥远（天津在外）	8
汉口	9
长江流域（上海、汉口在外）	23
上海	27
无锡	12
云南	1
总数	193

一百九十三家面粉工厂之中，一百六十五家之资本为三百十五万八千两，又三千六百十二万八千元，又一千八百四十二万三千日元，又一百零二万卢布，又一亿枚铜元，又二十万小洋，约共合国币六千万元。

榨油工业集中于东三省。依前经济讨论处之报告，一九二八年中国共有榨油工厂二百八十三所，其中设立于东三省者有一百七十六所，约占全数五分之三。从下表可以窥知中国榨油工厂之地域分配。

第二十九表　中国榨油工厂之地域分配（1928）

省名	厂数
东三省	176
大连	70
锦州	33
哈尔滨	19
牛庄	18
其他	36
河北	10
天津	8
其他	2
山东	25
青岛	20
其他	5
湖北	26
武汉	26
江苏	39
上海	23
无锡	9
其他	7
其余各省	7
总数	283

　　大连为东三省榨油工业之中心。在一九二五年时，有油厂八十四家。最早设立之油厂为双和栈，设立于一九〇六年。继之而起者为忠盛和及立新（译音）。立新为日人所设，有资本三百七十

五万日元。一九〇八年有张本政者,为东三省航业界之领袖,经营一油厂,名曰政记油坊。是年南满铁路公司划一运价,凡货无论自何地运往大连、安东、牛庄者,其运价相等。该公司之意,在使大连为一商业中心。自此以后,大连之油厂日增,渐变为大豆业之中心市场。豆饼与豆油之出口,该口有独揽之势。大连一埠榨油工业之发展情况见下表。

第三十表　大连各期榨油厂成立之数目(1925)

成立期	厂数
1906—1910	25
1911—1915	25
1916—1920	10
1921—1925	23
成立期未详者	1
总数	84

据一九二五年之调查,八十四家油厂之中,七十二厂共有资本一千二百五十六万三千元,又七百八十九万日元,总数约合国币二千一百万元。是年各厂共产豆饼二十六万一千二百片,又二十九万九千三百七十六斤。是年各厂共出豆油一百二十五万二千七百六十斤。

火柴工业亦为中国工业化中重要工业之一。火柴工业与以上所列举各种工业不同之处,在不集中于一地,而分立于各省。据前经济讨论处所制之统计,一九二八年中国共有火柴工厂一百八十九家,其地域之分配见下表。

第三十一表　中国火柴工厂之地域分配（1928）

省名	厂数
东三省	23
山东	27
河北	14
山西	9
甘肃	3
江苏	18
浙江	6
两广	41
陕西	3
福建	3
河南	11
两湖	6
安徽与江西	5
云南	7
四川	13
总数	189

一百八十九厂中，一百零三厂之资本总额为六百七十二万五千元，又三十八万五千两，又二百十九万五千日元，又福建台府元七万，约共合国币九百五十万元。七十三厂之总产额为每年六万零七百箱，又每月二万五千九百二十箱，又每日一百五十箱及一千四百六十五吨。

电气工业之兴起，亦为中国工业化进步之一证。一省电气工业发展之程度，颇足代表该省一般工业进步之情况。据一九二四年之调查，中国共有电气工厂二百十九家，分配于各省。详见下表。

第三十二表　中国电气工厂各地之分配（1924）

省名	厂数
江苏	61
浙江	34
河北	25
广东	16
东三省	13
山东	13
湖北	12
福建	11
其余各省	34
总数	219

上表之统计，与一九二七年英文中国年鉴之调查，颇为符合。据是年中国年鉴之调查，电气工业略有进步，由二百十九厂增至二百三十一厂。增加之厂，以东三省为最多。

第三十三表　一九二四年与一九二七年中国各省之电气工厂

省名	厂数	
	1924	1927
江苏	61	58
浙江	34	27
河北	25	21
广东	16	15
东三省	13	31
山东	13	13
湖北	12	12

（续表）

省名	厂数	
	1924	1927
福建	11	11
其余各省	34	43
总数	219	231

二百十九家电气工厂之中，一百八十二厂之资本总额，约合国币五千万元，其中包国币三千八百九十九万五千五百元，又小洋二百三十二万元，又银一百七十万零二千六百四十两，又一千四百二十五万法郎。二百十九厂中一百七十五厂共用电力八万零六百六十四基罗瓦特，每厂平均电力有四百六十一基罗瓦特。大概电气工厂，约有百分之七十六，其所有之电力，均在二百基罗瓦特之下，用电力在一百基罗瓦特或一百以下者，有一百十四厂，约居全数百分之六十一。一百八十七厂所用电力之大小见下表。

第三十四表　各电汽工厂所用之电力（1924）

（基罗瓦特）

每厂之基罗瓦特数	厂数
1—50	64
51—100	50
101—150	18
151—200	11
201—300	7
301—500	8

（续表）

每厂之基罗瓦特数	厂数
501—1,000	9
1,001—2,000	11
2,000 以上	9
总数	187

最大之电气厂设于湖北，该厂之资本额为二百五十万元，电力有六千五百基罗瓦特。较次之一厂设于江苏，有资本二百五十万元，电力亦有六千四百基罗瓦特。此等电气工业之统计，颇为粗陋。二百十九工厂之中，仅有一百八十八厂之电力与资本，有可靠之统计，余则尚付缺如。

（三）工业化之影响

设于中国工业化之程度，事前无详细之调查，而欲总述其影响，必为难能之事。居今日而讨论中国工业化之影响，仅可视为此项研究之发端，去可获切实结论之期，前途尚远。从各方面观之，工业化在中国之影响，与其百五十年前在西方之影响无以异。工业化社会的与经济的影响，曾见之于英法者，亦有一部已见之于现在之中国。工厂制度之逐渐采用，于上章已略述之。劳动界与劳动运动之兴起，已使中国进于一新时期。由手艺工业过渡至工厂工业，旧日铺主与手艺工人学徒之关系，均逐渐消灭，而渐以金钱代之。中国昔日铺主与手艺工人同为一会员之行会制度，现亦已代为发达未全之工会及雇工联合会。上海于一九二一年成立之华商纱厂联合会,具雇主联合会性质。日本资本家与英国资本家,亦继之而起,组织雇主联合会。天津、湖北、无锡等地,均有同样组织之成立。各联合会活动之范围,虽有大小之不同,然均为纱厂联络机关之用,一方供给同业者以报告,一方以团体之力量,抵制政府之苛征。

工会之兴起,约在欧战停止之时。因华工之归国,进行更速。自欧战停止至一九二一年,各城工厂工人组织工会者,约有二十万,为当时中国效力最大之团体。工会组织以人数之多少计,除工厂工人外,为矿业工人与铁路工人,其人数约有十八万五千。农人向较其他工人为保守,故其组织力亦最低。自一九二一年以后,中国各地工会,莫不如雨后春笋,及时兴起。中国南部,因受国民党指导,及与西人交际较早之故,工会组织之发达,几可与西方各国,并驾齐驱。长江流域一带之情形,较为复杂。有数地方,工会组织较为发达,而其余地方之工会,则鲜有进步可言。在北方则因军阀压迫,与工业不甚发达之故,工会组织较为薄弱。

自国民政府成立之后,指导工人组织工会一事,已为施政之既定政策。故在地方党部指导之下,各业工会均逐渐成立。

劳动运动既起之后,各业中之劳资纠纷,已成为司空见惯之事。据近来劳资纠纷之分析研究,自一九一八至一九二六年之九年间,罢工之总数为一千〇九十八次,平均每年有一百二十二次,以服用品业之罢工数为最多。在调查之九年中,服用品业一行,罢工至三百六十八次之多,居总罢工数百分之四十一。基本业中之罢工次数为最少,在过去之九年中,仅有二十五次,居全数百分之三。罢工之详细统计见下表。

第三十五表　罢工按工业分类(1918—1926)

类别年	服用业	饮食业	家具业	建筑业	器具制造业	交通运输业	基本实业	教育事业	卫生事业	奢侈品及装饰业	杂业	总数
1918	8	1	5	2	3	3			2	1		25
1919	13	3	6	3	13	15	2	3	1	2	5	66
1920	16	3	2	3	10	2	1	1	1	3	4	46
1921	10	7		4	1	13	1		4	3	5	49
1922	26	6	1	3	7	22	5	3	8	4	6	91
1923	8	6	1	3	3	14	4	1	2	2	3	47
1924	13	8	1	3	6	13		2	3	3	4	56
1925	73	11	7	9	8	30	7	14	3	6	15	183
1926	201	34	10	19	64	77	5	41	18	23	43	535
总数	368	79	33	49	115	189	25	66	42	47	85	1,098
每年平均数	40.9	8.8	3.7	5.4	12.8	21.0	2.8	7.3	4.7	5.2	9.4	122.0

工厂制度应用之后，不徒工会兴起，罢工次数增加，童工、女工亦随之而起。在中国童工并非罕见之事。手艺工业中，亦有童工，不过名之曰学徒而已。然工厂之童工，与手艺工业中之童工，其间差别甚大。手艺工业学徒之目的，在学习手艺，工厂之童工，则在谋生活。学徒与童工之统计，均感缺乏。然从上海童工委员会，一九二五年之调查中，各工厂使用童工之状况，亦可窥见一斑。据该会之调查，十二岁以下之童工，在六种不同之工厂中，有二万一千九百人。详情见下表。

第三十六表　一九二五年上海各工厂所用十二岁以下之童工

工厂种类	男童工	女童工	总数	
	数目	数目	数目	百分比
织染	3,520	16,737	20,257	92.5
机械器具	430	250	680	3.1
化学	……	60	60	0.3
饮食	247	318	565	2.6
杂业	108	230	338	1.5
特别	……	……	……	……
总数	4,305	17,595	21,900	100.00

上表中值得吾人特别注意之点，即织染之工厂所用之童工为最多一事。盖该类工厂之主要者为纺绩及缫丝。此二类工厂所用工人，既无须精巧之技能，亦无须强壮之体力，故最易引诱厂方使用童工。关于各工厂女工之统计，自一九一四年至一九二〇年，农商部曾经编制，然自一九二〇年之后，即行停止。依农商部所编制之统计织染业中之工人，女工有总数百分之四十七至六十五，饮食业中之女工，有总数百分之三十一至四十三，杂业中之女工，有总

数百分之十一至二十三,化学业中之女工。有总数百分之十二至二十二,机械器具业中之女工,有总数百分之一至四,特别业中之女工,有百分之一。自一九一四至一九二〇之七年间,各种工业中所用女工之百分比见下表。

第三十七表 中国工厂工业中所用之女工（1914—1920） （百分比）

工业种类 \ 年	1914	1915	1916	1917	1918	1919	1920
织染工业	57	58	59	65	61	62	47
机械器具业	1	4	1	1	3	2	1
化学工业	12	12	13	12	12	16	22
饮食工业	35	40	42	31	33	37	43
杂工业	13	13	11	13	23	13	16
特别工业	0	0	1	1	0	1	0

中国工业化于国外贸易及贸易政策上影响甚大。因中国工业之进步,昔日出口货以原料为大宗者,近则渐渐代以半制品或制成品。入口货适与此相反,棉纱入口数量之逐年减少,足为此事之明证。在一九一五年时,进口之棉纱为二百六十八万六千担,一九二七年时,则为二十九万五千担,与一九一五年之进口量相当,仅九分之一耳。棉纱进口量之所以大减,不外因自一九一五至一九二〇之十三年间,国内纺纱工厂,有极大之进步所致。在过去之十年内,纺锤增加,竟至四倍。自一九一五至一九二七年,每年之进口纱量见下表。

第三十八表　中国棉纱之进口量（1915—1927）

年	进口数量（以千担为单位）
1915	2,686
1916	2,467
1917	2,076
1918	1,120
1919	1,405
1920	1,325
1921	1,273
1922	1,219
1923	775
1924	576
1925	647
1926	449
1927	295

所谓贸易政策之变更者,即采用保护政策以培养中国现在幼稚之工业,以期促进发展之谓也。中国因受不平等条约之束缚,关税失其自主者,已数十年。夫以关税为武器,以防止外货之竞争,而培养一国之工业,不仅中国独然,即素以采用自由贸易政策著名之英国,亦何独不然。在中国工业初兴之期,国人不知关税可以供保护国内工业之用,今则国民莫不澈悟前非,而视之为振兴国内工业之必需政策矣。

中国工业发展之最后问题,为如何利用人力与天然富源。中国工业界已觉专门人才之急需,故实业家均相率不惜以巨款为造就专门家之用。张季直先生首先在南通州创设纺织学校,上海穆藕初先生亦曾以其私人之金钱,为遣送二十余青年留学之用,其他各处有专门训练之人,已逐渐为工业家收用。其工作之价值,亦渐为社会所公认。天然富源之开采,进行虽缓,然亦有与时俱进之概。大规模之矿业,为中国向来所无,近则各处均已着着进行。从一九二四年前农商部所发出之矿业执照中,可知矿业已经发展之梗概。一九二四年内,该部所发出之矿业执照为数共有二百件,其中六十三件为寻探权之允许,其余一百三十七件皆为营业权之允许。执照以河北、四川等省所得为最多,河北四十七,四川四十,湖北十九,山西十六,山东十五,河南十五,各省执照之详细分配情形见下表。

第三十九表　农商部所发出矿业执照之分配(1924)

省名	寻探权利	营业权利
河北	12	35
河南	9	6
山东	3	12
山西	6	10
湖北	8	11
江西	6	5
安徽	1	10
浙江		2
江苏	2	4
吉林		4
黑龙江		2
四川	6	34
察哈尔	1	1
热河	8	1
绥远	1	
总数	63	137

（四）结论

吾国工业化之情形，已如上述。就世界已往历史之所示，参以目前之事实，吾人皆知工业化之种种恶果，多产生此项经济蜕变之中。使此时而不谋救济之方，则欧西各工业化时，人民所受之痛苦，又将重演于吾国矣。然解决之法，须先有精确之研究。吾国今日关于工业情形之统计，多不可靠。恃之以为解决问题之资料，殆如扣盘为日，相隔殊远。故欲洞明真相，非实地调查不为功。盖如是始可获切实之统计，以为研究之用。惟实地调查之困难，亦有足令吾人注意者。吾国工商界对于所经营之工商业，多不肯以实况示人，殊为调查之障碍。即其深悉工业调查为学术之研究者，亦往往隐讳不以实告。不第浪费调查人之时间，亦工业研究前途之大难也。且此种调查需费甚巨，非一二人之独力所能举办。提而倡之，是在吾国工商界之先觉耳。是篇所载关于工业化之程度及其影响，材料范围，粗漏不赅。所载统计，其乖讹之处，亦所难免。第区区此心。特欲以此为提倡工业研究之前驱，揭而出之。倘邀国人赞助，则所望也。

中国工业化之统计的分析

(一)概论:工业化定义及范围,中国工业化之发展。(二)中国工业化之主因:富源,环境。(三)中国工业化之程度:农矿,制造,商业,金融及交通。(四)中国工业化之影响:生产地域化,人口集中,工厂制度之普遍,劳工阶级及劳工问题之兴起,国外贸易及其政策之改变,外国在华投资之性质及其范围。(五)结论:中国工业化之趋势。

(一) 概论

吾人欲分析吾国工业化之概况,须先对"工业化"名词之含义加以确定。工业化者,即生产技术及组织改进之过程,以期达于工业制度为目的者也。[①] 含义如斯,故每与日常通称之"经济现代化"相通用。所谓改进之过程即为由农业制度而入于工业制度之意。在工业制度之下,生产规模扩大,国民经济生活亦即建立于资本主义之基础上,其特征之最著者,即为制造业之发达,因此其他经济组织亦应运而起,乃至农业,矿业,商业,交通及金融等,罔不以工业化方法施行之。结果所致,乃成为今日之"工业制度"。本文对于中国之工业化,予以统计的分析,就所能搜集之统计材料,以抒述其发展之主因,程度,及其影响。

中国之工业化,始于一八六○年后,其发展迅速之期,则在欧战期间。溯自一八六一年吾国开放五口后,中外贸易,因而日繁,西方工业化之风气,遂以东渐,而吾国之工业化,亦因之萌芽于是

[①] Johnston, G. A.: "Industrialization and the Countries of the Pacific", in *International Labor Review*, June, 1930, p. 784.

时。一八六二年安庆军械局建造汽轮；三年后，上海设立江南制造局 即今日之江南造船所。一八七二年复设立招商局，为中国人设立之第一最大航业公司；四年后吴淞铁路修筑完竣，为我国最初修筑之铁路。是时以后，运输工具之现代化，既开其端，同时于制造业及矿业，亦多开始革新。如一八六三年上海设立碾米厂；一八七三年成立缫丝厂；一八七八年开平设立煤矿局；一八九〇年上海设立纺织厂；武昌设立钢铁厂；一八九四年汉口设立火柴厂；一八九五年营口设立榨油厂；一八九六年上海设立面粉厂等，皆其例也。

一八九五年中日战争之后，"马关和约"中许外人在中国通商口岸有设立工厂之权，故是后制造业之发展，颇为迅速。其时，邮政虽仍袭一八七八年之成法，隶属于海关，然二十年来，行之颇著成效。一八八一年上海天津间之电报线成立，一八九六年上海商业银行成立；后于一九〇七年及一九一二年，交通银行与中国银行相继成立。交易所之设立，开端于一八九一年，是年外人在上海设有外商证券交易所（Shanghai Sharebrokers' Association）；惟中国人尚无是项组织。及至一九二〇年，上海中国人始有证券物品交易所之设立。嗣后投机之风大开，中国资本家见有利可图，趋之若鹜，上海一隅，交易所竟设有一四〇处之多。终以投机事业，不可久持，故转瞬即逝。至一九二一年，多数交易所均相继瓦解。最近，全国上下，对于交通事业之发展，复极注意，尤于汽车路之修筑，航空线之开辟及无线电报之设置为甚。①

中国之工业化,发端虽早,然其变化迅速之期,则在欧战期间;盖因大战爆发,外货来源断绝,所有市场,遂为本国生产者所有,故吾国工业,乃因而勃兴。如第一表甲所示煤之产量于一九一三年设为百分之一〇〇,至一九二〇年增至百分之一五八.九;铁矿砂之产量于一九一三年设为百分之一〇〇,至一九二〇年增至百分之一九四.四;铁之产量于一九一三年设为百分之一〇〇,至一九二〇年增至百分之一六六.七。在中国矿业内,煤与铁占极大部份,故其产量之激增,可视为中国矿业发展之指数也。

至于制造业,其发展之速率尤大。如以一九一三年为一〇〇,于一九一九年,厂丝之出口量增至一六八.三;豆油之出口量增至四八〇.二;于一九二〇年,纺锤数增至三七一.七;烟草之输入量增至一四〇.七。丝与豆油既为吾国出口货之大宗,今虽缺乏关于二者产量之统计,但其出口额统计,亦足视为二业发展之指数也。在另一方面,烟草为卷烟制造业之原料,故其输入额,亦足视为卷烟制造业发展之指数也。

贸易与运输二者,在欧战期间,其发展之速,不及矿业或工业。吾国对外贸易,于一九一三年至一九二〇年期间,输入额仅增加百分之六.五,而输出额亦仅增加百分之一九.四;其较可乐观者,即欧战期间,吾国输出贸易之增加,较输入贸易为大耳。在另一方面,邮运铁道之长度,设以一九一三年所有为百分之一〇〇,至一

---

① *China Yearbook*,1929-30;吴承洛:《今世中国实业通志》,二卷,民一八。

九二〇年则增至百分之一〇七.八;邮政路线之增加,较为迅速,设以一九一三年之长度为百分之一〇〇,至一九二〇年则增至百分之一五〇。同时在此期间,各通商口岸之汽船吨数,亦增加百分之一三.七。

一九二〇年以后,矿业,制造业,商业及交通事业之发展,其趋势较以往稍异。论矿业,一九二〇年煤产量为一五八.九,至一九二八年增至一八七.六;一九二〇年铁矿砂产量为百分之一九四.四,至一九二八年增至百分之二〇八.八;而铁之产量则较前减低,于一九二〇年为百分之一六六.七,至一九二八,减至百分之一二一.七。论制造业,自一九二〇年至一九二九年期间,增加最大者,厥为烟草之输入额,于一九二〇年为百分之一四〇.七,至一九二九年增至百分之五六三.七;其次纺锤,自百分之三七一.七,增至百分之五〇四.六。厂丝之输出,于一九一九年为百分之一六八.三,至一九二九年增至百分之二一七.二;而豆油之输出,则因一九二七年来商业凋敝之故,致有减少,一九一九年为百分之四八〇.二,至一九二九年仅百分之二二六.七。论国外贸易,我国出口贸易之物量指数,一九二〇年为一一九.四,至一九二八增至一六五.五;而我国入口贸易之物量指数,于一九二〇年为一〇六.五,至一九二八年增至一八八.三。至于汽船吨数之增加特多,于一九二〇年为百分之一一三.七,至一九二九年增至百分之一七一.四。其次为铁路之增加,于一九二〇年为百分之一〇七.八,至一九二九年为百分之一三六.三。邮政路线,一九二〇年为百分之一五〇,至一九二九年增至百分之一七六.五。

第一表（甲） 自一九一二年至一九二九年间中国工业化之进展

年	煤产额① (吨)	铁矿砂产额② (吨)	铁产额③ (吨)	厂丝出口额④ (担)	豆油出口额④ (担)	棉纺锤⑤ (锭数)	烟草入口额④ (担)	出口量指数⑥	进口量指数⑥	铁路(邮运)长度 (公里)	邮政(邮政路线) (公里)	船只④ (进出口之汽轮) (吨)
1912	8,886,453	721,280	177,989	74,019	525,688	—	142,931	103.9	82.9	10,368	229,824	28,388,957
1913	13,379,007	959,711	256,513	70,150	491,817	836,828	161,586	100.0	100.0	10,944	264,384	87,613,967
1914	13,639,912	1,005,140	300,000	56,869	607,477	855,196	118,354	83.8	91.6	10,944	279,936	91,126,240
1915	14,480,348	1,095,555	336,061	87,364	1,017,922	976,620	76,726	96.5	92.1	10,944	283,738	84,641,227
1916	15,902,616	1,129,056	369,160	81,451	1,565,640	1,228,152	147,132	102.4	96.6	10,944	290,707	82,381,569
1917	17,299,583	1,139,845	357,632	87,413	1,891,353	1,280,672	153,927	108.3	103.1	11,232	299,578	80,266,725
1918	18,339,502	1,474,689	354,144	87,514	2,277,167	1,456,012	181,091	105.5	92.8	11,520	310,349	74,201,372
1919	20,054,513	1,861,230	446,588	118,028	2,361,633	2,366,722	159,824	140.1	105.9	11,695	344,407	89,844,371
1920	21,259,610	1,865,985	427,648	72,917	1,713,104	3,110,546	227,323	119.4	106.5	11,800	396,491	99,642,210
1921	20,459,411	1,462,988	402,787	118,895	1,148,357	3,191,546	221,281	127.0	132.9	12,259	424,874	109,319,714
1922	21,097,420	1,559,416	393,694	110,040	1,480,196	3,266,546	254,033	130.6	158.5	12,551	439,222	119,354,968
1923	24,552,029	1,733,226	343,442	106,827	2,126,928	3,380,000	315,312	137.4	155.0	12,901	445,707	127,279,000
1924	25,780,875	1,765,732	330,521	101,112	2,121,470	3,581,214	683,152	144.8	170.8	13,152	456,304	136,829,598
1925	24,255,042	1,519,021	369,617	136,324	1,989,302	3,587,978	551,685	140.9	157.0	13,480	463,891	124,516,464
1926	23,040,119	1,561,911	404,668	137,493	2,667,229	—	755,083	149.6	186.7	13,707	471,271	132,249,431
1927	24,172,009	1,710,135	411,148	126,582	2,469,734	3,674,690	633,003	163.4	157.2	14,199	462,237	112,048,073
1928	25,091,760	2,003,800	433,843	151,343	942,189	3,850,016	1,069,851	165.5	188.3	14,578	458,051	148,261,342
1929				152,360	1,115,047	4,223,956	910,940	—	—	14,021	466,548	150,203,488

① 北平地质调查所：《中国矿业纪要》第一次（民一〇）、二次、七、三一页；第二次；第三次（民一七至民一四），第二表，民元及民六年《全国产煤额》系根据民元至民六年《全国矿产额推定。在民五年此一六大煤矿此占全国矿产额百分之五。② 同上，第二次、第三次，二九八页。③ 同上，第二次、第三次，第一四表；第三次，第一四表；④《华海关民元至民一八年，《华洋贸易总册》，上卷（报告及统计辑要）。⑤《华商纱厂联合会，中国纱厂一览表，民一六》，第九次；Chinese Economic Journal, Feb., 1926;Apr., 1928,《华商纱厂联合会季刊》，民一二，元月，二至三页。⑥ 何廉：中国六十年进出口物量指数，物价指数及物物交易指数（一八七二至一九二八），民一九，第十四表。⑦ 王仲武：《中国邮政统计》《统计月报》，民一九，十月。

第一表（乙） 自一九一二年至一九二九年间中国工业化之指数

（以一九一三年为基数＝一〇〇）

年	煤产	铁矿砂产	铁产	厂丝出口	豆油出口	棉纺锤	烟草入口	出口量	入口量	铁路	邮政	汽船
1912	66.4	75.2	69.4	105.5	106.9	—	88.5	103.9	82.9	94.7	86.9	99.8
1913	100.0	100.0	100.0	100.0	100.0	100.0	100.0	100.0	100.0	100.0	100.0	100.0
1914	102.0	104.7	117.0	81.1	123.6	102.2	73.2	83.8	91.6	100.0	105.9	104.0
1915	108.2	114.2	131.0	124.5	207.0	116.7	47.5	96.5	92.1	100.0	107.3	97.0
1916	119.0	117.6	143.9	116.1	318.3	146.8	91.1	102.4	96.6	100.0	110.0	94.0
1917	129.3	118.8	139.4	124.6	384.6	153.0	95.3	108.3	103.1	102.6	113.3	91.6
1918	137.1	153.7	138.1	124.8	463.0	174.0	112.1	105.5	92.8	105.3	117.4	84.7
1919	149.9	193.9	174.1	168.3	480.2	282.8	98.9	140.1	105.9	106.9	130.3	102.5
1920	158.9	194.4	166.7	103.9	348.3	371.7	140.7	119.4	106.5	107.8	150.0	113.7
1921	152.9	152.4	157.0	169.5	233.5	381.4	136.9	127.0	132.9	112.0	160.7	124.8
1922	157.7	162.5	153.5	156.9	301.0	390.3	157.2	130.6	158.5	114.7	166.1	136.2
1923	183.5	180.6	133.9	152.3	432.5	403.9	195.1	137.4	155.0	117.9	168.6	156.0
1924	192.7	184.0	128.9	144.1	431.4	428.0	422.8	143.8	170.8	120.2	172.6	156.2
1925	181.3	158.3	144.1	194.3	404.5	428.8	341.4	140.9	157.0	123.2	175.5	142.1
1926	172.2	162.7	157.8	196.0	542.4	—	467.3	149.6	186.7	125.2	178.3	150.9
1927	180.7	178.2	160.3	180.4	502.2	439.8	391.7	163.4	157.2	129.7	174.8	128.8
1928	187.6	208.8	121.7	215.7	191.6	460.1	622.1	165.5	188.3	133.2	173.3	169.2
1929				217.2	226.7	504.6	563.7	—	—	136.3	176.5	171.4

(二) 中国工业化之主因

中国工业化之主因，以富源及环境二端为最要。首就富源论之。中国人口稠密，故为工业化适宜之处。据最近内政部陈正谟君之调查，全国三十省面积凡四，七八六，九一五方英里，人口共四八五，一六三，三八六，人口密度为每方英里一〇一人。但中有十七省，人口占百分之八五.八，而面积则仅占百分之二八.一，人口密度每方英里为三一一人。而在此十七省之中，复有十一省，人口占百分之六三.七，仅占面积百分之一五.六，人口密度每方英里为四一四人。[1]

中国以农立国，人口已如此稠密，毋怪年来因内争，饥荒，瘟疫，贫苦而死者，为数甚多。使能驱之服役工业，则促进国家之工业化，影响必非浅鲜也。据白克教授分析研究中国人口与土地统计之结果，揭示于一九一九年，美国每人有已耕田三.六英亩，中国则每人不过〇.四英亩而已；易言之，中国每人所有已耕地，仅及美国每人所有九分之一耳。[2] 氏谓"中国如能迅速发展其制造业，使农民服役工业者之增加率，能较生于乡间食于乡间之人数之增加率为速，则农业与制造业之效率始能增高，而同时中国之人口问题，亦将因之解决。"[3]

---

[1] 陈正谟：《中国户口统计研究》，《统计月报》，民一九，六月，一〇至一二页。
[2] Baker: "Land Utilization in China", in *Problems of the Pacific*, 1927, p. 329.
[3] 同上，三三八页。

人工富源，虽极丰富，足为促进国家工业化之资；不过其自然财富，则极有限，即语自给，犹嫌不足。就耕地言，据白克教授之估计，美国可耕田地现已开垦者约百分之三九，中国则不过百分之二六而已。① 中国未开垦田亩之成分，虽较美国为高，不过以每人所有耕地衡之，仅及美国每人所有九分之一。即使国内可耕地尽行开辟，每人所有耕田，仍较目前美国每人一半为少。

　　若言矿产，则中国工业化之前途，更为暗淡。据培恩氏云："以东方与西部之北美洲及南美洲比较，东方之矿产业不著名；而尤以远东矿产为最少。即澳大利亚及菲洲，其在世界矿业中所占之地位，亦较远东为重要。"② 兹据北平地质调查所之估计，亦明示目前中国矿产，在世界殊无地位。所产铁矿砂不过百分之〇.五，铜百分之〇.〇二，铅百分之〇.〇九，锌百分之〇.〇九，锡百分之六，煤百分之一.六，石油百分之〇.〇〇〇〇八。③ 其已开矿产如斯，即未开之重要矿产，亦复有限。据地质调查所之估计，中国煤矿储量不过二一七.六二六百万吨而已④，仅及全世界百分之四。⑤ 铁矿储量亦不过九五一百万吨，⑥仅及全世界百分之一.六而已。⑦ 石油储量，不过美国百分之一。⑧ 他如铜，铅，锌，及银等之储量，据地质

---

① 陈正谟：《中国户口统计研究》，《统计月报》，民一九，六月，三二九页。
② Bain, *Ores and Industry in the Far East*, 1927, p. 21.
③ 《中国矿业纪要》第三次，第二三表。
④ 同上，第二次，一四页。
⑤ Torgasheff, Boris, P.：*Coal, Iron and Oil in the Far East*, 1929, p. 13.
⑥ 《中国矿业纪要》第二次，一二三页。在第三次报告（见二九四页），此数已修正为九七九，〇〇〇，〇〇〇。
⑦ Torgasheff, op. cit., p. 33.
⑧ Bain, op. cit., p. 116.

调查所所长翁文灏氏之调查,俱不敷用,尤以银一项,最为欠缺。而在另一方面,许多不重要之金属,吾国所产极富,其于中国工业化之关系,实属有限。据翁氏云:"中国在短期间,已一跃而为世界产锑及钨最多之国。此二项产品,因其产量特多,故其价格之低廉,亦非他国所能比。"①据一九二七年该所估计中国之钨产值八,三六六,〇〇〇元,占全世界钨产额百分之六四.三,其锑产值七,〇〇四,五五〇元,占全世界锑产额百分之七七。②

除依土地及矿源之统计,为说明我国富源缺乏之指数外,更可依进口统计为其指数。据中央研究院杨端六氏之分析,一九二八年内,中国之饮食品烟酒等输入额,占入口总额百分之二七.四四,而原料及半成品之输入额占百分之一九.二三,总计占全入口额百分之四六.六七,值五万五千七百万两关银。③ 至于矿产,于一九二九年内中国钢铁之输入,值关银五三,二一六,〇九八两,占全进口额百分之四.二;煤油之输入,值关银六四,三二一,六九六两,占全额百分之五;合计二者之进口额占全进口额百分之九.三。

中国富源,不利于工业化,而其环境亦然。以社会环境言,则目前大家庭制度,适为工业化之障碍。④ 第一,家庭束缚甚重,冒险进取之心甚微,纵使有志青年,思图上进,然家庭大权,操之长者,而长者心理,方日怀抱孙之望,必促儿孙早日完婚,室家既成,壮志

---

① *China Yearbook*, 1925, p. 122.
② 《中国矿业纪要》第三次,第二三表。
③ 杨铨、侯厚培等:《六十五年来中国国际贸易统计》,民二〇,国立中央研究院社会科学研究所专刊第四号。
④ Lieu, D. K.: "The Social Transformation of China", in *Chinese Social and Political Science Revierw*, Sept., 1917, p. 81.

易矣,一生岁月,率在家庭间消游,而家庭之团结,亦由是益固。近年内地人民之移居于东三省,即为一最确切之例。虽此种人口移动之原因,系由东省发展机会之多,而主因则由冀鲁豫各省人民,受饥荒内战之逼,乃移徙他处谋生。但于一九二三年至一九二九年期间,内地移往东三省之人民计四,九五二,一九〇名,其于东省安家永居者,仅有二,四〇八,六四三名,占全数百分之四八.六而已;余百分之五一.四,则每届年终,即返原籍,其向东三省移殖,惟为一时谋生之计耳。① 第二,大家庭制度足以养成依赖习性,构成一种类似"家庭共产"之制度。普通若一家之中,一人致富,率全家籍以食。又如有一人在政界或商界,握有要职,则其他同宗或亲戚群趋之,甚或竟有弃其前业以谋仰托其亲戚之荫庇者。② 处此大家庭制度之下,富贫相济,相依为生,殆为惯例。且壮者须供养尊长,否则即目为不孝。此种制度,固能促成互助美德,然结果则消灭个人进取精神,养成依赖习性,致构成均产之趋势。而此种趋势,又因均分遗产之制而益强固。故一人于其生时,积有财富者,迨及其死,则其产业恒为子孙所耗散无遗也。

以政治环境言,则自民元以来,内战未息,税租繁重,中间虽得欧战之机会,然以自陷困境,亦未能充分利用,工业化终乏进展。据最近中央研究院社会科学研究所陈翰笙君之统计,自民国五年至十七年间军费加增五倍。最先不过一万五千三百万元,至后竟加至八万万元之巨。中央政府之开支,用于军事者在民国五年不

---

① 南开大学经济学院在《大公报》刊登之《经济研究周刊》,民一九,六月二九日。吾人所宜注意者,即东北移民之一部分,非为永久居住东北,而为逐年来往者。

② Lieu, D. K.; "The Chinese Family System", in *China Critic*, Sept. 20, 1928, pp. 330-331.

过百分之三四,至十二年则为百分之六四。各省政府之开支用于军事者更高:民国十四年,江西为百分之七八,十二年,山西为百分之八〇,河南为百分之八四,湖北为百分之九四,十一年,四川为百分之八八。如此巨额军费,洵足惊人。① 而究其来源,又无往而非出自厘税。二十年元旦以前,厘金尚未裁撤,大宗税源,即由此出。此外则为田赋。又加以巧为诛求之附加税及各种预征,卯粮寅收,税入动逾巨万。盐税之附加税亦然。他如强派公债,滥发纸钞,滥铸辅币等之间接税,有时更较直接税为尤烈。如目前铜元充斥,市面汇价日跌,非惟中等阶级蒙害极巨,即一般苦力,亦受损莫大焉。②

中国之经济环境,本最利于工业化。惜交通阻滞,运输不灵,工业化亦以纡缓。中国面积大过美国三分之一,③而铁路则不过一五,三〇〇公里。以全国人口四八五,一六三,三八六计,每百万人仅有铁路三一公里。在另一方面,于一九二〇年美国全国人口为一〇五,七一〇,六二〇,而铁路则有六一九,六一四公里,每百万人竟有铁路五,八六一公里。④ 换言之,中美两国每人所有铁路之比较,为一与一八六之比。处此情形之下,无怪旅行甚难。由桂阳至南京不过一,四〇四英里,旅行其间,需时兼旬。若筑有铁路,则经五七小时即至矣。由南宁至广州相距一,四九五英里,若筑有铁路,则昔之必行十日者,今仅五十小时可达矣。⑤

---

① 陈翰笙:"中国农民担负的租税",《东方杂志》,民一七,十月十日,九至十页。
② 同上,一三,一七至一九,二三页。
③ Encylopaedia Britannica, Fourteeth edition, 1929, Vol. 5, p. 509.
④ Statistical Abstract of the Unite States, 1924, pp. 2,357.
⑤ Sun Fo: "National Scheme of Construction", in *China Yearbook*, 1929-30, p. 362.

(三) 中国工业化之程度

就上述富源及环境二点,即可推见吾国工业化之程度。盖自农业方面观之,则农田技术,俱未受工业化之影响。收割耕耘,悉用手工。据白克氏之考查,中国农业一半利用人工,美国则不过百分之一。同时中国平均每一农家仅用四分之三马力,而美国则用八马力有奇,超过中国农家所用十倍。此因美国治农,多用机器,大抵全部工作五分之三,即由机器而成,若中国农民,则用机器之事,尚未多见也。①

中国农艺,虽多墨守旧法,然农业经营,则已渐由昔之自给政策而趋入近世之市场贸易。不但销行国内,亦且载售全球。数十年来丝茶即为我国大宗出口货品。近年来东三省产品极丰,赖中东,南满两路,运销外国。河北之棉花,海外销售,亦极畅旺。计在民国十八年中,豆丝茶棉四者,占中国全部出口货物一半,价值约五万万关两焉。其中大豆与豆制品,值关银二三二,一七九,六八二两,占全出口额百分之二二.九;生丝与蚕茧值关银一五一,八五三,四一七两,占全出口额百分之一四.九,茶值关银四一,二五二,四二八两,占全出口额百分之四.一;棉花,棉子及棉子饼值关银三五,五三二,一三六两,占全出口额百分之三.五;总值关银四六〇,八一七,六六三两,占是年全国出口额百分之四五.四。

---

① Baker, op. cit., pp. 330-332. 美国农田所有之动力五分之二,系由动物供给;中国农田所有动力之二分之一,系由动物供给。

至于矿业,则工业化风气已开。盖采矿事非轻易,非有机器设备及大规模资本,不易奏功。但中国矿业,目前未甚发达。计在民国十六年间,金属及非金属矿物之总产值,为二九八,八五〇,〇八七元,而煤铁锡三项产物所值,已占全部矿产百分之八〇.八(二四一,六二六,六一〇元)。其中煤产一项,即占百分之六六.二(一九七,九〇四,四八六元)等于全世界产值百分之一.六。铁占百分之七.六(二二,七五三,九二四元),等于全世界产值百分之〇.五。①

煤矿业中,有十一矿,在一九一二年至一九二八年之十七年间,此各矿中有一年或数年产额,每年均超过四十万吨。其于一九一六至一九二八年之十二年间,此十一煤矿每年平均产煤一二,五三五,〇〇〇吨,占全国煤产额百分之五七(一九一七年之统计付阙)②。只开滦与抚顺二矿,在此期间,每年平均产八,四四六,〇〇〇吨,占全额百分之三八.四。据地质调查所报告,年产五千吨以上之"大"煤矿,于一九二八年共产煤一七,二八六,五五一吨,占是年总产额(二五,〇九一,七六〇吨)百分之六八.九。中国现有"大"煤矿四十一处,其中年产一万吨以下者有二处;年产自一万零一吨至五万吨者十一处;五万零一吨至十万吨者十一处;十万零一吨至五十万吨者十四处;五十万吨以上者三处。③

铁矿业中,有十一矿,一九一六年至一九二八年之十二年间,(一九一七年除外)此各矿中有一年或数年产额每年均超过一万吨。当此期间铁矿之经开采者,最多之时有八处,最少之时亦有四

---

① 《中国矿业纪要》第三次,第二三表。
② 同上第一次,二六至二七页;第二次,第二表;第三次,第一表。
③ 同上第三次,第三至第四表,二三〇页。

处。在此十二年间，已开之矿，其铁矿砂之产额，计有一三，九三一，四四二吨，占全国产额（一，九六四，七四七，一九八吨）百分之七〇.九。其余百分之二九.一，均系以土法采自小矿者。一九二八年内，中国铁矿砂之总产额计二，〇〇三，八〇〇吨，其中一，四七四，九〇〇吨，占全额百分之七三.六，系八处新式铁矿所产者。八矿之中，以振新最大，汉冶萍次之，其于是年之铁矿砂产额，若以吨计，则为五四〇，〇〇〇；四一九，九五〇；二一二，五三三；一一五.〇〇〇；一一二，三九〇；六四，〇〇〇；一〇，五七三；四五四。①

第二表　一九二七年中国矿产值之分类

矿之名称	值（银圆）	金属及非金属之百分比	金属及非金属之百分比
金属	68,492,321	100.0	22.9
铁、铁矿砂	22,753,924	33.2	7.6
锡	20,968,200	30.6	7.0
钨矿砂	8,365,000	12.2	2.8
锑	7,004,550	10.2	2.3
金	4,065,320	5.9	1.4
锰矿砂	2,853,240	4.2	1.0
铋	720,900	1.1	0.2
其他	1,761,087	2.6	0.6
非金属	230,357,766	100.0	77.1
煤	197,904,486	85.9	66.2
盐	20,672,690	9.0	6.9

① 《中国矿业纪要》第一次，三六页；第二次二四至二五页，第一四表；第三次，二九六至二九八页。

（续表）

矿之名称	值（银圆）	金属或非金属之百分比	金属及非金属之百分比
碱	3,625,000	1.6	1.2
陶土	2,125,460	0.9	0.7
石	1,780,000	0.8	0.6
石灰	1,100,000	0.5	0.4
其他	3,150,130	1.3	1.1
总　　计	298,850,087		100.0

炼铁工业，在目前中国，更属幼稚。中国有铁厂九处，其每年之容量，产钢一一〇，〇〇〇吨，产铁九六七，四〇〇吨；于一九二八年，其开工者只四处，产铁二五四，九七三吨，占全国产铁额（四三三，八四三吨）百分之五八.八，其余百分之四一.二，系内地小矿所产。该四大矿厂之产额，南满铁路会社产一六〇，〇〇〇吨；本溪湖煤铁公司产八四，三四五吨；六河沟煤矿公司产五，八一四吨；保晋公司产四，八一四吨，九大厂之中，仅有汉冶萍，和兴，上海三处能炼钢，但自一九二六年以来，均已停工。目前炼钢之处，有上海之江南造船厂，沈阳及巩县之兵工厂，唐山之启新水泥厂等处，惟产额有限，每年尚不能超过二万至三万吨。①

制造业之工业化，则极明显。良以工业化一名词，通常恒指制造之技艺及其组织之改进，其他关系经济生活之变迁，则稍次焉。今日之工厂制度，可为制造业工业化之象征。但何谓工厂制度，则言人人殊。据民国十八年十二月三十日国民政府公布之工厂法定

---

① 《中国矿业纪要》第三次。一三二页；第三次，二九九至三〇〇页。

义,以通用汽力电力水力发动机器及雇佣工人三十人以上者,始得称为工厂。此种定义,未免过狭。许多制造厂坊应列为工厂者,均未及计入。最近实业部调查九省二九城市中之工厂工人,则以雇工三十人以上之工厂为调查单位,但于运用动力机器等,则不兼及。① 此种调查,本足为中国工业化之鉴镜,第因调查地域不广,殊不能包括全国耳。综计于民国十九年,在江苏,浙江,安徽,江西,湖北,山东,广东,广西,及福建九省中之二九城市,仅有工厂工人一,二〇四,三一八人。② 此类工人,按职业性质分为十二类。中以纺织工人最多,计占全体百分之四七,次之为饮食品,占百分之一四.七,衣服占百分之六.六,建筑占百分之六.五,化学品占百分之六,机械占百分之五.四,教育占百分之四.九,器具占百分之三.三,其余美术,公用,及交通三业,共占百分之一.四,杂项占百分之四.二。此十二类工业,更细分为一一一小类。纺织业二一,饮食品工业二〇,衣服五,建筑六,化学品二一,机械五,教育五,器具

---

① 工商部:《全国工人生活及工业生产调查统计报告书》,第一及第二号。工厂工人之定义,见第二号序文。
② 该调查包括九省二九市如下:江苏省之上海、无锡、苏州、南京、武进、南通、宜兴、镇江及扬州;浙江省之杭州、嘉兴及宁波;安徽省之芜湖、蚌埠及安庆;江西省之南昌及九江;湖北省之汉口、武昌及大冶;山东省之青岛;广东省之广州、顺德、佛山、潮安及汕头;广西省之梧州;及福建省之福州及厦门。换言之,其他二十一省,辽宁、吉林、黑龙江、热河、察哈尔、绥远、山西、陕西、甘肃、宁夏、河北、河南、外蒙、西藏、西康、新疆、青海、贵州、云南、四川及湖南,均未包括在内。在此二十一省中,至少有八省十八市,均为工业及矿业中心,理应包括在调查区域之内。辽宁省之大连、沈阳、营口、抚顺及本溪湖;吉林省之哈尔滨及长春;河北省之天津、北平、唐山、塘沽及石门;河南省之郑州;山西省之榆次及新绛(纱厂业中心);云南省之箇旧及四川省之重庆;此外即在已调查之九省中,尚有下列之工业及矿业中心,亦未包括在内:安徽省之当涂、江苏省之崇明、海门、常州、江阴、太仓及常熟;江西省之萍乡;山东省之泸南、周村及烟台;及福建省之三都澳。

五,美术三,公用四,交通二,杂类一四。中有六小类未详,所余一〇五类总共雇工一,〇二五,三六五人,占全体工人百分之八五.一四。若以雇工百分数之高下言,此等工业更可分为三类,第一类雇工当全体工人,(一,二〇四,三一八人)百分之一有奇者有十三业,计凡七七四,八三五人,共占全体工人百分之六四.三四。第二类雇工百分之〇.五至百分之一者有十七类,计凡一二八,一四七人,共占全体工人百分之一〇.六四。第三类雇工不及百分之〇.五者有七五业,计凡一二二,三八三人,共占全体工人百分之一〇.一六。在第一类之十三项工业中,有棉纺(百分之一七.一五),棉织(百分之九.一二),缫丝(百分之一二.三六),丝织(百分之二.二〇),卷烟(百分之四.〇一),机械(百分之三.一一)及金属器皿(百分之二.〇七)等七项,大部分都在此九省。其余六项如成衣(百分之三.四一),针织(百分之一.七八),靴鞋(百分之一.三〇),印刷(百分之四.一〇),木器(百分之二.六),火柴(百分之一.二七),虽在此九省外,亦甚发达,尤以火柴一业,到处可见。他如面粉(百分之〇.五二),榨油(无统计),碾米(百分之〇.五八)及电气(百分之〇.二三)诸业,因调查之省分不多,在第一类中皆未列入。榨油业以东三省为中心。面粉业除东三省外,山东及河北二省,亦极发达。在九省中碾米业应甚重要,然其雇工百分数竟如此低微,是或由于分类不详所致。盖杂粮业雇工八,六四五人,占全数百分之〇.七二,或者即为碾米工人,亦未可知。若然,则该业合计当有雇工一五,六五八人,占全数百分之一.三〇。电气业大都为电灯厂发电之用,亦为国内普通工业之一。鉴于上列诸业,对于中国之工业化,有极重要关系,故特将其中棉纺织,缫丝,丝织,面粉,榨油,火柴及电气等工业提出,从细分别论述如下。

第三表 一九三〇年中国之二十九城市中工厂工人之分配
（依工业种类分类）

工业名称	人数	百分比	工业名称	人数	百分比
纺织业	566,301	47.02	火柴	15,254	1.27
纺纱	206,532	17.15	造纸	8,526	0.71
缫丝	148,814	12.36	医药	7,796	0.65
棉织	109,809	9.12	漂染	6,893	0.57
针织	21,452	1.78	陶瓷	6,779	0.56
丝织	26,448	2.20	玻璃	6,664	0.55
织物杂类	8,019	0.67	其他十五类	20,108	1.67
轧花	6,510	0.54	机械工业	65,501	5.44
未分类者	16,597	1.38	机械制造	37,436	3.11
其他十三类	22,120	1.82	五金器具制造	24,961	2.07
饮食品工业	176,504	14.66	其他三类	3,104	0.26
烟叶	48,333	4.01	教育工业	59,006	4.90
调味	9,076	0.75	印刷	49,391	4.10
肉类	8,666	0.72	文具	8,173	0.68
杂粮	8,645	0.72	其他三类	1,442	0.12
碾米	7,013	0.58	器具	40,195	3.34
糖果饼干	6,330	0.53	木器	29,600	2.46
面粉	6,275	0.52	其他四类	10,595	0.88
未分类者	63,254	5.25	美术	10,216	0.85
其他十二类	18,912	1.58	刺绣	7,261	0.60
衣服工业	80,078	6.65	其他二类	2,955	0.25
成衣	41,124	3.41	公用	5,432	0.45
制鞋	15,681	1.30	未分类者	1,481	0.12
未分类者	18,404	1.53	其他三类	3,951	0.33
其他二类	4,869	0.41	交通二类	1,284	0.10
建筑工业	77,737	6.45	杂项	50,044	4.16
锯木	7,306	0.61	煤	8,215	0.68
未分类者	54,432	4.52	未分类者	24,785	2.06
其他四类	15,999	1.32	其他十二类	17,044	1.42
化学品工业	72,020	5.98	总计	1,204,138	100.99

棉纺织业在目前中国,为最大之工厂工业。据实部所调查之九省中,有七省从事纺纱业,计有工人二〇六,五三二人,从事织布业者有一〇九,八〇九人。在运用电力或汽力之大纱厂中,多系同时兼营纺织二业,惟在中等以下之工厂中,织布多系独立之工业。关于棉纺织业之情形,自一九二〇年以来,上海"华商纱厂联合会"编有统计,故知之较详。据一九三〇年之统计,中国已有纱厂一二七家,中只有两家系织布厂,其余一二五家均系纺纱厂或纺织厂。在此一二七厂中,有三家尚未开工,有一家已停工。是项统计经精细修正后,其中一二〇厂之资本及公积金计有二八八,三二八,一三八元;一二五厂之纺锤,计有四,二二三,九五六锭;五〇厂织机计有二九,二七二架;一一九厂之动力量计有一二六,五七四启罗瓦特及三八,五一一匹马力,共等于一五五,四五七启罗瓦特;一一九厂之工人数为二五二,〇三一人;一一六厂之消费棉花量为八,七五〇,〇一九担;纺纱量为二,四五五,一七七包(每包重约四百磅);四三厂之织布量为一四,七七九,五三八疋。

根据是项统计,可断定棉纺织业确系一种大规模工业,平均每厂须资本及公积金二,四〇二,七三五元,纺锤三三,七九二锭,动力一,三〇六启罗瓦特;工人二,一一八。此处所谓一厂,虽系指一个工厂而言,但有时一厂,亦有数家分厂者。中国所有棉纺织厂之中,有十四厂计设分厂六十一家。其中一厂,竟有分厂十六家之多,至少亦多有两家分厂。此六十一分厂计有纺锤二,四三四,二八〇枚(占全数百分之五七.七),织机一七,〇五八架(占全数百分之五八.三),动力八二,六六四启罗瓦特(占全数百分之三四.〇),雇工一三六,五三八人(占全数百分之五四.二),棉花消费量四,四四八,九〇七担(占全数百分之五〇.九),纺纱一,二五五,六五四包（占全数百分之五一.二），织布九，一七八，二三八疋（占全数百分之六二.一）。总计有资本及公积金一六五，一〇八，八九三元。①

纺织类中，除棉纺织业外，其次丝纺织类，亦为吾国最大之工厂工业。据实业部之调查，从事缫丝业之工人，有一四八，八一四人（占全工人数百分之一二.三六），从事丝织业者二六，四四八人，（占全数百分之二.二）。此外从事丝绒业者二，一八九人，从事丝棉混织业者三，二六五人，从事丝织品杂类者五，三六九人，总计有一〇，八二三人，占全体工人数百分之〇.九。换言之，从事丝纺织业之雇工，共有一八六，〇八五人，占全数百分之一五.四六。但实在尚不止此数。盖实业部调查范围内之各省，其统计既不完备，他如辽宁四川之丝业工人，亦未列入。一九二九年内，厂丝之输出额，值关银一三〇，六二一，一一八两，其中江苏输出者占百分之四四.二，广东占百分之三七.一，四川占百分之一四，辽宁占百分之六.九，山东占百分之四.三。江苏与广东多系白丝，四川系黄丝，山东系野蚕丝。

缫丝业之成为工厂工业，其肇始当在六十年前；目前机器缫丝，几已遍播全国。一九二九年输往外国之生丝计有一八九，九八〇担，值关银一四七，六八一，三三八两，其中厂丝有一五二，三六〇担，占全额百分之八〇.二，值关银一二八，五五七，一二九两，占全额百分之八七.一。机器缫丝之产额虽大，然缫丝厂之规模则甚小。据最近调查，一九二八年内，上海一处有缫丝厂九〇处，投资总额二，五〇一，九〇〇元，工人计五二，四六三人。故平均每厂资

---

① 详细统计，请阅已付梓之拙著《中国之棉纺织业》。

本为二七,七九九元,有工人五八三人。① 复据调查,一九二九年内,无锡有缫丝厂三八处,投资总额一,九三八,九六〇元,工人二七,二四五人。② 平均每厂资本为五一,〇二五元,工人七二二人,故较上海之缫丝厂为大。广东之缫丝厂,其规模亦较上海者为大。一九二九年内,上海有缫丝厂一〇四处,使用缫丝机二三,五八二架,平均每厂有二二七架,其中最小之厂,有缫丝机七〇架,最大者有六〇〇架。但最普通者,每厂有缫丝机二〇〇架至二九九架;此种最普通之厂有六〇处。③ 同年广东有缫丝厂一四六处,使用缫丝机七二,二四六架,平均每厂有四九五架,其中最小之厂,有二八〇架,最大者有七二〇架。但最普通者,每厂有四〇一架至五〇〇架;此种最普通之厂,有七八处。广东之缫丝厂,平均每处有缫丝机四九五架,而上海者,只有二二七架,故前者实较后者大两倍有余也。④

至于丝织业,在城市中尤以苏杭宁三处为最盛。工厂之组织,已经流行,但在穷乡僻壤之区,则仍系一种家庭工业。就以往十余年内观之,各工商业中心之区,丝织业殆已适用大规模生产之制度。如一九二八年上海有丝织厂五一处,其中四六处资本总额一,二七九,〇〇〇元,平均每处有资本二七,八〇五元;工人总数六,二六二人,平均每厂有工人一三六人。⑤ 然在南京,小规模之生产制度,则仍流行。一九二九年南京有丝厂六〇四处,资本总额九

---

① 《上海之工业》,上海特别市社会局,民一九。
② 《统计月报》,民一九,六月。
③ 《经济半月刊》,民一八,四月,一五,二二页。
④ 广东省政府统计事务处:《统计汇刊》,第一卷第四号。
⑤ 《上海之工业》。

〇三,七九〇元,工人一一,五三四人,平均每处仅有工人一九人,资本一,五〇〇元。惟缎织业一项,规模较大,平均每厂有工人三二,资本二,七五三元。从事缎织业者,有二九四处,资本总额为八〇九,四五〇元,占南京丝织业资本总额百分之八九.四;工人有九,四四六名,占南京丝织业工人全数百分之八一.九。①

饮食品工业中,以面粉业为目前我国之最大工厂工业。从事是业之工人,虽为数不多,然投资于是业之资本,为数殊有可观。一九二八年天津有五家面粉厂,资本总额为二,六五五,〇〇〇元,而工人仅有六七七人。② 平均每厂资本为五三一,〇〇〇元,工人一三五名。同年上海有面粉厂一九处,其中一三处之资本总额为七,九五〇,〇〇〇元,工人一,八七一名,③平均每厂有资本六一一,六四〇元,而工人仅一四四名。一九二九年无锡有面粉厂四处,资本总额为一,六八〇,〇〇〇元,工人四八五名,平均每厂有资本四二〇,〇〇〇元,工人一二一名。④ 在此三面粉业中心,共有面粉厂二二处,资本总额一二,二九五,〇〇〇元,工人三,〇三三名,平均每厂有资本五五九,〇〇〇元,工人一三八名。据实业部之调查,苏鄂赣皖鲁五省,共有面粉业工人六,二七五名,吾人如依上述津沪锡三处平均每厂之工人数一三八名衡之,则五省仅有面粉厂四五处。然事实上,于一九二二年,在全国一二三面粉厂中,

---

① 工商部技术厅:《首都丝绩业调查记》,民一九,九月,三九,四七,四九,六一,七七至七八页。
② 《天津特别市社会局周年报告》(民一七年八月至民一八年七月),五六四页。
③ 《上海之工业》,八六至八七页。
④ 《统计月报》,民一九,六月。

该五省已有六一处:江苏有四四处,湖北九,山东六,安徽及江西各一,可见前项估计,未免过低。① 据一九二八年之调查,中国共有面粉厂一九三家,其中一六五家,有资本银三,一五八,〇〇〇两,银圆三〇,一二八,〇〇〇圆,日金一八,四二三,〇〇〇元,卢布一,〇二〇,〇〇〇,钱一〇〇,〇〇〇,〇〇〇,小洋二〇〇,〇〇〇。其分布之地域,东三省有七三处,济南一二,山东(济南除外),山西,河南,及江苏之一部共有一四处,天津一四处,河北(天津除外)绥远八处,汉口九处,扬子江流域(上海汉口除外)二三处,上海二七处,无锡一二处,云南一处。②

饮食品工业中除面粉业外,榨油业亦为最大之工厂工业。据一九二八年前"经济讨论处"之调查,全国有油坊二八六处,其中五分之三(一七六所),均设于东三省。其余一一〇所,设于江苏省三九,湖北者二六,山东省者二七,河北者一一,其他各省者七所。中有九四所投资总额计日金一三,〇八〇,〇〇〇元,银洋七,六二三,〇〇〇圆,银二,二八〇,〇〇〇两,小洋四六五,〇〇〇元,奉票一〇〇,〇〇〇元,钱一二,〇〇〇,〇〇〇。③ 复据南满铁道会社调查部之调查,一九二九年内,东三省共有油坊四七二所。中有四〇四所设于南满,六八所设于北满,投资总额为日金三四,三四二,二五一元,平均每坊有资本七二,七五九元日金。共有榨油机一二,九一〇架,平均每坊有二七四架,所有油坊每天能产油饼五六九,九二一块,平均每坊产一,二〇七块。④

---

① 《农商公报》,民一一,一二月一五日。
② *Chinese Economic Journal*, June, 1928.
③ 同上。
④ 南满铁道会社调查课,满洲之油坊业,调查资料第一三五种,八至一六页。

化学品工业中,火柴制造为最大之工厂工业。据实业部调查之九省中有七省从事制造火柴,计有工人一五,二五四名;江苏有六,〇二八人,占全数百分之三九.五;广东有二,七一〇名,占百分之一七.八;山东有二,〇五六人,占百分之一三.五;浙江有一,七一三人,占百分之一一.二;湖北有一,二三〇人,占百分之八;安徽有一,一六七人,占百分之七.七;江西有三五〇人,占百分之二.三。是项工业,以其所供给者,系日常必需品,故极为普遍。据一九二八年七月前"经济讨论处"之调查,中国共有火柴厂一八九处,其地域之分布几及各省:设于广东广西者四一处,山东二七,东三省二三,江苏一八,河北一四,四川一三,河南一一,山西九,云南七,浙江六,湖北湖南六,安徽江西五,甘肃,陕西及福建各有三处。中有一〇三处(几为全数五分之三),其资本总额为六,七二六,〇〇〇元,银三八五,〇〇〇两,日金二,一九五,〇〇〇元,大福洋七〇,〇〇〇元。其中七三处,于一九二八年内,年造火柴六〇,七〇〇箱,月造二五,九二〇箱,日造一一五箱及一,四六五吨。①

第四表　一九二九年中国各大商埠贸易额之比较

埠名	直接国外贸易		总贸易		内地通过贸易	
	海关两	百分比	海关两	百分比	海关两	百分比
哈尔滨	55,617,170	2.4	55,197,506	1.5	290,479	0.2
安东	78,447,393	3.4	91,313,054	2.5	166,089	0.1
大连	389,086,056	16.9	473,665,052	13.1	2,221,788	1.2
天津	196,403,303	8.6	342,631,149	9.5	56,793,137	22.1
胶州	82,983,101	3.6	166,801,328	4.6	2,843,863	1.6

---

① *Chinese Economic Journal*, July, 1928.

（续表）

埠名	直接国外贸易		总贸易		内地通过贸易	
	海关两	百分比	海关两	百分比	海关两	百分比
汉口	62,613,588	2.7	265,519,529	7.3	4,100,902	2.3
上海	988,686,714	43.1	1,035,689,733	28.1	75,310,825	42.5
广州	116,855,787	5.1	183,589,036	5.1	2,801,748	1.6
其他	326,315,497	14.2	1,001,403,098	27.7	32,575,563	18.4
总值	2,297,008,609	100.0	3,615,809,485	100.0	177,104,394	100.0

供给电灯厂及工厂电力之发电事业，亦系大工业之一。据一九二九年之调查，中国共有发电厂六四五处，多数均系独立经营，非附属于工厂或矿局者。中有四九九处，有发电量六一四，八六〇启罗瓦特。有十五处，其发电量占全数百分之六二.三，余四八四处仅占全数百分之三七.七。此四八四厂中，每厂之发电力在一启罗瓦特至五〇启罗瓦特者有二一一处，占发电量全数百分之〇.九；在五一启罗瓦特至一〇〇启罗瓦特者九二处，占全数百分之一.一；在一〇一至五〇〇启罗瓦特者九一处，占全数百分之三.五；在五〇一至一，〇〇〇启罗瓦特者三一处，占全数百分之三.八；在一，〇〇一至五，〇〇〇启罗瓦特者五〇处，占全数百分之一七.四；在五，〇〇一至一〇，〇〇〇启罗瓦特者九处，占全数百分之一一。①

在商业交通及金融三方面，工业化之进行，尤为显著。商业大有集中数大商埠之趋向。计一九二九年上海一埠，占直接对外贸易值百分之四三.一，总贸易值百分之二八.七，及内地通过贸易值百分之四二.五。其次，大连占直接对外贸易值百分之一六.九，总

---

① 张家骧:《我国之电厂设备》,《统计月报》,民一八,九月。

贸易值百分一三.一,及内地通过贸易值百分之一.二。第三为天津占直接对外贸易值百分之八.六,总贸易值百分之九.五,及内地通过贸易值百分之三二.一。第四为广州,占直接对外贸易值百分之五.一,总贸易值百分之五.一,及内地通过贸易值百分之一.六。胶州,汉口,安东,哈尔滨四处,占直接对外贸易值百分之一二.一,总贸易值百分之一五.九及内地通过贸易值百分之四.二。总之,在四五通商大埠中,有八埠共占直接对贸易值百分之八五.八,及总贸易值百分之七二.三。在三八埠中有八埠占内地通过贸易百分之八一.六。至各埠之直接对外贸易,总贸易,及内地通过贸易,其详细分配情形,可参阅第四表。

交通方面,如汽船,铁路,汽车路,航空,邮政,及电报之发展,俱为工业化进步之象征。计民国十八年中,中国海关进出各商船总共一五四,六六七,九一○吨,其中汽船吨位占百分之九一。① 中国之铁路为数有限,其长不过一五,三○○公里,仅及汽车道长度三分之一(按汽车道长凡四八,六五六公里)②。航空为新兴事业,国内三大航线,曾与美商订约施行。其由西伯利亚飞航欧洲三线,则与德商缔约办理。然今日正式通商航线,则惟沪汉及平津间有之。邮政事业,尚称发达。统计在民国十八年中,寄递各种邮件七二四,五一二,三六○件,包裹六,八五七,二五四件,其有邮政局所一二,二六三所,邮路四六六,五四八公里,中以五四,八六九公里为水道,一四,九二一公里为铁道。③ 电报在民国十七年中,有陆路

---

① 沿岸商轮吨位,不包括航行各商埠及内港间之商轮吨位,或航行未与外人通商之沿岸商埠间之商轮吨位。
② *Chinese Economic Journal*, May, 1930.
③ 王仲武:《中国邮政统计》。

线九九,七九七公里,电线一七一,五〇一公里,河底电线八七.九二公里,地下电线一六.七公里。同时电机有摩斯机二,四四五具,费士吨机八一具,电报局一,一四〇所。计在该年,国内电报共发三,二五九,〇二五件,合计一三六,五六九,五八八字。①

至中国之金融,则今日之银行公司皆为工业化影响所形成。据前农商部自民元至民九所调查之最高投资额,计在民国五年旧式钱庄投资额凡二四六,二二九,二六二元,在民国八年投资于新式银行者不过五四,二四七,七一一元,仅占银行钱庄投资总额百分之一八而已。② 惟自此年起,银行事业,日益发达。至民国十四年,已有银行一四一家,中有三分之二或九三家,为自民国八年起陆续成立者,统计成立于民国八年者一一家,九年者一三家,十年者二三家,十一年者一八家,十二年者一五家,十三年者八家,截至十四年六月以前者五家。合计此一四一家之额定资本,凡三七五,一五〇,〇〇〇元,实付资本为一五八,一六〇,四七一元。除此一四一家本国银行外,其由中外合办之银行,亦有二〇家,总共额定资本计有二四,〇〇〇,〇〇〇元,四,五〇〇,〇〇〇两,五〇,〇〇〇,〇〇〇法郎,五五,〇〇〇,〇〇〇卢布,六〇,二七五,〇〇〇日金。实付资本计有一二,〇四五,二三〇元,四,五〇〇,〇〇〇两,一〇,〇〇〇,〇〇〇法郎,五五,〇〇〇,〇〇〇卢布,及二八,三五九,〇〇〇日金。外国银行共有四三家,其额定资本计有五〇,〇〇〇,〇〇〇元,一一,〇〇〇,〇〇〇金镑,一三,〇〇〇,〇〇〇美金,一〇,〇〇〇,〇〇〇两,一八二,〇〇〇,〇〇〇法

---

① 《民国十七年度交通部统计年报》,南京交通部,民二〇,一月。
② 何廉、方显廷:《中国工业化之程度及其影响》,民一九,一二至一三页。

郎，一四〇,〇〇〇,〇〇〇荷金，五四三,〇〇〇,〇〇〇日金。其实付资本，则有二〇,〇〇〇,〇〇〇元，六,六四四,一六〇金镑，八,〇〇〇,〇〇〇美金，七,五〇〇,〇〇〇两，一五〇,四〇〇,〇〇〇法郎，一三五,〇〇〇,〇〇〇荷金，及四一一,三七〇,九〇〇日金。① 至言公司，据前《农商部统计年报》所载，以民国元年为最多，合计九七七家，共有资本一千一百万元。营业范围，大抵不外农商制造及运输四类。自民国元年至九年间，此四业投资额之比例，大都无甚更变。中以制造业资本为最大，约占全体百分之六〇至七〇。运输及商业，则各占百分之一〇至一五。农业资本最少，仅与百分之五至一〇而已。各公司资本之大小，亦极悬殊，但最普通者，多在国币万元以下，计在民国元年至九年间，公司中资本只此数者，占全额百分之二五至五〇。次之为资本一万至五万元者，计占百分之二五至三〇。至资本超过五万以至十万元者，则不过百分之一〇。其余百分之一五至二五，大都为极大公司，资本数额，约在十万元至百万元以上也。②

（四）中国工业化之影响

不明中国工业化之程度，实无以尽知其工业化发生之影响。然居今日而言中国工业化之影响，仅可敷陈事实，以为学者鉴往知

---

① "Banking Institutions in China", in *Chinese Economic Monthly*, Jan, 1926, pp 21-22.
② 何廉、方显廷：《中国工业化之程度及其影响》，民一九，一五至一六页。

来之资,未可据以为定论也。细察目前工业化之影响,与泰西各国百余年前之情形相仿。所有社会及经济之变迁,曾一度风行于英法者,今皆重见于中国。中国工业化之第一影响,即为生产集中化。中国虽划分三十省,然生产荣繁之地,则不过集中于江苏,辽宁,河北,广东,山东,及湖北六省而已。此六省虽仅有全国面积百分之一〇,全国人口百分之三六.三,而矿业则占全国百分之五五.一,煤矿占百分之六四.九,铁矿占百分之六四.四,棉纺业占百分之九三,缫丝业占百分之九二.六,榨油业占百分之八六,运用电力占百分之八七.六,总贸易占百分之八四,对外直接贸易占百分之九二.五,内地通过贸易占百分之九一.九,铁路占百分之五三.四,汽车路占百分之四二.一,电线占百分之四二。在此六省中,又以江苏一省之工业化为最甚,于前言各种事业,大多数列居第一,工业商业俱占首要地位。上海为全国最大都市,无锡为腹地发达最盛之城市,二者实为构成江苏工业化之重心。辽宁之工商业,虽逊于江苏,然矿业则远过之。大连为华北巨埠,即在该省。河北为第二矿业省份,工业商业则居江苏辽宁二省之后。天津一埠,为华北工业重镇。① 如广东则有广州,以商业著称。山东则有青岛,工业最盛。湖北则有汉口,矿产极富。至于交通,辽宁及河北之铁道最长,山东及广东则以汽车道见称,电报则以江苏及山东最为发达。人口密度,亦以江苏为最高,每方英里有八〇一人。山东次之,每方英里有四六六人。再次为河北,每方英里有四五〇人。广东每方英里有三八〇人。湖北每方英里有三四一人。辽宁每方英里仅一二一人。

---

① 欲知河北省工业化之详情,请参阅拙著"Industrialzation and Labor in Hepei", in *Chinese Social and Political Science Review*, April, 1931, pp. 1-28.

第五表（甲） 中国各省工业化程度之比较

（百分比）

项　目	江苏	辽宁	河北	广东	山东	湖北	其他
面积	0.9	2.6	1.5	1.9	1.5	1.6	90.0
人口（民十九）	7.3	3.2	6.4	7.2	6.7	5.5	63.7
矿产（民十六）	2.2	29.2	15.4	1.5	5.0	1.8	44.9
煤产（民十七）	0.4	33.0	25.3	0.5	4.6	1.1	35.1
铁矿产（民十七）	—	32.7	—	0.1	—	31.6	35.6
制造业							
棉纺锭（民十九）	66.4	3.2	6.9		8.8	7.7	7.0
丝出口（民十八）	44.2	6.9	—	37.1	4.3	0.1	7.4
豆油豆饼出口（民十八）	0.1	85.5	—	—	0.3	0.1	14.0
发电量（民十八）	42.2	21.5	10.9	5.2	3.9	3.9	12.4
贸易							
总贸易（民十八）	30.8	17.8	10.4	10.6	5.7	8.7	16.0
对外贸易（民十八）	43.7	21.5	9.0	11.5	4.1	2.7	7.5
内地通过贸易（民十八）	47.4	3.1	34.6	2.9	1.6	2.3	8.1
交通							
铁路（民十三）	4.6	21.7	12.6	5.4	6.7	2.4	46.6
汽车路（民十九）	6.6	6.5	6.2	8.7	11.2	2.9	57.9
电报（民十七）	10.8	3.8	8.8	4.6	9.5	4.5	58.0

第五表（乙） 中国各省工业化程度之比较

项 目	江苏	辽宁	河北	广东	山东	湖北	其他	合计
面积(65)平方英里	44,346	126,326	69,358	91,872	69,812	78,449	4,306,752	4,786,915
人口①								
总数(民十九)	35,510,882	15,274,825	31,242,050	34,876,507	32,500,218	26,724,482	309,034,422	485,163,386
每平方英里密度(民十九)	801	121	450	380	466	341	72	101
矿业(民十六出产,元)②	6,605,726	87,310,560	45,978,974	4,564,970	14,939,280	5,254,564	134,196,013	298,850,087
煤(民十七出产,吨)③	117,477	8,280,646	6,335,630	150,000	1,157,488	317,982	8,732,537	25,091,760
铁(民十七铁矿砂出产,吨)④	—	655,000	—	1,600	—	633,983	713,217	2,003,800
制造业								
棉(民十九纱锭)⑤	2,804,770	135,764	291,756	—	371,668	324,070	295,928	4,223,956
丝(民十八厂丝出口,海关两)⑥	57,743,426	9,107,613	—	48,523,422	5,635,126	141,225	9,470,306	130,621,118

① 陈正谟:《中国矿业纪要》。
② 《中国矿业纪要》第三次,第二表。民一九年九月二九日之 Nankai Weekly Statistical Service.
③ 《中国矿业纪要》第三次,第二表。
④ 同上,二九六至二九八页。
⑤ 《中国纱厂一览表》第九次,民一九。
⑥ 《中国海关一八民洋贸易总册》,上下卷。

（续表）

	项 目	江苏	辽宁	河北	广水	山水	湖北	其他	合计
贸易	大豆(民十八,豆油,豆饼出口,海关两)①	44,293	68,787,575	2,276	1,360	240,506	73,929	11,261,840	80,411,779
	电力(民十八,启罗瓦特)②	259,285	131,954	67,037	32,109	23,721	24,081	76,673	614,860
	全部贸易(民十八,海关两)	1,113,258,218	643,105,885	374,886,169	383,045,020	206,456,575	312,537,331	582,520,287	3,615,809,485
	国外贸易(民十九,海关两)	1,002,941,727	494,231,294	206,105,579	264,333,488	94,887,994	62,863,961	171,644,566	2,397,008,609
	内地通过贸易(民十八,海关两)	83,873,638	5,408,742	61,267,087	5,073,845	2,868,503	4,101,522	14,511,057	177,014,394
交通	铁路(民十三,公里)③	700	3,320	1,930	822	1,024	363	7,141	15,300
	汽车路(民十九,公里)④	3,207	3,136	3,011	4,217	5,440	1,397	28,248	48,656
	电报(民十七,陆地线,公里)⑤	19,557	6,875	15,855	8,279	17,061	8,149	104,773	180,549

① 《中国海关民一八华洋贸易总册》,上下卷。
② 张家骧:《中国之电厂设备》。
③ 《统计月报》,民一八年九月二八页。
④ Nankai Weekly Statistical Service, June 16, 1930.
⑤ China Yearbook, 1929-30. p. 475.

人口集中为工业化之第二影响。据海关人口估计,在民国十八年人口数超过一〇〇,〇〇〇之二三埠中,有一九埠在光绪三十年计有人口六,六五六,〇〇〇,至民国十八年则增至一〇,三四三,〇二五,计每年中每一千人增加一七人。有二二埠之人口在宣统二年为七,〇六六,〇二〇,至民国十八年则增至一一,一七二,〇六五,计每年中每一千人增加二二人。有二三埠之人口民国九年为九,九四六,〇〇〇,至民国十八年则增至一一,三七四,九〇二,计每年中每一千人增加一四人。但在此二三埠中,有六埠人口,则由五,二三五,六〇〇减至二,八七七,八三二。若除此六埠不计其余一七埠之人口,每年增加率每千人中当为六一人矣。查各地人口增加最巨者为东三省各埠。计哈尔滨在宣统二年有人口三〇,〇〇〇,至民国十八年则增至二五二,九八八。大连人口在宣统二年为一六,〇〇〇,至民国十八年则增至二二〇,五八八。营口人口在光绪三十年为五〇,〇〇〇,至民国十八年则增至一〇六,二四二。① 观此人口猛增之现象,多为经济影响所促成,非皆由自然蕃殖所致。盖都市工业化愈甚,人口集中之趋势亦愈显著。虽然,人口集中,亦非漫无限止。待至一定额度,集中之事,亦有停止或衰减者,纯视一都市之经济和社会环境为依归也。

---

① 中国海关所估计之中国历年人口总数,固非完全可靠;但因缺乏其他同样之统计,亦可藉以表示中国人口增加之趋向矣。详细批评,请阅民二〇年二月二日之 *Nankai Weekly Statistical Service*。

第六表　一九二八年上海各业工厂按雇工人数之比较

工业名称	工厂数	每厂工人数	总工人数	工业名称	工厂数	每厂工人数	总工人数
棉纺业	55	1,715	94,342	印刷业	210	39	8,248
缫丝业	90	583	52,463	帽业	8	35	276
火柴业	7	391	2,737	化妆品业	20	32	630
衣服业	3	350	1,050	制皮业	18	31	554
制蛋业	1	287	287	机器业	163	31	5,122
水电业	8	223	1,781	藤竹木器业	13	30	391
造纸业	13	169	2,193	调味食品业	5	30	151
面粉业	12	156	1,871	其他化学品工业	9	28	254
轧花业	5	148	739	科学仪器业	3	28	84
卷烟业	69	137	9,478	糖果罐头业	47	27	1,251
丝织业	46	136	6,262	五金器具业	57	27	1,518
榨油业	12	125	1,501	皂业	23	24	555
毛织业	7	118	828	煤球业	8	22	173
棉织业	99	94	9,327	其他器具工业	5	21	106
珐琅业	8	82	652	磻砂业	47	20	930
玻璃业	16	78	1,243	文具工业	4	19	78
毛刷业	6	72	431	绳带工业	23	19	440
电器业	21	69	1,445	伞业	9	18	164
造船业	2	69	137	制药业	14	16	219
其他纺织业	13	60	774	其他食品工业	4	13	51
针织业	110	59	6,536	乐器玩具业	11	13	146
杂项	10	57	566	冰冷食品业	6	12	71
日常用品业	6	50	298	其他机器业	1	12	12
建筑材料业	21	46	968	碾米业	46	9	399
造漆业	3	44	131	眼镜业	5	7	37
制匣业	15	40	601	总　　计	1,498	149	223,691
漂染印花业	81	39	3,190				

工厂制之流行，为工业化之第三影响。民一九年实业部曾调查九省中之工厂工人，但于工厂本身之大小，则无稽考。不过前农商部，曾于民国元年至九年间，调查国内工厂之大小。此时工厂规

模极小，每厂雇工由七人至九人者，占百分之八〇至八五。其雇工由三〇人至九九人者，占百分之一〇。其余百分之一〇之工厂，规模较大，每厂雇工大约一〇〇人至一，〇〇〇人之间。① 上海市社会局曾经调查各工厂，计在民国十七年间，共有一，四九八工厂，雇工二二三，六九一人，按工业性质分为八大类及五二小类。② 计一三小类中共有工厂三二八所，当工厂全数百分之二一.九，每厂雇工由一〇〇人至一，〇〇〇有奇，合计为一七五，五三二人，当雇工全数百分之七八.四。另二一小类中，共有工厂八四八所，当工厂全数百分之五六.六，每厂雇工由三〇人至九九人，合计为四一，六七一人，当雇工全数百分之一八.七。最后一八小类中，共有工厂三二二所，当工厂全数百分之二一.五，每厂雇工由七人至二九人，合计为六，四八八人，当雇工全数百分之二.九。以雇工人数言，当以棉纺业工厂为第一（一，七一五），次之为缫丝（五八三），火柴（三九一），衣服（三五〇），制蛋（二八七），水电（二二三），制纸（一六九），面粉（一五六），轧棉（一四八），卷烟（一三七），丝织（一三六），榨油（一二五），毛织（一一八）。此类工业较大，雇工人数亦较多，恒自一〇〇以至一，〇〇〇以上焉。

工业化所发生之第四影响，即为新式劳工及劳工问题之兴起。近世工业勃兴，生产多用机器以代手工。所雇工人，仅责以司机职务，技术体力，俱非必需，故妇人孺子，亦相率入厂，积渐成为今日之新式劳工阶级。按上述实业部调查九省中之工厂工人中，女工占百分之四五（共计四三二，九四〇人），童工占百分之六（共计六

---

① 何廉、方显廷：《中国工业化之程度及其影响》，民一九，三五页。
② 《上海之工业》，上海各种工厂工人人数比较表。

三,二八七人)。计在调查之十一类工业中,纺织业有女工三六五,一五九人(百分之八四.三),饮食品业有四二,九五九人(百分之一〇),其余九类工业,共有女工二四,八二二人(百分之五.七):计化学品一〇,三一五人(百分之二.四),美术五,八六四人(百分之一.四),衣服四,九六四人(百分之一.一),器具一,二〇七人(百分之〇.三),建筑一五五人,机械一四三人,公用一〇八人,教育八三人,杂项一,九八三人(百分之〇.五)。至于童工,则在十二类工业中,仍以纺织业为最多,计占百分之七一.五(四五,二〇九人);衣服业次之,占百分之八(五,〇三九人)。此外化学品业占百分之五.八(三,六四三人),器具业占百分之三.五(二,一九五人),其余八类工业,共占百分之一一.二(七,二〇一人):计饮食品占百分之二.九(一,八三〇人),美术占百分之一.六(一,〇〇四人),机械占百分之一.五(九五三人),教育占百分之一.四(八七九人),建筑占百分之一.三(八三七人),交通及公用占百分之〇.一(五八人及一九人),杂项占百分之二.四(一,六二一人)。合计女工童工在纺织业中共占百分之八二.七,计凡四一〇,三六八人,饮食业共占百分之九,计凡四四,七八九人。其余十类工业中,女工童工共占百分之八.三,合计四一,〇七一人。①

新式劳工阶级日众,现代之劳工问题,亦愈演愈繁。时至今日,竟成一社会重要问题。第一,今日劳工之职业灾害,职业疾病,以及失业悲苦等,俱极可怜。据最近估计,上海工会工人在民国十七年间失业者,为百分之七.一九;十八年为百分之六.四五。在新式工厂中,如棉纺织厂及面粉厂,大都利用机器,然以安全设备未

---

① *Nankai Weekly Statistical Service*, Mar. 2, 1931.

周,工人以是而遭伤损甚至丧失性命者,不知凡几。他如职业疾病,亦极可畏。地毯业中之痧眼症,最为流行。在民国十四年火柴厂尚未禁用黄磷以前,业此工人,多患落颔惨疾。① 此外工时延长,工资微薄,亦皆为劳工之大问题。实业部调查九省二九城市中之工厂工人最普通之工资,每月约十元至十五元;最普通之工作时间,为每日十小时。② 劳工第三问题,即为女工及童工。据实业部调查九省中之十二类工业,女工即占全体百分之四五,童工占百分之六。雇用女工童工,影响国民健康至巨。政府为补救起见,在新颁工厂法内,虽明文规定女工童工工作每日不得超过八小时,童工年龄至低须满十四岁,女工生产时须与两月休息,以及禁止女工童工服役夜工等,但迄未严格施行。加以女工童工入厂日多,虽成年男工生计,亦即为彼辈所夺,然其工资,则随而减轻矣。

　　劳工问题,日趋繁重,政府及工人,俱力谋解决之道,如工会组织及劳工法规等是。据实业部对于九省工厂工人之调查,综计工会会员凡五七六,二五〇人,中以属于纺织业者为最多,计凡一三八,九四六人,占全体百分之二四.一。次之为交通,占百分之一八.四,机械占百分之一二.九,饮食品占百分之一〇.六,化学品占百分之七.五,建筑占百分之五.四,衣服占百分之四.七,器具占百分之二.四,教育占百分之二,公用占百分之一.一,美术占百分之〇.一,杂项占百分之一.〇,其他占百分之九.八。③ 劳工法规,则自国民政府成立后,曾先后颁布工会法,劳资争议法,工厂法,及工

---

① 见拙著之 *Industrialzation and Labor in Hepei*。
② 《全国工人生活及工业生产调查统计报告书》,第一号。
③ 同上第三号:*Nankai Weekly Statistical Service*, Mar. 9, 1931.

厂检察法四种。其工厂法及工厂检察法，仅就运用机械动力及雇工三十人以上之工厂而设。所定范围，既甚狭隘，且因事实上之困难，迄今尚未能施行也。

中国工业化之程度，既日益增高，其国外贸易及贸易政策，亦受更变。观其入口货物，第一以五金及机器为最多。计在民国二年，金属矿物进口不过二八，九七三，一五六关两，至十八年则增至七〇，八五五，一五二关两，前后增加二.四倍。同时期内，其输入钢铁，亦由一五一，二七六吨加至六三九，五二二吨，增加四.二倍。输入纺织机器，亦由八三六，八六四关两，增至八，九三一，七五一关两，增加一〇.七倍。输入电气物料，则由二，三二二，三三九关两，增至一三，二七八，五六七关两，增加五.七倍。第二点可注意者，即制造品之输入减少，而原料进口则逐渐增加。计自民国二年至十八年间，棉纱棉线之输入，竟由二，七〇二，八七六担（百分之一〇〇）减至二三四，一二六担（百分之八.七）。原棉则由一三三，二五五担（百分之一〇〇）增至二，五一四，七八六担（百分之一八八七）。以中国国民用棉之多，臆度棉织布疋之入口，必年有加增，而实际则不然。据海关报告，在民国二年为二八，四四五，七〇〇疋，至民国十八年仍不过二八，一〇五，一九一疋，无甚增减。此种无增无减现象，实为国内棉纺绩业发展之又一象征。卷烟业亦复如是。自民国二年以来，渐有增加烟草入口及减低卷烟入口之趋势。查民国二年卷烟输入共六，二〇九，〇三七，〇〇〇支，至十八年亦不过八，一三六，三二五，〇〇〇支，前后相比，不过增加一.三倍，极为有限。以国内卷烟之需要测之，其入口数量，断不止此。而在同时期间烟草入口，则由一六一，五八六担，增至九一〇，九四〇担，增加五.六倍矣。

第七表　一九一三年至一九二九年中国之进口贸易

货品	年	量		增或减(一九一三为一〇〇)	值(海关两)	增或减(一九一三为一〇〇)	占进口总值之百分比	
							一九一三	一九二九
棉布	1913	28,445,700	疋		101,732,770		17.8	
	1929	28,105,191	疋	98.8	164,611,609	161.8		13.0
棉纱棉线	1913	2,702,876	担		72,636,779		12.7	
	1929	234,126	担	8.7	14,346,750	19.8		1.1
棉花	1913	133,255	担		2,984,022		0.5	
	1929	2,514,786	担	1,877.2	91,123,857	3,053.7		7.2
卷烟	1913	6,209,037	千支		12,589,300		2.2	
	1929	8,126,325	千支	131.0	20,745,619	164.8	1.6	
烟草	1913	161,586	担		3,572,560		0.6	
	1929	910,940	担	563.7	26,642,392	745.8		2.1
金属及矿产	1913				28,973,156		5.1	
	1929				70,855,152	244.6		6.1
钢铁	1913	151,276	吨		13,823,194		2.4	
	1929	629,522	吨	422.8	53,216,098	385.0		4.2
纺织机械	1913				836,864		0.1	
	1929				8,931,751	1,067.3		0.7
电气材料及配件	1913				2,322,339		0.4	
	1929				13,278,567	571.8		1.0
总输入	1913				570,162,557		41.8	
	1929				1,265,778,821	222.0		37.0

第八表 一九一三年至一九二九年中国之出口贸易

货　品	年	量		增或减（一九一三为一〇〇）	值（海关两）	增或减（一九一三为一〇〇）	占出口总值之百分比	
							一九一三	一九二九
厂丝	1913	70,150	担		46,233,379		11.5	
	1929	152,360	担	217.2	128,557,129	278.1		12.7
丝	1913	78,865	担		27,276,296		6.8	
	1929	37,620	担	47.7	19,124,209	70.1		1.9
豆油	1913	491,817	担		3,732,012		0.6	
	1929	1,115,047	担	226.7	12,243,094	328.1		1.2
豆饼	1913	11,818,443	担		24,962,787		6.2	
	1929	18,715,729	担	158.4	51,209,060	205.1		5.0
大豆	1913	10,325,964	担		23,296,876		5.8	
	1929	45,192,478	担	437.7	164,739,605	707.1		16.2
棉花	1913	738,812	担		16,235,604		4.0	
	1929	943,786	担	127.7	29,603,791	182.3		2.9
煤	1913	1,489,128	吨		6,592,078		1.6	
	1929	4,123,281	吨	276.9	30,908,301	468.9		3.0
铁	1913	67,086	吨		1,430,528		0.4	
	1929	203,843	吨	303.9	6,440,256	450.2		0.6
铁矿砂	1913	271,810	吨		609,744		0.2	
	1929	971,990	吨	357.6	3,210,763	526.6		0.3
锑	1913	17,239	吨		1,092,510		0.3	
	1929	23,770	吨	137.9	4,225,997	386.8		0.4
总输出	1913				403,305,546		37.7	
	1929				1,015,687,318	251.8		44.2

至出口货物，近亦趋重于制造品，尤以纺织物为多。厂丝在民国二年时计输出七〇，一五〇担（百分之一〇〇），至十八年则增至一五二，三六〇担（百分之二一七.二）。他如非厂丝，则由七八，八五六担（百分之一〇〇）减至三七，六二〇担（百分之四七.七）。同时豆油之输出，亦由四九一，八一七担（百分之一〇〇），增至一，一一五，〇四七担（百分之二二六.七）。豆饼由一一，八一八，四四三担（百分之一〇〇），增至一八，七一五，七二九担（百分之一五八.四）。

在关税尚未自主以先，受不平等条约之束缚，税则莫能自定。入口税率，率为值百抽五。直至民国十八年关税主权恢复后，始行提高。然是年所行之税则，尚为民十四年与列强共组之特别税则委员所代筹者。真正国定税则之施行，则自民国二十年一月一日始。此次税则，为政府之国定税则委员会所订定，非如前之双方合定者可比也。此次新税则中，即采用保护原则。入口货物有为本国产品所不能竞争者，则加税至值百抽五十之多。其足以促进本国工业化之物品，则低至值百抽五。卷烟入口税，则按牌从量征收。中有数种，竟较最高从值税为尤高：每一千支值二一.八八金单位者（按每一金单位值美金四角），则从量征税一六金单位。丝织品多值百抽三五至四五。毛织品多值百抽三〇，地毯则值百抽三五。火柴值百抽四〇。茶值百抽三〇。国内棉业，虽日益发达，但棉布及棉纱，需要仍多，入口税率，多在值百抽七.五至一五之间。他如五金及机器，为中国工业化之必需品，则税率极微。大抵矿砂及农业机器为值百抽五，电机行擎及钢铁为值百抽七.五，铁路电车道及飞机用件，亦皆按值百抽五轻税征收。如此者尚多，不能悉举；但就上所言，已可见新税则中采用保护政策之一斑焉。

外人投资，在过去亦为中国工业化促进之原因，至今日中国工业化之基础已立，日在发扬光大之时，资本之需要孔巨，外人之投资，势将反因为果。盖资本之运用，常循供求原则，率由工业发达国家，向工业退化国家移动也。① 外人在华之投资，论者恒分政府公债，商业投资，及慈善事业投资三类。其中以商业投资一项，与中国工业化之关系最深。此类投资，以英日两国为最多，次之为德法美三国。据刘大钧氏之估计，在民国十八年中，英国在华投资合计一，四三三，九三六，五一六元。日本在华投资之估计甚多，各有出入。据支那实业发展会之估计，则为一，八三一，九六五，〇〇〇日金。但日本政府财政部之估计，则为一，〇三七，二五八，〇〇〇日金。② 他如美国之商业投资，据雷默氏估计，为一〇〇，〇〇〇，〇〇〇美金。③ 法国之商业投资，据刘君估计，为五一，八一五，〇〇〇法郎，三，八四〇，〇〇〇两，及三八九，〇〇〇元。④ 至其他各国之商业投资，则尚无统计可稽。

（五）中国工业化之将来

自欧风东渐，时习竞效西洋，论者多以中国经济组织受欧美工业化之熏陶，改进甚速。综观上述中国工业化之程度，主因，及其影响，可见其殊不尽然。第一，中国幅员辽阔，交通阻滞，民习守

---

① Remer: *American Investments in China*, 1929. p. 29.
② 刘大钧：《外人在华之投资统计》，《统计月报》，民一九年，二，三，五及一二月号。
③ Remer, op. cit., p. 34.
④ 刘大钧：《外人在华之投资统计》。

旧，泥于革新。工业化之传入垂七十年，而流行稍著者不过六省，仅占全国面积百分之十而已。且工业化之范围，亦极有限。以矿产言，在民国十六年产铁矿砂仅占世界百分之〇.五，产铜占百分之〇.〇二，产铅占百分之〇.〇九，产锌占百分之〇.〇九，产锡占百分之六，产煤占百分之一.六，产石油占百分之〇.〇〇〇〇八。棉纺业为中国工厂工业之最大者，计在民国十八年中，共有纺锭不过四，二二三，九五六枚，当全世界所有百分之二.六。① 动力织机，亦不过二九，二七二架，当全世界所有百分之〇.九而已。② 丝业为中国最古工业，近已日就凌替。昔日广袤市场，今多拱手让人。此因本国丝商，拘守旧法，不思改进。虽缫丝一项，业已采用机器，然较之日本，远落后着矣。计在民国十四年，世界运销茧丝共三九，八六〇，〇〇〇启罗格兰。其中华丝，不过八，一二〇，〇〇〇启罗格兰，仅占百分之二〇.四，而日丝则有二五，八四五，〇〇〇启罗格兰，竟占百分之六四.八焉。③ 在日本缫丝悉用机器，中国则机缫丝据十八年海关统计，不过百分之八〇而已。④ 中国之国外贸易，以全国人口平均计之，在民国十七年不过每人二.九一美金。若与太平洋各国相较，实极低微。计新西兰为三二七.三美金，加拿大

---

① 根据一九二八年出版之 *Cotton Facts*，全世界共有纱锭一六五，一〇三，〇〇〇。

② 根据第十四版第六卷之 *Encyclopaedia Britannica*，五四八页，民一六年全世界共有力织机三，一八三，〇〇〇架。

③ 同上，第二〇卷，六七六页。

④ 民十八年中国出口生丝一八九，九八〇担，中有一五二，三六〇担或百分之八〇为厂丝。

为二八〇. 四九美金,澳大利亚为二一八. 〇一美金,智利为九〇. 三〇美金,美国为七四. 七二美金,台湾为四八. 八三美金,秘鲁为三〇. 八五美金,墨西哥为三〇. 五八美金,日本为三〇. 四九美金,菲律滨为二四. 三〇美金,荷属东印度群岛为一九. 四四美金,高丽为一八. 一九美金,由瓜多为一一. 七三美金,安南为一〇. 三〇美金,苏俄为五. 一九美金。① 言及交通,中国益落人后。据民国十三年之统计,中国铁路不过世界百分之〇. 九五而已。若以每万人所有铁路线计之,则中国所有,仅〇. 二英里。除澳大利亚之康柏拉联合区 Canberra Federal District 为每万人〇. 〇二英里外,较世界任何国家为低。盖美国(阿拉斯加在内)每万人有二三. 六英里,法国八. 五英里,德国六英里,英国五. 五英里,俄国(欧洲部分)五. 三英里,意大利三. 三英里,日本一. 七英里,英属印度一. 二英里,俄国(亚洲部分)一英里,较之吾国,均倍蓰焉。②

　　中国之工业化,虽为救济过剩人口及提高国民生活程度必需之方剂,然以目前情形,推测将来,其进展之希望,似甚有限。盖中国财源既不甚富,加以家庭观念,入人过深,进取精神,不易发展。凡此诸端,俱为工业化发展极大之障碍。然使内战停息,政局稳定,最近数十年内之工业化,必有进展之望。但若欲其跻于泰西工业先进国之列则为势甚难。盖中国以农立国,今日之经济组织,仍多为中古式。工业之兴盛,仅限于数大都市,所关系于全国之经济

---

① League of Nations, *Memorandum on International Trade and Balances of Payments*, 1926-28.
② *Encyclopaedia Britannica*, XXI, p. 104.

生活甚微。倘能充分发达,或足以雄视东方,亦未可知。要于英美相较,必远不逮。至工业化进展后对于提高目前人民生活程度,则固极可能之事,无足疑也。

以国际情形衡之,则中国之工业化,极为需要。近世各国,莫不以生产过剩而起经济恐慌,以致市场萧条,商业疲敝。若果中国工业化,则各国过剩之生产,必为其所吸收,经济恐慌,或可藉之以免。虽然,此就经济方面言之耳,若以政治目光绳之,则又未必尽然也。

吾人对于工业化
应有之认识

一　工业化之意义及由来

"工业化"三字,含有广狭二义:就广义言之,工业化即产业化或产业革命,系指社会之经济组织,如农业、工业、商业、金融、财政等等之现代化;就狭义言之,工业化即制造工业之现代化,社会经济之组织之其他方面,如农业、商业、金融、财政等等之现代化勿与也。时人之谈工业化者,恒以二义互相混惑,辄致误会丛生。本文所指之工业化,系就狭义而言;至广义之工业化之探讨,容俟之于异日。

言及工业化之由来,吾人不能不追溯近代欧洲经济之发展,盖近代欧洲经济之发展,综合言之,系以制造工业之现代化为中心。制造工业现代化之兴起与扩张,亦即工业化之由来也。

中古时代欧洲之经济制度,颇为简单。国家以农业为重,地主与农民为社会上之主要阶级,除少数政治都会如伦敦巴黎外,市镇之大者为数颇少。手艺工人与商贾,散居各市镇,从事于工商业务。生产以需要为依归,需要则仅限于当地,故当时之生产与交易,为量颇微。是则工业实农业之附庸,工业化实无由产生也。

迨重商主义兴起，注重发展国外贸易，厥后放任主义创始，奖励个人竞争，航海事业因以进步，海外市场因以扩张，结果促进机械之发明，货物之大量出产，工业革命以来，向之以农业为重者，今则以工业为重，换言之，由农业国进而为工业国，由农业化进而为工业化矣。

欧洲工业化之行程，并非及于欧洲全部，南部及东部之国家，仍多保持其原始时代之农业经济；其工业化者，除东北部之俄国及东南部之意国外，仅西北部之英、法、德、比四国而已。英、德、法三国可称之为欧洲之工业领袖国家。在不同之时期内，在不同之情况下，均先后工业化矣。以工业化之时期论，英国最早，工业革命，于始于十八世纪末叶，约历八十年之过程，始由农业国一变而为工业国。法国工业化之开端，约肇始于一八二五年至一八三〇年间；沄国工业化之程度，与英国迥然不同，其国内之主要经济活动，仍为农业。德国之工业化，更迟于法国一二十年，约肇始于一八四八年左右，其进步极为敏速，不数十年，一跃而侪于近代高度工业化国家之林。欧洲大陆以外之国家，以工业化之程度论，首推美国。美国之工业化，约肇始于一八四〇年，一八六五年后，即有长足之发展。日本之工业化约发轫于明治维新之时，一八九四年中日战争后，日渐发展；欧战期中，发展更速。

二　工业化之程度及方向

世界各国工业化之进展，既有前后迟早之区别，则其发展之程度及方向，自亦互异。高度工业化之国家，国内经济，以工业为主；

低度工业化之国家,其国内经济,农工并重,或仍以农业为主。以工业为主之国家,工业化之程度甚高,矿业、钢铁及机械等"重工业",与夫制造日用品之"轻工业",并驾齐驱,皆大为发展。以农业为主之国家,工业化之程度极浅,其所有之工业,多为制造日用品之轻工业。以工业为主之高度工业化国家,有英、美、德等国;以农工并重或以农业为主之低度工业化国家,有法、日、俄及中国等。此七国工业化之程度不同;试比较之,以观一斑。重工业之基础为煤与铁;由煤铁之消费量,足可窥知其重工业发展之程度。一九三〇年各国之煤消费量,以每人计,英美德皆为四公吨,法国为二.一公吨,日本为〇.五公吨,苏俄为〇.三公吨,而中国仅〇.〇五五公吨。一九三〇年各国之钢铁消费量;以每人计,美国为五七〇公斤,法国为三八八公斤,英国为二八二公斤,德国为二八〇公斤,日本为四七公斤,中国仅为二公斤。

自电气发明后,电气与煤,同为工业之发动力,故自电气之消费量上,亦可略窥工业化之程度。一九三〇年之电气消费量,美国为最多,每人之消费量为九七七基罗小时(kWh),德国每人为四四二基罗小时,英国为三五八基罗小时,法国为三六六基罗小时,日本为二一六基罗小时,中国仅五基罗小时。

轻工业可以棉纺织业为代表,藉示一般。一九三一年之统计,以纺锤论,英国所有之纺锤占世界纺锤总额百分之三三.六,美国占百分之二〇.四,德国占百分之六.六,法国占百分之六.三,苏俄占百分之四.七,日本占百分之四.四,中国仅占百分之二.四。自另一方面观之,英国每千人有纺锤一,一九九,美国每千人有纺锤二七三,法国二四九,德国一六九,日本一一三,俄国四个,而中国每千人仅九个。

高度工业化之国家,国民多从事于工商业,其从事于耕种者,为数寥寥。故自其农民占全国人口之百分数观之,亦可窥知该国工业化之程度若何。以农民占全国人口百分数论,英国为最少,占百分之六.六,美、德、法较多,占百分之二六.三,百分之三〇.五,及百分之三八.三。日本及中国更多,占百分之五三.一及百分之七四.五。俄国为最多,占百分之八六.七。故即以农民人口多寡论,工业化之程度,英、美、德仍居首位也。

综上所述,无论以煤铁或电力之消费额论,以所有纺锤之比例论,或以农民人口论,英、美、德三国工业化之程度为最高,法、日次之,而以俄国及中国为最落后。

三　中国工业化之原因程度及今后亟应采取之途径

中国为工业化最幼稚之国家,无庸讳言。四千年来,以农为本,贱视工商,而自秦汉以降,厉行重农政策,国内所有之工业,重遭打击,完全以皇室消费所好为兴衰之归;重艺术而不重生产,民间工业,因以难兴。迨海禁大开,与欧美之工业接触,机器产品输来,国内手工业,渐被摧毁,压迫频来,不得不走上工业化之途径,故中国工业革命之开始,乃由于外力之压迫而出于被动者也。

年来国内经济萧条,农村破产,忧国之士,群起谋农村复兴之策。议论纷纷,主张迥异。综合言之,大致可分两派:一派系主张"振兴农业以发引工业",一派则主张"发展都市以救济农村"。仁者见仁,智者见智,各有其理由在。然细为探讨,此二者之主张,虽似各趋极端,实非无调剂之余地者。盖一国之经济建设为一整个问题,农业与工业有相互之连带关系;觭重觭轻,皆非所宜。工业无农业以供给原料,则工业不振,农业无工业以供给制成品,则农民之消费及生产二方面,均受损失。观乎以农立国之苏俄,而亟亟提倡工业化;一方面发展重工业,制造农业机械,以为苏俄农业工业化之张本;他方面发展轻工业,制造衣食用品,以补救农民之消费经济;其理由自明矣。年来国内高谈经济建设者,对于工业在国家整个经济组织上之地位,或少争执之处,然对于工业化三字,提倡之者固不在少数,反对之者,亦所在多有;考其致此之由,不外对于工业化之认识之互异。盖工业化之发展,其程度及方向,如上所述,均受时间与环境之支配,而各有不同;则中国之工业化,虽属必要,然究能发展到如何程度,并应发展重工业或轻工业,自非工业化三字所能解答。时人之反对中国工业化者,恒以英、美、德国之高度工业化国家为对象,藉以证明中国工业化之不可能,固属言之成理。若复由不可能进而倡说不可为,则非吾人之所愿赞同者。然则中国工业化之进展,其程度与方向,果以取法何国为最适宜乎?吾人上已言及,世界工业化之国家,以其工业化之程度论,有高度工业化(如美、法、德)及低度工业化(如法、日、俄、中)之分。如欲高度工业化,则必须具备的条件有三:一为原料,二为资本,三为人工。原料中之最重要者,为煤与铁;试问中国所有之煤铁若何?中国铁矿储量,据估计占世界总储量千分之六,约当美国储量七十二分之一,英国九分之一。煤之储量,虽占世界第三位,但碍于运输困难,大量开发,为期遥远;即现已开采者,矿权又多操诸外人之手。故原料之条件不备。以言资本,尤足令人悲观。年来农村破产,国内经济凋敝,农民之收支尚难相抵,遑论储蓄以作工业投资之用哉!是则中国所有者,仅为人工耳。若仅以劳力众多,工资低廉为基础，而谋高度之工业化；就目前商战剧烈之情形观之，亦非持久之策。条件不足，中国高度之工业化，势不可能。然则中国工业化所宜采取之途径，果以何者为宜耶？

就吾人拙见所及，中国工业化之程序，应先自轻工业入手，而渐及于重工业。然与国防有关，由政府创办者，则须当作别论。吾人深知，重工业乃轻工业之基础，若重工业不发展，则一国工业化之程度极其有限；但兴办重工业，须有充足之原料，雄厚之资本，及销售之市场。原料与资本不备，无庸讳言。姑退一步言之，设中国有如许之资本，创办重工业，并有相当之原料，以资开发；其出品能否在市场上与外货相角逐，则又系一大问题。且吾国历年自外洋输来之货物多为轻工业之制造品，故吾人认为中国工业化，宜先自轻工业着手也。

然则中国所宜创办之轻工业，究以何种轻工业为宜耶？吾人认为中国所宜创办之轻工业应以下列之四原则为准绳：

（一）工业品之销路，应以国内市场为基础。盖国外市场，久已为欧美工业先进国家瓜分净尽，工业落后之国家，起而与之相角逐，大非易事。国内市场，又应以农民为基础；中国人口，四分之三为农民，故工业品之运销，自宜以农民之购买力为转移。

（二）宜创办能利用小资本经营之工业。盖中国资本缺乏，至小资本，则尚易募集也。

（三）宜创办需用机器少而需用手工多之工业。盖中国之人工众多，工价低廉，则出品之成本轻；成本轻，则推销自易。

（四）创办能利用中国已有之天然产物（如农产、矿产）之工业，则原料一节，无须自外国输入，非惟成本因运费缩减而低廉，即原料之来源与价格，亦不至受外人之操纵。

中国为一农业国,故欲使工业发达,必须使农业发达。盖农业发达,农民之购买力因生产增加而始增加。农民之购买力增加,工业之基础始能日臻稳固。农业为一有季节性之实业,故除移民垦荒,改良耕种方法,铲除阻碍农村发展之种种障碍外,又须提倡乡村工业,利用农民余暇,以增加其收入,提高其购买力。至宜创办何种乡村工业,方不致为城市工业所排挤,尚须加以研究也。

总之,就吾人拙见所及,中国经济建设为一整个问题。目前中国所亟应创办者为轻工业而非重工业,为小工业而非为大工业,为城市与乡村并重之工业,而非仅偏重于城市之工业也。

一九三五年二月四日

INDUSTRIAL ORGANIZATION IN CHINA

Modern industries in China had their origin in the early sixties when Tseng Kuo-fan, realizing the impotence of Chinese military organization in face of western armaments and warships, for the first time persuaded the government to establish ammunition factories and shipyards in the coastal ports of Shanghai, Tientsin and Foochow. The early beginnings, however, were not followed up with developments that would lead to rapid industralization on a scale such as Germany or Japan had gone through during about the same period. The causes for retarded industrialization in China are beyond the scope of the present paper, but that such industrialization as China has already gone through has failed to produce a system of organization that may be considered modern will constitute the central thesis of our present analysis. The two distinguishing features of modern industries in China — the lack of organization and the small scale of operation — will first be outlined in the introductory section, while in the ensuing sections they will receive further confirmation and substantiation through a comprehensive survey of the various aspects of Chinese industrial production, namely raw materials, machinery and buildings, labor, and marketing.

I. FEATURES OF CHINESE INDUSTRIAL ORGANIZATION

A. *Lack of Organization.* Roughly speaking, three sets of factors have converged to make it practically impossible to introduce a full-fledged system of organization into modern industries in China; these include sudden growth of modern industries, persistence of the old gild and family system, and severe struggle for livelihood in a densely populated agricultural country.

(1) Sudden Growth of Modern Industries. —As one reads the early history of factory production in England in the light of China's more recent experience, certain factors stand out clearly as favorable circumstances which were present in the one case but lacking in the other. One cannot be unmindful, of course, of the social friction and the great economic losses which have marked the transition period there also.① But the principal difference is that in England that transition had a well-marked middle stage which is almost lacking in China, the factory conducted entirely with human and animal power. When steam power was introduced into England there were already in existence well-conducted factories with a disciplined labor force, with a far-going specialization of

---

① *Cf.* Karl Marx, *Das Kapital*, Volksausgabe, Berlin, 1923, Vol. II, pp. 314-315.

functions. ① In China, modern industry has entered almost full-grown with the use of the most intricate power-driven machinery which Western ingenuity had contrived at the end of the nineteenth century. Workers here were expected to obey the curt commands of the foreman who had never been regimented before and did not know what it was to keep the apparatus they were operating from standing still at whatever cost in physical or mental discomfort. The wage incentive was new to them, or at least to that large number who had not previously been engaged in manual labor on some organized job such as large-scale construction or the loading of ships. It was new to many of them to work at a job of which they could see neither the beginning nor the end but only that stage in the transformation of material on which they and others near them were engaged. Many of them had never used tools other than those they had been familiar with at home and farm from the days of their childhood.

Nor was the employer's role better prepared for such changes in previous experience. He came from the small store or the warehouse, sometimes from a native bank or from some clerical occupation. He saw how quickly the machine did its work but knew neither how it was made nor what conditions were required to keep it in good working order. He knew even leas of planning work when the output exceeded the easily calculable demands of an immediate market. His bookkeeping made no

---

① See, for instance, Heinrich Cunow. *Allgemeine Wirtschaftsgeschichte*, Berlin, 1931, Vol. IV, Chapter XII: " Wirtschaftsgestaitung Englands vom Ende der Revolution (1688) bis Mitte des 19. Jahrhunderts. "

allowance for depreciation. And he employed labor as he bought materials, for immediate use, with no thought of a human relationship between himself and his workers which had to be managed to insure effective mutual cooperation over a long period. He was entrepreneur more in the sense of a merchant who sets out with a bag of silver to purchase goods which he hopes to dispose of at a profit than in the sense of an organizer of an undertaking with laws derived from its own special nature. In England many large industrial enterprises started with unfree labor which was so expensive that before long it gave way to the wage system, long before steam power was used, a system which made it necessary to consider the output and competency of individual workers in relation to the wage paid. The Chinese employer in modern industry had not had that experience and took no thought of the constancy and reproduction of his labor supply, and even to this day uses up human beings as though they had for him no value at all.

Another difference, and a very important one. In England the introduction of power machinery was preceded by a period especially rich in inventions, particularly in the textile industries. In China transition was in most branches of industry straight from primitive to modern equipment. The psychological effect of this difference is worth noting. In the one case we have a mental alertness, a general expectation of, and readiness for, new changes; in the other a complete absence, right to the point of adopting the latest device, of any dissatisfaction with the tools that had served generations of ancestors. To the Chinese the introduction of power machinery meant a jump into a new world of steel and speed;

he had to throw over not only habits of work but a whole ideology; for, dissatisfaction with the ways of his fathers in one particular meant doubt of the fathers' way of life in all its aspects. If the old loom must be discarded, then a hundred other things must be discarded with it for which there are as yet no adequate substitutes — only a vague sense that foreign people somehow had them, and that they must be learned.

With modern industry came the growth of cities, in England as well as in China. But city and country in England had been connected by a thousand threads. Mills and factories had been spread along the streams, and small towns hummed busily with the turning of wheels. In China where water power is available only in very few districts, and where communications were few and difficult, there had been no such integration of urban and rural life. Rural exodus here meant, especially since the drift was to the port cities so largely made over by foreigners, a revolution in the habits of life.

None of these changes could take place without great mental strain. Adjustment was not a consciously sought process but forced upon the people. Even to this day most of them are hardly aware of the extent to which their present economic existence has alienated them from the ways and the thinking of their forebears, but tenaciously cling to many customs and institutions hallowed by their antiquity. Thus contradictions are set up, both in the external circumstances and in the inner cohesion of the individual life career, which occasion constant frictions and nervous ill-ease. For the casual observer there is a charming cultural stability in China to which writers do not fail to pay tribute in an endless stream of essays. The student cannot help but be impressed with the appalling cost in human well-being at which this dual nature of Chinese life is maintained. Much has been written also of the conflict between the older and the younger generation in China. But there is no such neat contrast as this in actual life where, even among advanced progressives, the longing for new things does not exclude much reverence for the old, and where even the crusty conservative is pleased enough to avail himself of new comforts and to let his mind play with new ideas.

In other countries all this has been more gradual, and there was not, to start from, so complete a satisfaction as there was in China with the civilization inherited from a long chain of ancestors. Some of the characteristics of the Chinese mind which have been observed, especially in economic relations, are not old but expressions of a present inner conflict. There are too many problems to solve. Imitation of Western strenuousness has its natural limits; and even the incongruity of old habits and new, of old tastes and newly acquired ones, of manners that are sanctioned by tradition and manners called forth by new types of human intercourse, all these are at least subconsciously entering into the reactions of intelligent people to the new tasks of adjustment that confront them.

(2) Persistence of Gild and Family System. —The sudden growth of modern industries in China, which under circumstances could not have availed itself of the opportunity for gradual adaptation afforded to industrial countries like England or France, is primarily responsible for the lack of an inner integration which in turn handicaps the rise of a

modern system of industrial organization. Another cause for the lack of organization in Chinese industries is the persistence of the gild and family system. Chinese economic organization, as represented by the gilds, has had a different development in China from that in Europe. In Europe the gild fulfilled certain governmental functions and was recognized as a strong link in the administration of local affairs. In China, the gild remained almost entirely a monopoly organization in defence of vested interests. In Europe, because of the diversity of their functions, the gilds have gradually been absorbed by other organs of the state and the community. In China they could not thus be absorbed, chiefly because the status of craftsman and merchant has not changed as it has in Europe. In China regional and local self-sufficiency has limited the economic activity of both; and limitation has not, as it has in Europe, been removed by a modern era of internal social peace and by the creation of a system of communications. Morse quotes the economic historian W. J. Ashley as saying that "as soon as in any industry the amassing of great capital became feasible, as in the great London companies, the gild system tended to become a mere form." [1]

"This condition," Morse continues, "has not yet been reached in China. Great fortunes derived from industry have been, and are, known there; but inquiry will show that they have invariably been made possible by the more or less direct connexion

---

[1] *The Gilds of China*, New York, Longmans, 1909, p. 4.

of the 'merchant' with the bureaucratic world; the merchant has in such cases worked through the gild, but the gird has been his servant, subserving his interests in any direction that he might dictate."①

One might add that the gild system survives in China because, in the main, it is associated with the handicrafts and with petty business, while the large fortunes that have flown into the capitalization of modern industry② have come mainly from other sources, including the overseas Chinese merchant who, because of his foreign residence, has also been able to emancipate himself to a considerable degree from the fetters of the family system.

For, the family system not only interferes with the building up of industrial capital, it also interferes at many points with the conduct of modern business of any sort including that of industry. One large employer of a highly skilled class of labor, not long ago, was moved by the obvious physical inefficiency of many of his employees and the large incidence of sickness among them to raise wages of his own accord. The only result, as he was able to discern not long afterwards, was that each of these men was now supporting an even larger number of relatives than a person of his position was expected before to look after. In China there has all along been the unavoidable tendency, so long as the family

---

① *The Gilds of China*, New York, Longmans, 1909, p. 4.
② See my article on "Industrial Capital in China", *Nankai Social & Economic Quarterly*, April, 1936.

system prevails, to place persons in responsible positions who are in no way qualified to fill them. And that is not all. For, when a modern factory is staffed in part with those who do not hold their job by virtue of their competency, a general laxity results. Internal intrigues take the place of objective standards in promotion. Considerations which have no place in business conducted for profit swing decisions and may land the enterprise in disaster.

(3) Severe Struggle for Livelihood. — The general condition of a severe struggle for livelihood among almost all classes which characterizes the period in which modern industry takes its start in China also may be named as one of the causes of its defective organization. Where labor is a large element in the cost of production—that is, where other charges, such as interest and depreciation, are moderate in comparison with the wage bill—there is a margin within which new forms and methods of industrial management can be tried out. Without too great a dislocation in the total labor cost, it is possible to substitute skilled for unskilled labor, or the reverse, to reduce labor by the introduction of labor-saving devices, and so forth. Where, however, the proportion of labor cost in the total cost of production is small, there is no flexible margin, and the established mode of operations tends to go on because the employer dare not experiment. In China, every favorable opportunity, such as the decrease of foreign imports during the World War, has at once led to cut-throat competition, all competitors operating with about the same major costs, including a wage cost at or below subsistence level for the workers. There was neither the internal flexibility of costs which

permits management to shift costs from one item to another, nor was there a margin of financial resources for any of the host of competing entrepreneurs which would enable them to place their operations on a much larger scale than those of their competitors and thus defeat them. A single blow at times could push all of these enterprises into a corner, whether it was a new competitor from without, or an absorption of one or more of the competing enterprises by a newcomer, usually a foreigner, with capital enough to install equipment that would cut down costs below the level at which these men could produce and come out even.

We see, thus, that it is not only the traditional industries which suffer from excessive internal competition; but under present general economic conditions even an entirely new or recent industry is weakened by a system which does not permit either a control or a joint planning to further the growth of the industry. Here is a typical example. The food flavoring sodium glutamate, extracted from wheat, is a chemical product which has given rise to a considerable Chinese industry under the name of gourmet powder. Originally a Japanese import, this product was made first in China in 1921, by a company with a capital of $200,000, which was soon followed by others, one of which produces an annual average of 400,000 lbs. valued at $2,500,000. Because of excessive competition, prices dropped by 10 to 15 per cent in 1934, and the industry is now faced with a crisis that has affected almost every new industry that does not require large capital outlay or etchnical equipment. ①

---

① *China Press*, *Double-Tenth Supplement*, October, 10, 1935, shanghai, p. 72.

B. *Small Scale of Operation.* The small scale of operation constitutes the second distinguishing feature of Chinese industrial organization. In this respect one might summarize the situation by saying that industries conducted on what would be regarded as a fairly large scale in Europe and America are only those which could not be conducted otherwise at all; and that all those enterprises which might be conducted theoretically either on a large or on a small scale are conducted on the latter. Instances of industries that are being conducted on a fairly large scale are cotton spinning, wool spinning, iron and steel works, shipbuilding, flour milling, sugar refining, power generation, and cement works. Industries conducted on a small scale include silk reeling, silk and cotton weaving, hosiery knitting, match making, printing, machine construction, cigarette making. Why this difference?

Cotton spinning has to be on a large scale because such equipment as bale breaker, feeder, opener and scutcher would stand idle if the unit did not permita certain minimum output. For, operation here has to be more or less continuous, and it is not possible for one set of these equipments to serve several mills, for example. The median number of spindles per mill in the Chinese-owned mills probably comes very close to the minimum at which efficient operation is possible. Reckoned in number of spindles per mill, it is 25,000, as against nearly 35,000 for Japanese-owned mills in China. Of eighty Chinese mills studied in 1930, one-half (39) had less than 25,000 spindles;[1] but there is reason to believe that in their

---

[1] H. D. Fong, *Cotton Industry and Trade in China*, Nankai Institute of Economics Industry Series, Bulletin No. 4. 1932, Vol. I, p. 195, 199.

operations they did not reach the efficiency minimum of scale. Of the British-owned mills none had less than 25,000 spindles. Capital investment is not a true criterion because it depends so largely on factors outside the scope of operation, such as land values and the availability of outside supplies of motive power.

As an opposite example, i. e. an industry where large-scale operation is of no particular advantage, one might quote hosiery knitting. It did not, as a matter of fact, originate in China in imitation of a full grown foreign industry, as did cotton spinning; but was organized, without such models of foreign enterprise, under the master-craftsman and merchant-employer system.

"The organization was highly flexible; for a workman could easily set up as a small master or as a middleman for the large establishments, the merchant employers. The small scale on which the industry is operated can be shown in many respects. Of the 154 establishments in the industry in Tientsin, five employed no worker, while the other 149 had altogether 1,610 workers, or an average of 11 workers per establishment. The commonest size, however, is that of 6 to 10 workers, applicable to 55 establishments. The amount of capital invested, too, is insignificant, the total for the industry being $180,140. Of this total, $106,000, or 59 per cent, was contributed by 49 establishments, the other 136 employing only $74,140, or an average of $560 per establishment. In respect to the number of knitting frames, 154 establishments employed a total 1,265, or an average of eight frames per establishment. The commonest size, however, is that of one to five frames, applicable to 78 establishments. With this small amount of labor, capital and knitting frame at disposal, the amount of raw materials consumed as well as that of the hosiery produced could not be large. The 154 establishments, accordingly, consumed only $ 963,674 worth of raw materials and produced $ 1,813,650 worth of hosiery articles. The latter sum, it may be recalled, is ten times that of the capital invested for the whole industry. "①

One might summarize the reasons for the small scale of this industry—which in these respects is typical of others—by saying; first, the amount of capital required is so small that almost any enterprising and experienced worker can raise that amount from among his relatives or other connections; second, the small man with practically no overhead expenses often can undersell the larger manufacturer who has no special advantages from producing on a larger scale, which here means only a multiplication of equipment but not substitution of machines which to any considerable extent reduce the cost of production; third, there is no great demand for large quantities of the product uniform in cost and quality; fourth, it is possible to employ unskilled labor such as may be idle in the worker's own family; fifth, the small master in times of slack demand can afford to let his equipment stand idle and employ himself at

---

① H. D. Fong, *Hosiery Knitting in Tientsin*, Nankai Institute of Economics Industry Series, Bulletin No. 3, Tientsin, 1930, p. 69.

more remunerative labor; sixth, he can still find a market for a product of a quality so poor that it would not pay to produce it in any large quantity, by this means also underselling the larger producer; and seventh, he may only nominally be an independent entrepreneur but actually in the position of a worker with a fixed clientele, or a sort of outworker producing for a merchant employer.

Similar conditions prevail in a number of Chinese industries which in their total output have reached noteworthy dimension but where the individual unit of operation has remained remarkably small. Take, for example, grain milling, another industry studied in Tientsin. The mills are not even instruments of separate business enterprises but simply part of the grain retail-trader's equipment. For example, maize flour was milled by 205 of 265 such shops; and the average output of such flour per shop was only $ 13,251. The average use of raw materials by the 265 retailing-and-milling shops in 1931 was only worth $ 13,528 as against $ 15,090 as the average value per shop per annum of the total output of all kinds.① Here again, it is doubtful whether operation in such small units is economically justified. For, the same retailers who now mill maize at one time also milled wheat but, on the reorganization, in 1925, of a large wheat flour mill in Japanese ownership, with a capital of $ 600,000, ceased to mill that flour themselves and instead subscribed

---

① H. D. Fong, *Grain Trade and Milling in Tientsin*, Nankai Institute of Econonmics Industry Series, Bulletin No. 6, Tientsin, 1934, pp. 572-574.

a large portion of that mill's capital. ① The explanation for this divergence in policy may, perhaps, be seen in the fact that maize flour has to a large extent remained a part of the native economy, and is produced almost entirely in the Chinese city at shops which sell the flour in small quantities to the native population, whereas wheat flour from the few large mills enters into a wholesale trade extending far outside the city, in Peiping for instance, in competition with imports.

The silk filatures of Shanghai offer another interesting example. They were from the very beginning operated on a small scale, with Italian expert assistance. The average capital is $50,000, subscribed by a dozen or so partners, most of them relatives or friends of each other. These establishments commonly lease the buildings where they operate, sometimes on bank credit. The lease is dissolved or renewed — and so is the partnership! — each year at the gathering of the spring crop of cocoons in May. The fixed capital is, thus, very limited. Some filatures can manage with only $20,000 or $30,000 of capital of their own, being able—no doubt because of the relative value of the raw material as security—to borrow from the native banks as much as five and even ten times their own capital. ② Here the nature of the market for the product is certainly no factor in the small scale of operations, since about nine-tenths of the output is exported, chiefly to the United States and France,

---

① H. D. Fong, *Grain Trade and Milling in Tientsin*, Nankai Institute of Econonmics Industry Series, Bulletin No. 6, Tientsin, 1934, p. 553.

② *Chinese Economic Journal*, Vol. III, No. 1, July, 1928, pp. 590-591.

even though the manufacturers deal with the exporters through Chinese brokers who often are financially interested in the filatures. ① It lies, rather, at the other end of the procedure, in the connection of the industry with an unorganized market in its raw material. For, these filatures are financed largely by native banks which are primarily interested in marketing the cocoons and only quite secondarily in the filatures. ② These banks are closely related to the primitive economic structure of the rural hinterland and neither in a position nor fitted by their experience and traditions to take part in such large-scale ventures as the establishment of large modern plants in Shanghai — the more so since in this case, because of the relative cheapness of the unit of machinery required, there is no obvious advantage in producing on more than a very moderate scale. ③

In short, in regard to scale of operations, as to so many other things, the key to understanding the form which industrial developments in China have taken since modern methods were introduced must be looked for in the general structure of economic procedure, and not in the short-comings of particular groups or their lack of understanding of the

---

① *Chinese Economic Journal*, Vol. III, No. 1, July, 1928, pp. 602-603.

② D. K. Lieu, *The Silk Recling Industry in Shanghai*, China Institute of Economic and Statistical Research, Shanghai, 1933, pp. 47-48.

③ For a detailed account of the nature and operations of native banks in the Province of Kiangsu, where Shanghai is situated, see *China Industrial Handbooks: Kiangsu*, Bureau of Foreign Trade, Ministry of Industry, Shanghai, 1933, pp. 911-930. It is shown there that of 72 such banks in Shanghai only 22 have a total capital of more than Tls. 200,000, which amount is, in fact, the mode, with 27 banks, and twice what it was ten years ago (p. 915). Outside of Shanghai, only 34 of 271 native banks have a capital of more than $40,000, and seven out of every ten have less than $20,000 (p. 916).

problems that have to be faced. The conditions of Chinese industry simply are different from those which have confronted other countries when they entered into competition with the industrially more advanced countries.

II. RAW MATERIALS

The lack of organization and the small scale of operation are distinguishing features that permeate almost every aspect of Chinese industrial organization, related whether to the purchase of raw materials, installation of machinery, power and buildings, supply and management of labor, or disposal of industrial products. In the purchase of raw materials, these two features give rise to three sets of difficulties which often incline the manufacturer to prefer imported to domestic sources of supply, namely, lack of standards, prohibitive cost of transport, and uncertainty of prices.

A. *Lack of Standards.* In so far as the greater part of the raw materials which go into Chinese industry is derived from farming, the complete lack of any sort of control to ensure some sort of uniformity or united action over a large part of China is noteworthy. Each farming household uses the land as it sees fit, except in so far as it is influenced by the requirements of landlords, tax authorities, creditors, and, of course, the state of the market. In some parts of the country, one or other of these indirect controls is at times as effective as would be a government order enforced by police power. There are even occasions when such power practically is applied, as was the case so extensively when the tax on opium was a large item in the National and provincial governments' revenues. Incidentally, under present political conditions, efforts on the part of various Chinese and foreign interests to impose controls upon agricultural production are viewed with great alarm by economists, since the farmers' present relative freedom to produce food for themselves and their families in addition to money crops is the only insurance against even worse famines than large parts of the country have suffered in recent years. While a larger proportion of land utilization for money crops might introduce for a time a larger total income for farmers, even a benevolent government would have no control over the price level which, for the more important products, is set by world movements outside its control; and a discrepancy between higher prices for food crops and lower prices for industrial crops would have calamitous consequences for millions of households. ① However, the present forms of control are not in the interest of a steady market for purchasers of industrial raw material, since they are dictated by passing and arbitrary demands, apt to change quite suddenly. Nor is the peasant's present relative freedom in his own interest, since he has no means of predicting the movement of prices and is not, in this respect, helped either by the government or by the wholesale trade. Of co-operative organization to control agricultural production and marketing there are as yet mere beginnings. ②

---

① Franklin L. Ho., "World Cotton War and China", in *Ta Kung Pao*, Aug. 11, 1935 (in Chinese).

② See my "Co-operative Movement in China", in *Monthly Bulletin on Economic China*, May, 1934; "Co-operative Marketing of Cotton in Hopei", *Nankai Social & Economic Quarterly*, October, 1935.

In short, whether he has to buy wheat or rape seed, cotton or soya beans, rice straw or hides, tobacco or cocoons, the Chinese manufacturer fumbles in the dark; he has no means of knowing what quantities will come on the market or of estimating the trend of prices.

Moreover, the producer of raw materials has no inducement to supply standard commodities. If he were to market all that part of his product which is not consumed by the household in an independent market, even the primitive country fair would be an occasion for experiencing the buyer's appreciation for goods of higher or of even quality. But actually a large part of the peasants' produce goes in payment of rent, since the system of share farming is widespread. ① And another large part goes to creditors who may be landlords, produce merchants or simply money lenders. ② Since under credit arrangements, payments are stipulated quantitatively, the producer will attempt to "get by", that is to deliver goods not markedly inferior to the expected average; he will not be induced to do his best to improve the quality of his product since, in most cases, he can expect no additional payment for higher value. Even if he sells independently in the local market, he has often no means of having quality recognized in the price, since often the distant buyer has a general idea of the average quality to be expected from a given locality or neighborhood and instructs his agent accordingly.

---

① D. K. Lieu, "Land Tenure Systems in China", *Chinese Economic Journal*, II: 457-474, June, 1928.

② Chen Han-seng, *The Present Agrarian Problem in China*, China Institute of Pacific Relations, Shanghai, 1933.

Thus, for example, qualities of cotton are often known to manufacturers only by the name of the place of origin and are valued accordingly; the individual producer gets no more if he offers a superior grade of cotton; nor is his product bought at a lower price if it is inferior, in which case the producer in the circumstances runs the risk, rather, of not being able to sell his goods at all through the regular channels. Eventually, of course, the trade of the whole region suffers.

In the cotton industry, the lack of standards in the qualities of cotton offered by Chinese growers and merchants is regarded as "an intolerable curse to the trade."①

"Absence of grading standards for cotton has, on the one hand, brought about many disputes and lawsuits between buyers and dealers, with the result that direct and indirect losses are inflicted on both; while, on the other hand, it has necessitated sampling in big quantities for each transaction, a source of not inconsiderable loss which dealers have been eager to eliminate."②

In this industry, deliberate adulteration adds to the unpleasantness of using the domestic raw material.

"The farmer may splash water on the ground first, and then cover it with newly ginned cotton for a night or so in order to absorb

---

① Fong, *Cotton Trade and Industry in China*, I:34.
② T. S. Chu and T. Chin, *Marketing of Cotton in Hopei Province*, Institute of Social Research, Peiping, 1929, p. 53.

sufficient moisture. Another method is to spread water upon each layer of lint cotton, and then pack all these layers together into a bale. A third method, which is more injurious to cotton, is to pound it with a thong, so as to break apart the wax layer on the fibre and thus to facilitate the absorption of moisture, Lately it is reported that even a mechanical splasher has been invented in order to perpetuate the abuse."①

Foreign solid substance are also sometimes introduced, to add to the weight. In this, indeed, the simple peasant of North China shows a singular ingenuity.

"Since the establishment of the Cotton Testing House in Tientsin, it has become difficult for adulterated cotton to appear on the Tientsin market. Nevertheless, the practice still prevails at primary markets where there are no testing houses, and, what is more serious, there even happens occasionally adulteration with sand, pebbles, and other foreign matter which can hardly be detected by testing."②

The same or similar complaints come from buyers of wool③ and of many other raw materials of industry. In fact, the tendency to attempt substitutions and adulterations is probably as old in China as it is

---

① Fong, *Cotton Industry and Trade in China*, I:29.
② Chu and Chin, *op. cit.*, p. 53.
③ "Shanghai Woolen Textile Factories", *Chinese Economic Journal*, Vol. XI, No. 6, December, 1932, pp. 438-439.

universal.

Speaking of the loss of markets for so many Chinese products, Tsao Lien-en writes:

> "Short-sighted men of the co-hongs, selfish, self-centered and greedy, whose vision of trade prosperity was limited to immediate and personal gains, ruined their own market by corrupt practices, shipping goods of inferior quality, and other evils. There was no systematized practice between the Chinese sellers and foreign buyers. The sellers were alleged to have added water to silk and tea so as to increase their weight to assure better profits, with the result that on arrival after a long voyage... the goods became unfit for use... Tea and silk have since been consumed largely at home...
>
> "Exactly the same thing is happening to the Manchurian soya beans and bean oil at present." ①

The total effect of the lack of standards on the industries that have to use these Chinese raw materials is not difficult to imagine, though no one can compute the total loss from this cause — not least of which is that of additional operation costs to remove impurities or to regrade. One effect is that China imports far more raw materials, e. g. wheat, cotton, wool, than would be the case if the domestic supplies were more reliable in quality.

---

① *Chinese Economic Journal*, Vol. VII, No. 3. September, 1930, pp. 941-943. See also A. V. Marakueff, "The Export of Soya Beans from Manchuria and Its Financing", *Ibid*, Vol. II, No. 6, June, 1928, p. 483.

Another consequence of unstandardized raw materials is that the industries themselves cannot put out a standardized product. Even Chinese consumers increasingly prefer to buy commodities which they need not examine minutely at each purchase. One cannot test sugar, salt, flour, each time a purchase is made; and so prices of foreign products often are higher in relation to those of domestic products, not to the degree of difference in average quality but because they are more reliable.

Another consequence is that frequent variations in the qualities of raw materials make impossible an orderly plan of production.

"Standard materials are of advantage to the manufacturing department for the following reasons. Greater uniformity in purchased materials under carefully drawn specifications makes possible greater refinement in technical designing and better utilization of the material. Workmen will thereby achieve more uniform and better results in both manual and machine operations. Waste and spoilage will decrease, the effectiveness of machines be increased, and the average quality of the output raised. Necessary production time will show less variation, a most important factor because of its effect on employee earnings and plant morale.

"The ultimate user of the commodity will get uniformity in his purchases, and find that advertisements and selling appeals prove dependable. Because of this the dealer will find sales easier, fewer adjustments to make with disgruntled customers, and collections more prompt. This favorable situation will be reflected to the manufacturer in easier collections, and increased sales will be obtained at less cost."①

B. *Transportation Difficulties.* The lack of standards more or less sums up why it is impossible, often, for the Chinese manufacturer, quite as much as for the foreign manufacturer in China, to rely on Chinese raw materials—greatly to the benefit of the importer and to the disadvantage of the Chinese peasant. There is, however, another reason, perhaps equally strong; and that is the chaotic state of China's internal communications. There are many Chinese products which stand comparison with similar imported goods when price as well as quality is taken into consideration; but again and again the manufacturer finds himself compelled to buy the imported material because he cannot rely upon existing channels of inland transportation to bring these products to his doors in time, in good condition, or at all.

There is also the high cost of inland transportation which at times eats up the difference in cost between a Chinese and a foreign product. This is given as one reason, for example, by Kiangsu flour mills for the large proportion of foreign wheat they use. ② Similarly, salt, limestone, and iron pyrites, the chief raw ingredients for the manufacture of acids, could be supplied in China in adequate quantities for the acid-

---

① Arthur G. Anderson, *Industrial Engineering and Factory Management.* New York, 1923, pp. 273-274.

② *Chinese Economic Journal*, Vol. XIII, No. 1, July, 1933, p. 42.

manufacturing and using industries; but because of the distance over which these materials have to be carried to the centers of industry and the resulting high cost of transportation, the domestic product cannot compete with foreign products. ①

The Minister of Communications, in 1925, submitted a memorandum to the Provisional Chief Executive, in which he pointed to some of the difficulties which stood in the way of a more systematic attempt to solve the problem of efficient transportation and others connected with it.

"Since the Sixth Year of the Republic (1917)", he wrote, "internal wars have been numerous. High military leaders in the provinces mistake the systems of communication for their own instruments of warfare and place these systems under their own control. They have commandeered railway rolling stock, telegraph lines, and vessels. Still worse, they have often operated the official systems of communication for their own profit with great detriment to trade and industry. Even revenues needed by the railways and telegraph offices for their own maintenance have been seized. As a result, wages are not paid, and there is no money to buy materials urgently required for repairing equipment. Worst of all, administrative officials and accountants of the railway and telegraph administrations are appointed directly by the provincial

---

① *China Press Double-Tenth Supplement*, October 10, 1935, Shanghai, p. 72.

authorities who recklessly exploit the properties and revenues of communications."①

While there have been improvements in these respects, the communist troubles and the alienation of Chinese territories by the Japanese have again in recent times introduced new disruptions and uncertainties. Requisitions of rolling stock have been frequent.② Goods have been rotting, protested only by frail matting against sun, sand and rain; and the improvement of some of the main lines notwithstanding, manufacturers in the port cities find it impossible to rely upon the regularity of supplies from the interior. Divided control, in spite of considerable efforts on the part of the National Government, still directly or indirectly makes possible a multiplicity of charges which makes it hazardous for the manufacturer to estimate closely what the transport of raw materials carried by the railways will cost him.③

There is also still the difficulty that, with foreign capitalization, many of the Chinese railways were forced to adopt gauges and other

---

① *Chinese Economic Monthly*, Vol. II, No. 14, Novembtar, 1925, p. 32.

② "In 1932, the total operating revenues amounted to $ 137,400,147, out of which $ 8,350,879 was on account of military transportation for which the railways received no cash payment. In addition to free military transportation, the railways in 1932 made to the military authorities a present of $ 5,508,500 in the way of subsidies. These two items make a total of $ 13,359,379, or more than 10 per cent of total operating revenues of the year." Cheng Lin, *The Chinese Railways*, Shanghai, 1935, p. 105.

③ See Wang Peh-chun, Minister of Communications, "The Reconstruction of China's Communications," *Chinese Economic Journal*, Vol. IV, No. 3, March, 1929, p. 266 *et seq.*

specifications which gave the lending country a quasi-monopoly of the supply of rolling stock and equipment, so that to this day attempts at exchanges and trans-shipment meet with the greatest difficulty, in so far as they are not actually impossible. [1] The latest example is the Chekiang-Kiangsi Railway, which, although built entirely with Chinese capital, has great difficulty in transhipments over the Shanghai-Hangchow-Ningpo Railway which, unlike itself, is not a light railway.

Apart from such ostensible and well-known handicaps, the railway system of China, because of the long history of civil strife and usurpation of power by sectional authorities, is saddled also with a tradition of corruption[2] which leaves the shipper of small quantities of goods, more especially, exposed to exceptional hazards. While the large concern, transporting in car loads, can often smooth the path of his supplies by oiling in appropriate places, the small man suffers many delays. The Government has attempted to make the difference between rates for car loads and smaller shipments less unjust than it has been in the past, (providing that it must cost only the actual extra charge in handling) but it is still generally believed that there is no equality of opportunity in getting the goods shipped at all. One need only travel in the interior to see the quantities of miscellaneous goods piled up at or near the goods stations, especially in time of civil war or during seasonal movement of

---

[1] For details see Chapter IV of H. Stringer, *The Chinese Railway System*, London, 1925.

[2] See Cheng Lin, *op. cit.*, p. 112.

agricultural commodities, to get some impression of the serious losses and anxieties from this source. Depreciation, theft, and robbery are risks which enter into the cost accounts of any industry that relies largely upon materials brought from a distance. And this especially, of course, where goods must be transferred and handled repeatedly.

The railways are, of course only a part of the Chinese transportation system, in view of the endless processions of human and animal carriers and of wheeled vehicles of all sorts that move goods over distances ranging from a few fundred yards to many miles. ① The total length of roads in China is officially given as 84,809 kilometres, ② but only a small part of it is surfaced; and though figuring in official statistics, a good part of the other is not much better than the tracks and furrowed lanes which for ages have served the traffic between towns and provinces.

Apart from the flimsy and often quite temporary form of road construction which often precludes the possibility of permitting the sharp-wheeled peasant carts to use the new roads, two factors lessen their usefulness: the monopolies often created on motor bus transportation to secure a revenue in lump, and the high toll charges often made. In some cases the toll taxes on motor trucks equal the operating cost. ③ Actually the total number of such trucks seen on Chinese roads is as yet

---

① See John Earl Baker, "Transportation in China", *Annals of the American Academy of Political and Social Science*, Vol. 152, November 1930, p. 160 *et seq.*

② *Chinese Yearbook, 1935-36*, p. 307.

③ Baker, *op. cit.* p. 165.

INDUSTRIAL ORGANIZATION IN CHINA

surprisingly small. ① The bulk of foreign sales of this kind of vehicle being to rival warlords. Because of the flimsy road construction, heavy trucks with trailors are rarely seen.

The achievement of bringing a substantial part of the marketable raw products out of the immediate region of their production to their destination for fabrication or export is, in the chaotic state of the Chinese road system, an achievement of endless labor, patience, and taking of risks.

"The tremendous supply of cheap coolic labor available in China", writes one of the well-informed foreign observers of the country's system of road transportation, "has often given rise to the belief that this constitutes cheap transportation. The fallacy of this idea has frequently been commented upon, but perhaps has nowhere been more cogently stated than in *Some Bigger Issues in China's Problems*, a recent publication by Julean Arnold, American commercial attache to China. Mr. Arnold states therein that the human beast of burden of China is 'fifteen times as costly as the luxurious railway train in America,' and estimates that an

---

① Sir. Arthur Salter, in his investigation of conditions in Chekiang province, remarked as follows: "In four days' motoring over the roads round Hangchow — over some 700 kilometres — the traffic observed by two of our party on the roads consisted only of five motor buses, carrying passengers only, and only half full; four private motor-cars; some 40 or 50 wheel barrows; a few handpushed trucks and rickshas; and several hundred coolies carrying baskets on poles slung across the shoulder." See *Annexes to the Report to the Council of the League of Nations of Its Technical Delegate on His Mission in China from Date of Appointment until April 1 ,1934*, Nanking,1934,p. 76.

American railway will haul a ton of wheat for what it costs to haul a picul $\left(133\frac{1}{8} \text{ pounds}\right)$ the same distance by coolie carrier in China. Transportation by pack animals and carts in Shansi Province averages about 16 cents a ton-mile; motor transportation from 20 to 25 cents a ton-mile; whereas railways should be able to carry cargo at less than 3 cents a ton-mile."①

The defective road system and the absence of railways are in themselves a cause of many other difficulties and costs in transportation, such as the infestation of the country with bandits.② Again, road transportation means reliance upon many small and independable carriers in place of a large transportation company or a government that can be held to account. Take Chekiang, for example. Here "the total gross income of the business [of the old-fashioned transportation firms] in a year amounts to five to six million dollars, much larger than that of the modern express companies in the province."③

Speaking of traffic on China's inland waterways suggests many difficulties which have been discussed from time to time in respect of them but rarely with direct reference to the problems of the industrialist who is helplessly at the mercy of the transportation agencies that bring

---

① A. Viola Smith, *Motor Roads in China*, U. S. Department of Commerce Trade Promotion Series No. 120, Washington, 1931, p. 2.
② Stringer, *The Chinese Railway System*, 1925, p. 121.
③ "Means of Communications in Chekiang", *Chinese Economic Journal*, Vol. I, No. 1, January, 1927, pp. 120-123.

his needed raw materials to the doors of his plant. To begin with, less than one-third (29.1%) of the tonnage carried by vessels entered and cleared at Chinese ports in 1935 are carried under the Chinese flag, though the total number of Chinese vessels so engaged (104,450) is larger than that of foreign vessels (78,555). ①The large extent to which goods are still carried on small Chinese steam vessels,—and this in spite of a hazard from piracy which adds an important cost item — is partly owing to the special nature of their trade but also, apparently, not a little a consequence of the general lack of economic organization and the ability of many small shipowners to take advantage of it. On the other hand, the aggressiveness with which foregn interests have extended navigation by vessels of their own nationality in Chinese inland waters, as well as along the coast, has been caused to a large extent by the unreliability and the insufficiency of the existing facilities, not only for exporters but also for manufacturers in the port cities. ② The same causes of inadequate organization which we have found in other respects here also are held responsible for obvious difficulties: lack of system, commandeering, "squeeze", the family system, and so on—in short, a primitive, pre-capitalistic type of business. This lack of what Chinese enterprise provides in services to the user of Chinese raw products, with which alone we are here concerned, is not, however, due entirely to

---

① *The Trade of China*, *1935*, I:102, also see Mingchien Joshua Bau, *Foreign Navigation in Chinese Waters*, Institute of Pacific Relations, 1931, pp. 18-19.

② See statement by G. Warren Swire, *Problems of the Pacific*, *1931*, p. 363.

internal causes; it has been rendered far more serious by foreign interference with a natural process of development. British, and in recent times especially Japanese interests have again and again stood in the way of effective organization. Those concerns which they control give preference to shipping of their own nationality not only because in many cases it is cheaper or more reliable but often with the deliberate purpose, as their spokesmen have admitted, to prevent the growth of a Chinese mercantile marine after a modern pattern. They particularly feared that such a fleet would eventually be used for military purposes and so deprive them of rights assumed often under the threat of their own gunboats. ①

Whatever the more important causes, the fact remains that today it is frequently cheaper for the flour miller in Tientsin to bring wheat all the way from Canada than to secure grain of the same quality and at the same price from his own country. Wool in abundance and at a low price could be secured from the Northwest; and it is not only because of difference in quality, (for the demand is as yet largely for the cheaper grades) that the manufacturer on the coast often turns to Australia for his supplies. Here we have, then, reason enough to contend that the backwardness of Chinese industry is to a considerable extent linked with that of the general economy as it affects its supply of materials.

C. *Uncertainty of Prices.* There is, of course, the factor of price itself, as affected by other influence as well. With the virtual wall

---

① J. P. Chamberlain, *Foreign Flags in China's Internal Navigation*, Institute of Pacific Relations, 1931, pp. 18-19.

around each local or regional market, the manufacturer must keep himself informed about a dozen price movements if he is interested in a particular kind and quality of material; if it is an agricultural product and the margin is small, he must keep himself informed if possible of weather and crop conditions in a dozen places — and not this alone but also of military conditions and the state of banditry, whether roads are passable or boats have been commandeered. If he is not informed that a new surtax has been imposed on the sale of the commodity he is interested in or that there is an impending minor war in the neighborhood, he is likely to buy at the wrong time and at the wrong price. Now all this, it will be said, does not normally affect the industrialist who buys through a middleman. But the fact is that a market quotation from Chicago or Liverpool is reliable, but a quotation given in good faith locally concerning a product yet to be shipped from the interior or yet on the fields is not reliable because somewhere in the chain from producer to plant there will be the weak link of someone who, because of some unforeseen condition, cannot keep his contract or puts on some charge which to a Chinese arbitrator would seem equitable, no matter what the working of the sales contract.

All along the line, too, there is speculation. We need not here go into the alleged gambling spirit of the Chinese as part of the national character, for which there are adequate explanations in the average man's adjustment to the hazards of his environment. But whereaa speculation in futures in foreign grains, wool, cotton, hemp, sugar, and many other materials can be made a fine art, based on concrete and reliable information about past experiences in the relations between price movement and supply, in connection with Chinese future deliveries such speculation is apt to be pure guess. Domestic prices must follow world prices to some extent, but the margin of difference may be entirely lost by unpredictable circumstances and events.

And the chief reason for this as for many other difficulties which have here been touched upon is the diffused nature of the trade in any given commodity as a whole. To begin with, production of the raw material itself is on a small scale. The middleman has to collect from many sources. This means a high cost of his services; it means wasteful buying, uncertainty of volume of supply, and lack of uniformity in the material where a fairly large quantity is required to put out a standard product. The small scale of production in Chinese plants, as compared with that in foreign-owned plants in most industries, interferes with the stability of the product for another reason, namely that the manufacturer is rarely in a financial position to order and store a volume of material of uniform quality in advance of his needs. The paper on which the present study is printed is a good case in point. With the best will in the world, the Chinese printer, even when operating on a relatively large scale, cannot give his clients a continuous supply of the same paper at the same price; either he or the wholesaler from whom he buys is forced to purchase only what he can be more or less sure to dispose of in a short time. This is as true of imported as of domestic materials. The difficulty here is partly lack of capital and partly the uncertainty of the demand. It is this difficulty again which in turn gives the Chinese manufacturer the reputation for unreliable quality in his product. He often has not the possibility of assuring himself of a supply of stable quality because the industry and the wholesale trade that supplies it are broken up into many competing small units any one of which may succeed in securing a part of the diffused orders of an equally divided demand.

III. MACHINERY, POWER AND BUILDINGS

The difficulties that have confronted the Chinese manufacturer in the purchase of raw materials have been repeated, although not exactly in the same manner but nevertheless traceable to the same lack of organization and small scale of operation that are characteristic of Chinese industrial organization, in his provision for machinery, power and buildings. Machinery still has to be purchased largely from abroad despite the early growth of industrialization back in the sixties, while with the exception of leading industrial centres such as Shanghai and Wusih, motive power supply is as yet inadequately provided for by the manufacturer himself or by several competing plants operated in nearly every case on a small and inefficient scale. Buildings are poorly constructed wherever they constitute an item of investment in the manufacturer's budget, while often enough they are leased from an outside proprietor at the payment of a rental.

A. *Machinery*. In regard to the availability of modern machinery to the progressive Chinese manufacturer, we shall note that some of his problems spring from the recentness of modern industry in this country, others from the suddenness with which traditional processes were discarded in favor of technically complicated ones or need for a precision which the old type of equipment could not afford. Both causes converge to increase the difficulty of planning production. Theoretically, industrialization should have started with the development of the heavy industries, as it started in Russia under the Soviet regime. But the Chinese Government never was in a position to plan industrial production as a whole. When its most progressive leaders became "machine-minded" in the sixties, this was entirely in relation to quite specific national needs, especially armaments and navigation. The concern for inland transportation and for the building up of miscellaneous industries came much later —and in some respects has remained neglected to this day.

Since the need was great, industry started, not with the building of machines, but with their importation. The value of machinery, however, did not reach a million Hk. Tls. before 1894 nor five million before 1905. In 1887, the first year for which imports of machinery are listed by the Maritime Customs, the value of that item was Hk. Tls. 398,000, but it fell again in the following two years and reached an average of only Hk. Tls. 382,000 for the four years 1887-1890. Taking this period for index, the rate of increase in the following five-year periods was as follows: ①

---

① Based on figures given in C. Yang and others, *Statistics of China's Foreign Trade during the Last 65 Years*, National Research Institute of Social Sciences, Academia Sinica, 1931, Table V, and *Customs Reports for the Years 1929-1934*.

CHINA'S NET IMPORT OF MACHINERY, 1887-1934

Period	1,000 Hk. Tls.	Rate of Increase	Period	1,000 Hk. Tls.	Rate of Increase
1887-1890	382	100	1911-1915	6,908	108
1891-1895	1,186	310	1916-1920	11,947	173
1896-1900	1,903	160	1927-1925	35,371	296
1901-1905	2,544	133	1926-1930	27,824	79
1906-1910	6,406	252	1931-1934	35,376	127

These figures show a great rise — for which, however, a very few government shops and private plants may easily have been responsible — just before general permission to manufacture in the open ports was granted foreign firms. The increase in the next two five-year periods (1896-1905) was not quite as striking as one might have expected, though still amounting to nearly 150 per cent. The two five-year periods of largest increase are from 1906 to 1910 and from 1921 to 1925 when, after the impetus of the wartime shortage of foreign imports in manufactured commodities, the development of Chinese industries was larger than at any time before or since. [1] In 1913, there were 245 factories in China, by 1920 their number had increased to 673, by 1925 to 1,009, and by 1930 to 1,975. [2] Actually, these figures do not in

---

[1] *Modern Industries in Shanghai* (in Chinese), Shanghai Bureau of Social Affairs, Shanghai, 1933. Kung, Chen, *History of Modern Industrial Development in China* (in Chinese), Commercial Press, Shanghai, 1933.

[2] R. H. Tawney, *Land and Labor in China*, London, 1932, p. 196.

any clear manner illustrate the growth of Chinese industries, first because there have been great differences in the scale of individual manufacturing units importing machinery in these different periods, and second because prices and exchange rates also vary and make the imports in some periods appear smaller in comparative tables based on value than they actually were.

Omitting agricultural machinery and pumps, the proportions in value of machinery imported between 1918 and 1934 for different categories will give a slightly better picture of the nature of these imports.

The outstanding features to be noted after an analysis of the above table are, on the one hand, the great importance of textile and power (including both electrical machinery and prime-movers) machinery in the total import, which during the last decade 1925-34 reached an average annual import of 13.6 million Haikwan taels or 83% of the total import of industrial machinery, and on the other hand, the increasing import of these items, interrupted only since the depression in 1933. These features reflect adequately the trend of China's recent industrialization, although we are not unaware, especially in respect of growth, of the unreliability of value index. ①

---

① Such growth is to be discounted by the fact that the wholesale price index in Shanghai increased, for instance, from 99.3 in 1925 to 126.7 in 1931, the peak figure, and then fell successively to 112.4, 103.8, 97.1, and 96.4 during the following four years 1932-35.

VALUE OF PRINCIPAL CATEGORIES OF INDUSTRIAL MACHINERY IMPORTED, 1918-34

(in 1,000 Haikwan Taels)

	Electrical	Printing	Primemovers	Textile	Brewing and Refining	Cigar and Cigarette	Machine Tools	Sewing Knitting & Embroidering
1918			646	1,650	19	33	282	
1919			1,589	3,744	3	491	610	
1920			2,348	6,904	28	711	1,015	
1921			5,109	26,723	645	931	648	
1922			2,395	30,484	269	634	769	
1923			1,474	12,316	103	463	702	
1924	808	1,032	1,963	5,511	1,391	455	878	
1925	858	651	1,920	3,407	6	23	404	
1926	832	580	1,901	4,058	4	291	651	
1927	1,292	435	2,980	3,709	9	315	767	
1928	1,316	769	2,566	4,105	100	442	1,047	
1929	2,532	1,230	3,441	8,932	63	219	734	1,516
1930	3,538	1,116	3,757	13,995	71	753	849	796
1931	3,677	732	5,671	13,801	62	824	1,271	645
1932	3,607	730	4,464	10,337	*	597	1,086	587
1933	3,207	495	2,519	5,829	*	164	1,053	691
1934	3,698	885	5,274	9,118	2,691	92	1,373	897
(1928-34)								
Total	24,557	7,623	34,493	77,291	3,006	2,649	7,437	8,001
Average	2,456	762	3,449	7,729	301	265	744	800
Percentage	14.9	4.6	20.9	46.8	1.8	1.6	4.5	4.9

Of every type of industrial machinery here named, the port of Shanghai receives the largest proportion. Cause and effect here are difficult to extricate: because Shanghai is the principal Chinese port of call for foreign shipping, it has seen the greatest development of industries using imported materials, hence also machinery. But the growth of these industries again is one cause among others for the continuing supremacy of this port. ①

We thus come to the part played by the machine industry in China itself in the building up of its industries. According to a report of the China Institute of Economic and Statistical Research, machinery and metal tools and utensils combined make up Shanghai's second largest industry in number of establishments, fifth largest in number of workers employed and seventh largest in capitalization, there being (in 1932) about 300 shops and factories, about 11,000 workers, and over $4,000,000 invested capital. ② This separate enumeration of works devoted to machine manufacture does not take account of the large number of shops that are auxiliary to other industries, though some of them may be included if under separate management and on separate premises even though belonging to a company mainly engaged in the manufacture of some commodity, shipping, or the like.

Most of the machine works, including foundries, are quite small

---

① For a more detailed analysis of China's imports of machinery see *Chinese Economic Journal* Vol. XII, No. 1, January, 1933, pp. 65-77.

② D. K. Lieu, *A Preliminary Report on Shanghai Industrialization*. China Institute of Economic and Statistical Research, Shanghai, 1933.

shops; even of the repair shops only a dozen or so operate on a sufficiently large scale to employ a number of mechanics. The smallness of the industry and its diffusion are explained with lack of capital and of technically trained personnel. Men with a little mechanical skill and enterprise who could not command larger credits or loans, can often obtain sufficient backing to open a small repair shop where the capital is kept fluid, where the overhead is small, and where most of the work is done by apprentices. The result is that there is severe competition between many small shops, none of them able to tackle a difficult or big job. Of the larger machine factories a number have failed for reasons which it would be tedious to enumerate since they have here been described so often already for similar ventures. For example, the well-known publishing and printing house, the Commercial Press, had a subsidiary, the Hua-tung (华东) Machine Works, which made for it much of the smaller and less complicated printing machinery. Chiefly because of labor troubles, this concern has had to be dissolved. The China Iron Works (中国铁工厂) was engaged on a fairly large scale in making textile machinery but failed owing to excessive indebtedness and litigation.[1] There is a saying in the cotton industry that the Chinese industrialist tries to run a two million business with one million, and this is especially true of the machine industry. Even the one million tends to be frozen in fixed equipment and buildings so that the plan of operations cannot easily adapt itself to variety and change of demand. The smaller

---

[1] *Modern Industries in Shanghai*, *op. cit.*

shops, in spite of their number, have no difficulty in keeping, going when business is good because at such a time they can usually get the credit they need; but they collapse very quickly in hard times.

On the whole, the machine shops in China " are now able to manufacture many kinds of machinery which are usually imported from abroad. For the textile industry, they supply gins, looms, spindles, silk reeling and doubling machines, cocoon heaters and boilers, etc. Machinery for the knitting, printing, rubber, flour, vegetable oil, tobacco, and rice-milling industries is now manufactured in China, especially Shanghai. Steam and petrol engines are supplied to all industries, while lathes, drills, vises, punches, planers, cranes, pumps, etc., have also a good market in the country. " Of these works several larger ones in Shanghai specialize in some of the branches here mentioned. For instance, Ming Tsing specializes in the manufacturing of printing machines; Lao Ka Hsin, knitting machines; Hwan Chiu, silk reeling and weaving machines; Sze Ho Kee, cigarette-making machines; Chung Kuo, spinning, weaving and dyeing machines; and Ta Lung, textile machinery and agricultural implements. ①

B. *Motive Power.* The supply of power produces problems of its own. In such large centers of industry as Shanghai and Tientsin, electric power is very popular with manufacturers. In the interior, the smaller factories more often generate their own power from kerosene with internal combustion engines. Only the larger plants use steam or electric power.

---

① *Chinese Yearbook*, *1935-36*, Shanghai, 1936, p. 1932.

In the cotton industry, electric power is more popular than steam power. In a recent survey of 45 Chinese-owned mills, electric power is in use in 29, steam in 12, and both electric and steam power in 4 mills. The total capacity amounts to 92,255 H. P., of which 82% is electric and 18% steam. Generally speaking, the older and smaller mills resort to steam, while the newer and larger mills use electric power, which is generated by commercial companies as in Shanghai and Wusih but by own plants as in the interior. ①

The silk filatures of Shanghai all use steam which supplies not only power but also hot water for boiling the cocoons. Sometimes small auxiliary petrol engines or electric generators are installed. A curious system in the silk filatures is the "farming out" of the engine room and the supply of motive power to a man called *laokwei*, the "old devil",

> "Who undertakes to supply power enough to run all the reels of the filature at a fixed sum a month. He is generally something of a skilled mechanic who knows how to handle the steam engine, including the cost of running it and of keeping it in repair. The *laokwei* engages his own assistants and buys all the necessary supplies except coal, while the firm gives him only a fixed sum. For the supply of motive power to each reel the sum allowed is usually $ 0.55 silver a month.
>
> "Another peculiarity about the engine room is that the

---

① Wang Tse-chien and Wang Chen-chung, *A Survey of Chinese-owned Cotton Mills in Seven Provinces*, (in Chinese) Commercial Press, 1935, pp. 83-85.

laokwei, is seldom changed when the filature changes hands. The firm usually farms out the engine room to the same man who has probably been there since the plant was first built. He knows the particular engine as well as a rider knows his favorite horse, how well it can work, and how it is to be kept in repair. For major repairs, of course the owner of the plant will be responsible, but all minor work is done by the *laokwei* without extra charge to the operating firm...

"Sometimes the *laokwei* farms out engine rooms in different localities, and at each plant an assistant is placed in charge of the operation, who is called the *erkwei* or ' No. 2 devil. ' Under the *laokwei* and the *erkwei* are usually a brass-smith, a carpenter, an attendant of the water pump, a man to filter the water through the sand bath, and a few to look after the engine itself... The *laokwei* also receives a commission of 30 to 40 cents per ton of coal bought by the filature. "①

In the country as a whole, there are 194 power companies of which two-thirds are in two provinces, 65 in Kiangsu and 66 in Chekiang. Numbers, however, are unimportant; only two of the plants, the Hangchow Power Company, and the Chapei Electricity and Water Works, are large by western standards, and eight more are of moderate size. The National Reconstruction Commission lists as operating early in

---

① Lieu, *The Silk Reeling Industry in Shanghai*, pp. 69-70.

1934 about 150 industrial power plants, nearly all of them steam-driven. A few of the 500 or so electric utility companies, primarily organized to supply current for lighting, also supply power in a small way for driving industrial and agricultural machinery. ①

That "almost 95 per cent of the prime movers are steam-driven, 4.8 per cent are internal combustion engines, and the rest 0.2 per cent rely on water power"② emphasizes the importance of coal as the source of power fuel. A recent estimate shows that as much as one-third of the coal consumption in China is devoted to industrial purposes, with the following distribution among the various industries: electric light plants 10%, cotton mills 4.7%, flour mills 3.3%, iron works 1.8%, cement works 0.8%, other factories 12%. ③

So far as the use of coal is concerned, there is no application of economy at all, except in the very largest plants that produce power for themselves or others. Systems of farming out the supply of fuel, such as described above for the silk filatures, exist, no doubt, in other industries also. But the chief problem is that there is no standardization in the coal supply, and the small manufacturer has no way of checking on the quality of the coal he gets. ④ Even experienced men who have a "feel" for the quality of fuel supplied to them are rarely employed in any but the

---

① T'ang Leang-li, *Reconstruction in China*, Shanghai, 1935, pp. 66-67.

② *Ibid.*, p. 67.

③ *Coal and Coal Industry* (in Chinese), Shanghai Commercial and Savings Bank Research Department, Commodity Series, No. 10, 1935, p. 110.

④ *Ibid.*, p. 27 et seq.

largest plants. The usual engine room attendants have never learned how to economize and are more concerned in their commission from the coal merchant than in the quality of his supplies.

In regard to power economy it must not be forgotten, either, that the supply of coal for steam and electric power generation is made unnecessarily expensive through the inefficiency of the production process and, especially the same inadequacy of the transportation system which, as we have seen, is so great an obstacle to the use of raw materials produced inland, in place of imported materials. There are not only different distances but also different freight rates for the same distance.

On the same railway the rate charged per ton will be different for different companies. According to the manager of one coal company, on the Peiping-Hankow railway there are four different freight rates for the seven mining companies using the line. Similar conditions exist on the Tientsin-Pukow and Chengting-Taiyuan lines. ①

Because of this high cost of transportation, but originally no doubt to avoid extortionate road charges, visitors to Peiping still see coal brought into that city in minute quantities, though in a large total volume, on the backs of camels. Elsewhere, coal is occasionally carried

---

① T. H. Hwang, "Notes on Coal Mining in China," *Chinese Economic Journal*, Vol. XII, No. 4, April 1, 1933, p. 445.

by primitive means simply because sufficient railway cars cannot be had and the high rates make coal transportation on carts and vessels of all sorts a paying proposition.

C. *Premises*.   As might be expected, the physical conditions under which industries are conducted in China vary enormously. Some of the modern cotton mills of Shanghai, Tsingtao, and Tientsin are definltely superior to the average to be seen in Lancashire or in Massachusetts. But among the Chinese mills, especially the old ones, the buildings are with rare exceptions in a bad state. In his *Report on Inspection of Chinese Cotton Mills*, Major H. Bancroft, a textile expert from Lancashire, made the following remark:

> The old mills are nor of much use, and to recondition them is throwing good money after bad. The buildings themselves are very poor, and not able to stand the load of modern machinery without drastic structural alterations, and even then, the buildings would not lend themselves readily to modern methods. The lighting of the old mills leaves a lot to be desired, and during my visits, so as to examine slivers etc. in the middle of the rooms, I have had to request the management to switch on the lights. No operative can work efficiently in the dark, and it is necessary for good work to have good light. This was during the middle of the day. At night time, in the old mills, I have found the lighting to be deplorable.

In other industries the conditions are even worse. The multitude of small plants and shops offer a sad contrast to the larger and newer cotton mills built whether by the Japanese or by the Chinese. The following remark by a member of the International Labor Office still holds even after almost a decade:

> Even such westerners as cannot be accused of speaking of the miseries of Asia in ignorance of those of their own country, cannot but be moved to pity at the sight of one of the many workshops operating under the old industrial regime, to be met with in all Chinese towns, on the coasts as well as in the interior. The entrance is littered with filth, factory waste, and ordure of all kinds, the buildings are black with dirt inside and out, the narrow windows closed summer and winter alike, and the earthen floors covered with mud and dust.
>
> Match factories are particularly bad: large sheds seething with women and children who shiver with cold in winter and suffocate with heat in summer, so dark that artificial light is necessary even at high noon. In the old filatures of Shantung the ceilings are barely man-high, and the workshops are so narrow that there is scarcely room for two rows abreast of the primitive looms, separated only by a narrow passage with an earthen floor full of accumulated rubbish. The atmosphere is steaming hot summer and winter, so that the men have to work stripped to the waist; and if they have to go outside, they do not take the trouble to cover themselves, even in the bitter

cold common in northern China during several months of the year. The prevalence of tuberculosis is hardly surprising in these circumstances. ①

There is, with premises and conditions of this sort, a hazard of industrial accidents and fires far in excess of that in most industrial countries, particularly when the lack of industrial experience and discipline of a large part of China's industrial working population is taken into consideration. In spite of safety movements and inspection, even in the International Settlement the accident rate is very high. In not a few cases explosions and fires cause an appalling death rate because safety exits have been carelessly barred or even kept locked in contravention of municipal regulations. In the larger centers, accidents occur daily from disregard of the law in regard to safety devices. The construction of factories itself is often an affair of jerry-building and faulty planning with no consideration to the most elementary requirements of safety. To describe the various inadequacies in these respects is no purpose of the present paper. ②

---

① Henry, *op. cit.*, pp. 14-15. For similar evidence see A. M. Anderson, *Humanity and Labour in China*, London, 1928, pp. 154, 171-172, 186-187, 190; Sidney D. Gamble, *Peking: A Social Survey*, New York, 1921, p. 219.

② See works already cited, also Herbert D. Lamson, *Social Pathology in China*, Shanghai, 1934, p. 114 *et seq.* : *China Yearbook*, 1934, p. 271 ; Ministry of Industries, *China Labor Yearbook*, 1934 (in Chinese) ; Ta Chen, " Toward Factory Legislation in China", *Chinese Social and Political Science Review*, Vol. XV, 1931, pp. 542-544.

IV. LABOR

In older days only two kinds of paid labor were known — common labor, which was to be found everywhere in abundance, and skilled labor of various sorts which was also abundant unless the skill was in part based upon a knowledge which could be kept secret and thus monopolized on behalf of sons and other apprentices. ① In modern industry this kind of special knowledge is of little importance; at least it no longer can be kept, with a few exceptions, a family or gild secret; and so far as China is concerned, the trained skill recruited from foreign countries with long experience in some branch of industry or other, and not skill available in China which could not be readily reproduced, has been indispensable to the introduction of new processes. In short, industries have been established irrespective of the labor supply which has never been expected to give any trouble. Nevertheless, we must here deal with certain phases of labor recruiting and management as part of the total picture of modern industrial organization in China.

A. *Labor Recruiting.* Whereas the manufacturer in Birmingham or Cleveland can count on a vast reserve of available common labor, of men who have worked for years in other factories and need only be shown a few tricks, perhaps, to make their labor effective in the functions to

---

① Among the gold-beaters of Ningpo, for example.

which they will be assigned, the manufacturer in a Chinese center of industry as yet often has to start with a personnel entirely unaccustomed to working with machinery or of the discipline of a manufacturing plant. This is particularly so in the smaller towns, of course; but in the coastal cities, too, during the time of most rapid expansion of industries, men were recruited from the docks—where, to be sure, they had undergone an industrial discipline of a different sort—and from among the crowds of country and city-born who had never worked even in a gang.

At the present time, with the world economic depression, an employer who desires to do so can recruit additions to his staff entirely from among unemployed workers with previous industrial experience. On opening a new plant, the manager will endeavor, by the offer of a slightly better wage, to take workers away from works already engaged in his proposed branch of industry or in some similar line. In this he will have no difficulty; for there is no recognized code of business ethics, much less an established convention, to prevent his doing so by any means that commends itself to him as likely to produce results. In the interior, the proportion of skilled labor required in the predominant industries is too small to present serious difficulties. If necessary, men with some general industrial training are brought in as mechanics and somehow manage to keep the machinery going, while those acquainted with the manufacturing process, usually not far removed from the craftsman stage, manage the production, generally without awareness even of the existence of different methods of organizing it.

In the absence of trained skills, it may be said that, generally speaking, the Chinese factory substitutes number for efficiency. A foreign visitor recently complained that even in the foreign-owned hotels in China" one positively falls over the servants, there are so many of them hanging around everywhere. No one ever seems to be fired; if he does not do his job properly one or two more will be borought in to help him." This multitude of assistants has its cause, of course, in social conditions for which the individual employer is not to blame; it reflects merely the transition stage between a traditional and a modern mode of operation. When a craftsman takes his job home from the merchant employer it is natural that the whole family assists is carrying it out. In the early factory, likewise, the worker is still more or less the boss of his own loom or apparatus, and it is regarded as perfectly natural if a son or a younger brother is brought in to help him work more quickly. When it comes to power-driven machines, the determination of the speed of operation is no longer entirely in the worker's control; but since nine times out of ten he is on a piece-rate wage, it still is to his advantage to work fast. While women in cotton mills frequently bring in their children to help them, male operatives in a variety of industries often develop a sort of sense of temporary ownership of their job which entitles them to bring in assistants of their own choosing. In fact, the chief form of recruiting labor in Chinese industry today is, especially in the smaller plants, this method of experienced operatives gradually developing into shop bosses with the right to engage their help. This right means that in times of good trade they more and more emancipate themselves from working themselves and live, instead, largely on commissions charged their helpers for giving them the job; whereas in times of lowered production, such straw bosses, with a diminished number of helpers, must again do a larger part of the work themselves. Thus also among the female operatives of the cotton spinning mill, there will be brought into the shop a friend as helper to be trained; and this girl will pay for this introduction either with a gift or by substituting; and eventually, while Mrs. Chang's name stays on the firm's payroll her work will more and more be done by Miss Wang, with a still younger Miss Li starting as a beginner to learn the job. In the other textile industries, likewise, one never gets far away from the familial origins of the system of labor recruiting.

In the more modern mills, particularly those in Japanese and other foreign ownership, the tradition has developed into a contract system under which it is the recognized duty of the Chinese foreman to bring in new workers as needed. Usually he is most successful in his own home town where the people trust him; but if considerable numbers of new workers are required at one time, this boss may go into some poverty-stricken town in the interior, the less touched by progress the better, and there, with promise of a small loan to the family and of a wage payment sufficient to send a small amount home each month, ensnare a son or a daughter in this family and that to follow him to the distant city, here to work for him for a mere pittance. Once the young rustic has entered the Shanghai mill, and on a twelve-hour shift, direct communication with the home soon ceases altogether; what letters or moneys are sent go through the contractor-boss's hands. If the young worker is useful, little chance is given him or her to return home at the end of the year, as promised, or as long as he can be prevented from doing so.

Too often, since his methods of procedure do not lend themselves to strict control, the small boss contractor becomes simply a racketeer who lives as a parasite on the work of others, and particularly of children. The evils of this indirect system of hiring labor are so well known that it has been almost entirely done away with in industrially more advanced countries. In China, the origins of modern industry under foreign ownership or with foreign participation did not, of course, permit of the introduction of modern methods of hiring labor but, as in so many other matters, made the Chinese intermediary indispensable. The effects of the labor contract system are worse in China than in most countries from specifically Chinese causes: first and foremost, the pressure and misery of the population generally which gives enormous power to anyone who manages to get control of the giving out of jobs; second, the family system with its sacrifice of the individual for the good of the family on the one hand, and, on the other, the almost unbelievable inhumanity toward those helpless because lacking family protection. This goes through all of Chinese economic life. For example, in the coal mines of Shansi one finds miners who work twelve hours a day underground for a wage of 10 cents a day, and have been doing so for fifteen and twenty years in individual cases, without ever getting away. How did they get recruited in the first place for such living hell, and how does it come they are still there? They were recruited just as are the young cotton-mill workers and the apprentices for the multitude of small industries, by contract between some boss and the parents. There was some debt to be paid, or there simply was not enough to eat to support the whole family. So one boy or two went to the mine. There was no escape afterwards because the contractor controls the worker's expenses and never permits him to get out of debt.

As the overwhelming majority of Chinese mines use contract labor, it should always be borne in mind that the amount paid out for wages by the mine administration is never that which is actually received by the miners. According to the authoritative estimate of the China Geological Survey, there is a difference of about *twenty per cent*, on the average, which still is—we regret to state it plainly—an entirely legitimate. extremely heavy toll on the miners' earnings for a hardly justified benefit of the contractors, who are nothing but entirely superfluous middlemen. [1]

Commenting on this and other first-hand studies, Lamson says:

In addition to this percentage on wages, the contractor also feeds the workers and manages to get a large profit on that. Furthermore, the contractor is paid by the owners in big dollars but he pays his men on the basis of small money and makes from two to eight per cent on this exchange transaction. Thus all the squeezes

---

[1] Boris P. Torgashoff, *Mining Labor in China*, Ministry of Industry, Commerce and Labor, Shanghai, 1930, p. 119. See also Lowe Chuan-hua, *Facing Labor Issues in China*, London, 1934, pp. 21-23.

and profits which the contractor exacts from his laborers may amount to from 40 to 60 per cent of the basic wage. The experience of those companies which have tried to shake off the contract system and do their own hiring directly has shown the deep-rooted nature of the system. Some have tried to break away but have been compelled to go back to the old system. ①

Mining is, perhaps, one of the worst examples of the effects of the system, because the distance of the mine from the workers' home often gives the contractor who has advanced the railway fare a hold over his victims from the very start. But this is often equally true of other industries. For example, many of the smaller industries of Shanghai do not recruit their labor in the city or even in the immediate rural neighborhood, but go deliberately further afield to do so in a more distant famine-ravaged part of the country. As in mining, so also in other industries, living-in arrangements frequently permit the boss-contractor to deprive the workers of a large part of their earnings; and in this respect likewise the degree which insensitiveness to the suffering of others may reach is psychologically conditioned by the sense of social distance — in this case the absence of family ties, in America more often the freedom felt from responsibility for the welfare of immigrants, in colonial dependencies the indifference of members of the dominant for those of the indigenous race.

---

① Lamson, *op. cit.*, pp. 129-30.

Another way of exploiting human misery open to the labor contractor is the attraction of the foreign concessions and settlements for refugees of all sorts. Here on the outskirts of the factory sections he can find peasant families driven from their homes by famine, banditry, or other ills, supporting a precarious livelihood by whatever means are available, living in mud-or grass-huts, surrounded by filthy pools, social outcasts sometimes feared by the local authorities, sometimes aided, more often simply abandoned to their fate. These people will let the contractor have their children without asking too many questions; or the children will simply be absorbed in the smaller shops without an agreed apprenticeship and without any responsibility of the employer for them. Others drift into the building trade where sub-contractors board apprentices and kill many of them off in a few years by overwork and bad food while living on their wages. ① Conditions in all these respects, incidentally, are equally bad in industrial centers under Chinese and under foreign control, so that a throwing of stones would produce considerable work for the glazier on either side.

How, it may be asked, does this class of labor contractors itself come to be recruited? In the cotton industry it is usually some experienced operative who at a time of relatively good trade and hearing that wages are higher or conditions better in some other mill, seeks and finds employment there. If he does not change again he will try to get

---

① *Report of Shanghai Child Labor Commission*, Shanghai Municipal Council,1924, reprinted in *China Yearbook 1925*, p.551.

friends and relatives to join him. When thus he has made himself the leader of a small group of workers, he more or less automatically comes to be promoted as a strawboss whose business it is to supervise others while still, perhaps, at first also engaged on work himself. Gradually as he gets more persons working for him, the portion of his income from "squeeze" and commissions rises and that from his piece work drops, until he succeeds in securing a regular foremanship and goes further afield to hire labor. In fact. the practical inability to secure work other than through one of these men is one cause of the peculiar nature of trade unionism in China, since it forces the individual work-seeker to join some existing clique.

There is, of course, also a good deal of haphazard hiring, more especially of casual and seasonal workers. When cotton shipment comes in, men are taken on at random to move it about the plant. In the case of a Tientsin mill this is described as follows:

> Every morning at about six o'clock, a group of coolies are seen waiting in front of the mill's gateway. In a few minutes a staff member comes forth with a bundle of numbered sticks and throws them toward the coolies. A struggle immediately ensues, and those coolies are employed for the day who are in possession of the sticks. The method employed is repeated day after day, and is evidently against the interests of the coolies. But in view of the keen competition for jobs, the mill is able to retain the method and to dispense with the obligation of having to maintain the casual staff on

the regular payroll. ①

There is, in most Chinese factories, almost no selection for efficiency except for men claiming some special skill or experience entitling them to a wage above that for common labor. A record of names is kept, and attendance is checked by means of bamboo tablets. The name and address of each worker is recorded also on a wage-book, together with the wage-rate by means of which each worker is theoretically able to check for himself that he is receiving the proper pay for his output. But since the hiring is left almost entirely to foremen, the employer has no means to insure the efficiency or desirable character of the persons engaged, except in so far as his standards of desirability coincide with those of the foremen.

The number of workers hired also is often somewhat outside the control of the employer and does not necessarily coincide with the optimum number required for a given volume of output. The rate of absences is so high that foremen reassure themselves against loss of output by having from about ten per cent more persons on the payroll than are required. With the long shifts, still largely of twelve hour, overwork and substitutions of workers from day to night shift and *vice*

---

① Fong, *Cotton Industry and Trade in China*, I: 120. The final remark of the passage quoted does not overlook the fact that orderly procedures are possible in the hiring of casual workers — as has been demonstrated by the success with which many European and American ports have managed to regularize and systematize the temporary employment of dock labor; but with the complete lack of organization between employers such a method of job regularization is obviously not possible in China as yet.

versa are difficult to manage, and since piece-rate wages are the rule, and the demand for work, at any rate in the last ten years, is always greater than the demand for labor, it is economical to keep on hand an over-supply of workers.① For the same reason, that of keeping a margin of workers on hand, slackness in work is usually, in the cotton mills at any rate, met by short-time arrangements rather than by dismissals.

  B. *Wages.*   There is no scientific setting of wage rates. Just as piece rates are lowered when conditions are favorable for doing so, they are raised when too many good workers are being lost to other firms or when it seems desirable to attract experienced operatives from other plants. In no industry do the employers have scientific information as a basis for setting wage rates. Attempt is seldom made to bring these in harmony with prevailing standards or with demand and supply or with changes in the cost of living. In the cotton industry those categories of workers usually are on a time-wage whose output is subject to controls outside their own speed or efficiency—such as mixers, scutchers, card tenders, balers, mechanics, smiths, carpenters, power tenders, sizers, finishers, and coolies. Certain categories are placed on a time-plus-piece basis to assure the worker of a minimum income, yet provide some incentive to increase output; among them are rovers, spinners, reelers, bundlers, warp and filling winders, warpers, drawers and weavers. In some mills, nearly all these operations are, however, on a pure piece-

---

  ① Fong, *Cotton Industry and Trade in China*, I:122-24.

rate basis. ①

Since studies of wage-rates have, for the most part, been made in the more highly developed industries where time-rates predominate, comparisons are usually given in terms of actual or computed time-rates, either per hour or per day. Although in each occupation there is a wide range of wages this does not represent a complex classification of jobs with separate wage-rates but rather the recognition of differences in degrees of skill—as is but natural in a country where uniformity in wage-setting is not influenced by widely extending agreements. As between different occupations, there is some similarity it wage-rates when these are assorted according to similarity of skills. Since the workers are usually unorganized there is a much greater variety, apparently, than in other countries between the average rate of wages for one year and another, reflecting more closely the trend of the labor market and the directness with which employers can throw the fall of prices upon the wage-earners. Thus, the highest paid workers in China's modern industries, the warping workers in the silk weaving industry, were paid an hourly rate averaging 15.8 cents in 1930, 20.3 cents in 1931 and in 1932, 24.9 cents in 1933, but only 16.8 cents in 1934, when because of the foreign exchange situation, the industry was near complete collapse. In the silk industry are to be found also workers who receive only 2.5 cents an hour (basin workers), and a large number whose

---

① Fong, *Cotton Industry and Trade in China*, I: 127 ff; *Wang Rates in Shanghai*, compiled by Shanghai Bureau of Social Affairs and published by Commercial Press, Shanghai, 1935.

wage is 4.5 cents an hour — reelers. ①Taking Shanghai industry as a whole, wage rates above 10 cents an hour are rare. As among the silk weavers named above, so also for all the industries the employment curve is reflected by a rise in wage rates from 1930 to 1933, followed by a considerable fall in 1934, the actual average hourly wage rates for Shanghai male industrial workers amounting to 8.5 cents in 1930, 8.6 cents in 1931 and 1932, 8.7 cents in 1933, and 8.3 cents in 1934. In the case of female workers the fall in the average wage rate between 1933 and 1934 was less pronounced, presumably because most female workers are already employed at wages far below the subsistence level. As might be expected, the wage rates for male workers are higher than those for female workers, and piece workers earn a higher rate, when reduced to their equivalent per hour, than time workers. The low level of wage rates generally in the cotton spinning and silk reeling industries is explained in part by the large number of female workers employed. ②

The average wage rates do not reveal another peculiarity of industrial remuneration in China, the enormous variety of wages paid by different factories, often in the same town and neighborhood. This also can be explained only by the excessive competition and lack of organization, the fact that as soon as a concern has become well established and has trained up a force of workers, a number of small mushroom factories are

---

① T. Y. Tsha, "A Study of the Wage Rates in Shanghai, 1930-34", *Nankai Social & Economic Quarterly*, Vol. VIII, No. 3, October 1935, pp. 492-493, from which are taken also most of the following data.

② *Ibid.*, pp. 496-497.

likely to spring up around it to cut into its trade by lower prices and hence, with lower-paid and less efficient labor. ①Differences in policy also account for a considerable variation in wage rates as between several companies in the same line of manufacture. Some employers attempt to build up a small and loyal permanent staff with relatively high pay and treat the rest of their personnel with indifference; others are more concerned with providing a general stimulus to high output. In setting wage-rates, employers in certain centers, such as Nantung, Chenchow and Tientsin, also have to reckon with the difficulty of reducing the personnel in times of bad trade because of unreasonable demands on the part of the workers backed by political party officials. Dismissals in more than one recent case have led to strikes; and it has been found necessary to keep the whole plant closed for half a year or so, until a majority of

---

① This is well illustrated in the actual wages paid in various Shanghai cotton spinning mills by Arno S. Pearse, who made a study for the International Federation of Master Cotton Spinners' and Manufacturers' Association in 1929 (*The Cotton Industry of Japan and China*, Manchester, 1929, p. 175 *et. seq.*) and recorded average wages for drawing, for example, varying from 35 to 70 cents, ring tenting 50 to 80 cents, reeling 45 to 90 cents, etc. Pearse (*ibid.* , p. 169) found wages in the interior substantially lower than in Shanghai, as one would expect, quoting also the *Chinese Economic Bulletin* of June 15, 1929 to this effect. For example, the respective Wusih wages are 32 cents for drawing, 35 cents for ring tenting, and 29 cents for reeling. These enormous differences — space does not permit to give a more complete comparison between various accounts — are explained in part by different proportions in the employment of male and female labor, in part by the much higher living costs in Shanghai; while they are lessened, on the other hand, by the larger overhead item for welfare in some of the Shanghai mills which does not appear in the wage rates but undoubtedly keeps them lower than otherwise they would be. More recent data on labor costs in Shanghai and other parts of China are given of cotton mills in Wang and Wang, *op. cit.* , Chap. X.

the workers were dispersed, before it was possible to continue operations with a reduced staff. Compensation for dismissal, even travelling expenses to the home town of the workers, often are among the traditional responsibilities of the employer in one trade when no such conditions are recognized in other trade. Then again, industries may be burdened with other surviving traditions in employer-employee relations dating back to pre-capitalistic times. In short, the whole system of labor management is permeated with old folkways which do not readily give way to the methods brought back from western practice by foreign-trained managers and engineers.

C. *Hours of Labor.* Thus also in the matter of hours of work, days off, over-time and short-time, at first glance chaos seems to reign over the whole realm of Chinese industry. On closer inspection one finds, however, that what seem divergent and even contradictory practices all have their origin in a public opinion which forces upon industrialists conditions which no doubt have proved their worth in the familiarity of the small craftman's shop but would be considered unbearable burdens by the western scientific manager of to-day.

Thus, for example, there is no obvious reason why in cotton spinning and flour milling a working day of twelve hours should survive, a working period which a large body of experiment and demonstration has proved ineffective in producing maximum output, while match makers and tobacco workers work only seven and eight hours respectively; or why the average hours of labor among hosiery knitters, for example, should have varied within a margin of two and half hours per working day in the five years 1930-34. ① The long hours in cotton spinning and flour milling are explained, of course, by continuous operation in two shifts, but one would expect a reasonably short working day in printing, with its relatively large employment of fairly skilled operatives. In the case of match making and tobacco rolling, the statement that "the industries where long working hours prevailed were at the same time those where low wage rates were paid", ② hardly seems to hold good, since the wage rates in these occupations are not conspicuously high. More probable is the explanation that the effect of cyclical depressions on the length of the working day is particularly noticeable in the case of piece workers.

Owing to a lack of raw materials, partial suspension of certain jobs and whatever causes, piece workers often found in time of depress on their chance of work much curtailed, while the workers, so long as their employment contract continued, could keep up with the official working hours. Hence, the hours of work for piece workers were more liable to changes than those for time workers, and short working days were often found in those industries where piece workers predominated.

"The range of difference between longest and shortest working hours for time workers was 2.98 hours in 1930, 3.21 in 1931, 3.15 in 1932, 3.18 in 1933 and 2.76 in 1934; while that for

---

① Tsha. *op. cit.*, p. 499.
② *Ibid.*, p. 498.

piece workers was 4.94, 5.29, 4.20, 4.47, and 4.56 hours respectively. ①

Chinese employers, in the matter of working hours, are in direct opposition to their Government which, it its factory law, stipulates a maximum working day of eight hours which, under certain conditions provided for, may be extended to ten hours, a law which to enforce there exists as yet neither machinery nor the pre-requisite psychological possibility. Although these employers have for their excuse the fact that enforcement would place them at a disadvantage in competition with foreign employers who under extrality are not subject to Chinese law, the foreign employers, likewise, the experience of their own countries notwithstanding, consider it impracticable to reduce the daily or weekly working period in China. Thus, Japanese cotton spinners, when confronted with the discrepancy between their policies in this respect as applied in Japan and in China, allege that the difference in efficiency and output as between Japanese and Chinese workers does not permit of uniformity. Professor Ta Chen summarizes the result or a study in Shanghai by saying:

> A group of cotton mills estimates the loss from all causes if the working day were reduced to ten hours as 9 per cent, the reduction in output alone would amount to 17 per cent if the working hours were changed from 12 to 10 per day. A large manufacturing

---

○ Tsha. *op. cit.*, pp. 498-500.

concern which two years ago reduced its hours of work from 10 to 9 per day did so at a cost of 10 per cent. This firm estimates that reduction to 8 hours would cost 12.5 per cent. One public utility company inaugurated eight-hour shifts two years ago at a cost of $8,400 per annum. The number of workers involved was more than 950. ①

When pressed for further explanations, industrial managers usually admit that an increased output per hour, which has made possible the reduction of the working day in most European and American industries, could be achieved in China only by almost revolutionary changes in the system of labor management grenerally, including a more scientific selection of workers, better working conditions, more up-to-date machinery, more systematic planning, more artificial stimuli of various sorts, in short a greatly increased expenditure on the capital and overhead accounts. In other words, the long working day fits into the pattern of an industrial management which has not yet completely emerged from its primitive origin. Illiteracy and more especially lack of understanding for economic processes of which they see only a small part, makes the Chinese factory employees careless of waste of material and of spoilage. On a piece rate they appreciate the need for speed; but because of the humble and dreary condition of their lives, additional leisure time has less attraction for them than it has for the workers of

---

① *Chinese Social and Political Science Review*, Vol XV, No. 4, January, 1932, pp. 515-516.

western countries. The fact that such appreciations have not come yet with the introduction of modern industrial methods is, of course, chiefly due to the low level of wages which, for the great majority, makes impossible a life of moderate comfort, dignity, and varied enjoyments.

Differences in the efficiency of Chinese industrial workers and those of other lands, thus, are both cause and effect of long hours and low wages. Many stories are current about Chinese factory operatives found asleep at their work or wasting time in trifling conversation. Those who note instances of this sort do not always take the trouble to inquire into the surrounding facts. For example, a Chinese student of labor problems writes:

> When last month I visited a certain mine and went underground with the engineer to see how hard the miners worked, I came out quite disappointed. For, I discovered some of the miners sleeping soundly in this place far below the surface. In one place where eight miners were supposed to be at work, only two were actually cutting coal; two were asleep; two were taking a rest; where the other two had gone, I do not know. The engineer said to me: "You see why we cannot treat Chinese miners like human beings. The mules that pull the coal-cars never loaf. I am not surprised to hear people say that in other countries a miner can produce as much as four Chinese miners. With such men as these who go to sleep because the boss does not happen to be around to stand over them, how did we ever come to abolish the old piece-rate system and adopt instead a wage

system based on the number of hours underground?"

a statement which, apparently, convinced the recorder who introduces this experience with the words: "Can we blame the capitalists for things like this? No, a large part of the responsibility rests on the laborers themselves." ①

This writer probably was not among those present when the mangled body of a boy, seven or eight years of age, was, it is reported, recovered from a cotton-mixing machine in a Shanghai mill. The little boy, tired of picking bobbins, went into an adjoining room and fell asleep on a pile of cotton. Unfortunately that pile soon was lifted on the conveyor that fed it into the mixing machine. One more victim to the unregulated Chinese working day. The reports telling of preventable accidents due to overtiredness of the workers follow each other in quick suecession. One time it is the hair of a girl that is caught by the grip of a roller machine. Another time a man's hand is torn off because a machine is insensitive to its slackening speed at the zero hour. These are matters of daily experience.

"The evils of long hours", writes S. K. Sheldon Tso, "are intensified by the evil practice of night shifts. This has been

---

① Kai-lu Huang, "What Are the Labor Problems of China?", *Independent Critic*, No. 156, June 23,1935,p. 19(in Chinese). See also the callous remarks in a report of a British consular officer, reproduced in *Papers Respecting Labour Conditions in China*, H. M. Stationery Office,1925, Cmd. 2442. pp. 45-46. "The average worker," he writes, does not "grudge the time spent in labour. He, or she, works just as long as strength and daylight permit."

common in textile factories. The workers in these factories work day and night in turns. Other leading industries in China, like tobacco, match, and silk works, have also adopted the night-shift system. The result is inevitable fatigue and serious accidents."①

This author also draws attention to the inadequacies in the distribution of the working hours and in the matter of holidays:

> In each industrially developed country there is a rule regulating hours for rest, which usually ranges from one to one and one-half hours, but in China there is no definite rule for lunch or rest. Generally speaking, only half an hour is allowed for both, and in some of the factories the time allowed for lunch never exceeds twenty minutes. In many of the textile factories, women often bring meals into the factories for the workers,② for oftentimes there are no rest or dining rooms in factories, and the workers eat their food beside the machines.
>
> There are but few holidays, especially in those industries owned by foreign capitalists. Strangely enough, these foreign capitalists forget their habit of observing Sunday, and no holiday is allowed. Among the factories owned by Chinese, the holidays for the New Year festival range from ten to fifteen days. Holidays of

---

① *The Labor Movement in China*, Shanghai, 1928, pp. 57-58.
② Reversely, it is quite customary for children to be brought twice a day to their mothers in the factory nursing infants for their meals! See Fang Fu-an *Chinese Labour*, Shanghai, 1931, p. 38.

one or two days are given for the Chinese spring and summer solstices, for the May 15th or Dragon Festival, for the mid-annual, for mid-autumn, for the October "double-ten" or national holiday, for the winter solstice. etc. ①

In the most modern Chinese-owned mills and factories, apparently both seven-and ten-day weeks are observed by the interposition of a rest day; the New Year's vacation is shorter, and more national holidays take the place of the traditional ones.

"Rest days", writes Arno S. Pearse, "are arranged to suit individual cases. Some stop every Sunday afternoon, others every tenth day, again others allow two days per month ... The Chinese has accustomed himself to absent himself every now and then from his work and to take holidays when it suits his convenience, that is the reason why more people than necessary are on the wage list and why mill owners pay one day's wage extra, as a bonus, to anyone who for 14 consecutive days has not absented himself from his work." ②

D. *Labor Management.* With the primitiveness of the basic conditions, the finer points of labor management have not, as yet, received much attention in China. Foreigners have interested themselves in methods of more skillful regimenting of masses of workers but too often

---

① Tso, *op. cit.*, p. 58.
② *The Cotton Industry in Japan and China*, Manchester, 1929, p. 164.

have given up again any attempt to apply the results of western science in this respect when confronted with attitudes among the workers which they could not understand. Among Chinese managers there is often such understanding, but the demands of their employers or their financial backers do not conduce to the introduction of methods which cannot be expected to produce financial results at once. It is true, there has been established some years ago an Institute of Industrial and Business Management at the suggestion of the International Institute of Scientific Management, but as yet it does little more than acquaint Chinese employers with the results of western study and experience in this field and has had little influence on the prevailling practices. ①

Wage rates, we have already seen, are even more than in the west relied upon to provide the needed incentive. Promotion is individualistic; while in western industries wage-rates are set for different occupations in such way as to make simultaneous increase of earnings and advance to a more desired type of work, in China the individual is rewarded for special diligence, but there is much less of a systematic promotion to a higher status, except through the achievement, either of a transfer to more desirable work by a show of special aptitude, or of a foremanship through the skilful formation of a little group which, as a team, responds to the manager's requirements. There are no sharp

---

① A magazine entitled *Iudustrial and Business Management Monthly* has been publis hed by the Institute since May of 1934, in Chinese.

differentiations between classes of wage-earners. ① The employer's personal observation in the case of small factories, the recorded output in that of larger ones, are the usual grounds for promotion. In the absence of rigorous standards, it is natural that, on the one hand, the employer's personal prejudices, and, on the other, ability to coax and flatter on the part of the worker plays no small part in this process.

Thus foremanship also often does not represent a selection entirely on the grounds of special aptitude for its functions, especially of ability in handling men. The "long-gown" foreman in Chinese factories is essentially a member of the office force who knows how to keep accounts and is the scribe of the shop, responsible for checking stores and output, the wage-accounts of individual workers, the receipting of supplies and the marking off of outgoing products. In cotton mills, for example, the shop is usually supervised by such a long-gown foreman; but the actual work is assigned to that functionary in western countries is, for the most part, done by a boss selected from among the operatives. The long-gown foreman or shop superintendent is attended, as in cotton mills, by a group of apprentices, also belonging to the clerical rather than the operating staff. They are boys who have had a little education and assist in keeping the written records and accounts, responsible under their boss for keeping what little order there is in the shop procedure. These apprentices know next to nothing of machinery or processess except what they pick up in the course of the day's observations. It must not be

---

① Tsha, *op. cit.*, p. 465.

thought however, that this foreman with his group of apprentices constitutes a sort of embryo drafting office. Hardly any of them, as a rule, will have received enough education to want to read a book on industrial management or to prepare themselves by study for large responsibilities. Besides, this class exists only where operations on a fairly large scale necessitate some sort of orderly procedure. In the smaller factories everything is managed by men risen from the ranks of operatives; and such long-gown foremen as are around do not interfere with the shop procedure at all but are limited to clerical work. The shop superintendent also is usually a man who has risen to his rank because of his experience in the plant. He knows *what* must be done but usually has no theoretical knowledge of *why* it is done.

The whole system of management among Chinese-owned mills is usually polluted by ignorance, favoritism and squeeze. In particular, the mills established by inexperienced men who were attracted solely by the magnetism of huge profits during the War period are utterly inefficient. The whole plant, worth millions of dollars, may be entrusted to a manager who knows nothing about spinning. The latter, usually the trusted appointee of the most influential stockholder, has frequently neither a grasp of the technical complexity of spinning and weaving, nor a knowledge of cost accounting, financing and marketing. Instead, he delegates his duties to the subordinates, and relies upon the good turn of luck for the mill's profits. In such a mill, the head of the spinning or weaving department, oftentimes a close friend or relative of the manager or the stockholder, considers his job as a source of squeeze, but delegates in turn his duties to one of the foremen who, although skilled in mechanics, lacks scientific training. Consequently, machinery is not well-kept, and is not running in an efficient order. Laborers are not well-selected and trained, but recruited under the notorious contract system. The finished products deteriorate in quality, while their cost mounts higher and higher. ①

In the larger cotton mills, a new type of foreman and shop superintendent has been introduced by the successful training given for such posts in the Nantung Textile Institute, started and supported by Chang Chien, erstwhile Minister of Industry. The training given is of the type found in technical schools abroad. The graduates usually serve at first on the long-gown staff and are drawn upon to fill vacancies in the superintendence of various departments.

With the prevailing attitude of mill and factory owners, already referred to, that is, their almost exclusive attention to large profits rather than continued solidity of the manufacturing business, the successes of factory management in China lie mainly in the field of speeded production—and even here, as we have seen, the common complaint is about the long way which Chinese industries have yet to go to reach European and American standards. However, the fault for this does not

---

① Fong, *Cotton Industry and Trade in China*, I:319.

lie with the foremen whose ruthlessness in driving the workers is not a whit behind that of those of their class elsewhere.

The outstanding failure of foremanship in China—for which, again, not the functionaries but the system, or the lack of it, is to be blamed— lies in its inefficacy to produce loyal and willing cooperation on the part of the workers. Fear may have sufficed as a stimulus to build in record times portions of the Great Wall of China or later to build military roads; it may spurn the worker to great effort where, with primitive equipment, the volume of the output depends entirely on his speed. But where delicate machinery must be managed, where the product is the joint work of groups engaged upon various operations, where profit is so limited by competition that it melts away with excessive waste of raw material or careless damaging of the product, where a larger labor turnover means time and money lost in training new-comers, in short in industries carried on with modern methods and on a large scale, the attitudes of the workers are a factor of primary importance to efficiency.

And in this respect it often seems as though China has reached the stage through which western industrial countries have had to pass when the attitude of the wage-earners was as yet predomminantly one of blind, non-comprehending hostility.

> "Complaint is often made," writes H. D. Lamson, " of the leisurely fashion in which men or women work, especially if on time rate. By idleness, wasting of time, unwillingness to improve leisure hours with productive effort, many persons lose opportunities for

advancement. Dignity and easy-going use of leisure are delightful characteristics of the Chinese people; yet if these qualities are carried over into industrial undertakings, the result is economically undesirable. ①

Placing the blame for low labor efficiency squarely upon those responsible for backward technical equipment, the contract system of hiring, lack of training, illiteracy, impermanence of employment, and low wages, Torgasheff concludes:

> It is unanimously testified by most of the foreign manufacturers, with experience in China, that the Chinese workman, if taught the way in which an operation should be done by a uniform mechanical process, does exactly as he is taught. In several industries, where there is no need for any special muscular power and where the mechanical process is minutely uniform, as for instance in the textile industry, the Chinese workmen were able, it is said, to produce, in some instances, an efficiency almost ninety per cent of western labor. ②

To this one might add the regret commonly expressed by former employers of Chinese labor in Hawaii and continental United States over the loss, owing to the operation of the American immigration law, of an exceptionally efficient labor force, and the fact that Chinese labor is still

---

① Fong, *Cotton Industry and Trade in China*, p. 131.
② *op. cit.*, p. 52.

preferred to other available labor supplies in the largest industries of the neighboring countries to the South.

The long history of exploitation which has preceded industrialization in China and the pressure of population which produces the severest competition for labor opportunities known in the modern world to some extent obscure the dissatisfaction of the Chinese workers with their lot. Nor can we under the extraordinary circumstances in which the Nation has found itself expect clear-cut direct expressions of this discontent. This is discernible rather, on the one hand, in the general behavior of wage-earners toward the persons and properties of their employers and, on the other, in such disputes as come to the attention of the public authorities.

As regards the former, one may perhaps adduce as evidence a complaint characteristic of large rather than small employers. Traditionally, the Chinese laborer who works for an employer for the time being regards himself as a member of his household. Just as Chinese servants are known as very rarely stealing from their employers, so also in the small shops apprentices and laborers are too much still under the influence of the traditional attitude as to place their selfish interest in opposition to that of their master in such a flagrant way. In the large factories, however, one hears constant complaints about the thievery of workers. A certain mill manager finds that even the belts are cut down by workers who convert them into shoe soles. Fire doors are locked lest some out-side accomplice receive through them stolen loot. Women operatives have been known to wad their gowns with cotton yarn. Visits from children, common in the smaller factories and workshops, are frowned upon in the larger plants because too much loot went out with the little visitors.

It is strange to find each exit of a mill in China provided with wooden barricades in zig-zag form. Through these the operatives have to pass, one by one, to be thoroughly searched for anything they may have taken out of the mill. The Chinese can sell any trivial thing; he finds a customer for a bit of string, for cotton waste, a screw; he is by instinct a petty trader. That such a search is absolutely necessary is another indication of the low state of civilization which the Chinese mill operatives occupy. At one Japanese mill there were red boxes attached to pillars near the barricades, a large white hand was pointing to the opening of the box, and underneath was an inscription to the following effect: "Have you something in your pocket? Ask your heart. You do not want to steal. If the answer is yes, put it at once into this box." In about 14 days every box is full with all kinds of waste, bobbins, bits of cloth, etc. [1]

A manager of a modern mill which provides housing for employees and their families has had to cut off electric current supplied for lighting

---

[1] Pearse, *op. cit.*, p. 172. A more adequate interpretation of this situation than that given by the author would be that only one element prevents from complete collapse the civilization of slums and extreme inhumanity created largely by foreign exploitation in Shanghai (as to this, see for example, the evidence of S. H. Peek, an officer of the Shanghai Municipatl Council, in an article on "Super-Slums", *The China Critic*, Vol. X. No. 12, September 19, 1935, p. 271, and elsewhere), namely the traditional ethics preserved even in the humblest homes.

because the tenants used it also for cooking and heating. Guards are employed to search suspiciously bulging operatives on their way out of the mill gates. Cotton waste is taken out by the ton.

We were visiting a large coal mine. Passing through a large tunnel through which many miners had to come and go, I noticed that it was very long and entirely dark. I could not see my own hands. "Why don't you put some electric lights in here?" I asked the engineer. "It would not only be more convenient than this groping in the dark, but it might also save you losses from the collision of coal cars?" He snorted. "So say you," he answered. "It is simply because these miners are a worthless lot. At one time there was an electric lamp in this tunnel every 50 steps. Then, because the miners kept on stealing the bulbs, we left the passage dark for a while. But this was inconvenient, so we shifted the connections and placed the lights in the roof of the tunnel, four meters high, where they could not be reached by hand. There was no more theft after that. But we had to put in new bulbs every day because these miners made targets of the bulbs and shied pieces of coal at them every time they passed. So what could the company do? We decided we would have to do without lights."①

Sabotage is, of course, a familiar device of workers too weak, through lack of effective organization, to express their dissatisfaction with

---

① Kai-lu Huang. *op. cit.*, pp. 19-20.

working conditions in an orderly manner and through recognized channels. The surprising thing is not its occurrence in China but its rarity in this country. The amazing patience of the Chinese laborer in the face of intolerable working conditions has often been commented upon by Chinese and foreign students alike.

E. *Labor Organization and Disputes.* It is not this patience, however, but the recent transformation of an agricultural society which has made the growth of an effective labor movement impossible in China. This is not the place to recount the varied history of this movement, since the days when the Kuomintang party itself may almost be said to have sprung from it — at any rate had the most intimate relations with both its leadership and its ideals. [1] Since the suppression of the more aggressive type of trade unionism, organized labor has an extremely small influence on labour conditions, except in some of the southern ports, particularly in relation to engineering and to dock labor. The survival of unionism in these occupations must be ascribed to different reasons — in the one case it represents, no doubt an aristocracy of skill difficult to replace, and thus enjoys the same position which similar unions have always enjoyed in industrial countries. Ship-owners, particularly, complain about union tactics among unskilled workers, including, both firemen and dock labor. Here the relative power of the workers which is by no means large rests upon the relatively high losses which the withholding of their labor occasions to ship-owners, not only through the idleness of a valuable unit

---

[1] See Lowe, *op. cit.*, Chaps. III to VI.

of capital but also through the ongoing charges for wharfage, etc. Unfortunately no recent statistics of trade union membership are available, nor are those occasionally published for Shanghai or other cities reliable, and this for obvious reasons. The statistics disregard the obviously necessary distinction between company unions and free unions; moreover, secret unions of an aggressive type undoubtedly exist which have been driven underground by the suppression of undesirable radical activities. The company unions are established in individual plants under a leadership often in close connection with, even appointed by, the party machinery. The leadership, while sometimes irksome to the management of the plant is, as a rule, wholly innocuous and opposes employers of labor only on questions relating to the dismissal of employees or the spreading of employment in times of slackness. Often without even a loose federation, such units have little influence, generally speaking, either on labor conditions or on the framing of labor policies. While they are not necessarily "yellow unions" in the European and American sense, i. e. controlled by the employing class, they are nevertheless liable to dicker with employers chiefly to the advantage of the union officials rather than that of the rank and file, in this way comparable, perhaps, with many of the unions in the building trades in the United States, the venality of whose leaders has at times led to publle scandals but to some extent always determines the policies on both sides. ①

---

① Bureau of Social Affairs, City Government of Greater Shanghai, *Industrial Disputes in Shanghai since 1918*, 1934, p. 30.

With these explanations, it seems hardly necessary here to reprint such statistics of trade unions and trade union membership as the reader may find them in the reports of the Ministry of Industry, Commerce, and Labor.① The weakness of trade unionism which explains the fact that it easily falls into the hands of outside professional organizers who use it for ulterior purposes, is, as already intimated, caused by lack of those fundamental social attitudes which elsewhere have created a strong labor movement in spite of many difficulties. The shop still is too close to that of the master craftsman with the traditional feeling of "belonging", strengthened by the inability of the industrial worker, in China today to get a job at all, unless he is willing to subject all his interests to those of the boss who, with the pressure for jobs, can make far greater demands on the loyalty of the assistants whom he himself selects than the foreman in a European or American plant can make on that of his workers. The traditional family organization also stands in the way of a strong feeling of fellowship developing among wage-earners on the basis of their common interest. Just as in most industries there is as yet no effective organization among the capitalists who rather fight each other to the knife, so it is even more difficult for a poor and uneducated wage-earner to realize that his welfare is more closely connected with that of his fellow workers than with that of the man who happens to offer him a job.

In spite of this weakness of organized labor, industrial relations in China are by no means harmonious. On the subject of labor disputes, no

---

① See the comment on these statistics by Ta Chen in *China Yearbook 1934*, p. 247.

reliable statistics are available either. The fullest and most recent are those collected by the Bureau of Social Affairs of the Municipality of Greater Shanghai. Of 194 disputes in that city reported in 1934, 120 were connected with employment, and only 38 directly with wages. As might be expected, demands for higher wages are inconspicuous in these disputes in a year of trade depression. Apparently, as in so many other aspects of Chinese social life, compromise is the usual outcome of negotiations. In only 42 of the 194 cases did the workers get what they asked for, and in only 19 did they fail altogether. Thirty-three cases were still unsettled or without results at the end of the year. ①

Changes in government policy, the effect of the world economic depression, and a relative strengthening of employers' organizations are given as causes for the declining effectiveness of labor organization by the Shanghai Bureau. ② Taking the five years, 1928-32, one-third of the strikes and lockouts, 517 in number, concerned wages, over one-fourth engagement or dismissal of workers, one-seventh collective agreement. ③

---

① Cheng Hai-feng in *China Yearbook*, 1935, pp. 352-353. The *1935-36 Chinese Yearbook* gives, on pages 927-929. a total of 183 industrial disputes for the four provinces of Kiangsu, Hupeh, Anhui and Kiangsi and five cities of Nanking, Shanghai, Tsingtao, Hankow and Tientsin during the first part of 1934, of which Shanghai alone claimed 138,970 establishments were involved in these 183 cases, affecting altogether 24,390 male, 15,987 female and 2,325 child workers—a total of 42,702 workers. Textile industry led with 61 cases, followed by food and drinks with 20, leather, and rubber with 16, etc.

② *op. cit.*, pp. 28-29.

③ *Strikes and Lockouts in Shanghai since 1918*, compiled by the Bureau of Social Affairs, City Government of Greater Shanghai and published by the Chung Hua Book Company, Shanghai, 1933, pp. 64-65.

The major causes of industrial disputes (1,491) during the same period[1] were engagement or dismissal of workers: two-thirds; wages: over one-tenth; collective agreement: less than one-tenth. Forty-four per cent of the strikes and lockouts were settled with a partial and 23 per cent with a total victory for the workers, a remarkably favorable showing, considering the industrial situation during this period, and pointing to a somewhat different nature of resort to strikes and lockouts than is customary in other industrial countries. It may be, however, that, in part, this favorable showing reflects no more than a limitation in reporting, since no less than 87 per cent of the industrial disputes and 53 per cent of the strikes and lockouts included in these statistics were settled by the City Bureau which records these cases. That is to say, the resort to conciliation or arbitration by a public body may be responsible for the large proportion of settlements partially in favor of the wage-earners. Strikes and lockouts as well as disputes in Chinese-owned establishments appear to be both numerically and proportionally more frequent than in foreign-owned ones; a fact which, without further information, does not suffice to conclude that labor management in the one is more fair or more efficient than in the other. [2]

Perhaps because of the depressed condition of labor or possibly because of the better control of the Government, semi-political strikes,

---

[1] Labor disputes in the Shanghai reports do not include strikes and lockouts. but only those ended by negotiation. See *Industrial Disputes in Shanghai Since 1918*, p. 55.

[2] Ibid.

which at one time were frequent and serious because of their interference with public services, seem to have been few in recent years. It is noteworthy, for example, that a widespread opposition to persistent Japanese aggression has produced little labor unrest, whereas formerly it frequently took the expression of strikes. ①

F. *Welfare Work.* What part does determined improvement in labor conditions play in the lessened virility of labor disputes and in the weakening of the trade union movement? That this has been the case in Japan, is beyond question. In that country, labor legislation, a national economic policy favorable to industrial workers at the expense of the farmers, and the working out of welfare plans in particular industries and plants have combined with the suppression of radical activities and of "dangerous thoughts" to reduce the labor movement to a mere shadow of what it was fifteen years ago, and this in spite of a very low standard of real wages. Of the sort of labor policies to which industries in other countries have resorted to ensure greater satisfaction and loyalty on the part of the workers, there is very little to report from China. There is not a single industry which has voluntarily introduced far-sighted schemes for dividing part of the profits among the wage-earners. The physical condition under which work is being done, still, as we have seen, leaves much to be desired. Pension funds on a scale comparable with those of great American plants, housing schemes like those of some of the great British industrial concerns, generous provision for recreation or for

---

① *Strikes and Lockouts in Shanghai since 1918*, pp. 64-65.

guarding the health of the workers are, if not unknown, at any rate as yet in an embryo stage of development. It would, in fact, be an irony if plants which do not as yet take all possible precautions against preventable accidents were to establish dental clinics for their employees, or if those which run on twelve-hour shifts were to build reading and recreation rooms for them. However, there are beginnings in every direction. One group of mill owners has established a group insurance plan on a modest scale, as yet without an actuarial basis. Bonus and premium payments are occasionally heard of. In a few cases schools have been established for child workers. And a peculiarly Chinese institution is the payment of "coffin money" in case of death. ① Another is the New Year's bonus, in addition to which there are occasionally small attendance and efficiency bonus payments. In an inexpensive way, especially foreign employers sometimes do provide for recreation, perhaps by laying out a playing field.

Where housing is provided for mill operatives, it is of a very primitive kind.

> ...The Chinese mills provide only cheap houses, two-storied brick houses in the neighborhood of the mills. These houses are back to front with very narrow alleys between them. According to Western ideas they are slum property, but according to Oriental views they are little palaces. The writer has been inside one or two

---

① Fong, *Cotton Industry and Trade in China*, I: 158.

of these houses and was appalled at the stench which emanated from them.

The rent charged is only a nominal one, say three to five tyels per month, which includes free supply of water and sometimes lighting. and this is divided amongst the various occupiers, say three families or 12 to 15 girls. The space occupied by such houses is very small, 20 by 11 feet. ①

All efforts of this sort are necessarily on a small scale, so long as there is no agreement on policies among a majority of employers in any one industry, and so long as individual activities of this sort are not generally demanded by public opinion.

G. *Labor Legislation.* While both the National Government and local governments have encouraged a greater regard for the welfare of employees, the non-enforcement of the factory act makes it difficult for a well-meaning employer to saddle himself with the expenses of even a minimum program of welfare work. And the factory act cannot be enforced for two reasons — on the one hand the inability of the Government to arrive at binding agreements with foreign employers not under its jurisdiction, on the other, the cheapness of labor generally and the attitudes directly arising from that fact. Here again, progress is hampered by the chaotic state in which industry as yet finds itself, and by the weakness of the Central Government. Many of the factories, even

---

① *The Cotton Industry of Japan and China*, Manchester, 1929, p. 165.

if they were brought to account for non-compliance with the law, are so precarious in their capitalization that they could not pay an appropriate fine. Adequate factory inspection even if it were politically feasible would be too expensive an item just now to add to the Government budget. Complete plans have, in fact, been made for a system of factory inspection under the Factory Act of 1931. and a small number of persons have been trained for that function. The International Labor Office has been invited to assist in the introduction of such a system and made preliminary studies before advising the Government.

"The general impression which we quickly reached", writes C. Pone, chief of section of the International Labour Office, was that the conditions of labour in the factories we visited was generally far from satisfying the rules laid down in the new Factory Act, and that the observance of those rules, however desirable and even urgent it might be, wound require very considerable modifications in the organisation and methods of working of a large number of factories... The New Chinese Factory Act deals with the most varied questions all at the same time, and right at the outset adopts the most modern solutions which have only been reached in other parts of the world by a more or less slow and gradual process of development. [1]

For this reason, a modification of the regulations and of the program as a

---

[1] *International Labour Review*, Vol. XXV, No. 5, May. 1932, p. 596.

whole was recommended and adopted, providing for several stages in the enforcement of the Act, and the Act itself was amended the following year. ①

Even so, it cannot be said that much progress has been made in enforcement, or even in the routine of factory inspection, and this partly because of the unwillingness of foreign capitalists, as represented by their consular courts and by the governments of their settlements and concesssions, to co-operate with Chinese National or local governments. Foreign employers consider the Factory Act even in its present form impracticable and against the best interests of industrial development — forgetful, perhaps, that in large continental countries, such as China and the United States, legislation is necessarily more idealistic and designed to set up standards rather than limited to possibilities of immediate enforcement, as is the case in small island countries, such as Japan and Great Britain. ②

A deeper difficulty, however, lies in the impossibility of enforcing even a modest installment of the law in a society so little motivated by social considerations as is industrial China. Even the strongest advocates of a forceful beginning with such enforcement admit this difficulty.

Those who are familiar with the practices of Chinese business men can easily perceive that the backwardness of China's industries

---

① *Chinese Economic Journal*, Vol. XII, No. 3, March 1, 1933, pp. 178-283.
② See Lowe Chuan-hua, "Factory Inspection as a Political Football", *China Critic*, Vol. VI, No. 19, May 11, 1933, pp. 471-473.

is due not so much to any burdens imposed upon them by Government regulations as to their own obsolete and rotten methods of management. The problem with Chinese industrialists is not so much the Factory Law as the lack of a scientific spirit and modern methods of administration. Governed largely by traditions and family ties, Chinese employers are usually reluctant to employ experts to improve their plants. ①

The recentness of the whole undertaking must, of course, also be taken into consideration. There was no legislative protection for labor of any kind in China before 1914, when for the first time regulations were decreed for the employment of miners. The reason for the continuing opposition to labor legislation is only ostensibly that it introduces fanciful and unnecessary provisions; actually it is much more honorable to the intentions and efforts of the Government: the various laws have been opposed precisely because they were fundamental, and necessitate a wholly different attitude of employers from that which at present prevails. The impetus to legislation in this field was given originally by the Revolutionary movement itself and the personal influence of Dr. Sun Yat-sen. The successes of British labor, the scientific and practical approach of the International Labour Office, and later the successful introduction of sweeping reforms not only in Russia but also in other European countries, have all contributed to the energy with which it has been taken up. But no

---

① Lowe Chuan-hua, "Enforcing China's Factory Law", *China Critic*, Vol. V, No. 34, August 25, 1932, p. 874.

government can produce a forceful control over labor conditions when it has neither a trained inspectorate, nor a strong organization of the workers themselves, and against it the apathy of the leaders of public opinion. ①

V. MARKETING

A. *Industrial Products.*　　No one knows or can even approximately estimate the total volume of China's industrial production. The reason for this is that there are no clear lines of demarcation between products that may be said to emanate from modern plants and those that come from traditional crafts. It is not even possible to make a fine distinction between commodities that are manufactured at all and those better described as "raw" materials, since the degrees of manipulation and change shade over from a mere process of sorting and cleaning into processes of complete transformation by degrees almost imperceptible because the same application of human or mechanical energy to the raw product may at one time take place in a primitive farmstead and at another in a modern plant. Moreover, so large a portion of China's production either enters only into local trade which is of a primitive, unorganied

---

① See Jefferson D. H. Lamb, *The Origin and Development of Social Legislation in China*. Yenching University. Peiping, Series C., No. 24, March, 1930.

character, or is consumed without entering into trade at all, that any attempted estimate may be wide of the mark.

What we do know is that only a small portion of manufactured articles if we adopt any standard definition of that term is produced by modern industry. A further factor confusing to the statistician who likes neat distinctions is that often a raw product —cotton or silk, for example may undergo early stages of its manufacture in a modern plants, only to be turned back again to craftsmen with old-fashioned tools for those processes which turn it into consumer commodities. Similar situations also exist in western countries, to be sure, but nowhere to the extent as in China in relation to the total volume of its manufactures under modern conditions. And the reason for this lies in the history of its industrial development. For Chinese industry is almost in its whole extent based upon beginnings introduced by foreigners; and these were at no time interested in producing either for Chinese consumption or for export finished products from Chinese raw materials. We thus find that the great bulk of Chinese exports represents raw materials which have undergone some preliminary form of treatment or have been extracted with the aid of modern equipment; and this is equally true of materials prepared for foreign markets by plants in Chinese or in foreign ownership. Although they do not indicate the basis for their classification, Chien Tsai and Kwan-wai Chan are undoubtedly right in estimating Chinese exports of unmanufactured and

sem.-manufactured goods as larger than those of manufactured goods. ①
They also show that the export of unmanufactured and semi-manufactured
goods has greatly increased at the expense of that of manufactured goods
between 1912 and 1931 when given in proportions of the total. But in the
import figures, this trend is even more marked,②so that it does not signify
a relative weakening of Chinese industry in competition with the
importation of manufactured articles.

CHINESE IMPORTS AND EXPORTS CLASSIFIED BY STAGES OF PRODUCTION, 1912-1931

(in percentages)

	1912	1931	1912-31
Import			average
Manufactured	51.8 ⎫	46.2 ⎫	55.2 ⎫
Semi-manufactured	26.3 ⎬ 34.8	19.7 ⎬ 52.2	23.7 ⎬ 41.5
Unmanufactured	8.5 ⎭	32.5 ⎭	17.8 ⎭
Export			
Manufactured	25.6 ⎫	24.3 ⎫	24.3 ⎫
Semi-manufactured	37.7 ⎬ 71.8	32.5 ⎬ 75.3	38.6 ⎬ 74.1
Unmanufactured	34.1 ⎭	42.8 ⎭	35.5 ⎭

For China's internal trade we have no comprehensive data to
indicate the relative importance of manufactured, or semi-manufactured
and unmanufactured, articles. Nor are there any inclusive figures

---

① *Trend and Character of China's Foreign Trade*, Institute of Pacific Relations, 1933. pp. 10-11 and 34.

② *Ibid.*, pp. 13-15 and 35.

indicative of the output, except perhaps for coal and minerals which are of greater interest as potential raw materials for our present study than they are in the sense of being industrial products themselves. However, the local study made by D. K. Lieu in 1930 for Shanghai, China's industrial capital, may help to give some indication of what the totality of these products probably is. According to that study, the textile industries came first, with 43.1 per cent of the total output of 431 million dollars; foods, drink and tobacco came next with 31.8 per cent; paper, bookinding, and printing, 6.6 per cent; chemicals and allied products, 4 per cent; clothing, 3.6 per cent; machinery and miscellaneous metal products, 2.6 per cent; leathers, skins and rubber 2.2%; gas, electricity and water, 1.6%; boats, ships and vehicles, 1.5%; other seven groups, 3%.[1] A further examination of the able shows that even in this industrial capital of the country, where one would expect to find manufacture most advanced and best equipped to put the materials through all the necessary processes to transform them into articles for consumption, the output of those branches of industry which deal with raw materials is much greater, in most cases, than that of the branches concerned with finishing processes and this in spite of the fact that the proportionate value of the output in relation to volume is, of course, much larger in the latter than in the former. For example, in the woodworking industry, the output of saw mills is 94 per cent of the total in

---

[1] *A Preliminary Report on Shanghai Industrialization.* Table V; *Nankai Weekly Statistical Service*, Vol. VI, No. 41, Oct. 9, 1933.

value, or 50 per cent if the whole furniture manufactory, which uses also many other materials, is counted in. In the group composed of non-metallic mineral products, including bricks and tiles, glass and glasswares, cement, stone powder and lime, building materials other than bricks and tiles alone make up more than five-sixths of the total. In the cotton industry, the output of the spinning mills, including a considerable proportion of weaving also, is ten times as large in value as that of the weaving mills. In the silk industry, the value of the product of the filatures is five times that of the weaving mills. Wool spinning produces almost twice as much output in value as wool weaving. Leather and skin manufacturing, which includes the making of complete uppers and soles, almost equals in value the output of leather goods. In the food, drink, and tobacco group, the output of the flour mills alone is one-half of the total in value. Even as the country's greatest center of the printing and publishing industries, Shanghai has a paper and card-board manufacture with an output almost equalling in value that of newspaper printing and publishing.

There are no other local studies of similar comprehensiveness. However, taking Wusih as an example of smaller industrial centers, some figures obtained in 1929 are interesting. Of the total output of that city's industries, amounting to 81 million dollars, cotton spinning (also including some weaving), silk reeling, flour milling, rice cleaning, and oil pressing which formed the principal raw material transforming

INDUSTRIAL ORGANIZATION IN CHINA

industries, made up more than ninetenths of the total. ①

One fact stands out from these data, that modern industry has not yet started in China to supplant the traditional methods of supplying the country with consumers' goods. In this respect a comparison with Japan is interesting. In both countries, modern industry sprang in the first instance from the needs of national defense and then was further developed, first, by the importers' desire for larger profits and then by native competition with importers. It was foreign, specifically European and American goods, which a rapidly increasing section of the buying public wanted; and it was for the purpose of making these essentially alien commodities more widely and more cheaply available that industries were started. Those commodities, naturally the vast bulk even in an alert and progressive country, which were traditionally part of the standard of living, continued to be manufactured as before. So, in Japan as in China, the great majority and the largest volume of consumers' goods are still produced by small shops and factories, a considerable proportion on a craftsman rather than a capitalistic basis. What one sees in the world of the great variety of Japanese industrial finished products does not represent the consumer buying of Japan. The fact that such goods are produced on a large scale for export has, however, also inundated the home market with them and is deteriorating the Japanese standard of living — as may be said of the five and ten-cent stores in America and of certain types of department stores which the National-Socialists are

---

① *Nankai Weekly Statistical Service*, Vol. III, No. 50, December 15, 1930, p. 241.

combating for this reason in Germany. But the every-day needs of the Japanese peasant and *Kleinbuerger* are still being met by industries which produce with a regard to quality as well as to price and which, in fact, cannot enlarge and thereby cheapen their production because the product is in the main a part of the national culture and cannot, except by some accident of foreign fashion, enter into world trade.

But whereas a similar situation in China has meant that almost all consumer goods are still being made in the traditional way without benefit of modern machinery or organization, there are two important differences in that situation compared with that of Japan. First, from a desire for western-style goods, Japanese consumer demand has much more rapidly advanced toward a desire for the cheapness and standardization of quality which mass production by machines makes possible, so that many of the small industries producing only goods for home consumption and not for export have been mechanized. In China the western-style article is, in the main, still an article of luxury. Second, not so much the extremely low purchasing power of the masses as lack of capital, of means of transportation, of possibilities of organization, have prevented small producers from adopting for the manufacture of native articles the advantages of machine production. Japan has been forced by its economic situation, and under the guidance of a purposeful government with strong control over the whole economic life of the people, to direct its production toward a rapid increase in exportation of manufactured articles and thus has automatically given the whole population more of a training in the production and consumption of new-style goods. In

China, the internal economy has hardly been affected at all by industrial production for export; and whatever stimulus has come from this course to change consumer and producer habits has been too small to affect in any appreciable way the general economic life. In the circumstances, only a disregard of the actual surrounding facts can lead writers to conclusions about the relative progressiveness or backwardness of the Japanese and the Chinese as producers or consumers. It cannot be said that Chinese consumers are more tradition-minded than are Japanese; for in those groups for which a comparison is possible, the opposite conclusion would seem nearer to the truth. For our present purpose, it only needs to be pointed out that in those few Chinese industries which, because of some specialized foreign consumer demand, produce a finished article for the world market, there also develops a corresponding domestic demand, This is, perhaps, seen most clearly in the rug industry of Peiping and Tientsin, but is also true of ceramics, piece goods, and knitted wares. The last named represents a new consumer commodity which finds a rapidly increasing demand in China as a result of a production introduced and stimulated by foreign interests. The other commodities named have undergone significant changes as production for home consumption adapted itself to new forms of production for foreign markets.

Only in exceptional circumstances have consumer habits changed directly in imitation of foreign ones. The most noteworthy examples of this are to be found in those spheres of the public welfare where philanthropic and commercial motives have made a joint attack upon tradition, particularly in matters of health and sanitation and in education. Modern industries, though often retaining their small-scale operations, are substituting new implements for old and are transforming even the equipment and the stock-in-trade of the old-style Chinese physician and druggist.

There are few available data as yet to illustrate in detail the changing nature of factory production so far as they represent a transition from traditional or native to modern or cosmopolitan articles of use. Just because modern industrial processes, for the reasons given, are as yet applied more to crude than to refined processes, and the manufacture of consumers' goods is distributed over vast numbers of small factories and shops, reliable records on this subject are practically non-existent.

B. *Marketing.* Almost wholly uninformed about the domestic market, most Chinese industries are further handicapped by being unable, as we have seen, to predict for any length of time the extent to which they can count upon a steady production to make worth while a purposeful campaign of sales promotion. Not only this, but buying from an unorganized, primitive market and selling in large part to such a market, they cannot build up a modern machinery of sales. Supposing an American producer had his modern technical equipment, but this surrounded by a chaotic scramble, with no certainty that materials of a given kind and quality could be obtained within a reasonably limited range of prices, with no way of selling except to almost illiterate peddlers and small retailers who keep no books and have no assets other than their good name among their immediate neighbors, with transportation facilities which may be available today and commandeered for troop movements tomorrow, with taxes which may suddenly be doubled by local impositions, with a large demand for his product in one state, suddenly swept away by a famine, and a steady increase of sales in another faced with equal suddenress by the competition of a cheaper product using a style of packing and a trade name similar to its own — how long would such a manu facturer be able to use that technical equipment to advantage? Well, the reader cannot answer this conundrum because American industry as carried on today simply is not imaginable apart from a marketing organization as technically systematized as is the producing organization. Mechanization on a large scale, scientific planning, long-range policies of purchase and production are possible only because there is an organized wholesale trade with standardized weights, measures and currency, banking institutions which give credit on a basis of impersonal criteria, reliable transportation facilities, with rates that do not suddenly change, with taxes which, though heavy, are predictable, with outlets as thoroughly organized as are the industries themselves, including great chains of stores and department stores which are managed on more or less scientific principles. Though there is competition it is regulated by conventions and laws. When an American industry plans expansions it does so on the basis of scientific inquiries, knowing that for every practical problem in the working out of a policy competent specialists can be hired.

Now, it is perfectly true that in all this there are many shades of accomplishment, that some industries, even in the Soviet Union which makes so much of scientific planning, are more thoroughly mechanized and systematized than others, that some quite important industrial countries of Europe are still close to early phases of capitalistic development, and that traditionalism is pronounced in some aspects of industrial life even in highly organized countries. But when the modern industries of China are seen against their background, it is obvious that here even foreign concerns when they have tried to introduce scientific methods have succeeded in doing so only to the extent to which their products are for export, or when the machinery of distribution in China itself remains under strong foreign control, as for example, in the case of the foreign-owned cigarette industry. ① One neglected fact in Chinese economic history is that many foreign concerns which at one time tried to introduce marketing methods familiar to them from experience in their own country, have had to give up this attempt and either assimilate their practices to Chinese customs or else make use of Chinese intermediaries. In recent times, this latter tendency is again weakening, because now it is possible for foreign concerns to employ Chinese trained in western commercial methods, yet conscious of Chinese customs, who can work out new intermediate methods and adjustments, and also because many of the larger foreign concerns have on their staffs more foreigners familiar with the Chinese language who themselves obtain a more intimate

---

① Petroleum products and sewing machines also have been introduced largely by the direct sales method.

knowledge of Chinese trade methods and psychology. ① Nevertheless, the picture of marketing organization for industries in China created by a glib use in many Chinese studies of western technical terms is often very misleading. It is not even quite true to say that in this as in other matters China is in a state of transition; it is much more in a state of inner conflict between old and new methods, each deeply embedded in an ancient culture; and unless quite fundamental conditions undergo a change, there is no inevitability at present that western methods, more scientific and therefore superior as they are, will make great headway.

(1) Sales Machinery. —With the above preliminary remarks, we may proceed to analyze the three kinds of sales methods employed for the disposal of the products of China's modern industries, namely, export, nation-wide distribution, and local distribution. The first of these is almost entirely in the hands of foreign firms. Indeed, some of the largest industries in China are either owned by foreign concerns or under contractual obligations to them—as particularly in the case of iron mines—to place at their proposal either a definite volume of output or a given proportion of their total output. In recent years, particularly Japanese enterprise has taken unto itself a large part of the output of certain industries which, though on Chinese soil and using both Chinese raw materials and Chinese labor, are in every other respect foreign enterprises. ② Many other

---

① Frank R. Eldridge, *Oriental Trade Methods*, New York, 1923, pp. 100-101.

② H. D. Fong, Industrial Capital in China, *Nankai Social & Economic Quarterly*, April, 1936.

industries, though conducted entirely under Chinese ownership and management, produce in the main for export through foreign houses. Among these might be mentioned more especially raw silk, soda, bristles (also a partly manufactured product), bean oil and cakes, egg products, and rugs. So far, no large Chinese export industry, with the exception of soda and to a certain extent of rugs, has established a full system of its own to conduct and promote foreign sales. Nor is there any agency of Government sufficiently equipped to assist them. Their own capital is insufficient, even in the case of luxury articles much appreciated abroad, to establish foreign branches or agencies. The only noteworthy exception to this is in the trade of those southern countries where Chinese enterprise more or less controls the retail trade or where Chinese residents themselves are large consumers of Chinese industrial products. Here the responsibility for financing the trade in Chinese products falls, however, upon the Chinese importer rather than upon the manufacturer; and it is more frequently the case that the import firm has purchasing agencies in China than that the Chinese manufacturer has agencies even in these countries where his products have found a ready market.

  It is in those industries which cater either to a nation-wide market in China or at least to a large part of it that we find the most highly developed system of sales planning and the most thoroughly organized machinery for selling. Such system and machinery are often comhined, however, with traditional methods of serving the nearer markets. Thus, for example, in the rayon and cotton weaving industry of Tientsin, the middlemen in nearby eastern provinces, until recently including those of Manchuria, send their own agents to the manufacturing center where they take their temporary abode in native hotels. Here "runners" from the various manufacturing firms wait upon them with samples and quotations. Purchases are paid for, in the traditional way, at the middle or end of the month during which goods are delivered, or during one of the three festivals when settlement of accounts is customary. Merchants in the more distant western provinces are served by sales offices established there by individual Tientsin manufacturers if the market is an important one or concentrated in a single city, such as the provincial capital. This method, however, has declined because of its cost and because of difficulties experienced in dealing directly with large number of local piece-goods merchants. In addition to these methods of distribution, the manufacturers also count upon a considerable local trade, through piece goods firms, department stores or bazaars. The smaller factories may supplement such sales by encouraging numbers of peddlers to purchase directly from them on cash terms, or on credit if the peddler can find a reputable local person to serve as his guarantor. Such peddlers may come to Tientsin several times in a month and established temporary offices in the small native hotels, thus in the aggregate constitiuting a not negligible channel of distribution. ①

The sales methods for the hosiery knitting industry of Tientsin are

---

① H. D. Fong, *Rayon and Cotton Weaving in Tientsin*, Nankai Institute of Economics Industry Series, Bulletin No. 2, 1930, pp. 45-46.

similar. However, since the industry is relatively new and deals in relatively small transactions, cash payments by visiting merchants from a distance are more frequent; and the local merchant, who in the case of the rayon purchaser plays the part of the guarantor, here becomes a commission agent or broker who is paid a commission for introducing the client. The method of establishing sales branches to conduct a wholesale trade with merchants in the more distant provinces also is resorted to. Some of the manufacturers have separate sales offices in Tientsin itself, particularly also because in this industry the local retail market is a large one and requires considerable attention. In fact, the local sales departments often resemble small department stores with a preponderance of imported articles in the clothing line. ①

What about the cotton industries? Since they are in very direct competition with importers of cotton yarns and cotton goods, they naturally use to a considerable extent the machinery established originally for the sale of imports. Moreover, the size of these industries has introduced more specialization in methods of marketing. Both the trade in yarn and that in piece goods have given rise to a considerable wholesale trade which is the principal channel for the distribution of Chinese-made as well as imported manufacturers. In 1929, there were 63 dealers in yarn established in Shanghai and 32 in Tientsin; and 87 dealers in cloth in Shanghai and 44 in Tientsin. They are, for the most part, substantial firms with a paid-up capital ranging from $50,000 to

---

① H. D. Fong, *Hosiery Knitting in Tientsin*, p. 52.

$200,000, and are able to finance their purchases on a cash basis, often by drawing upon their credit with native banks, secured by the assets or deposits of the owners themselves or of relatives and friends. These dealers buy either directly from the mills or through the Chinese Cotton Goods Exchange in Shanghai and sell either directly to their customers or through agents. They may also act as brokers or commission agents and trade in both spots and futures. On the Exchange only cotton yarn, not cotton piece goods, is being transacted. The unit of trading is 50 bales of 40 bundles each, the quantity unit for quotation being one bale. ①

The exchange is the major method also for disposing of the products of Chinese flour mills. This exchange, established in Shanghai in 1921, has a capital of $500,000, and 55 registered brokers. On its floor both spots and futures are transacted, the latter with a three months' limit. In addition to machine-milled flour, bran also is traded in, the unit of trading for each being 1,000 bags. ② In Tientsin, the flour exchange deals only in spots, not in futures. Trading is carried on in private on the exchange floor, without formal regulations; it is based on sample, and paid for in cash for Shanghai or imported flour but on two weeks' credit for local flour. Retail trade here is carried on by retail grain shops engaged in the sale of flour as well as of other grains such as rice,

---

① H. D. Fong, *Cotton Industry and Trade in China*, I:103-105.

② Y. P. Yang, *On the Exchanges in China* (in Chinese), Commercial Press, Shanghai, 1930, p. 46.

maize, millet bean, etc. Flour, however, occupied the leading position, claiming 51% of a total sale of 23.7 million dollars in 1929. There were 509 shops in that year, of which 31 alone handled 44% of the total sales, each having a sale record of over one hundred thousand dollars during the year. ①

Shanghai also has an exchange for transactions in grain, oil, and oil cake, established in 1921, with a capital of $2,000,000. This is a joint stock enterprise with 100 registered brokers. The principal articles of trade are beans, bean oil, and bean cakes — the last two only being of interest in the present connection as products of Chinese industry. Future trading is limited to four months. ②

(2) Sales Promotion. — Chinese manufacturers have not yet learned the art, and usually do not have the means, of encouraging trade by educating consumers in the uses of their products. Sending out samples is almost unknown. Students of Chinese business often have paid tribute to the ingeniousness with which retail trade is advanced; ③ but there is as yet no corresponding development of the art of wholesale selling.

Advertising is, of course, the weapon peculiar to the salesmanship

---

① H. D. Fong, *Grain Trade and Milling in Tientsin*, pp. 403-488, 571.

② Yang, *op. cit.*

③ "Customs and Practices of Nanking Shops", *Chinese Economic Journal*, Vol. I, No. 9, September, 1927, p. 796 *ct seq.*; "Business Practices of Foochow Merchants", *ibid.*, No. 11, November, 1927, p. 941 *ct seq.*; James A. Thomas, *A Pioneer Tobacco Merchant in the Orient*, Durham, N. C., 1928.

of modern industry, in China as elsewhere. In its main features it follows western examples, and its practioners are obviously western-trained. In the traditional Chinese trade the seal or "chop" of the maker or merchant was and is the only advertising means in general use. It still has a high reputation as a guarantee of quality, and no Chinese manufacturer would lightly disregard the confidence placed in this trade mark. Correspondingly there is, of course, much imitation of established trade names and trade marks, against which there is as yet little redress because of the complications and recentness of the trade-mark law. ①

A study made of advertising in five prominent newspapers ten years ago showed in every case but one a large preponderance of patent medicine items, amounting to a proportion ranging from one-quarter to almost one-half. In some cases, economic items including banks, savings, insurance, industries, communications, etc., took second place, in others educational or amusement items. Among manufactured goods, which here especially interest us, luxury items, such as toilet articles, jewelry, and cigarettes, tend to occupy more space than daily necessity items, such as clothing, furniture and foodstuffs. ②

While display advertising uses western lay-outs, it is interesting to note that it makes many concessions to Chinese traditions. The more

---

① Passed in 1930. See S. H. Hung, *Commercial Law of China*, Shanghai, 1932, Chap V and Appendix I.
② "An Analytical Study of Advertisements in Chinese Newspapers", *Chinese Economic Monthly*, Vol. III, No. 4, April, 1926, pp. 139-143.

popular the distribution of the article, the more likely the pictorial content will make use of Chinese scenes and portraits, of legendary and historical figures, well-known land scapes, favorite biological symbols, Chinese rather than foreign concepts of female beauty, etc. Trade names and even company names are chosen which have favorable associations in the minds of the people, with a predominance of references to good luck, longevity, wealth, harmony, etc. ① Striking conventionalized pictures or symbols are used to fix a product in the memory of potential customers; and as in the west, identifying calligraphic devices are used to connect advertising of different. kinds with the trade name on the product itself.

It was estimated a few years ago that the amount spent annually in advertising in China was at least ten and a half million silver dollars a year②; and it has certainly not decreased since then. Probably both the eight million dollars then estimated for newspaper advertising and the two and a half million for outdoor advertising have greatly increased. Both are regarded as the essence of that modernity so greatly desired by progressive Chinese; and any proposal to curtail the latter as a matter of public comity would probably be laughed at. Advertising agencies have

---

① Even translations of foreign trade and firm names are made with a view to suitable connotations. Thus the Chinese name of one of the largest British importers reads " Harmony and Peace" , the largest importer of machinery calls himself " Careful and Prosperous" , an American beverage — with only a slight change in sound — becomes " Palatable and Enjoyable".

② C. A. Bacon. "Advertising in China." *Chinese Economic Journal*, Vol. V. No. 3, September, 1929, p. 754.

the same optimism which this type of business displays in the west; and so far they may be said to have been justified, as the Chinese public, for reasons deeply imbedded in the national culture, is particularly susceptible both to the impact of well-chosen words and to the visual appeal of pictures and written characters. In fact, the magical association of both is still so powerful that those unacquainted with Chinese folklore are apt to produce unforeseen results. ①

The whole range of known tricks to encourage sales is resorted to by smart young Chinese advertising men. Prizes are enclosed in packages, solvers of puzzles and collectors of series of coupons or picture cards are rewarded, popular articles are featured in such a way as to draw less popular ones with them into public favor; and so on. But in these matters also Chinese psychology introduces variations; specifically the Chinese penchant for gambling. Moreover, only foreign firms and large Chinese concerns have capital enough to engage in advertising of any sort in dimensions comparable with those in which the art is practised in western countries. Of industry generally it must be said that, for all the reasons already enumerated to show why its products cannot reach more than a fraction of the millions of people, it cannot use advertising

---

① See James A. Thomas, *Trailing Trade a Million Miles*, Durham, N. C., 1931, pp. 203- 205. In Canton the glaring eyes of a tiger poster of a well-known Chinese manufacturer of drugs, electrically lighted by night, so frightened the customers of a business house opposite that the proprietor sought redress from the local authority. This being refused, he fastened over his door a huge display of some legendary warrior gods whose bows and arrows, extending over the side-walk, now hold at bay the tiger and have brought back the menaced trade.

extensively enough to build upon it a large expansion of trade. Moreover, much of the present advertising is unquestionably uneconomical since it is not, as a rule, connected with a real planning of sales policy. Numerous instances are of advertising which over-shoots the mark by inviting customers which the advertising manufacturing concern cannot satisfy, of advertising which precedes organization enabling a prompt delivery of the goods advertised, of advertising which serves to establish individual prestige rather than increased sales, of advertising which blindly follows precedents, often inapplicable on practical grounds, and of advertising which, though expensive, does not reach, or reaches without force, the group which contains the potential customers.

In the modernization of Chinese sales methods, two movements, commercial education and visual demonstration, are important as being especially of help to the distribution of industrial products. Advertising, like other commercial subjects, is now being taught in a number of modern institutions, chiefly departments of commerce in colleges and universities, but also in commercial schools, though the last named do not often go beyond elementary subjects. The art of commercial exhibiting also is being fostered by chambers of commerce, usually with no regard at all to the actual distribution of local producta and more with the aim of inspiring the local population generally to patronize Chinese industries. Commercial organizations also route exhibits to various cities, and these demonstrations are usually more inclusive and more educational, though not to be compared in the craftsmanship of display with similar shows in the west. The National Government on several occasions has given special encouragement to such enterprises, not only with the aim of promoting Chinese industrial products but also with the larger aim of introducing modern consumer habits generally and of overcoming a conservatism, in this respect, which to the western-educated men who dominate the Government seem to stand in the way of progress. ①

Generally speaking, the statement must be reiterated that in this as in other aspects of salesmanship, different methods are not sufficiently coordinated to produce the desired results. Exhibits are more often gestures than effective means of reaching the buying public to which a particular industry must make its appeal. "Complimentary" advertising takes too large a share of the expenditure which should go in purposeful sales promotion. Local advertising is bought in publications with national circulation. Foreign examples are thoughtlessly imitated. In all these respects it is possible to sense more of an admiration for modern methods than a thorough grounding in their principles. As in production so also in salesmanship, the conflict between tradition and recognition of new needs produces anachronisms and inefficiency.

(3) Sales Financing. —One of the difficulties in sales promotion is that few Chinese manufacturers know exactly what a given unit of their products costs them to manufacture. A teacher of accounting and factory management declares that he has never come across a modern cost

---

① See, e. g. , "The National Products Exhibition", *Chinese Economic Journal*, Vol. IV, No. 1, January, 1929, pp. 1-20.

accounting sheet in a Chinese plant. No one seems to know, more especially, what it costs to sell a given unit of production, and what the margin between production cost and selling price must be to leave a reasonable profit. The fact of the matter is that the typical Chinese manufacturer is not interested in "reasonable" profits. He desires to get everything the traffic will bear and to produce at the lowest possible cost. If in any one year or on any particular article of production that margin should happen to be 100 per cent, he is not alarmed at this evidence of a price-setting which will invite competitors and possibly ruin his chances of a gradually expanding business, but on the contrary congratulates himself on his business acumen. Since most manufacturing business is conducted by partnership firms with financial backing from a bank unaccustomed to modern business, short-term views prevail; and just as there is rarely, as we have seen, a sufficient appreciation for the necessity of providing for depreciation, there is even less appreciation for the demands of building up a trade by careful price setting. In a study of costs in the manufacture and sale of cotton yarns①, we find the statement that in 1932 it cost, on an average, 44 cents to market a bale of cotton yarn of 16's in Shanghai and $1.16 to market the same yarn elsewhere. ② The information given is too apocryphal to make sure

---

① Wang and Wang, *op. cit.*, p. 215.

② For yarns of different counts, the difference in selling cost per bale, ascertained for three Shanghai mills and seven mills in the interior, is as follows: ten counts, 0.275 and 0.724 dollars; twelve counts, 0.330 and 0.824 dollars; sixteen counts, 0.440 and 1.158 dollars; twenty counts, 0.550 and 1.336 dollars. (*Ibid.*)

whether the calculation in both cases is entirely parallel. ① Why should there be this great discrepancy in sales costs? Possibly it is because the Shanghai mill has an established channel through the local exchange, and dealers from nearby come to stay at Shanghai yarn dealers' establishments when coming to purchase, while for sales inland agencies and branch establishments are necessary. The example only goes to show the great need for more studies in the this field before reliable and fully explanatory statements can be made which would have general validity. If a comparison were to be attermpted between different industries, account would have to be taken not only of the difference in the cost of different sales methods, but also in the extent to which the respective industries are driven to unusual promotion efforts by competition, especially also with imported products, and also in the extent to which traditional or other organized channels can be relied upon automatically to dispose of most of the output.

One element in the cost of sales on which more definite information is, or ought to be, available is that of taxation. Excise taxes are payable on five products of modern industry, cigarettes, wheat flour, cotton yarn, matches, and cement. Those on cigarettes and flour, first levied in 1928, antedate the abolition of *likin*, while the other three are in substitution for it, dating from February 1, 1931. How evenly or

---

① Foreign published accounts, being more interested in comparisons of production costs than of prices, also almost invariably omit the comparison of selling costs. See e. g., Pearse, *op. cit.*, p. 162 ff.

effectively these excise taxes or *tung shui* are being collected, it is impossible to say. The rates are as follows:

For cigarettes, since December 5th of 1933, a tax of $160 per box of 50,000 pieces selling at about $300 per box and of $80 per box of 50,000 valued at less than $300, is levied. Chinese manufacturers complain that these tax rates favor the foreign manufacturer who produces the better qualities and pays a tax of about 50 per cent of the value, while the product of Chinese factories, often of much lower value, is taxed up to over 80 per cent of the value.

For wheat flour a uniform rate of 10 cents per bag of 49 lbs. or 22.23 kg, is levied. The same rate is paid on imported wheat flour on top of the import duty. Chinese flour on being exported is entitled to a rebate of one-half of the excise tax, 5 cents per bag.

The excise tax on cotton yarn is simpler: under the 1931 law, only two rates are applied, $2.75 per picul on grey yarn of counts up to and including 23, and $3.25 on that of counts above 23. Here also Chinese manufacturers complain that the two rates work in favor of the foreign manufacturer who makes the more costly product.

Of safety matches, three different grades or categories of quality are recognized since December of 1933, and the excise tax is accordingly imposed at three rates: $13.50, $17.40, and $21.00 per case (of 50 gross boxes). Of sulphuric phosphorus matches two grades are recognized: $10.80 and $13.50 per large case.

The excise tax on cement is uniformly at the rate of $1.20 per barrel of 170 kg. ①

While the excise taxes in theory represent consolidations of a variety of previous impositions, actually there is always a tendency for new local, provincial, and national taxes to be imposed upon any industry that seems to be profitable. Any calculation of sales costs on the basis of known tax rates for different localities or products would, however, be a purely academic exercise, since it is a common saying that what one man pays in taxes another pays in "squeeze".

The export duty, now abolished in almost every enlightened nation, is still being levied in China. The rate, according to the 1934 schedule, varies between $2\frac{1}{2}\%$ and $7\frac{1}{2}$ *ad valorem*. For most of the manufactured goods, e.g. silk, flour, cigarettes, cotton yarn, the duty is now abolished. For others, the duty when levied is light, and specific instead of *ad valorem*. Thus, the duty per 100 kg. amounts to $4.10 for wood oil, $0.26 for bean oil, and 0.083 for beancake. ②

A far greater tax on the distribution of China's manufactured products is the unorganized nature of the credit arrangements with its hazards and losses. The foreign manufacturer, like the importer, pays

---

① *Chinese Yearbook 1935-36*, pp. 1343, 1346, 1348-1349; also *Yearbook of Public Finance* (in Chinese), Ministry of Finance, Nanking, 1935, I: 935 ff.

② *Chinese Yearbook 1935-36*, p. 1868 *et seq.*

heavily for assuring himself of the dealer's payments, either through commission payments to a compradore who is held responsible or through the establishment of an elaborate sales organization which must be equipped with the necessary machinery for ascertaining the standing of would-be customers. If distribution takes place from an inland center, disputes over the quality of the product or failure to take delivery from other causes may absorb the entire margin of profit. The Chinese manufacturer still largely finds his security in the traditional personal ethical attitudes of the trade, financing his sales, as he does his purchases, with the aid of native banks.

The difficulties in the way of extended credit are due to lack of law and scarcity of communications. The defaulting debtor cannot be traced; moreover, local officials, too, often find hard cash (otherwise bribery) more attractive than the punishment of the culprit. And yet this great and commercial people produce men who, on the death of a brother, will carry out his verbal promises even if to their own detriment.... They will carry out the promise of a relative as if it were their own obligation. ①

There are many similar testimonies. "Most Chinese business", writes Miss Ware, "depends upon friendly relations, or cash guarantees, not on law in the Western sense." ② And again:

---

① C. A. Middleton Smith, *The British in China and Far Eastern Trade*. London, 1927, pp. 34-35.

② *op. cit.*, p. 40.

INDUSTRIAL ORGANIZATION IN CHINA

All Chinese banks acknowledge that in China money is loaned on friendship and reputation as much as, or more than, on collateral; this is the age-old Chinese method. In the Bank of China in Tientsin, for example, there is a bank visitor who reports three or four times a week the condition of clients' business. This knowledge is accepted in lieu of collateral. ①

The greatest handicap of the Chinese manufacturer is that no machinery exists, with the limited extent of modern banking, of promoting acceptance business. Chinese custom of settling accounts during the three festivals of the year has so permeated the business mores that any attempt to substitute it by a familiar modern device such as trade acceptance would have been confronted with considerable difficulties. Bank acceptance, which has always found favor with the native banks in a slightly modified form, is on the contrary not common among modern banks. Recently, however, the Shanghai Banks' Joint Reserve Board has inaugurated a Bank Acceptance Guaranteeing Union with a capital fund of $50,000,000 which is divided into 1,000 shares of $50,000 each. This Union, which undertakes to guarantee the loss sustained from the defaulting of the acceptances endorsed by the member banks, may prove to be an important step forward in the introduction of acceptance business into Chinese industrial life. ②

The contribution of modern banks toward the financing of industrial

---

① C. A. Middleton Smith, *The British in China and Far Eastern Trade*. London, p. 48 See also p. 73 *et seq.*

② *Economic Weekly* of *Ta Kung Pao* (in Chinese) No. 128, August. 28,1935.

sales is as yet limited to larger enterprises, amounting to 11-13 per cent of the loans of the Bank of China for the four years 1931-34, and to 24-41 per cent of the total loans of the Shanghai Commercial and Savings Bank for the same period. ①

  The increase in the granting of industrial loans by the banks arises partly out of the necessity on the part of the banks to establish a more diversified portfolio. Impelled by a steady increase in deposits through the drain of funds from the interior to the commercial ports and by a realization of the need for seeking new forms of earning assets and new channels of investment, Chinese banks have in the last few years become actively engaged not only in the establishment of insurance companies, the extension of credit to rural cooperatives, the building of warehouses, and the development of real estate for residential and business uses, but also in the financing of manufacturing industries. ②

The Shanghai Commercial and Savings Bank, in 1933, secured as much as 60 per cent of its loans to industry on commodities, a very large proportion in consideration of the relative recentness of extension in this direction, but perhaps more directly caused by the overbuilding of Shanghai and the decline in real estate values than by a permanent policy. Moreover, so far cotton and flour mills are the only industries

---

  ① Leonard G. Ting, "Chinese Modern Banks and the Finance of Government and Industry", *Nankai Social & Economic Quarterly*, Vol. VIII, No. 3, October, 1935, p. 604.
  ② *Ibid.*, pp. 604-605.

which have to any very large extent been able to take advantage of the bank facilities thus made available. ① In general, and especially for the manufacturing centers of the interior, it still holds true that the producer must secure cash payment or borrow in diverse and expensive ways, chiefly through the agency of native banks, to finance his sales as well as his operation costs.

In summary, it may be said that the organization of marketing in China matches that of production as characteristic of a phase of development in which strong contrasts between old and new wring for supremacy. We do not have here simply traditional and modern forms of enterprise side by side, but the conflict between those forms which belong to the inherited culture and those which belong to an alien culture is being fought out even in the most highly developed branches of industrial enterprise. While Japan in its industrial organization either has completely gone over to western models or has retained the craftsman and other early stages of organization and operation, in China there is a medley in which even the Chinese entrepreneur has difficulty of moving. The result is an immense addition to costs; opportunities of expansion and improvement cannot be taken advantage of; a semblance of modernity takes the place of a real application of modern methods; the coastal manufacturing centers have to reckon with two types of markets essentially different in their requirements, not only in regard to the nature of the product but even more so in regard to the nature of the sales

---

① Leonard G. Ting, "Chinese Modern Banks and the Finance of Government and Industry", p. 605.

apparatus: the nearby markets, largely cosmopolitan and influenced by new ideas and methods, and the inland markets, as yet medieval and wholly unrelated to modern economic principles and methods.

Not only this, but too often in the industrial concern itself, old and new are in constant conflict—the long-gowned partners and the managing staff chosen by them representative of a tradition which is breaking down under the impact of new forms of competition on the one hand; the young engineer and the graduate of a western-type school of business on the other hand, handicapped by ever recurring difficulties in applying what they know to the material, the men, the circumstances they have to deal with. The one type cannot easily find his way in the complexity of modern life; the other cannot find his way in the obscurity of an old business life which has not in any of its aspects been sufficiently studied and analysed.

Foreign enterprise and Chinese enterprise modelled upon it have shown vitality, so far, only when secured by the special privileges and safeguards of the treaty ports. Those who pin their faith for the development of modern industry in China upon these models and the support given such enterprise as has grown up behind the protecting wall of extraterritoriality by foreign political power, think in purely colonial terms. A policy of industrial development which can command the support of the Chinese Government and which has prospects of gaining over the inertia and opposition of old-established traditional ways and attitudes must of necessity be rooted in the Chinese economy — in the broad acres of the Chinese land, and not in the narrow garden patches of the concessions and settlements.

中国工业资本问题

目　　录

自序 ··· 235
  一　绪论 ·· 236
  二　中国工业中中外资本所占之地位 ················ 236
  三　外人对中国工业之投资 ·························· 239
    （甲）重工业 ······································ 239
    （乙）轻工业 ······································ 246
  四　民族工业资本之发展 ···························· 259
    （甲）公有资本 ···································· 260
    （乙）私人资本 ···································· 263
  五　二业资本之筹集与运用 ·························· 274
    （甲）以往之错误 ·································· 274
    （乙）今后之途径 ·································· 278
  参考书目 ·· 287

自 序

资本为生产三要素之一。而工业乃近代生产业之中坚；其非资本莫办，尤属自明之理。顾有资本而集之不由其道，用之不得其当，则其于工业，于国民经济，利害参半，甚或害超于利。吾国近百年来之新工业乃正坐此弊：大部资本出自外人；喧宾夺主，利权日丧，而病及民生。资本之投放几全在轻工业；重工业微不足道，而危及国脉。抗战师兴，捉襟见肘。今后苟不急起直追，牢守自力更生之原则以筹资，国防第一之主旨以用资；则国家前途殊堪危惧。是殆非过甚之辞也。

作者深感此问题之重要，尝草"中国之工业资本"一文，载南开《社会经济季刊》（英文）一九三六年四月号，其于中国工业资本之来源，用途以往危机，与今后出路，已粗陈梗概。兹辱艺文丛书编者之征，爰依曩作规模而扩充之，为更详尽之探讨，成兹小册以应。惟以旅寄贵筑，参考资料异常缺乏，挂漏舛误，自知不免，容俟异日补正。书中引用处有未及注明者，另于编末附列参考文籍全目，读者或不难循而索之。又属稿时，刘君悉规曾为校阅一过，不无助力。书将付梓，谨志其缘起如右。

方显廷序于南开大学经济研究所贵阳办事处
二十八年元月二十五日

一 绪论

现代工业之特征有二,即用机械代替手工,大规模组织代替小规模组织以从事于集中生产是。机械之运用与大规模之生产,均有赖于资本之巨量供给,此产业革命以来不易之定律,其在我国,自亦难居例外。我国之有现代工业,已达九十年,而进展程度,则仍极幼稚。重工业之基础尚在树立中,轻工业虽已略具端倪,然自抗战以来,先后被暴日摧毁殆尽。百年来内忧外患之频仍,诚为工业进展迟滞之主要原因,而工业资本之未能自给,在在均为外资利用而不能利用外资自亦不容忽视也。

二 中国工业中中外资本所占之地位

外人在华投资之方式不一,据雷玛教授(Prof. R. F. Remer)之研究,分直接商业投资与政治投资二种,而前者又分运输、制造、地产、进出口、银行、矿业、交通及公用业七种。据雷氏之估计,一九三一年外人在华投资总额为英金三十三万万元,其详细分配如下表。

第一表　外人在华投资按业之分配(民国二十年)

(百分比)

一　政治投资	22.1
二　直接商业投资	77.9
(1)运输业	26.1
(2)制造业	11.6
(3)地产业	10.5
(4)进出口贸易业	14.9
(5)银行业	6.6
(6)矿业	4.0
(7)交通及公用事业	4.0
合计	100.0

外人对于中国工业之投资,若按广义分析之,除制造业投资为百分之一一.六外,尚应包括矿业投资之百分之四,交通及公用事业投资之百分之四,合计为百分之一九.六。节言之,中国工业之外资占外人在华投资总额三十三万万美元之五分之一,或六万万五千万元美金,金额不为不巨。

中国工业资本之总额,尚无统计可资参考,是以外资在中国工业资本中所占成分,亦难直接测知。唯以上海之工业投资为例,则知外资所占成分,较华资约大出一倍,如表二所示,民国十七年上海工业投资总额为二九三.六兆元,内外资为一九〇兆元,占总额百分之六五,华资一〇三.六兆元,占总额百分之三五(见《上海之工业》一书。)

第二表　民国十七年上海工业之投资（元）

业别	外资		华资		合计	
	兆元	%	兆元	%	兆元	%
纺织	152.7	77.2	45.1	22.8	197.8	100
化学	2.0	21.1	7.4	78.9	9.4	100
食品	23.8	47.9	25.9	52.1	49.7	100
印刷	0.6	6.4	10.5	93.6	11.1	100
水电	10.0	52.8	8.9	47.2	18.9	100
其他	0.9	13.2	5.8	86.8	6.7	100
合计	190.0	64.7	103.6	35.3	293.6	100

在矿业方面，亦有与上海工业投资类似之情形。我国矿业中，发展最速产量最巨者，首推煤矿业。据地质调查所之统计，民国十九年我国各大煤矿之产量，共为一九,四七一,〇九一吨，占全国煤矿总产额四分之三（或百分之七四.八）。以言其投资国别之分配，则一九,四七一,〇九一吨之煤产量中，华矿占百分之五一，日矿占百分之三三，英矿占百分之一四，俄德矿合占百分之二。

外商对于我国工业之投资，托始于鸦片战争以后之五口通商条约，而渐盛于中日战争以后之《马关条约》。该约第六条第四节订明："日本臣民得在中国通商口岸城邑任便从事各项工艺制造，又得将各项机器任便装运进口，只交所定进口税。"又"日本臣民在中国制造一切货物，其于内地运送税内地税钞课杂派以及在中国内地沾及寄存栈房之益，即照日本臣民运入中国之货物，一体办理。"自此以后，其他各国均援引最惠国待遇，向我国取得同等权利，于是外国之工业资本遂在我国获得法律之根据，而更积极流入我国矣。欧战期间，日本复乘欧美无东顾之暇，向我国作巨量之投资，天津、青岛、上海及东北各重要商埠如哈尔滨、大连等处，莫不有日商厂矿之兴起，于是外资之侵入我国工业界，较前更甚。据雷玛教授估计，一九三一年外人在华之全部投资，英占百分之三七，日占百分之三五，俄占百分之八，英法各占百分之六，德比各占百分之三，其他各国占百分之二。此种投资之分配率，若专就工业论，容不免稍有出入，然要亦大同小异也。

三　外人对中国工业之投资

外资对于我国工业之投资，按方式言，有自营，合资及借款三种。按种类言，有重工业及轻工业之别。兹就后者分述外资在我国工业上之发展情形如下：

（甲）重工业　重工业种类繁多，其在我国，可分燃料、电气、钢铁、机器及化学五类，依次论之：

燃料工业中，以煤之开采较为重要。煤矿在我国现代矿业中，无论就事业历史言或就开采量值言，均占首要地位。而外资之投于煤矿亦最早，其经营之积极，更有令人怵目惊心者。盖煤为动力之源。自五口通商以来，外轮来华贸易者，每苦我国煤矿规模既小，又多偏在内地；运输上所需大量之煤恒赖国外长途接济，费时耗财，甚不合算。故自甲午一败于日之后，外人先后与我所订条约，莫不以煤矿开采权之取得为重要条文之一。计自一八九八至一九〇二之五年间，可名外人竞争采矿权时期，英、德、日、俄等无不处心积虑，以图攫取我国煤铁及其他重要矿产之开采权。至其所采手段，不外：（一）取得铁路附近之采矿权，如一八九八年中德

《胶澳租界条约》第二条第四款所云："于所开各铁路附近之处相距三十里内……允准德商开掘煤觔等项"及一九〇二年中俄协约中所订"俄国中东铁路附近扎赍诺尔（黑龙江）地方及吉林某某数处之矿产，皆有采掘权"是也。（二）外国私人或团体与中国政府交涉，求得某某省全省或一部之采矿权。如英商福公司请中国政府将山西几县煤铁矿采取权让与该公司。德商瑞记洋行要求山东五矿采取权。（三）中国中央政府或省政府特许外商以某某数矿之采掘权。如一九〇二年安徽南部铜官山煤矿，及一八九八年四川江北煤矿采取权之让与。（四）外国公司先与中国私人订立合同，共营矿业，事后迫我政府追认。如中英之开滦煤矿，中德之井陉煤矿及临城煤矿皆是。上述（一）、（二）、（三）三项，虽实际出于外人之强迫，名义上犹可云中国政府之自动让与。且其政治的意义较为浓厚。故一旦瓜分之议未成，上述要求权利之各公司均未开办，山东、山西、安徽、湖北各省矿权皆得逐渐收回。至第（四）项则经济的意义为多，然政治背景亦未尝不存在也。一九〇三至一九一〇年，为人民反对外资侵略时期，亦即政府收回矿权时期，尤以一九〇七至一九一〇之四年间为最盛。福公司之山西采矿权，德国在山东之五矿，中英企业公司之安徽南部铜官山，以及湖北炭山湾之煤矿，皆由政府以千余万元之巨资收回自办，所费亦自不赀矣。一九一一年起为外人利用矿业法律时期。在此时期内，如北京政府颁布矿业法规，规定外人可以投资吾国矿业，但其资本数不能超过百分之五十，为此后矿业法之根据。中央政治会议第一七九次会议通过之"确定利用外资方式及实施实业计划乙项原则，"且谓华股须占全部股份百分之五十以上。于是民国十九年之矿业法，遂规定华股至少须加至百分之五十一，较前更有进步。颁布后，外人尚能遵守法律，从事采矿。其在煤矿方面，除前此完全让与外人经营者，如日营之抚顺、烟台等煤矿，及中英开滦煤矿，各有特殊原因不遵守中国法律外，其余概照法规办理；可使外人侵略时代，一变而为中外合作时代，各占半资平等经营。然其后仍有二次例外，一为民国四年日人提出所谓二十一条，无理要求让与东三省数处采矿权，及加入汉冶萍煤铁公司。又一次则因热河华人杀害一日籍工程师而有阜新煤矿开采权之让与，名义上为中日合办，实际无异日人独办。

九一八以前外资煤矿在我国煤产上所占之地位，前已述及。九一八以还，东北煤矿尽沦日手，若以一九三三年之统计为例，则我国煤产取自外资或中外合资之煤矿者乃占十分之六，详见表三。

第三表 我国煤产按煤矿所有权国别之分布（百分比）

	1930	1933
华资	63	40
大矿	38	17
小矿	25	23
外资	37	60
东北四省（日资）		33
中国本部（中外合资）		27

据翁文灏氏在一九三五至一九三六年英文《中国年鉴》中所述，除东北四省现在日人统制下外，我国中外合资经营之煤矿，首推河北省之开滦矿务局，年产额四五百万吨。次为豫西焦作之中福两公司联合办事处，年产白煤约一百万吨。上述两矿，一如年产三十万吨之平西门头沟公司，均为中英合资。中日合办煤矿（东北四省除外）之最大者，为沿胶济路淄川及潍县之鲁大公司，年产煤

七十万吨。但淄川煤矿于民二十四年被洪水冲刷,损坏甚巨。沿正太路之井陉矿务局为中德合办,年产煤约八万吨,并在石家庄设厂炼焦,日产八十吨,实为吾国惟一之炼焦处。

我国电气事业,多赖外人之投资与经营而逐渐发展,此在上海、天津及东北四省为尤甚。如上海电力公司(前上海工部局电气处),为我国电气方面最大之发电厂。自光绪十九年英租界当局以银六万余两收并华商上海电气公司以后,该厂规模日以扩充,最初所有电力,仅二千五百瓩,欧战终结时,增至二万一千二百瓩,民国十六年竟增至十二万一千瓩,最近且增加至十六万二千瓩,资本一一三兆元。此外,外资电气公司之较著者,上海有法租界之法商电灯电车公司,成立于光绪三十二年,资本十兆元,发电量一二,五〇〇瓩;天津有比商天津电车电灯公司,成立于光绪三十年,发电量一五,八〇〇瓩;大连有日商之南满电气会社,共三厂,成立于光绪三十三年,资本二〇兆元,发电容量三五,〇〇〇瓩。据建设委员会二十三年之统计,我国(东三省在外)电厂共四六〇家,内外厂一〇家;发电量五四二,三九九瓩,外厂占二七三,三四五瓩或百分之五〇.四;发电度数一,六九四,一六七千度,外厂占一,〇〇六,八〇三千度或百分之五九.四。准此,外商厂数虽仅十家,而其发电容量及发电度数,均胜过四百五十家华厂。且华厂资本,共计不过一〇八兆元,而外商仅上海电力公司一家,其资本已达一一三兆元,是可知外资在我国电气工业所占地位之重要,及华资之幼稚而亟待培植矣。

钢铁工业分铁矿,冶铁及炼钢三部分,几全为外资——日资——所垄断。考外人之投资我国铁矿,一如前述之煤矿,其方法有四:(一)敷设铁路而要求路旁若干里内之矿山开采权,如依光绪二十四年(一八九八)中德《胶澳租界条约》,即许德人开采山东金岭镇之铁矿。(二)与政府直接交涉,取得全省或一部分之矿权,如英商福公司获得山西若干县煤铁矿之采取权。(三)指定矿地得政府之特许者,如凯约翰之于安徽铜官山铁矿。(四)以武力为后盾,提出条款,迫吾国应允者,如辽宁鞍山铁矿之让与乃由于民国四年日本二十一条之提出。缘此四途,我国铁矿被侵殆尽,计国内铁矿共十四处,兹将其中与外资有关之七处表列其情况于下:

第四表 一九三三年我国与外资有关七铁矿之统计

一 中日合办者			
矿 区	公 司	储量(%)	备考
(1)鞍山等处(辽宁)	振兴公司	41.2	采
(2)庙儿沟(辽宁)	本溪湖公司	7.0	采
(3)金岭镇(山东)	鲁大公司	1.4	停
(4)弓长岭(辽宁)	弓长岭铁矿公司	27.0	未采
二 向日本借款订有售砂合同者			
(5)大冶(湖北)	汉冶萍公司	1.7	采
(6)繁昌(安徽)	裕繁公司	0.5	采
(7)当涂(安徽)	宝兴益华福利民公司等	0.6	采
合计	7	79.4	

(注)中国独资创办者有七处,除象鼻山(湖北)及保晋(山西)已开采,修武(河南)已停采外,铜官山(安徽),凤凰山(江苏),滦县(河北)及宣化龙关(察哈尔)等四处均未开采。至英商福公司之山西煤铁矿权。凯约翰之安徽铜官山铁矿,及英商立德约之四川江北县煤铁矿,均经政府赎回,又外商于光绪二十五年曾开采贵州铜仁县之煤铁水银矿,因经营失败而自动停止。

以上正在进行(不论中外资)之鞍山、本溪湖、大冶、繁昌、当涂、象鼻山及山西保晋公司七处铁矿,自民十六至民二十,五年中共采八,四二七,五八七吨,其中鞍山占百分之四一,本溪湖占百分之七，大冶百分之二三，象鼻山百分之八，繁昌百分之一一，当涂及保晋共占百分之一〇。据此可知，国内铁矿产量，以鞍山为最多，大冶次之。鞍山、本溪湖，均为中日合办；大冶、繁昌、当涂等矿，皆与日本有借款售砂合同。故除象鼻山及保晋公司所产之微量外（约占总产量十分之一），国内铁砂产量几尽入日人之手，可不惧哉！

我国冶铁工厂，以汉冶萍煤铁公司为最大，该公司成立于一九〇八年，系由一八九〇年成立之汉阳铁厂，一八九一年开采之大冶铁矿，及一八九八年开采之萍乡煤矿合并而成。在该公司尚未成立前，已于一九〇三年九月与日本制铁所签订借用日币三百万元之合同。至民国元年，积欠日款达一千万元以上，是年且有中日合办之说，卒因国人反对而未克实现。然借款之议卒又复活，计自民国二年起至十三年止，举债一十二次，借款共达日金五千七百万元之多。欧战期间，该公司虽曾因钢铁价格高涨，一度繁荣；卒以内而经营无方，外受条约束缚，不得不将铁砂低价售与日本，而日趋衰落。汉阳铁厂之化铁炉于民国八年及十一年先后停炼。大冶新铁厂，早在民国二年借日款建筑，至民十二年始竣工，四月间开始炼铗，十三年底即停炼。另有同式之一炉。十四年五月开炼，十月停炼。民十四年，萍乡煤矿，因汉冶两厂息炉，不需用焦炭，便亦停采。于是我国三十余年来惨淡经营之惟一钢铁厂遂陷于完全停顿之境矣。民十六至二十年五年中，炼铁工厂，仅鞍山、本溪湖、扬子及保晋四处，共计炼铁一，四九七，八八七吨，内中日合资之鞍山（成立于一九一五年）及本溪湖（成立于一九一〇年），分别占一，〇八二，五五六吨或百分之七二及三七四，五四九吨或百分之二五，而华资之扬子及保晋两公司合计，仅占四〇，七八二吨或百分之三。今东北失守，鞍山及本溪湖两厂，已全入日人之手，我国炼铁事业更一落千丈矣。

至于钢之产量，在民十以前汉冶萍公司尚可年出四五万吨，厥后该公司停止冶炼，仅上海浦东之和兴钢铁厂及其他各处之电气炼钢炉，平均年出三万吨而已。观此，与外资有关之炼钢厂，虽只汉冶萍一家，然我国钢之供给，则几什九仰赖舶来品之输入，又为不可掩饰之事实焉。（见方显廷：《中国经济研究》，下册，我国钢铁工业之鸟瞰章）

外人对于我国机器工业之投资，为数甚微，上海为我国现代工业之中心，而二，四四一，四五〇元之机器工业总投资额中，尚未见外资插足其间。夷考其因，厥为我国钢铁业异常幼稚，致机器工业所需原料，不得不仰给于舶来品，而大规模之机器制造，尚为不可能之事。况就外人立场言，机器价格既较钢铁为贵，其担负长途运费之能力自亦较高，在华投资机器制造，尚不如经营机器进口贸易之有利。故我国新兴工业之机器几全然来自海外，而在国内制造者微不足道；目前我国所谓机器工业，只限于简单舶来机器之仿造及一般舶来机器之修理而已。

化学工业之堪称为重工业者，厥惟酸碱工业。是乃一切化学工业之基础，而为国防化学原料之所从出。酸分有机无机两类，有机酸又分硫酸，盐酸，及硝酸，简称三酸。我国酸类向赖外洋供给，近年来国内制酸工业始渐见发达，全国在民二十二年共有六厂，内仅上海之江苏药水厂系英商经营，年产硫酸四万五千担，在市上占有相当地位。至最近在南京附近成立之华资硫酸铔厂，论规模虽首屈一指，惜二十六年冬南京失守，该厂在日军炮火下，不免同付一炬，至可慨也。碱分天然与人造两种，我国除人造碱之一部分系舶来外，其余尚堪自给，外资亦无插足该业者。

（乙）**轻工业** 轻工业分纺织、食品、及化学三类，外资对于我匡轻工业之发展，参加甚早，投资亦颇可观，兹依次论之。

纺织业按采用原料之不同可分为棉、丝、毛、麻及人造丝等五业。外人对于棉丝毛三业，均有相当投资，而以棉业为尤甚。

我国棉纺织业之发展，分草创（一八九〇—），渐兴（一八九五—），勃兴（一九一四—），衰落（一九二五—）及复兴（一九三三—）五期。外资之参加我国棉纺织业，始自渐兴时期。是期初年，即一八九五年，日人迫我签订《马关条约》，开放制造权，于是外资之投入我国工业，遂得法律之根据。而各国商人，在华设立工厂者，亦接踵而来。就棉纺织业言，在本期中，英人设立者有一八九五年之怡和及一八九六年之老公茂，德人设立者有一八九六年之瑞记；美人设立者有一八九七年之鸿源，此等外资纱厂除英商者外，虽以后有转售与他国人民经营者，但其能在我国旺盛一时，自不得不归因于《马关条约》。日人为首先获得在我国境内设立工厂之权利者，其时日人在华初未设有工厂，乃采用收买华商纱厂之政策，一九〇二年大纯与三泰两厂。均由华人转售与日人，前者更名为上海纺织株式会社第一厂，后者称为上海株式会社第二厂。此后外人在上海相继设立纱厂，年有数起。计自一九〇五至一九一三年期间，日人设立者有二，英人设立者有一。

一九一四年欧战发生，为我国棉纺织业之发展辟一新纪元。盖战事既起，欧美物品来源断绝，我国与日本均乘机设立纱厂，而造成棉纺织业之勃兴时期。在此期内，华商纱厂虽处领袖地位，但日商纱厂之势力则更形重要。盖彼等多数均组为大联合，资本雄厚；而华商纱厂，除少数外，均系孤军奋斗，其财力多不充实。总计此期内，全国共设有纱厂八十七家，其中属于华商者五十三，属于日商者三十三，属于英商者一。五十三家华商纱厂共有纺锤一，七六八，五〇〇锭，平均每家三三，三六八锭。日商厂数虽为三十三家，但纺锤则有一，二三九，一五六锭，平均每家达三七，五五〇锭，复次，三十三家日商纱厂隶属于十七个公司，而五十三家之华商纱厂则隶于四十个公司。又在日商公司内，有四处各领两厂或两厂以上，如内外有十三厂，日华有三厂，大康同兴各有二厂；华商纺织公司之领两厂以上者则有六处，如申新有五厂，华新有四厂，宝成、永安各有三厂，大生、溥益各有二厂。华商纱厂之转售与日商者有三家，同时日商纱厂亦有一家售与华商。

一九二五年以后为我国棉纺织业之衰落时期。因大战告终，欧美纱布复源源输入我国，华商纱厂之在欧战期内兴起者，多因资本薄弱，受外货竞争之威胁，相继倒闭。加之民十六年以来，国共分裂，内战又起，农村购买力减低，纱布销路因亦大受影响。一九三三年政府为挽救计，于全国经济委员会下设立棉业统制委员会，一方求原棉之推广与改良，以图原料之自给；一方谋制造上之改革，以促进技术之合理化；棉纺织业始稍见起色，而转入复兴时期。不幸，九一八事变以来，日人谋我更急，东北之棉纺织业既尽沦入日手，华北方面，如天津纱厂，多有因经营不良，迫于债负而出售与日商者。长此以往，行见我国之棉纺织业，将尽受日人操纵而无余矣。

据一九三三至一九三六年四年间之统计，全国纱锭自五，一七二千锭增至五，五四六千锭，内华厂（东北在内）纱锭自二，八八六千锭减至二，八二五千锭；日厂者则自二，〇九八千锭增至二，四八八千锭。英厂纱锭亦自一八八千锭增至二三四千锭。若以一九三三年之纺锭为基数（等于一〇〇），则一九三六年之指数，全国纺锭为一〇七，华厂纺锭为九八，日厂纺锭为一一九，英厂纺锭为一二四。由是可知近年来外资在我国经营之棉纺业渐有压倒华资之趋势焉。（见《十年来之中国》，一五七至一五八页。）

我国缫丝工业之发展，所资于外力者亦甚大。盖生丝为我国主要输出品之一，丝质之良窳，直接影响国外市场之需要，间接影响在华出口外商之营业，故外商之于我国缫丝工业，或直接投资开厂，或间接协助技术改良，均不遗余力。远在同治元年（一八六二），外人即在上海试办百釜之机器缫丝工场。旋因试验失败，于同治五年倒闭。同年，又有某外人在上海设立十釜缫丝工场，亦于数月后歇业。考当时外商在华设立丝厂之动机，完全为在中国作蚕丝改良之试验。因中国七里丝条份不均，不合彼国之用，故利用中国工价之廉，成本之低，而自行设厂制造。但几经试办，迄未成功。至光绪四年（一八七八），法人卜鲁纳氏又于上海设二百釜之新式缫丝工厂，名曰宝昌丝厂，始渐有成效，是为我国缫丝工业之先导。一八八一年上海方面复有怡和与公平两英商丝厂之设立，次年开工，多聘意人为技师。

光宣之交，我国生丝出口贸易，已为日本所压倒。彼国自叠颁防除蚕病条例以来，其缫丝业之进步，更非我国所能企及。民国初年，日本在我国之缫丝业，已有长足进展。上海、汉口、青岛、烟台、安东等处，均有日商丝厂之设立。上海一区，日商丝厂尤多，其最著者，则为钟渊纺织株式会社所经营之上海制造绢丝公司，资本达四十万两，较任何华厂为多。一九一七年日商三井洋行在汉口创设中日合办之意大利式三井丝厂。不久停业，一九二二年由国人接盘，改名成和丝厂。一九二〇年日人小川爱次郎在同地创设日本式中华丝厂。惟是日人之注意点不在沪汉,经营最力之地,山东则烟台青岛,东北则安东等处。其规模最大者当推富士瓦纺绩株式会社在安东所设之工厂,该厂系合并安东数个日商工厂而成,资本日金四百五十二万元,每年出丝六十余万斤,其势力之雄厚,诚非华厂所能望其项背也。

外人除直接投资于我国之丝业外,其于技术上之改良,亦有足称述者。中外合设之改良华丝机关为数不少,其最脍炙人口者,厥为合众蚕桑改良会。该会由各洋商商会代表及丝茧总公所联合组织,成立于民国九年。会中经费由中央政府补助,年达九万六千两,自丝类出口增加关税项下拨发。会址设于上海,并在上海、苏州、横林、南京、嘉兴、诸暨、青阳等七地,设立制种场。会中专门技术上之设施,皆出法技师费咸尔氏之手。每年制造无病蚕种约百万张,更由意法两国购入约三百万张。往常江、浙、皖三省旧式蚕种,十之七八为有病者;自该会所制无病种行销以后,三省蚕病之比例年见递减。其次烟台方面,民国十年亦有芝罘万国蚕丝改良会之创立。该会除研究地质,购地植桑,检验蚕体外,并设一男女同学之蚕桑学校,一九二二年四月开办。是年年底又设一缫丝实验所。其在附近所设之蚕桑试验场,规模之大,在我国堪称首屈一指。此外,教会学校如南京金陵大学及广州岭南大学,均设有蚕桑系,关于我国蚕桑改良之研究,颇著成绩。一九三三年国联蚕桑专家意人玛利博士复应全国经济委员会之聘,来华擘划蚕丝改良事宜,可谓更进一步之新发展。

此外有上海生丝检验所,为华美丝界中人合办之机关,专事检验及保证出口生丝之品质,有裨益于生丝贸易者尤非浅鲜。盖自该所成立以后,输往美国生丝,得其保险证明,信用昭著,销售较

易。唯自国民政府成立以后,该所工作已移交各重要商埠之商品检验局经办矣。(见曾同春:《中国丝业》,第三编第三章)

外人对于我国毛纺织业之投资,多集中于天津、辽宁两处。盖北方所产羊毛,均荟萃于天津,由毛店批发与洋商;洋商加以整理,始行运输出口。津埠输运羊毛出口之洋商,大小约二十余家,其中以此为专业者,则仅英商隆茂洋行与高林洋行,美商新泰兴洋行与仁记洋行等四家;均设有打毛厂,其设备虽各不同,然大致均备有打土机,干毛机及打包机等。至洋商之经营毛纺者在天津有美商海京,倪克及达绅三家,前两家且兼营地毯之织造。海京为用机器纺制毛线之第一工厂,有纺锭一,五〇〇枚,民国三年开始营业。除纺毛线织地毯外,兼营制毯所用之棉线及毛呢制造事业。达绅于民国四年始用机器纺制毛线,有纺锭一,三五〇枚。倪克有纺锭二,一六〇枚,自民国六年起纺织地毯。在上述三厂中,除纺毛线外,其他如羊毛之洗涤,除净,及着色,皆以机器为之。(方显廷:《天津地毯工业》,页三一至三二。)

外商在华最大之毛织厂,当推民国七年在辽宁成立之满蒙毛织株式会社,亦我国最大之毛织工厂也。该厂名为中日合办,实则全系日营,由东洋拓殖会社代表及东京千住制绒所等创办,原定资本为日金千万元,专以中国之羊毛及驼呢制造毛呢及绒线等。并在天津设立羊毛整理厂,从事选毛,洗毛,打包等工作。至民十三年,辽宁总厂失慎,烧去厂屋之大半,乃减资金为日金三百万元,收足一百九十五万元。民十四年三月重行开工,计划每年出毛呢四十五万码,毛线十万磅。所出粗呢,多售于我国军队,作被服之用,毛线则在东三省及天津等处推销。该厂规模宏大,有线锭七千二百枚,织呢机一百六十架,允称我国各厂之冠。

外人对于我国食品工业之投资以面粉,精盐,精糖,制茶,蛋品及卷烟等业较为重要,兹依次分述之。

英、法、日、俄等国,对于我国面粉业,均有相当之投资,而以日资为尤甚。光绪十二年(一八八六),德人在沪设立正裕面粉厂,实开我国机制面粉业之先声。然该厂是否即光绪二十二年改组之英商增裕面粉公司,无从考证。光绪二十六年,俄人以侵略旅大为日本所忌,故增益北满驻军,以资防御。旋以食料缺乏,乃于哈尔滨设一满洲制粉公司(广源盛),以赡军需,资本三十四万卢布。该公司不特为俄人在华设立面粉厂之嚆矢,亦即哈尔滨跃为北满面粉工业中心之起点也。三十年法商设立永胜公司,三十一年俄商设立满洲联合制粉厂,三十二年俄商设立松花江制粉公司。同年,日商在铁岭设立满洲制粉会社。惟此时以原料供给关系,面粉业全盛于北满;南满所需之面粉,则什九取给于美国及上海。然自民国以来,日商在东三省之势力,突飞猛进。民国元年满洲制粉会社即设分厂于长春,民国二年,中俄边界自由通商线取消后(在五十俄里内,原设有自由贸易地),开征关税,一普特(一 Pud 十六公斤)征四十五戈比(一〇〇戈比 = 一卢布),北满之面粉业,遂竟以南满市场为尾闾。其在南满,因运费之多寡及中外人士口味嗜好之不同,外来面粉渐被排斥,而本地面粉业因以愈趋兴盛。加之欧战勃发,日本遂乘此时机,在东三省广设工厂。民国三年富顺设日本面粉厂;民国八年大连设大陆面粉公司;同年十月开源设亚细亚制粉会社(中日合办);民国九年长春设中华制粉株式会社(中日合资)。此外,辽阳有中日面粉公司,亦系日资。日本面粉业之插足于哈尔滨,始自民国七年,即俄国大革命之后一年。其年满洲制粉会社设工厂于哈尔滨,北满制粉会社亦于同年设立。其由中日合办之面粉厂,则有傅家甸之万福兴,成立于民国六年。

东三省诸厂之中,以满洲制粉会社规模为最大,该厂除在铁岭、长春、哈尔滨设有工厂外,民国七年(或云九年),在济南亦设分厂,其重要机器,皆由美国购入。然犹以为未足,民国九年三月该公司在东京召集股东特别大会,议决增加资本为四百二十五万元;四月又开特别会议,决与朝鲜大陆两面粉厂合并,增资本为五百七十五万元。九十年间,又与北满制粉会社合并,故该公司不特为东三省第一之大规模面粉企业,即推之中国全境,亦当首屈一指也。

日商对中国之面粉事业,除东三省外,在山东之济南、青岛、江苏之上海,湖北之汉口,亦均有投资。天津之寿星,于民国十四年已改归华商,兹姑不论。济南之满洲制粉会社分厂,上文已述及。其在汉口者有和丰面粉公司,系中日合办,成立于光绪三十一年。其在青岛者,有青岛制粉会社,成立于民国七年。其在上海者,有三井制粉工厂及内外棉经营之面粉工厂。三井制粉工厂原系英商之增裕面粉公司,民国六年由三井洋行出资收买;于是英商在中国面粉工业之地位遂完全消失。内外棉株式会社所经营之面粉厂,即光绪三十二年华商设立之裕顺面粉公司,不幸于民国七年,正我国面粉工业最发达之际,该厂竟以出售于内外棉闻矣。由此以观,日商在中国所营面粉工业,规模之大,分布之广,均非任何国所能及,国人可不知所惧哉!

外人对于我国精盐业之投资地,仅限于山东及东三省。光绪二十四年(一八九八)德占青岛后,即从事精盐业之经营。三十年营业渐盛,政府始加注意,规定每担征税四元。欧战期间,日人接管青岛,对于精盐业更积极加以扩充。民国十二年,青岛收复,在德日经管时期设立之精盐厂,政府乃招商投标承购,结果由商人张成勋所组成之永裕公司承办。其时工厂计有十七处,惟厂屋敝坏,多不适用,其存者仅小港一厂,台西两厂。该公司法定资本为三百二十万元,应缴盐田及工厂全部价值三百万元,分十五年缴清;于民国十四年二月开工制盐。(见《中国实业志:山东省》,页四四一)东三省之日商精盐工厂有四,规模较大者为东洋拓殖会社之旅顺双岛湾再制盐工场,设于民国十六年,资本四百万元,年产粉碎盐,洗涤盐三千万斤,值三十万元。又日本制盐业会社之普兰店工场,资本亦四百万元,年产精盐一千万斤,值十万元。

我国精糖业,以外人经营者为最早,至今仍操于外人之手,但其发展则尚极幼稚。初英商怡和洋行于光绪四年(一八七八)在香港设中华精糖公司。至三十年英商太古洋行又于香港设立太古精糖公司,规模均甚宏大。其后数年太古洋行复在汕头崎碌地方创设分厂,收购韩江流域之甘蔗为原料,以期独占广东之糖业,然未及开工而停业。至甜菜糖厂,则创始于宣统元年波兰人在哈尔滨以东阿什河所设立之工厂,资本一百万卢布。由波兰购买机器,次年始开工制糖。最初三年,未能获利。入民国后,始见起色。民国八年,俄境内乱,运输不便,该厂乃多制白糖。后因经营不善,十二年改树法旗,现已归哈尔滨著名商人阔干所有。与阿什河糖厂同年(即宣统元年)设立者尚有呼兰之华资富华公司。然该厂于未设工场以前,资本已耗大半,乃向德商借款五十万卢布,并借垫机器费十万卢布,仍以经费不足,迄未开工。至民国元年,始由东三省当轴摊还所欠德款,收归官办,改名东三省呼兰制糖厂。后因经营无方,于民国七年完全停办,十二年始行复工,每月消费甜菜根三百五十吨。宣统三年,日本南满铁道会社所设立之产糖试验场,试植甜菜,已大有成效,因于民国五年设厂于沈阳车站之西南,资本定金一千万元,先收三分之一,续收一百五十万元,共约五百万元。机器为日本及中国所制。所需甜菜,概由该社自行种植,不虞缺乏。民国八年,种菜面积为二万五千亩(东省亩),十一年增至六万亩,十三年增至七万亩,十四年略减。因菜量之增加,于十一年在铁岭设立分厂,同年又设酒精厂于总厂附近。该厂每日能制糖五百吨,酒精一百五十斤,规模在我国为第一。但自民国十五、十六年,铁岭及沈阳工厂,先后停工;至十八年资产复归债权者——朝鲜银行——管理,现在是否复工,因缺乏资料,无法查明。至前述之英商太古及中华两厂,每日各产糖一二,五〇〇及四,〇〇〇吨云。(《东三省物产资源与化学工业》,上册)

茶为我国出口之大宗,英俄商人对于我国之制茶业,在清光绪年间已开始投资于汉口、九江、福州等处,而以汉口为尤甚。汉口为我国输俄砖茶之中心。是项砖茶,在一八七七年即有俄商阜昌洋行设厂制造。迨一八七九年,俄商顺丰洋行继之。一八九九年,俄商新泰洋行又继之而起。此三厂者,资金均在一二百万两左右,年制砖茶最少亦有数十万担,可云极一时之盛。但自俄国革命后,彼等相继停业,惟新泰茶行停闭数年后,十九年由英商继续营业,改名太平茶砖厂,制造红茶砖及青茶砖,每年营业达三十万元之谱,二十年水灾时,损失颇巨,水退后,仍复原状。(朱美予:《中国茶业》,一一七至一一八页。)

我国制蛋工业之兴起,多赖外人之提倡。考蛋品之制造,创于欧洲;至光宣年间,传入我国。其时英商和记公司在南京、汉口、天津分设大规模之打蛋厂三处,营业极形发达。于是外人之经营斯业者,接踵而起,尤以德人为最力。迨欧战发生,在华德人全数回国。德商蛋厂同时歇业;其在汉口、青岛蛋业所占之地位,遂由日人取而代之。当时欧美各国以面粉或牛肉粉和蛋粉制成饼干,以为军食,故蛋粉之行销极畅,市价亦高,赢利常在一倍以上,是为蛋业之黄金时代。欧战告终,各国一方极力提倡养鸡,以谋自给,一方借口卫生,限制外货进口。我国蛋业,尤其国人经营者,因规模较小而渐见衰落。其尚能继续发展者,多属外人所办。上海蛋厂较大者有六家,外商占其四,即英商培林,资本二百万元,年产量一万吨;美商班达与海宁及英商怡和,资本各五十万两,年产量各五千吨。汉口外商蛋厂十一家,内以和记洋行开设者为最大,在我国亦为第一,其在汉口与天津二厂年各生产五千吨,足以垄断汉口之蛋业。该行在我国各地所设采办鸡卵等原料之机关不下一百五十余处。其南京分行每日生产力达三百吨(约五千担),年产百余万担,超过上海六家蛋厂生产力之总额,每日需蛋四百万个。影响所及,苏、皖两省之蛋价,较之他省乃高出数倍。近虽因国外销路不佳,存货颇多,生产力已渐减低,然其力量之雄厚,仍为国内各厂之冠。(第一次《中国经济年鉴》,K一六三页。)青岛现有蛋厂五家,外商居其四,以英商培林公司为最大,总厂在英国;上海、汉口均有分厂,青岛亦有一分厂;所出为冻蛋及鲜蛋,年产共值三百十五万元。其余三厂,规模较小,即美商美丰与华北及德商保和,保和且因资本亏折殆尽,今已停业矣。(《中国实业志:山东省》)

洋商在中国经营卷烟业者,首推英美烟公司。该公司于光绪二十八年(一九〇二)在英伦注册,为英美两国六公司所合办,资本总额达英金二千二百五十万镑。在华经营者,有中国英美烟公司,大英烟公司,及其他附属公司。在上海、汉口、天津、沈阳、哈尔滨、坊子(山东)等处,均设有工厂,六厂之中以上海、汉口两厂为最大。上海工厂二百亩,工人七千五百,并附设完美之印刷部。汉厂虽较沪厂稍逊,然每日亦能出卷烟六百万枝。该公司并在潍县坊子一带,租地栽种烟草。制造而外,兼营卷烟输入事业。其资力之雄厚,即首屈一指之华资南洋兄弟烟草公司,亦难企及。(见《上海之工业》,九九——一〇〇页。)次于英美烟草公司者,有日商东亚烟草株式会社,成立于光绪三十二年(一九〇六),初仅为南满高丽之烟草输出商,资本约日金一百万元;至宣统元年,乃于汉城及奉天之营口设立制造厂,宣统三年复于平壤(高丽)设立分工厂,民国初年又于全州(高丽)设立分工厂;自后营业区域,日益扩张,故至民国六年,乃于上海收买希腊人经营之安利泰制烟厂,又于天津设立分厂。该公司目下资本为日金一千万元,已缴足五百八十万元,营口一厂之生产力,每日可达卷烟一千万枝,故其在东北方面,势力非常雄厚。

外人对于我国化学工业之投资,有水泥、火柴、玻璃、制革、油类等业。兹依次分述之。

外人之投资水泥工业,最早者为英商青州水泥公司,于光绪十二年(一八八六)在香港成立,设制造厂于澳门(青州岛)及九龙。光绪二十四年,开平矿务局复就其煤矿附近设立水泥厂。该厂延聘英人为技师,用旧式直窑烧制,旋以管理不善,致亏本停工,光绪三十二年,乃让归华商经营,更名为启新洋灰公司。光绪三十四年日本小野田水门汀会社设分厂于大连之周水子地方。民国六年日人设山东水泥会社于青岛。二十二年日人复筹设吉林洋灰公司于吉林。统计三十余年间,国内先后已设及筹设之外商水泥厂共五家,为日商三,英商二。至每年产量,则大连为一百五十万桶,仅次于启新之一百六十万桶;而青州为一百二十万桶,山东为十万桶。(方显廷:《中国经济研究》,下册;中国水泥工业之鸟瞰章。)

火柴业之有外资,肇始于光绪二十七年(一九〇一)中日在重庆合办之有燐火柴厂。其次则为光绪三十二年中日在奉天合办之日清燐寸株式会社。自兹而后,日人单独设立者,如吉林燐寸株式会社、东亚燐寸会社、奉天燐寸会社、大连燐寸会社等。其中以吉林燐寸株式会社为最大,设分厂于永吉及长春,后又卖与瑞典火柴商,为瑞典火柴业侵入吾国之根据。此外日商更设东亚燐寸会社分厂于天津、济南,并于青岛设明石、山东、华祥及青岛等火柴厂,又于上海及镇江设立燧生火柴厂。此日商在吾国设立火柴厂之大略情形也。至瑞典火柴商之侵略我国火柴业尤甚。缘该国瑞典火柴股份公司,本握有国际火柴业之霸权;其势力及于二十八国,足以支配全世界之火柴业,其资金之雄厚,消息之灵通,及技术之精良,远非吾国火柴业所能与竞。自其与日本燐寸会社合并后,即向吾国同业进攻,以吾国火柴业不为利诱,乃收买东三省日清、吉林、大连等燐寸会社之股票、占十之六七;以大股东之资格,主持厂政,设办事处于哈尔滨及香港,以事侵略。吾国东三省及广东之火柴业,于此受一重大之打击。其在长江方面者,则以巨金投资于日商燧生火柴厂,从事制造,并以贱价倾销其出品,以期打倒吾国火柴业。其经营之机关,为瑞中洋行及民光公司;所出火柴,或称欧制,或称华制,更或称德法等国制,以淆惑视听,借避攻击,此皆瑞典火柴业侵略之大概情形也。

外人在我国设立之玻璃工厂,为数虽甚有限,然以规模宏大,影响所及,亦颇可观。秦皇岛之耀华玻璃厂,成立于民国十年,为中英合办之开滦矿务局所经营,资本一百五十万元。此外,日人在上海、天津、大连、安东、汉口等处均设有工厂,资金共约四百余万元,每年出品,约值六七百万元。其中上海之宝山玻璃株式会社,有资金五十万元；大连之昌光硝子株式会社，有资本三百万元；南满洲硝子株式会社有资金三十万元。

　　我国之外商制革工厂，天津、上海等处共有六家，内日商四家，意商二家，皆资本雄厚，生产力极强，任何华厂不能望其项背。六家之中，以中日于民国七年在天津合办之裕津制革公司为最大，资本五十万元，产量年约三千余担，占天津各厂出口总额半数以上。其次为日商在上海创办之中华皮革厂及江南制革厂，资本各五十万元。意人所设立之上海皮革厂，资本十四万元。其他在上海之外商制革厂：一为意商大利皮革厂，尚未开工；一为日商宫崎制革厂，现已停闭。综上所述，外商皮革厂，寥寥数家，合计资本将及三百万元，生产数量，几占我国各厂产量之半。华商工厂财力薄弱，统计数百家制革厂，资本满五十万元者，不过三两家，诚不免相形见绌矣。

　　外商在华所经营之油类工业，有桐油、豆油及烛皂等。我国桐油，多集中汉口，以便外运。国内油行有精炼厂者甚少，所有毛货，往往由出口洋行代炼，或向洋行借厂提炼。汉口各洋行所设油厂，具备炼净机及储油池者颇多；计十六家洋行，共有油池容积一五、六五〇吨，内以其来、美孚、福中、三井、三菱、怡和、安利、立兴等八家为较大，其油池容量均在千吨以上，合计已达一一、六五〇吨，此外，万县油行有德商瑞记及永利，日商武林等数家。上海有奥地利人所创办之东方油厂，直接运货出国，不经洋行之手。民国十八年该厂联合十四家油行，集股二十万元，开办振业机器榨油公司；并拟在浙江各县设法劝导，推广桐树种植，改良桐农生计，就地收买桐子，用机器榨油，运至上海，经该厂精炼后出口，销售欧美，卒以金贵银贱之影响而停止进行。

豆油业盛行于东三省，北有哈尔滨，南有大连与营口，均为榨油业之中心。日商对于榨油业之投资，初颇积极，卒以油业富投机性，而工作及待遇均非日本工人所能堪，故榨油业仍全在华人掌握中。然日人对于榨油业之促进及操纵，则不遗余力。南满铁路之兴建，予豆油及豆饼之外输以交通上之便利，油业中心之渐由营口移往大连，职是之故；繁荣一时之营口，遂见衰落。以是油品制造，虽多属华人经营，其输出则由日商经手，大连交易所及油厂公会均受日人统制。东省油坊产额年为五六万万元，而经由大连日商输出者，达二万万元云。

新式制皂工业，首由德人于宣统元年在沪创办固本制皂厂。至民国三年，欧战爆发，德人返国，因欠有华人张某少数款项，乃托其代为暂管。迨至民国六年，该德人返沪，拟再经营，遂为张某所拒；几经交涉，卒偿其值，另招华股，由五洲大药房经理，更名五洲固本制皂厂，于是一变而为纯粹之华商矣。五洲自接办以来，成绩斐然，资本亦激增至百余万元。目下外商在华所开设之皂厂，其较著者有日商上海油脂株式会社，资本五十万。英商中国肥皂公司与白礼氏洋烛厂，均规模宏大，设备齐全，为我国新法烛皂业之劲敌。除五洲外，我国烛皂业工厂虽多，然资本有限，多者不过三四十万元，少者仅一千元耳。

四　民族工业资本之发展

我国工业除外资经营部分外，其由自身积聚资本而经营之民族工业，亦堪一述。民族资本可分公有私有两大类。公有资本，或为国有，或为省市县所有。私有资本之供给者，不外官僚（包括军人），买办，华侨，商人，以及银行钱庄等等。兹请依次分陈之。

（甲）**公有资本** 公有资本经营之工业，按行政单位之不同，分国营，省营及市县营三种。国营工业发展最早，范围亦最广，然成效则甚微。考我国新工业之发展，其第一期（一八六二——一八七七）为军用工业兴起时期，亦即官办时期；期中主要事业，如制炮局（一八六二），江南制造总局（一八六五），马尾船政局（一八六六），及天津机器制造局（一八六六）等，均由国款创办。至第二时期（一八七八——一八九四）即商品工业兴起时期，完全国营或官办工业，虽因国款之支绌，新兴者渐见减少；然官商合办或官督商办者，则方兴未艾。在此期内之工业，虽有官办，商办，官督商办乃至外人经办者，而以官督商办为最著，故又称官督商办时期。计本期官办工业有甘肃织呢总局（一八七八），湖北织布纺纱制麻缫丝四局（一八九三），及各省兵工厂（其中如汉阳兵工厂，尤为卓著）等。官督商办之工业，则有织布局（一八九〇），机器纺织总局（一八九三），开平煤矿公司（一八七八），漠河金矿（一八八八），大冶铁矿（一八九一），及汉阳铁厂（一八九三）等。自此以后，国营工业日趋衰落。民营工业渐有取而代之之势。然国有铁路之机厂，造币厂，兵工厂，印刷厂，织呢厂等，则仍均为国营。单就各路机厂而言，据第一次《中国经济年鉴》工业章所述：吾国国有铁道，"计有北宁（一九〇四年开工），平汉（一八九七），平绥（一九〇五），津浦（一九〇八）胶济（一八九九），京沪（一九〇三），及沪杭甬（一九〇七）七线。北宁线之机厂有姑皇屯，山海关及唐山三处。平汉线则只长辛店一处。平绥线只南口一处。津浦线有西沽，济南及浦镇三处。胶济线之机厂在四方。京沪线之机厂在吴淞。沪杭甬线之机厂在闸口"(K六三八页。)国府成立以来,党政军当轴,秉承　总理实业计划,发展国家资本,节制私人资本,于是国营工业又复抬头。军事委员会设资源委员会(现改隶经济部)兴办国防或基本工业如煤铁、机械、电气、化学等。国府复有建设委员会(现已归并于经济部)主办电气工业及煤矿。而行政院实业部在抗战期前亦拟有实业四年计划:关于工业方面,拟举办钢铁厂,硫酸铔厂,机器厂,及细纱厂等。其中除硫酸铔厂已在南京附近开工,不幸于南京失守前被日机炸毁外,余于抗战发生前,亦均在进行中。此我国国有工业之概况也。

省营工业以矿业及电业较为普遍。光绪二十一年(一八九六)湖南设立官矿局。三十一年江西赣州举办铜矿。宣统元年直省又开办鸡鸣山煤矿。二年湖南官矿局以新法采水口山铅锌。此皆各省官业之要者。入民国后,此数矿中,其未停办而仍获利者,惟湖南一处耳。近年来,各省官营之矿业为数又渐多;最著者有河南之中原煤矿,陕西之延长石油矿,湖南之水口山铅锌矿及黑铅炼厂,湖北之象鼻山铁矿,河北之临城煤矿,广西之富贺钟锡矿,贵州之铜仁县大峒喇汞砂厂,安徽之烈山煤矿,以及辽宁之黑山县八道壕官矿等。其营业情形则各省不同;有因亏累而不振者,如贵州铜仁之汞砂厂,有仅能勉强支持者,如陕西之延长油矿,亦有获赢颇为可观者,如湖南之水口山铅锌矿及黑铅炼厂,河南之中原煤矿(地质调查所编:《第四次中国矿业纪要》)。此外各省官商合办之矿业,较著者有云南之箇旧锡务公司及察哈尔之龙烟铁矿公司。中外合办者,有河北省政府与德商合办之井陉矿务局,辽宁省政府与日商合办之本溪湖煤铁公司,弓长岭铁矿公司等。此我国近年来各省官办矿业之概况也。

我国电厂，据民二十一年十月之统计，共五一八处，资本三一一兆元，发电容量五五六，〇四八瓩。内公营（包括国营，省营，市营，县营）者二七家，资本三一兆元，发电量七七，七七五瓩。此等公营电厂之分布，有如下表：

第五表　民国二十一年中国公营电厂之分布

省别	厂数	投资额（千元）	发电容量（千瓦）	备考
江苏	3	6,008	24,236	国营二　县营一
浙江	5	5,150	21,640	省营四　县营一
安徽	1	300	640	省营
四川	1	20	100	市营
广西	2	595	1,088	市营
贵州	1	200	150	市营
河北	2	6,000	3,100	国营一　市营一
山东	1	70	100	国营
甘肃	1	32	80	省营
辽宁	3	150	10,275	省营一　县营二（官商合办）
吉林	3	11,960	15,800	省市县营各一
黑龙江	4	330	566	市营一　县营三
合计	27	30,815	77,775	

照上表所列，公有电厂之国营者四家，省营者八，市营者七，县营者八。公有电业之不发达，由上述统计已可窥见一斑。吾人若进而考察各地之大电厂，可知多数均为外资或民营，如上海、南满（只沈阳有省营者一家），广州、天津、武汉、哈尔滨、青岛等处均无公营电厂；而有公营电厂者，只北平、杭州、南京、武进（戚野堰）、苏州等地而已。

市营工业，除电业外，尚有自来水。我国自来水厂，分外资，商办，官办及官商合办四种。外资及商办者不论，其官商合办者有广州增步水厂(一九〇五)及昆明自来水公司(一九〇二)。官办者有南京市自来水厂(一九三三),杭州市自来水厂(一九三一),青岛自来水厂(一九〇五),及吉林省城自来水厂(一九二九)。此外,广西之柳州梧州,安徽之蚌埠安庆,江苏之苏州常州,河南之开封,及湖北之武昌,亦均有自来水厂之设置,或办有成效,或未及完成而中断。

(乙)私人资本　私人对于工业之投资,分官僚,买办,华侨,商人及银行钱庄五种。官僚阶级,起源于周末之士大夫。其时诸侯及贵族虽为自治体之支配者;然因政治与社会之混乱,政治实权渐旁落于士大夫之手,是为官僚阶级发生之萌芽。秦采中央集权制,彼等一时虽消声匿迹,然不久秦亡汉兴,彼等又重整旗鼓,掌握政权。此种阶级,由于历代之注重考试,故能踵起继进,永久延续;不似欧洲之贵族阶级,随时代之变迁而没落。即民国以来,士大夫之地位仍未衰替。彼等在朝为官,在野为绅,无形中把持中央与地方政权,且互相勾结以榨削平民,积聚资本。往昔我国经济落后,产业未兴,故官僚阶级之资本,尽以土地投资为出路。逮鸦片战争以后,工商百业受帝国主义经济侵略之刺激,日益发展。官僚资本逐渐由土地之买卖转向工商业之经营,而形成民族工业资本之首要源泉。新工业之由官僚兴办者,自官督商办时期后,日以滋多。如聂潞生设恒丰纺织新局于上海(一八九〇);李鸿章设伦章纸厂于上海(一八九一);盛宣怀设华盛纱厂(一八九三)及大德机器榨油厂(一八九六)于上海;张謇设大生纱厂于南通(一八九八及一九二四);崇明(一九〇七);海门(一九二一),及耀徐玻璃公司于宿迁(一九〇八);鲁督胡廷干设博山玻璃公司于博山(一九〇四);熊希龄设醴陵瓷业公司于醴陵(一九〇五);郑孝胥设日晖毡呢厂于上海(一九〇六);两江总督端方设江西瓷业公司于鄱阳(一九〇七);黎元洪设中兴煤矿于山东峄县(一九〇八)及鲁丰纺织公司于济南;周学熙设华新纱厂于天津(一九一八),青岛,卫辉及唐山(一九二二),倪嗣冲等在欧战期间设纱厂于天津;如此等等,均其较著之例也。

私人资本之第二来源为买办。买办(Compradore)一语,源于西班牙文之 Compar; Compar 在英语为 to buy, 有购买之意。吾国译作买办, 谓其代人买卖也;于原义尚能吻合。买办制之起源, 说者谓为西历一七〇二年, 由我政府正式批准之特许商人(其初此种特许商人仅只一名,嗣后名额渐次增加,在一七二〇年达十三名,有公行 Cohong 之组织)之变体。惟征之史乘, 外人在华早有使用买办之事实。自《南京条约》(一八四二)承认外人自由贸易, 废止特许商人后, 外人利用买办之范围亦随之而扩张。买办至此,亦变其本来之性质,且侵入从前公行之业务范围矣。

往时欧洲人来华经商者,悉以南方之广东为中心。自我国政府开放南方各港为商埠以来,南方之对外贸易,乃有急激之发展,同时更促进利用买办之机会。故买办制之发达以南方为最早且盛;而买办职务殆为广东人所独占。斯时之买办咸以外人不谙华语,不明吾国商业习惯及一般社会情形,乃居奇制胜,往往过索佣金,或于买卖价格上,播弄手段,获利颇为可观。于是各省人士,苟能通晓外国语言,莫不竞趋斯业,以求致富,甘为外商执役而不辞。然就人数言,依然以历史上对外贸易中心地之广东人占多数,其次当推宁波人。此两地人本以长于商略闻;其多操斯业,非无故也。

如上述买办以粤浙两省籍居多数,故现代资本之积聚,亦以两省为较巨。日人长野朗氏至谓我国财阀可分粤浙两派;虽不免过甚其辞,要亦有相当之理由在焉。该氏且谓:"中国的财阀,是由与外国通商而产生的;其发展地为通商口岸及生命财产有安全保障之租界。随着开港场之发展,他们的势力便愈扩大。所以中国财阀,在目前的状况,与租界及开港场是有着重大关系的。"(长野朗著,胡雪译:《中国资本主义发达史》,页三四〇。)职是之故,经营工业者亦以粤浙两省人为多。据长野朗氏统计,上海工业财阀势力之分布:在纺织工厂之一七家中,浙江系占六家,广东系占四家。缫丝业之九家中,浙江系占四家,广东系占一家。(见长野朗书,三六〇页。)

私有资本之第三来源为华侨。据陈达氏之调查,我国海外侨民分布五十余处,合计在一千二百万人以上;其中有万人以上者二十二处,分列如下(以千为单位):台湾四,三〇〇;暹罗一,一〇〇;荷属东印度群岛一,〇〇〇;香港八二一;马来联邦七一二;印度支那四〇〇;西比利亚三五一;缅甸三四九;印度一〇八;美国七五;澳门七一;日本与高丽七一;菲律宾七〇;英属北婆罗洲四八;加拿大四〇;夏威夷群岛二七;巴西二〇;澳大利亚一七;墨西哥一五;比鲁一五;古巴一二;法国一〇。(见陈达:《人口问题》,页三五五。)观此,华侨之分布区域虽广,然多数集中于南洋一带;其经济发展,亦以南洋为最显著。盖其他地方,物质文化进展至相当程度,工商业均甚发展者,华侨颇难有插足之余地也。南洋华侨在产业上之势力介乎欧人与土民之间,如法属安南之西贡一带,粤人经营者有绸缎店,米店,制板店,材木店,及砖瓦,石灰,平底帆船之制造,毛皮,兽骨,雄黄,小豆蔻等特殊土产之输出,及舢板船修理用材之制造等。闽人亦以西贡为中心,从事活动。图伦之工场与米商,多在彼等掌握中。暹罗经济全权,亦操于华人之手。华人不但经营输出入业,且设有保险公司十余家,与欧美及日人竞争而无逊色。银行业虽不发达,亦设有三家之多。航业亦曾一度经营,不幸失败。农业以园艺为主。暹罗之主要物产为米,而米之贸易,自熟米以至输出,均由华人经理。制材业亦以华人最占势力,且有兼营木器制造者。其他器具及机器工厂,亦颇不少;盖暹罗工业,尚甚幼稚,华人精巧的小工业自易发展也。英领马来半岛华人之经济地位,亦极巩固;橡皮制造业者,交易商,零卖商及劳动者占多数;富豪亦不少。至锡矿之开采,亦以华人为较多而有成效。荷属东印度诸岛及英领婆罗洲之华人,以经营贸易为主,在欧人与土人之间,形成一种中间商人。菲律宾华侨之经济地位亦甚高。岛内之小商业,什九在华人之手;趸卖亦然。彼等握有主要产物之收买权,且设有一千万元资本之中兴银行,以为金融周转之中心。

华侨在海外经济势力之雄厚,已如前述。其对于祖国经济发展之影响,除在国外推销国货并年输巨额资金回国以补偿历年来国际收支之不平衡外;对于祖国工业之促进,在资金与技术方面,更有莫大之助力。考华侨返国作工业之投资者以潮州人张振勋氏为最早。张本南洋华侨,因事晤法领,得葡萄酒饮之甚甘,回国后,访得天津烟台地方多产葡萄,乃出资三百万元,在烟台购地三千余亩,采集各种葡萄植之。最初十年所植美法等国葡萄种多不能活,后用接种之法,始获成功。又延聘造酒名师,在烟台开设张裕酿酒公司,从事酿造。于是销路大畅,名闻遐迩;其出品每年输出新嘉坡等处者,为额殊巨;且曾陈列中外博览会多次,获有金牌证书甚夥。政府为提倡国内实业起见,特许注册,免其厘税。该公司并附设有玻璃厂,制售酒瓶。

继张氏而起者为简照南昆仲,创办南洋兄弟烟草公司。该公司肇始于光绪二十八年(一九〇二),名为南洋烟草公司,三十二年始在香港正式注册,资本十万元。未及一年,资本告罄,乃宣布停业,并决将机器及生财拍卖。宣统元年,简氏昆仲鉴于纸烟输入日多,利权外溢日甚,遂自合资接办,改称今名。简氏之叔某饶于财,投资该公司亦甚巨。于是,营业日有起色。其出品极得两广及港粤人士之欢迎。欧战起后,外国烟草及材料输入减少,该公司乘机扩展营业,于上海、广州、北京、汉口各处皆设分公司。继而内地各行省及南洋群岛等地,亦有代销处。其时资本已增至一百万元。上海方面已增设规模甚大之卷烟厂;并聘海外烟业专家来厂烤制纸烟。民国七年,南洋获利益丰,资本扩充至五百万元。翌年,国内各商会各团体及海外华侨海内巨商,皆以英美烟公司之在吾国,实力雄厚,欲与其竞争营业,非集合巨额资本,组织规模宏备之工厂,不克有济;于是南洋应时势之要求,遂以公司公诸国人,而成为一股份有限公司。不数月而一千五百万元之资本,遂告收齐。改组以后,惨淡经营,年有盈余。惜以年来沪上烟厂林立,竞争销路,外商如英美烟公司则利用其大量之资本,低价求售,不惜亏本。加以烟税增加,工潮迭起,原料昂贵,出品迟缓,种种原因,该公司乃渐有动摇之势。其在国内之工厂,上海有第三第四两厂,汉口有第六厂,余均在香港。第三厂设于民国五年,为各厂之最大者。浦东之第四厂系因民国十四年五卅事变时英人限制电力而设立,叠受罢工影响,于十七年十一月停闭。汉口一厂,成立于十五年,只以近年营业欠佳,迄未开工。

  国人自办之新式制糖厂,以宣统元年南洋华侨郭桢祥氏在闽南所设之华祥公司为嚆矢,资本四十五万元。设立之初,由爪哇菲律宾购入蔗苗二百五十万株,在龙溪县之王四爷洲及田边与同安县之水头等处设甘蔗栽培场,于水头及浒头设制糖工场二所,其水头工场每日可用蔗八十吨。

国内之有新式针钉业,始于光绪三十四年张之洞在汉阳创办之湖北针钉厂。所购机器共值银二十一万两。开办数年,未能获利。宣统三年五月,由南洋华侨梁祖禄承租续办,仅制针而不制钉。

华侨对国内工业之又一投资,为上海之永安纺织公司。该公司为沪滨著名百货商店永安公司之附属事业。永安乃四十余年前澳洲雪黎金山(Sydney)华侨所经营之百货商店,今在广州、上海、香港等处,均有店号。民国九年,该公司董事议决拨盈余之一部,在上海创立纺织工场,次年遂在杨树浦引翔港购地筑厂,十一年秋竣工,是年十月即开始纺纱。十四年又收买吴淞蕴藻滨大中华纱厂为第二厂。第三厂在上海麦根路,系民国十七年该公司收买者。三厂资本,共六百万两,管理工程者均美国留学生。为我国华侨归国经营之最大纱厂。

树胶业为华侨投资之又一工业。初南洋归国华侨某目睹树胶业工资之廉,获利之厚,乃携款回国,于民国六年就广州河南之鳌州设立广东兄弟树胶公司,营业发展,获利颇巨。十七年又有留日华侨薛福基纠股设立大中华橡胶厂于上海,发展颇为神速,资本达百余万元,工人二千余,执橡胶界之牛耳。

华侨对于化妆品业之投资,除著名之先施公司而外,尚有上海之香亚化妆品公司,为美国华侨所创办,民国四年设立于美国旧金山,七年迁至上海,出品数十种;几经改组,始臻稳定。

东三省毛织厂兴起最早者:辽宁有裕华毛织工厂、哈尔滨有裕庆德毛织工厂,均为海参崴鲁籍华侨所创办。裕华发起于民国九年,至十一年正式开工。有英国纺毛机两部,共一,○二○锭,每一昼夜可出毛线一千磅；木制织毯机六千架，每架每日按十小时工作计，可出长六英尺半宽四英尺之绒毯五条；销售于东三省及天津等处，颇博一般人之称誉。裕庆德发起于民国十年，至十四年始正式成立，资本六十五万元。购德国纺织机七百二十锭，铁制织机十架；所出毛线及绒毯，在天津市场亦颇有名。

酒精制造业亦为我国新兴工业之一，以上海为中心。上海各酒精厂之规模及产量，以民国二十三年实业部与爪哇华侨黄氏合资创办之中国酒精厂为最大。黄氏在爪哇素称巨富，其财产达三万万之巨。酒精厂资本一百五十万，在黄氏创办之事业中，尚属规模较小者。该厂机器购自英国，所用蒸气电力及水等，均系自备。厂内设有一百万公斤之酒精储藏槽。全年产量为一百二十万加伦，占上海六厂总产量（二百二十二万加伦）二分之一以上。

华侨而外，国内商人对工业投资之较著者，有无锡商人荣宗敬氏之于纺纱与面粉业，宁波商人刘鸿生氏之于火柴水泥及手织业。荣氏在我国有面粉及纱厂大王之称。刘氏亦有火柴大王之称。兹请分述荣刘两氏所手创之工业于次。此外则仅加列举，不及详陈。

荣宗敬氏所办之申新纱厂，为华商纱厂之最大者计有六厂：第一、二、五、七等厂在上海，第三在无锡，第四在汉口。第一厂创立于民国五年。第二厂原为中日合办之久成厂，曾一度全属日人，旋以亏耗过巨，至民国五年停办，次年由无锡祝兰舫氏收买，改名恒昌源纱厂，民国八年始归申新。改今名。第三、第四两厂，均创于民国十年。第五厂本名德大，成立于民国三年，至十四年始由申新收买，改今名。第七厂本为英商之东方纱厂，十七年申新以一百七十万两买得。六厂以外，尚有申新第六厂，在江苏常州，系十四年向常州纺织公司租办。故申新经营之纱厂，实际上达七家之多，资本达六百万元，三十万两。各厂均为半合股有限公司性质，资本大半为荣氏亲属所摊，故其实际情形，外间难知底细。

中国最大之面粉事业，当推荣氏所经营之茂新福新面粉公司，资本在五百万元以上，每日生产量逾三万三千六百袋（每袋五十磅，）由十四所面粉工厂制造，其中公司自行经营者十二所，租与他人经营者二所。自行经营之厂，以福新名者八，以茂新名者四。福新有七所在上海，一所在汉口。茂新有三所在无锡，一所在济南。租与他人经营之厂，为上海之元丰及无锡之泰隆。其自营之十二厂除茂新第一厂成立于光绪二十六年（一九〇〇）外，其余十一厂均成立于民国年间。茂新第一厂最初之资本为二十万两，每日生产力为二千六百袋。其始经营困难，颇多亏折。入民国后，渐臻佳境。欧战期间，获利尤丰。于是在无锡设立第一、第二分厂，旋于民国六年在济南设第三分厂。民国九、十年间，茂新总厂之资本已增至五十万元，近复增至六十万元。而第一、第二分厂，亦自三十万增至四十万。福新第一厂创于民国二年，第二厂成立于民国三年，时值欧战爆发，面粉之需要陡增。原有各厂，无不获利，于是又有第三、第四两厂之设。民国七年又设第五厂于汉口；旋又于上海设第六、七、八三厂。以第八厂最为新式。各厂所备机器，以购自美国者为最多；购自英国者仅两架，购自德国者仅一架耳。

吾国火柴工业，起源于同光时代。欧战起后，因外货来源断绝而大盛。欧战告终，欧货复来，而日货复形活跃，大事跌价倾销，国内资本微弱之小厂，受此打击，遂多停顿。十六年以后，瑞典火柴商又挟其雄厚资本及国际火柴霸权之势力，加入竞争。国内火柴业更岌岌不可终日。上海巨商刘鸿生氏有鉴于此，乃集资组织大中华火柴公司，先事收买小厂，集零成整，一方借此免除同类相残，一方厚其实力以与外资抗衡。故该公司系由上海镇江荣昌火柴厂,上海中华火柴厂,苏州鸿生火柴厂等发起,合并为大中华火柴股份有限公司,于民国十九年七月一日成立,共计股本一百九十一万零八十元。嗣于二十年二月收买汉口荣昌厂,更名为大中华火柴公司炎昌厂,同年十月成立。是年五月,益以九江裕生公司,于七月一日成立。其资本扩充至二百三十六万七千三百元。更于浦东设厂一所,专制梗片,以供各厂之用。该公司现有工厂共七所,资产总额达五百六十六万余元。民二十年纯益为五十四万元。其总事务所设于上海,分总务、营业、会计、厂务、考工、技术等六科,各厂组织,亦有条不紊。出口销路遍于长江流域及南方诸省,诸如福州、厦门、汕头、宁波、南京、芜湖等处,皆设有分销处,实吾国火柴工厂中最有希望者也。

刘鸿生氏除以火柴大王著称外,复从事于毛织及水泥业之经营。民国七年筹设上海水泥公司。经理刘伯烈氏曾费四五年之时间,游历欧美,访购机器,卒以马克价低,向德国之秘鲁苏斯厂购得,价约五十万元。直至民国十一年,始兴工筑厂,十二年完工,开始出货,年达三十六万桶以上。厂中聘有德籍工程师三,化学师一。此外,刘氏复于民国十八年创办章华毛织厂于上海,资本八十万元;其大部机器系接收日晖织呢厂者,新机则购自比国。该厂现有毛织机七十二架,利用国产羊毛,从事织造,每年出品约值二十万元左右。

上述二氏而外,商人之投资工业者,不胜枚举。如光绪初年有沪商祝大椿以资本十万两在上海设立源昌机器五金工厂,植我国商办工业之基。光绪二十三年(一八九七),夏瑞芳、高凤池、鲍咸恩、鲍咸昌等共集股银四千元,在上海创立商务印书馆有限公司,开我国印刷界之先河。民国七年上海棉商吴麟书集资一百万两在上海创办溥益纺织公司第一厂,十三年复以一百五十万两之资本创设第二厂。与溥益第一厂同年成立者有沪商陆伯鸿在上海浦东所办之和兴钢铁厂,资本五十万,欧战期间获利独厚,复增资至一百万元。民国十四年丝商朱节香等以二十五万两之资本设立上海中孚绢丝厂,购日、意、法、德国等式机器,以制造绢丝。同年甬商虞洽卿在上海设立江南造纸股份有限公司,资本四十万元;十七年添装大造纸器一部,扩充资本为八十万元。

上述商人所营工业,均在上海。此外内地商人亦有作同样之经营者。例如宣统二年浙江平湖有高姓者,以织机有利可图,其时上海以外,尚无织袜机;乃购机数架,仿制洋袜。以出品价廉,供不应求,业务发达,工人日众,无法容纳;乃以织机分租与各农户,给以原料,而收其租金。不数年间,营业益盛,至民国十五年,平湖共有织袜机一万架,而高姓一家即占一千具左右。嘉兴、嘉善、石门、硖石诸地竞相仿效。福州附近,亦有类似情形。直隶之高阳县,早在光绪二十八年(一九〇二),即有士绅向天津购织布机,仿造洋货,其机均分租与农户。宣统二年,有合记者,以资本二万元购置织机。复逐渐扩充,至民国二年,租出之织机有二百余架,日出布百余疋;其留在工场内之织机仅八架耳。及十五年,高阳布业年产至少二百万元,以合记为巨擘;其余五家,共仅有机四十架。

我国金融界,分新旧两大类。旧者曰钱庄(或银号);新者曰银行。金融界对于工业之投资,恒为短期信用或抵押借款,而极少长期固定之投资。至新旧两类之于工业:在通商大埠,银行较钱庄为重要;其在内地,则适得其反。

钱庄对于工业之投资,在上海一带,以丝厂、碾米厂及其他规模较小之工厂为多。其投资于纱厂面粉厂及规模较大之工厂者,在欧战期间,亦尚不少;今则渐有被资本雄厚之银行取而代之之势矣。吾国丝厂之金融流通,恒唯钱庄是赖。因钱庄之放款与银行不同,毋须先缴担保品,放款数量,全视缫丝厂之信用为转移。在民国二十年以前,如丝商有资本二三万元,即可借款七八万元。其手续通常系将资本存入钱庄,作为垫款,至购茧时,向钱庄零星挪用,收茧完毕后,其收得之茧存贮于附近仓库,将仓库存单交与钱庄,以为担保,至其丝售脱,复以售价购茧。如此转辗流通,不断循环。上海缫丝业之克臻繁盛,实有赖于金融组织之完善也。(见沈文纬:《中国蚕丝业与社会化经营》,页四六。)

钱庄对于内地工业之投资,可以高阳之织布业为例。高阳工业组织,以布线庄为中坚。其业务为:(一)直接从外埠(如天津、青岛、上海)大批购入原料,或在高阳线市及布线庄购入,以备撒机之用;(二)散发原料与四乡织户,令其依照规定标准,织成布疋,送布线庄验收,布线庄即给以预定之工资;(三)布疋收来后,如需经过染色或轧光拉宽等手续,则即发交染坊或整理工厂为之;(四)在各埠择地设立分庄,推销本店货品,以求赢利。布线庄在天津购纱时,即与天津银号发生借贷关系:由银号垫借纱款之一部或全部,迨其在外埠售布得款后,即汇至天津银号归还借款,或更存款。不过九一八以后,东省市场丧失,布业因之衰落;而银号放款,亦较前更紧矣。(吴知:《乡村织布工业的一个研究》,页五七。)

银行对于工业之投资向不重视。北京政府时代,大小银行,几竞以政治借款之投机为务。近年来,识见较远大之银行对工业投资虽渐加注意,然为量尚甚有限。试就中国银行放款之性质言,民十九至二十一三年中,工业放款,占放款总额之百分比,仅分别为六.五七,一〇.一四,及一一.四六。我国银行之业务范围,以中国银行为最广;而该行对于工业之放款,已如此其微,其他殆不难想像而知。新进活跃如上海银行,民二十与二十一两年之工业放款,亦只及全行抵押放款总额百分之三四.三〇及四一.四四。交通银行,系政府特许之实业银行,但该行民二十一年所有"货物抵押及其他工商业投资"之数额,亦仅"约占总数百分之九",则银行业与工业关系之浅,概可想见。

吾国银行对于工业之投资,不但为量太少,其分布于各业亦极不均匀。例如二十一年中国银行营业报告书,对于国内各业放款三八、四三五、四二三元之分布,曾有下列简括之统计:

表六　民国二十一年中国银行工业放款按业务之分布(百分比)

纱厂	61.9	火柴厂	0.7
面粉厂	11.9	衣着厂	0.5
丝厂绸厂	5.5	布厂	0.5
蛋厂	4.9	染织厂	0.4
饮食厂	4.0	铁工厂	0.3
化学工厂	2.6	橡胶厂	0.2
烟厂	1.5	纸厂	0.2
建筑材料厂	1.1	其他	2.8
手工业	1.0		

(见吴承禧:《中国的银行》,页五五〇。)

五　工业资本之筹集与运用

(甲)以往之错误　我国之有新工业,历九十余年;惟就工业资本之筹集与运用言,则以往之错误至少有二:即在筹集方面被外资利用而未能利用外资；在运用方面为民生工业之发展而非国防工业之树立是也。

外资利用我国工业之方式,第一在以其雄厚力量把持我国工业之领导权；第二在其决定投资门类与地域时,一惟彼方利益是视,而于我国之权利,则漠不顾及。此征之外资工业在华发展之实况,固灼然可见者。考外资之侵入我国工业；为时颇早。远在同治元年（一八六二）,上海即有外人设立之百釜机器缫丝工场。此后外人于吾国各地开设工厂者时有所闻。洎甲午一役（一八九四）,我国败北；迫于日人之要求,签订《马关条约》,许其在华有制造权。于是各国纷纷援例,外资工业遂如雨后春笋,蓬勃滋长,而造成今日外商在我国工业上之霸权,几于牢不可破。仅就上海一埠而言,外资工业势力之雄厚,已非国人所能望其项背。据该市社会局民十七年之统计,全市工业投资总额三万万元中,外商即占二万万元,或三分之二。上海为我国工业中心,全国二分一至三分二之工业荟萃于此。上海如是,其他各埠自不待言。观以上各章所述,可知我国主要工业如煤铁、电气、棉毛纺织、精糖、制茶、制蛋、卷烟、水泥、火柴、玻璃、制革、桐油等,均以外资占优势,而最大之工业组织,如煤矿业之抚顺与开滦,电气业之上海电力公司,钢铁业之振兴（鞍山）与本溪湖（宿儿沟）,棉纺织业之内外棉（上海十一厂,青岛三,辽宁锦州二）,缫丝业之富士瓦（安东）及上海制造绢丝公司,毛纺织业之满蒙（辽宁）,面粉业之满洲制粉会社（铁岭、长春、哈尔滨、济南）,精糖业之南满（铁岭、沈阳）,砖茶业之太平（汉口）,制蛋业之和记（南京、汉口、天津）,烟卷业之英美烟公司（上海、汉口、天津、沈阳、哈尔滨、坊子）,火柴业之瑞典火柴股份有限公司（东三省、上海、镇江）,玻璃业之耀华（秦皇岛）及昌光（大连）,制革业之裕津（天津），及桐油业之其来洋行（汉口），亦全系外资经营。其中以日英两国资本为尤巨。

各项外资工业兴办之动机，莫不以外人之利益为前提。析言之，计有下列四大类：第一，输出品如丝、茶、蛋品、桐油、豆油及豆饼等之加工；第二，输入品如棉毛纺织品、面粉、精糖、卷烟、水泥、火柴、玻璃、皮革、烛皂、硫酸等之仿造；第三，外国工业基本原料如铁砂、盐、油等之采掘与加工；第四，在华外资工厂所需动力（如电气）及燃料（如煤）之供给。具此四种动机，故其兴办之工业，类无关我国国防之巩固，而一以民生消费之促进为主眼。其中虽亦有煤铁及电气等有关我国国防之重工业，然全由彼等操纵，华人无插足余地，或屈居附庸地位。其地域之分布，则以集中沿海沿铁路之通商大埠为原则，藉便收集原料，推销制品，且易与其本国往来，而劳力供给之集中，与商业金融机构之灵便，犹其余事也。七七事变起，我国弱点悉露；不惟国防工业之基础，十分薄弱，即经营有年之民主工业，亦因位于交通线附近，首当其冲而次第沦毁。九十年来利用外资之结果如是；良堪痛心！

其次，我国以往工业资本之运用，偏于民生工业之发展而忽于国防工业之树立。其铸错之主因，首为内忧外患之频仍，造成恶劣之工业环境；次为朝野上下之昏庸，缺乏经营现代工业之才识。考我国新工业初兴于同治元年。时值英法联军及太平天国二役之后，国人既慑于机器文明之威力，益以曾李等军政大员之提倡，军用工业，遂以勃兴；国防工业之基础始见萌芽。惜乎尚未数年，而内忧外患，纷至沓来。光绪十一十二两年，安南缅甸相继失守。甲午之耻未雪，辛丑之约又缔。鼎革以还，袁氏称帝；南北纷争；国共阋墙；东省沦陷。数十年来，国势日削，国库日绌。军用工业在此恶劣环境中，未及发育滋长而已摧残殆尽。同时外人援引《马关条约》，取得在华工业制造权，骎且握有我国工业领导权。驯致消耗民财之民生工业日见兴旺，充实国力之国防工业乃益无由树立矣。

至朝野上下对于现代工业之经营，缺乏远大之才识，只就近年来硕果仅存，具有悠久历史与巨大规模之汉冶萍公司而言。即可窥见一斑。吴景超氏于分析该公司之档案后，曾作如下沉痛之断语："汉阳铁厂的开办，距今将近五十年；汉冶萍公司的正式成立（一九○八），距今也有三十年。在这个时期里，假如主持这种事业的人，有眼光，有能力，勤谨的去工作，那么中国的钢铁事业，应该很早便有基础。果能如此，中国的工业化，一定早已突飞猛进；中国的国防力量，一定比现在要坚强巩固。可惜事与愿违，中国现在的钢铁工业，比张之洞的时代，相差无几，比盛宣怀的时代，还要退化。我们真是虚度了五十年！"（《新经济》一卷四期，一○六至一○七页）考汉冶萍失败之因，除环境不良如前节所陈外，据吴氏之分析，尚有三端：第一，计划不周。张之洞开办汉阳铁厂时，"度地则取便耳目，不问其适用与否；汉阳沙松土湿，填土埋桩之费，至二百余万两之多。造炉则任取一式，不问矿质之适宜与否。购机则谓大须可以造舟车，小须可以制针钉。喜功好大，以意为师，致所置机器，半归无用。"第二，用人不当。"汉冶萍事业，矿分煤铁，工兼冶铸；非独工程之事，赖有专家，即经理佐辅之人，亦须略具工商知识。乃公司中人，率皆闲散官绅，夤缘张之洞盛宣怀而来，只图一己之分肥，与公司无利害之关系。"至"职员技师，类无学识经验，暗中摸索。即实力经营，已不免多所贻误，况再加以有心朦混，任意开销，其流弊自不可胜纪。"第三，管理不善。此又可分为人事与帐目两方面。人事方面，股东既未监督董事与经理，而董事与经理，亦未严密的监督公司属员。是以民国元年，"公司亏耗之数，已逾千万，问诸股东，殆无知者。"盖总公司与董事会，均"设在上海，距各厂矿两千余里；消息不灵，鞭长莫及。况复事权各执，手续纷糅，凭三数坐办，一纸呈报，真伪是非，无从辨晰。"账目方面，"公司在开股东会时，有时也作账目之报告，其不可靠之程度，"张轶欧氏于民国七年二月，于代表政府参加该公司股东大会后，曾有如下之报告："上海公司收入总计不过一千一百二十六万二千余两，其支出则有一千一百十七万九千余两，出入相较，所赢无几。其所以称有盈余一百三十三万三千余两，得发股息六厘者，谓盘存项下，各厂矿较上届均有加存之故。及观其所谓盘存，则除所存钢铁及煤焦可以待时而沽，然所值亦属有限外，余皆厂屋基地炉机舟车之类。此类财产，照外国厂矿通例，除地价外，均应逐年折旧，递减其值。而该公司则十余年前设备之旧物，尚照原值开列，其历年所添之物，尤必纤毫具载。故虽通国皆知其亏累不堪，股票市价不及额面之半，而就其账略通收支存三项计之，往往有盈无绌，或所绌无几。"汉冶萍公司之经营如此，其他厂矿，亦不免有类似情形。盖我国工业，官营者，厂矿即为衙门之变形，而私营者，又何以别于封建式之大家庭。荣宗敬氏经营纱厂业及面粉业，在我国首屈一指；而其成绩除范围之庞大，亲友僚属之众多，与汉冶萍公司不相上下外，他无可述焉。总之，经营者不得其人，事业无不失败。我国国防工业之不振，岂尽环境使然耶？

（乙）今后之途径　今后我国工业经营，苟欲惩前毖后，趋回合理之途，则在筹集方面，应仿苏联先例，力事积聚民族资本；虽间亦利用外资，但务须保持主动地位。在运用方面，应适应世界现势及本国急需，以国防高于一切之原则，定事业之缓急先后。兹请依次分述于后：

民族资本之积聚，除鼓励华侨投资外，其在国内，不外促进生产与节制消费两端。我国应促进之生产事业甚多。惟今后之工业建设当以重工业为主；而重工业所需之机械，在最近期内，势须仰给外国。则为平衡贸易收支计，自惟有于输出产品换取外汇之要求下，从事生产之促进。此据过去情形，应为下列二类：（一）农林渔牧业。其产品如桐油、猪鬃、鸡蛋及蛋制品、生丝、茶叶、牛皮、羊皮、羊毛、肠衣、芝麻、棉花、杂粮等物，每年输出总值，在过去放任政策下，已达二万万元；此后政府如能采行鼓励与扶植政策，则其输出量值，自必大有增进。苏联在第一五年计划下所需外汇，其大部分亦系借农产品之外输而筹得，堪供吾人借镜。（二）矿业。我国矿藏甚富，亟须开发。矿产如煤铁铜石油等等，当留供自用，以建立国防工业。但其他工业上必需之矿物如钨锑锡及煤之一部，或为我国特产而目前尚不急需；或自用有余，外销较为合算；则不妨酌量输出，以换取外汇也。

所谓换取外汇，大部分实即换得重工业机器。第国防工业之促进，不仅在置备机器而已；尚须建筑厂屋，购置原料，付给工资，及应付其他必要开支。凡此在在需款，诸待筹集。筹集之方，依苏联之经验，最有效者为消费之节制。惟此有一先决问题，即筹集之款能否尽供国防工业建设之用是。欲实现此点，则政府对于生产事业——尤其工业之投资，应加统制。按我国私有资本之运用，素乏统制。资本所有者得专以个人利益为前提，任意投资，虽与社会利益相背者如投机性或浪费性之事业，亦可任便经营。今后欲矫此弊，当一反以住之放任政策，而仿效德国之严格统制。考德国之第二个四年计划，将拟办事业，按其轻重缓急，定一次序。最重要者为军需工业,其次为粮食供给,其三为工业原料之自制,第四为输出品之增加,第五为工人卫生宿舍之建筑。私人投资,须经政府核准,尽先投入较重较急之事业;凡政府认为不必举办者,私人即不得投资。我国情形,与德不同,虽不能如彼等之严格;但必需采用其原则,俾国内有限之资本,得适应目前迫切之需要。限制之后,更当继以鼓励,或保息,或津贴;如去年六月七日府令修正之特种工业(指制造电机,原动机,工业机及运输器材,冶制金属材料,采炼液体燃料而言。)保息及补助条例,即其一例。该法规定保息之限度,实收资本年息五厘,债票年息六厘,至多以七年为限。补助则以各品类每年生产费及市价为标准,酌量给予现金。至十一月二十五日立法院更进一步,通过非常时期工矿业奖助条例,规定中华民国人民在后方所办有关国防民生之重要工矿业,实收资本已达必要数额需要扶助者,得受下列一种或数种之奖助:(一)保息:以实收资本年息五厘债票年息六厘为限度,期限至多五年;(二)补助,以出品每年出产费及市价为标准,酌量给予现金;(三)减低或免除出口税;(四)减低或免除原料税;(五)减低或免除转口税及其他地方税捐;(六)减低国营交通事业交通费;(七)租用公有土地,免除地租;以五年为限,免租期满,得按照当地租金标准酌减,但减低之数,不得超过租金标准二分之一;(八)协助向银行或以其他方法借用低利贷款;(九)协助向交通机关谋材料成品机件及工人生活必需品运输之便利。

用途既定,请言节制消费之方法。此等方法多少含强制性,其最理想者当为定量分配。欧战时英、法、德、比等国曾一度行之。我国自抗战以来,对于外汇及汽油等,亦颁有同样办法。然以民众组织之不健全及统制机构之欠完备,尚难应用于衣食住等方面之大宗生活用品。迩来全国上下所提倡之节约运动，意义虽佳，而多赖国民自动实行，亦颇难收预期之效果。今退而求其次，惟有先后输入统制，及强制储蓄两端入手。

关于输入物品，我国素乏统制，是以民元后二十三个年度中，进口之奢侈品仅装饰品（如香水脂粉等）饮食品（如雪茄烟查古律糖白兰地酒等）两项平均，每日已达二一七，五〇〇元，每年约为七九，四〇〇，〇〇〇元，合计为一，八二六，一一〇，〇〇〇元，占同时期内入超总值百分之二二.三五，诚属惊人之巨量。而其他奢侈品如衣服方面之丝织，毛织及人造丝等，尚未计入。至必需之消费品如米棉等，本应自给者，输入亦不少。反观生产物品之输入，则为数甚微。二十三年机械输入为二八，〇五一，一〇八金单位，而最多之民二十年，亦仅为八〇，一一六，〇〇〇元，民七以前最多之年，则不过八百六十四万元而已。今后欲谋补救，当实行统制。一方增加农矿产品之输出，一方减少奢侈品及其他消费品之输入，而增加生产物如机械等之入口，庶资本有积聚之可能也。

其次关于储蓄，较易实行之方式有二：一曰摊派建设公债，一曰强制建国储金。

抗战以来，沦陷区域日广；其中工商百业，均已停顿，国内巨额流动资金，因亦无法利用。政府正可乘此时机，发行建设公债，令各工商机关——尤其金融机关——按照规定标准，如金融机关吸收得来或代人保管之现款至少提出百分之几，购买债券。故二十三年七月四日国府公布之储蓄银行法，规定凡办理储蓄业务之银行，对于农村合作社之放款及农产抵押放款总额，不得少于存款总额五分之一，允为饶有意义之立法。

强制建国储金之举办，可先就各类所得税，依其应缴税率，加收相当倍数,作为储金;即由所得税机关负责收存,不需另设机关,以免增加财务行政之负担。按我国自二十五年十月开征所得税以来,税收年有增加,计二十五年度平均月收为七十二万,二十六年度为一百六十五万,二十七年度(七至十月)则略减为一百十四万。即照二十七年度之统计,年收亦可达一千三百六十八万;加倍储蓄便可达二千七百三十六万。其于资金之积聚,亦不无相当裨益也。

促进生产与节制消费而外,华侨资金之招致,亦为积聚民族资本之主要方法。过去华侨现款之输入国内者为数亦颇不赀,历年来国际贸易入超之抵补,多赖此项为挹注。据去年十二月二十六日《大公报》中央社福州专电称:"海外侨胞以往汇款回国年约三万万元,本年以侨胞热烈拥护祖国抗战,益以中央再三鼓励,中、中、交、农四行及闽粤两省银行复予以汇款上之便利,汇款数额骤增;截至十一月份,总额已达五万万元,预计至年终止,可达六万万元。"至华侨汇款之用途分配,尚乏统计可查;然据前章所述,用于工业者自亦不在少数。吾人固知侨胞中不乏拥有巨赀而愿回国投资工业者,如在上海开设中国酒精厂之黄氏,素称爪哇巨富,其财产达三万万元之谱;其以一百五十万元办酒精厂,尚属小规模事业。以后国内他项工业之发展,借助于黄氏之处正多。目下黄氏在沪所办工厂,虽已为暴日强占,政府正可予以特殊便利,俾得继续投资西南西北等省工业。

国府为奖励华侨投资祖国工业起见,曾于十八年二月二十七日,颁布华侨回国兴办实业奖励法,对于华侨兴办之建筑、交通、制造、农矿及其他依法允许人民经营之事业,予以下述之便利:一、当地官署关于安全上之特别保护;二、交通机关于其所需材料及出产物予以运输上之便利;三、由侨务委员会派遣专员或行知地方官署予以指导保护;四、华侨兴办实业确有成绩者得由侨务委员会呈请国民政府给予奖章褒状。该项奖励法,用意至善。设能再进一步,予以非常时期工矿业奖助暂行条例中对于国内同胞所定奖助之一部或全部,则华侨回国兴办实业者,自将源源而至矣。

此外,为补充民族资本之不足,外资自不妨利用。即中山先生之实业计划亦主利用外资。然必利用得法,庶不致造成过去被外资利用之恶果。考实业计划中明订利用外资之原则,为平等与互惠,务在不妨碍中国之主权及行政范围内,双方各得其利。中央政治会议第二二二次会议,依据上项原则,曾有如下三种方式之决定:一、借款与中国政府,外人仅居债主地位;二、外人与中国政府合办各项事业,可居股东地位;三、特许外人在中国法律范围内,完全使用其资本与技术,以事经营,如开矿等,但期满后产权须无偿的交还中国。依第一方式,中国政府可向外国银行团或私人厂商借款,兴办实业。在第二方式之下,外商虽可与中国政府共同经营,唯外商须负为中国设计及供给机械设备之责任;盖不如此,则中国不能得合作之实益也。第三方式系就特种实业而言,于特许期内,外人得代中国创办各种事业,如开采金矿之类。以中国资本与经验之缺乏,特许外人经营,自亦有相当利益。惟享有特许权者,对于特许事业,必有长久经验,并能供给丰富资本而后可。

凡按上述三种方式组成之公司,必须遵守中国法律如公司法等。过去外人享有之领事裁判权,今后自不能适用,否则仍将受不平等条件之束缚,不如不用外资之为愈也。(见马寅初:《中国经济改造》,下册,三三二至三三四页。)

今后我国工业资本之运用,宜以国防工业为首要。而民生工业次之。盖立国于兹武力压倒公理之世界,欲图富强,自必先强而后富。国防工业之建树,乃致强之唯一途径;正如民生工业之发展,为致富之要道也。观乎欧战以还,苏德两国之卧薪尝胆,亟亟于国防工业之树立,其理更见显然。苏联在资本主义风行全世界之环境中,独行社会主义。执政当局,于推翻旧政权之后,即感有被外界攻击之危险;故于内政渐上轨道,秩序渐见恢复时,即着手实施五年计划。第一五年计划完成后,立继以同样之第二第三计划。其计划之内容,均以国防工业为主体。列宁且谓:"苏联之前途,不系于农产之丰收或轻工业之发展,而系于重工业之及早完成;盖无重工业,即无独立之苏联也。"是以在过去十余年中,苏联人民之物质享受,远在英美诸国之下,而其国防事业,却有惊人之进展;最短期内,一跃而为世界一等强国之一。此由其工业生产与投资之统计,更可窥见大略。如一九三四年,工业生产总值中,消费品只占百分之四二.六,生产品则占百分之五七.四。同年度苏联政府之支出预算中,重工业占百分之二一.五,轻工业只占百分之二.六。是以吴景超氏于考察苏联返国后,曾有如下之结语:"苏联把重工业放在轻工业之上,乃是显而易见的。所以在西比利亚一带居住的人民,可以没有鞋袜可穿,但苏联的飞机,却可从莫斯科绕过北极而达美国旧金山之南。莫斯科的房子可以不够住;但等到阅兵的一天,莫斯科的红场上,坦克车却是成群结队的。"

德国自希特勒执政以来,数年之内,由一战败受压之国家,一跃而为独立自主气焰逼人之强国。考其致此之因,端在善用德国已有之工业基础,以发展国防工业。是故德国近数年来,重工业日在猛晋途中,轻工业却进展甚缓。如以一九二八年工业生产指数为一百;重工业指数竟由一九三二年之三五.四激涨至一九三五年之一〇二.四;一九三六年十月更升至一二三.七。轻工业生产指数，一九三二年跌至七四.〇，一九三五年，仍为八五.六，一九三六年十月，亦升至一〇二.四。要之，自一九二八至一九三六年之九年间，德国重工业生产已增加四分之一，而轻工业则并无若何变动。一方面政府又持工资不动政策；故德国人民之物质享受，近年来因物价高涨，反较一九二八年为低。其刻苦奋斗之精神实不亚于苏联，而尤为我国所急应效法者也。

我国自国府成立以来，即于军事委员会下设立国防委员会，旋易称资源委员会，以从事于国防工业之树立。去年正月中枢改组，该会改隶行政院经济部。按照二十七年八月一日府令修正公布之组织条例，会中分设工业、矿业、电力、技术、经济研究及购料等处室，司掌（一）创办及管理经营基本工业；（二）开发及管理经营重要矿业；（三）创办及管理经营动力事业，及（四）办理政府指定之其他事业等项。据去年十一月一日国民参政会议开会时经济部翁部长之报告，上述各种工业，多为国营；且已进展至相当程度。如钢铁方面，将汉阳钢铁厂及大冶铁矿之重要机件，酌量运入四川，六河沟化铁炉，亦商购运入，运费逾一千万元；期在择地另建钢铁厂，继续炼制。又因国产纯铜，亟须增加，故早在长沙设厂，兹又在川省另建，并收购川康原铜，兴办滇北铜矿，以期所得产额，至少可供一部分之需要。至采运出口以换取外汇之锡锑钨等矿亦在集中管理，设法改良。关于锡矿，并已与桂省政府合办平桂矿务局，资本五百万元，拟以电气炼锡，产锡量预计年达千吨。机器方面，以五百万元之设备在云南创设机器厂，即可开始制造工业机械、工具、及发动机。而在桂滇之电工器材厂四处，资本合五百万元，能制电线电话、收发音管、灯泡、电池、变压机等件。化学方面，则在四川设立酒精厂，制造强度酒精。动力方面，近数月内，迭在兰州万县贵阳等处,增加电力;又在汉中辰溪沅陵昆明等处新设发电厂,共费约三百万元。

民生工业建设,在目前之中国,其重要虽远逊于国防工业,然亦未可因噎废食,而完全停顿。故抗战以来,政府于此方面亦有相当措施。战事初起时,军事委员会即有工矿调整委员会之设立,去年元月中枢改组,该会易名工矿调整处,隶经济部。该处依去年九月二日部令公布之"办事细则",分总务、业务、财务、秘书、及会计等三组室。其主要工作,在协助轻重工业之重要厂矿,由接近战区之前方移至比较安全之后方,并于其到达后,予以金融技术或行政上种种扶助。计截至十月二十九日止,经政府协助迁移内地之厂矿 除汉阳钢铁厂及六河沟化铁炉外,共计三四一家,机件共重六三,四〇〇吨。并汉阳钢铁厂内迁机件计,当达十二三万吨之多。此中纺织机件占三万一千六百余吨,机器五金机件八千余吨,电气机件三千二百余吨,陶磁机料三千四百余吨,化学机料二千二百余吨,煤矿机件三千六百余吨。各厂内迁后,除汉阳钢铁厂系由国营外,工矿调整处对于各民营工厂,共贷出款项四百五十万元;又为代向银行借款,购置供一年用之材料,共三百五十万元。

此外,小工业方面,亦有相当进展。党政当轴鉴于小工业之不容忽视,故"抗战建国纲领"中,有"发展各地手工业"之规定。经济、教育、内政三部,复于去年八月十二日会同公布章程,组织推广小工业设计委员会,俾负此方面之专责。去年夏季中外人士所主张以五百万元资本组织三万个工业合作社,以为抗战期间轻工业生产主体之议,亦蒙当局采纳,由国库如数拨发资金,成立中国工业合作协会,全国暂分西北、西南、东南、华中四区,每区设办事处。除华中区办事处尚在筹备中外,其他三区办事处,已分在东南之赣县,西南之重庆及西北之宝鸡等地,先后成立分会矣。

参考书目

实业部编:《中国经济年鉴》,第一、二、三次,民二十三、二十四、二十五年,商务出版。

《中国实业志》:江苏、浙江、山东、湖北等省,实业部国际贸易局编。

Chinese Yearbook, 1936-37 and 1937 issues, Chinese Yearbook Publishing Company

《十年来的中国》,中国文化建设协会编,商务,民二十六年。

马寅初:《中国经济改造》,商务,民二十四年。

方显廷:《中国经济研究》,商务,民二十七年。

长野朗著,胡雪译:《中国资本主义发展史》,中华,民二十五年。

漆树芬:《经济侵略下之中国》,民十四年。

Remer, C. F.: Foreign Investments in China, 1933.

《日本对沪投资》,中国国民经济研究所编,商务,民二十六年。

Fong, H. D.: *Industrial Capital in China*, Nankai Institute of Economics, Industry series bulletin no. 9, Tientsin, 1936.

吴景超:《中国工业化的途径》,艺文丛书之五,商务,民二十七年。

龚骏:《中国新工业发展史大纲》,商务,民二十二年。

吴承洛:《今世中国实业通志》,商务,民十八年。

杨大金:《中国实业志》,商务,民二十七年。

方显廷著,有泽广已译:《支那工业论》,东亚,昭和十一年。

刘百川编:《国防与军需工业》,上海汗血书店,民二十五年。

胡博渊等:《中国工业自给计划》,中华,民二十四年。

李雪纯等:《民族工业的前途》,中华,民二十四年。

《东三省物产资源与化学工业》,日本工业化学会满洲支部编,沈学沅译,商务,民二十五年。

《上海之工业》,上海特别市社会局编,民十九年。

《上海之机制工业》,上海市社会局编,中华,民二十二年。

《矿业纪要》,地质调查所。

Ting, Leonard G.: "The Coal Industry in China", Nankai Instituto of Economics, Industry series bulletin No. 11, Tientsin, 1937.

方显廷:《中国之棉纺织业》,商务,民二十三年。

王子建、王镇中:《七省华商纱厂调查报告》,中央研究院社会科学研究所丛刊,民二十四年。

吴知:《乡村织布工业的一个研究》,南开大学经济研究所专刊,商务,民二十五年。

曾同春:《中国丝业》,商务,民二十二年。

沈文纬:《中国蚕丝业与社会化经营》,生活书店,民二十六年。

方显廷:《天津地毯工业》,天津,民十九年。

朱美予:《中国茶业》,中华,民二十六年。

吴觉农、范和钧著:《中国茶业问题》,商务,民二十六年。

李昌隆:《中国桐油贸易概论》,商务,民二十三年。

吴承禧:《中国的银行》,中央研究院社会研究所丛刊,商务,民二十三年。

陈达:《中国人口问题》,商务,民二十三年。

沙为楷:《中国买办制》,商务,民十九年。

丘汉平撰述、庄祖同助编:《华侨问题》,商务,民二十五年。

《新经济半月刊》,民二十七年十一月一日创刊。

《经济动员》(半月刊),民二十七年六月十五日创刊。

第二编
中国工业化与乡村工业

中国之乡村工业

方显廷 吴 知

（一）乡村工业与乡村实业——（二）乡村工业在国家经济中所占之地位——（三）中国乡村工业之衰落——（四）中国乡村工业之现在情形——（五）河北省之乡村工业——（六）中国乡村工业与中国建设

(一) 乡村工业与乡村实业

实业者,其意义与人类之经济活动相埒,即满足人类物质的或非物质的欲望之努力也。其类别凡三:曰初级实业,次级实业,及自由职业。初级实业或为采取,如渔,猎,牧畜,伐木,采矿;或为种植,如耕稼,如养鱼。次级实业则或为制造及建筑,如纺织,炼钢,工程,营造,修路;或为商业,如交通,贩卖,堆栈,银行,保险等。至自由职业则包括医药,教育,保护,传教,管理,娱乐等。[①]

乡村实业者,泛言之即乡村之各式实业,而以农业为主。至乡村之定义,各国因人数而异。如英国为千人或千人以下,始谓为一乡村;德国及法国则为二千人或二千人以下;而美国之乡村则为二千五百人或二千五百人以下。如此乡村人口占英威全人口之百分之二〇.七(一九二一),在德国则占百分之三五.六(一九二五),在美国则占百分之四八.六(一九二〇),在法国则占百分之五三.

[①] Bogart Ernest L. and London, Charles E.: *Modern Industry*. New York, Longmans, 1927, p. 214.

六(一九二一)。① 惟以人数为乡村之定义,因工业化程度之不同,适压于甲国者每不适用于乙国。如日本在二千人或二千人以下之区域内之人口,不过全国人口之百分之六.五。② 若以德国或法国所规定之乡村人口衡之,日本之工业化或城市化之程度虽不如德法二国,而其乡村人口反占较小之成数。故在日本,规定以万人或万人以下之区域为乡村,如是则乡村人口占全国人口百分之六三.四。③ 印度之乡村,规定为人口五千人或五千人以下之区域,依一九二一年之统计,其乡村人口当全国人口百分之八九.八。④ 与日本相当人数之区域(占日本人口百分之四四.二)相比,约为二倍以上。

中国之人口调查极不完整,乡村人口之确定,因极困难。但其约晷之成数,或可于中国人口职业分配之分析中得之。依据刘大钧、陈重民二氏之估计,中国农民为 345,780,000 人,当全国人口 485,508,000(一九二六年中华邮政局之估计)中百分之七一,与立法院统计处一九三〇年之估计百分之七四.五者相合。⑤ 然与今日之已工业化或半工业化之国家如英威之百分之六.八(一九二一),比国之一九.一(一九二〇),美国之二六.三(一九二〇),德国之

---

① Birnie, A.: *Economic History of Europe* 1760—1930, London, Methuen, 1931, p. 278; *Statistical Abstract of the United States*, 1930. p. 46; Carr-Saunders. A. M. and Jones, D. C: *A Survey of the Social Structure of England and Wales*, 1927, p. 36.
② 内阁统计局编:《日本帝国统计摘要》第四十四回,东京,1930 年,7 页。
③ 东京政治研究所编:《1920—1930 政治经济年鉴》,东京日本评论社出版,1931 年,261 页。
④ Narain, Brij: *Indian Economic Life*, Lahore, 1929, p. 343.
⑤ 《历代田亩统计》,《经济半月刊》,一卷四期及二卷一期,民一六,一二及民一七,一: Nankal Weekly Statistical Service, March 16, 1931; April 22, 1932;国民政府主计处统计局编:《统计月报》,民国二十一年一二月号合刊。

三〇.五(一九二五),法国之三八.三(一九二六),日本之五三.一(一九二〇),意大利之五六.一,相去远甚。与印度之七二.三(一九二一),则极相近;而较苏俄之八六.七(一九二六)者为低也。①

第一表　主要国家农民及乡村人口占全国人口百分数表

国别	乡村人口占全国人口之百分数	农民占全国人口之百分数
英	20.7(1921)	6.8(1921)
德	35.6(1925)	30.5(1925)
美	48.6(1920)	26.3(1920)
法	53.6(1921)	38.3(1926)
日	63.4(1925)	53.1(1920)
印	89.8(1921)	72.3(1921)
中		74.5(1930)
俄		86.7(1926)

注:包括英格兰及威尔斯。

乡村实业中自以农业为主要,在上述诸国中乡村人民之业农者为十四分之一至六分之五。但国家愈工业化,则其乡村人民之从事于农业者之成数愈少。如英国为世界工业化程度最高之国家,乡村人口占全人口之百分之二〇.七,而农民仅占百分之六.八。印度为工业落后之国家,乡村人口占全人口之百分八九.八,而农民则占百分之七二.三。

除农业而外,其他乡村实业尚属极多,惟官厅机关尚无乡村实业分类统计之编制,于说明各种乡村实业之相对的重要时,尚感困

---

① League of Nations, *Statistical Yearbook*, 1931-32, pp. 44-45;《日本帝国统计摘要》,10—11 页。

难。吾人于此,惟有采取乡村实业之较狭的意义,仅就乡村中之制造业或工业而研究之。此乡村之制造工业,可依其存在之主要原素如原料,市场及劳工之供给,为之分类。以当地原料为工业存在之主因者为陶业,如造砖制瓦;为食品业,如酿酒,榨油,磨粉;为木器业,如农具;为编织业,如以稻秆,柳条,荆,桑所编之筐篮等什物;为纺织业,如棉,毛及丝之纺织是也。是当地市场,为存在之主因者有修理及制造之工匠,如造车匠,木匠,泥瓦匠,铁匠,成衣匠等。以当地劳工之供给为其存在之主因者,则有手织,针织及花边等工业。①

乡村制造工业更可依雇工之久暂为准则,而分为整工及零工。此种分类,尤为重要,盖有季节性之农业,农民当农忙终了时,率与家庭从事于乡村之制造工业也。

中国农业季节之变化,金陵大学卜凯教授(J. L. Buck)研究綦详。卜氏就安徽,直隶(今河北),河南,山西,江苏,福建中之九县调查研究之结果,发现七种主要农作物如米,小麦,高粱,玉蜀黍,小米,大豆,棉花之百分之八三.七之全年工作,成于五月至十月六个月中。自十一月至四月六个月中,不过为全年工作中百分之一六.三。其月际变化亦巨。如棉花最忙之月为八月,一月中成全年工作之百分之三七.三;玉蜀黍为七月,成全年工作之百分之三五.〇;大豆为九月,成百分之三一.三;小麦为六月,成百分之二九.二;米为六月,成百分之二八.一;小米为十月,成百分之二六.三;高粱为五月,成百分之一六.七。而此九县中所有之农产物,其工

---

① Woods. K. S.:*The Rural Industries Round Oxford*, Clarendon Press, Oxford, 1921, Chap. I.

作集于五月至十月中者为百分之八五,其余百分之一五,则分散于十一月至四月中。有数县之中,各种谷物之大部工作往往麇集于最忙之一月,如江苏江宁有百分之三一.四(六月),山西五台有百分之三〇.五(十月),河南新郑有百分之二九.四(六月),江苏武进百分之二七.五(十月),安徽怀远百分之二五.三(六月),直隶平乡百分之二〇.〇(八月),安徽宿县百分之一九.七,直隶盐山百分之一九.五(八月),福建连江百分之一六.八(六月)。①

第二表 华北及华东六省九县中种植七种主要谷物之农田数,1922—1924

县别	米	小麦	高粱	小米	玉蜀黍	大豆	棉花
安徽							
怀远	124	124	124	124		124	124
宿县		286	286	286		286	286
直隶							
平乡		152	152	152		152	
盐山		133	133	133	133		
河南							
新郑		144	144	144	144	144	
山西							
五台		226	226	226			
福建							
连江	161						
江苏							
江宁	217	217			217	217	217
武进	300	300				300	
总计	802	1,582	1,065	1,065	494	1,223	627

① Buck, J. Lossing: *Chinese Farm Economy*. Shanghai, Commercial Press, 1930, pp. 238-244.

吾人试查每年中国农民实际工作时间数量之小,则中国农业之季节性更昭然若揭。据卜凯氏在华北及华东之农场经济研究:"华北及华东各县农家每年所成之人工单位(即每一工人在一日十小时内所能成就之工作量)最小之农田为112工,最大者则为519工,其平均之中数为190工。如以每家农田平均雇工二人计,每人每年所成之工作仅八十五工。设每年中只此少量之生产工作,则农人或其家庭闲暇时间之长,当不言而喻。即有因其他工可作及坏天气与放假日而休工者,此种休工时间之总和,决不能提高全年四分之一之实际工作量至任何程度也。"①

(二) 乡村工业在国家经济中所占之地位

工业革命前,制造业率生息于乡村。厥后工厂制度兴起,制造业乃自乡村移至城市,若英德法美,皆其明证。一八四四年顾戴洛氏(Cooke-Taylor)之言曰:"英国之各种工业,惟而至欧美之各种工业,采用工厂之组织者日多,其趋势若风之向,若潮之流,人类之戒备及立法鲜能统驭之,故制法者之态度,应助此制度之完成,而不应阻得其进展。"②此语极为赅覈,征之欧西各国之情形,亦诚无误。然一察工业革命后社会及经济之变迁,则容有问题。此项问题极邀经济学及政治家之注意,而工厂制度之创始者及应用者固熟视无睹也。早在一八九八年克鲁泡特金氏(Prince Kropetkin)在其《田园工场及手工场》一书中,即有工业分化之拟议,其言曰:

---

① Buck, J. Lossing: *Chinese Farm Economy*. Shanghai, Commercial Press, 1930, p. 231.
② 引自方显廷著之 *Triumph of Factory System in England*,天津南开大学经济学院,1930年,22页。

"将来，你们可以住在你们喜欢的地方，每日在新鲜空气中种些田，门口可以设个小工厂，清洁而卫生的小工厂，随便作些你们所喜欢的工。至于那些大工厂呢？应该设在'自然'指定的地方，如铁矿，造船等，自然不是随便可以设立的；而到处设立的，是可以满足文明人的趣味的无数种类的手工场。这种手工场并不和现在的大工厂一样，小孩子在工业的地狱空气中失了人形；而是很通风的，很卫生的，很经济的工厂。在这种工厂中，人类的生命较之机械与剩余利润贵重得多。在这种工厂中的男女与小孩并不是饥寒所迫而来劳动的，是因为与他们趣味相合而来活动的。在这里有发动机与机器的帮助，他们便将要选择一个与他们的个性最相宜的部门而从事活动。"[1]又曰："各个国家——她自己兼有农业者和工业者；各个人从事耕作，也事工艺；各个人有科学的知识，也有手工的知识——这才是我们所说的文明国家的倾向。"[2]此语诚然，并已有多数事实之证明。法德俄英各国之"大工业中心附近所兴起各种小工业为数极多"，即是其例。且电气事业，一日千里，今已推至乡村，则克氏之建议，当更有新发展矣。

迩者过分工业化之国家，如英国，为乡村之开发并垦殖问题，乡村工业已大受注意。一九一九至一九二〇年间，牛津农业经济研究会秉垦殖委员会之意旨，开始调查牛津附近乡村工业之状况；但此次不过为试验之性质，以测有无彻底研究之可能。后三年（一九二〇—二三）垦殖委员会及农业部约定将此调查推广，及于英格兰及威尔士之全部主要乡村工业。其调查完成报告之引言，极宜重视，其言曰："当审量乡村发展时，乡村工业之地位及职务在乡村生活中，实不容

---

[1] 克鲁泡特金著，汉南译：《田园工厂及手工场》，上海，民一八，三八九页。
[2] 同上书，七页。

漠视。在乡村自足时代其重要固极明显,即在今日亦有绝大贡献,如充实乡村居民之生活,阻遏人民自乡间向城市之流动,并解决现代工业化之各种问题是。故对调查其现在情形之需要,亦日益明显,以测视因社会经济情形之变迁,而乡村工业被淘汰之原因,及发展乡村工业使之适应并服役于同样情形之可能。矧乡村工业为农工及小田主之副业,予乡村人民以在家作工之机会,且供给农业以应用之物品。故乡村工业者,实纯真之乡村社会中农业之良辅。丁兹经济原理及制度之革命中,乡村工业之人事的利益,直可与城市中大规模之生产之利益相衡而有余。且较小之工业单位能使工人明了其制造品由制造至使用过程中之关系,使一人之工作,不但与其个人之生命有关,同时与其所处之社会,亦有关系。"①

其他各国对于小规模乡村工业之组织及发展,亦正在探讨之中。如瑞士于一九二四年十二月二日瑞士联邦议会开会时,设特别委员会以研究瑞士山区居民减少之原因,及促进其经济情形以为救济之方策。此委员会所研究之第一救济策,即为鼓励小规模工业,以为辅佐或季节之职业,但以不损农业所需之劳工,而为此辈劳工各置副业为指归。更组织委员分会以研究达此目的之最适当之方法。此委员会亦已于一九二六年七月开始工作,对北欧各国如瑞典,挪威,丹麦,芬兰等国之小规模乡村工业,加以特别之注意矣。②

---

① *The Rural Industries of England and Wales*: II, by Helen E. Fitzrandolph and M. Doriel Hay, Clarendon Press, Oxford, see Preface by C. S. Orwin of the Agricultural Economics Research Institute, 1926.

② Laur, E. Die baeuerliche heimarbeit in den nordischen Staaten Europas, Berne, 1928. 此报告之摘要见于"北欧及瑞士小规模之乡村工业"一文中,*International Labor Review*, May 1929, pp. 704-708.

印度之乡村人口占全人口之百分之八九.八,而农民为百分之七二.三,前已言之。且据报告,印度之农人每年之闲暇时间,最少为两月至四月,故对可为农余副业之乡村工业,似为非常需要。然一九二八年印度皇家农业委员会(Royal Commission on Agriculture of India)之报告结论,洵令人惊异。其言曰:"虽有新观念之协助,训练与推销之辅佐,乡村工业之于解决人口过剩问题之贡献,仍极渺小,而他项有组织之工业之竞争,日甚一日,乡村工业欲与匹敌,亦属至难。吾人常恐时人对发展乡村工业之重要,过于重视;苟假以严密考虑,亦即知发展乡村工业之可能性,实极为有限也。"此种观点,不无可议;盖此委员会对"农民问题之主要解决方法,为集约耕种或分散耕种"(Intensification and diversification of agriculture)之议,持之过烈,对"有组织之工业之渐剧之竞争",又过分信之也。① 唯吾人所不应忽视者,为此委员会所陈述之"印度手织业在国家经济中,仍占极冲要之地位,且至今日,仍可与工厂之出品分庭抗礼"之语是也。②

(三) 中国乡村工业之衰落

虽欧西各国多方致力以求乡村工业之复兴,③但因工业革命之进展,乡村工业竟日渐消灭。"需要既集中于大工商业之中心,以手艺制度下之小规模生产以应供给,殊不经济。大工业如工程及造船等,为技术及经济之原因,固为促进手艺工业消灭之重要因

---

① *Report of the Royal Commission on Agriculture in India*, 1928, Cmd. 3132, pp. 566,575.
② 同上书,第569,576页。
③ 为简便起见,本文用"乡村工业"以代"乡村制造工业"。

素。出品之统一化(实为近世制造业如机械业之先决条件),亦只能在大规模之工厂生产下有之。即消费者对现成品及必需品需要上之增加,亦有以促进工厂制度之采用。"① 此虽为对英国百年前工业情形之结论,未足适用于仍为中世纪国家之中国,但中国乡村工业因欧西通商各国现代工业化之影响而逐渐减少,实亦不可讳言。取中国之棉纺,缫丝,制茶三种基本乡村工业稍加检讨,便可了然,而无须另寻其他证据。外国棉纱进口之增长,显示国内手工棉纺业之衰落。当一八二一年英国首先输入机制纱时,进口额不过五千镑,合三十八担,至一八六七年猛涨至三三,五〇七担。② 自此以后,年有增涨,直至一八九〇年中国国内纺纱厂兴起,其势稍杀。但一八六七年之三三,五〇七担之进口,已为一八二一年之九百倍。一八六九年为一三一,五二五担,一八八七年为五九三,七二八担,一八九九年之二,七四八,六四四担,则为历年来进口之最高峰,已当一八六七年之进口额八十二倍有余矣。一八九九年以后,纱遂始见缩减,至一九三一年,已为七四,五六五担。但此种棉口量之缩减,非因手纺业之复兴,实为国内新式纱厂勃兴之结果。中国纱厂之棉纺锤,一八九〇年初设时,凡一一四,七一二锭,至一九三〇年暴进至四,二二三,九五六锭,增四十倍有奇。在国外机纺纱及国内机纺纱之竞争下,手纺纱已受淘汰。在昔势力几占满乡村之手纺业,亦寂焉无闻。吾人愿引一八三三年英国民众对纱厂兴起之呼吁,以作比观,其言曰:"纺论竿及棉纺锤竟在何处?……

---

① 方显廷著之 *Triumph of Factory System in England*,10 页。
② 方显廷著之 *Cotton Industry and Trade in China*,天津南开大学经济学院,1932,卷一,245 页。

妇人儿童昔日皆能在'家庭'度其舒适独立之生活,今也彼辈之雇佣安在?——皆为机器所兼并而为'贱'的呼声所牺牲。"①

第五表　中国棉纱及棉线之净进口(1867—1932)

(以1913为基年＝100)

年	棉纱及棉线		年	棉纱及棉线	
	担数	指数		担数	指数
1867	33,507	1.24	1886	384,582	14.23
1868	54,212	2.01	1887	593,728	21.97
1869	131,525	4.87	1888	684,959	25.34
1870	52,083	1.93	1889	679,728	25.15
1871	69,816	2.58	1890	1,083,405	40.08
1872	49,809	1.84	1891	1,212,921	44.88
1873	67,833	2.51	1892	1,305,572	48.30
1874	68,819	2.55	1893	983,399	36.38
1875	91,403	3.38	1894	1,161,694	42.98
1876	112,908	4.18	1895	1,134,110	41.96
1877	116,163	4.30	1896	1,624,806	60.11
1878	108,360	4.01	1897	1,573,116	58.20
1879	137,889	5.10	1898	1,962,537	72.61
1880	151,519	5.61	1899	2,748,644	101.69
1881	172,482	6.38	1900	1,490,732	55.15
1882	184,940	6.84	1901	2,276,309	84.22
1883	228,006	8.44	1902	2,452,864	90.75
1884	261,458	9.67	1903	2,744,974	101.56
1885	387,820	14.35	1904	2,289,842	84.72

① 引自 Burrows' article on "Machinery", In The Advocate, or Artizans' and Laborers' Friend, 1833, No. 7, p. 55.

（续表）

年	棉纱及棉线		年	棉纱及棉线	
	担数	指数		担数	指数
1905	2,569,644	95.07	1919	1,432,553	53.00
1906	2,551,027	94.28	1920	1,345,101	49.77
1907	2,281,657	84.42	1921	1,296,640	47.97
1908	1,831,624	67.77	1922	1,242,038	45.95
1909	2,419,404	89.51	1923	787,649	29.14
1910	2,298,012	85.02	1924	587,058	21.72
1911	1,877,166	69.45	1925	656,132	24.27
1912	2,312,528	85.56	1926	460,230	17.03
1913	2,702,851	100.00	1927	304,272	11.26
1914	2,559,443	94.69	1928	294,125	10.88
1915	2,700,592	99.92	1929	241,819	8.95
1916	2,486,004	91.98	1930	169,620	6.28
1917	2,102,335	77.78	1931	74,565	2.76
1918	1,152,881	42.65	1932	102,806	3.80

第六表 中国之棉纺锤及力织机数（1890—1930）

（以 1913 为基年 = 100）

年	棉纺锤		棉织机	
	数目	指数	数目	指数
1890	114,712	11.67	1,612	17.17
1891	204,712	20.83	1,612	17.17
1892	204,712	20.83	1,612	17.17
1893	204,712	20.83	1,612	17.17
1894	204,712	20.83	2,267	24.15
1895	316,488	32.20	3,827	40.76
1896	519,908	52.90	7,655	81.53
1897	546,036	55.56	8,155	86.86
1898	546,036	55.56	8,155	86.86
1899	637,976	64.91	8,875	94.53

(续表)

年	棉纺锤		棉织机	
	数目	指数	数目	指数
1900	637,976	64.91	8,875	94.53
1901	637,976	64.91	8,875	94.53
1902	637,976	64.91	8,875	94.53
1903	637,976	64.91	8,875	94.53
1904	637,976	64.91	8,875	94.53
1905	706,056	71.84	8,875	94.53
1906	729,256	74.20	8,875	94.53
1907	843,380	85.81	9,389	100.00
1908	869,972	88.52	9,389	100.00
1909	898,972	91.47	9,389	100.00
1910	922,012	93.81	9,389	100.00
1911	922,012	93.81	9,389	100.00
1912	922,012	93.81	9,389	100.00
1913	982,812	100.00	9,389	100.00
1914	1,148,332	116.84	10,079	107.35
1915	1,148,332	116.84	10,079	107.35
1916	1,278,028	130.04	11,429	121.73
1917	1,388,396	141.27	11,511	122.60
1918	1,602,668	163.07	14,231	151.57
1919	1,781,972	181.31	15,741	167.65
1920	2,052,624	208.85	16,993	180.99
1921	2,805,748	285.48	20,662	220.07
1922	3,483,434	354.44	23,672	252.12
1923	3,749,288	381.49	25,818	274.98
1924	3,912,124	398.05	29,232	311.34
1925	4,046,100	411.69	29,272	311.77
1926	4,066,580	413.77	29,272	311.77
1927	4,076,626	414.79	29,272	311.77
1928	4,115,316	418.73	29,272	311.77
1929	4,132,756	420.50	29,272	311.77
1930	4,223,956	429.78	29,272	311.77

手工缫丝业之低落，非若手工棉纺业之显著。一八九五年海关对厂丝之出口始有统计时，手缫黄白丝之出口量为六七，六二二担，占生丝之全出口量之百分之七一.四。嗣后厂丝出口之百分比数逐年加增，一九〇〇年为百分之四五.一；一九一〇年为百分之五八.一；一九二〇年为百分之六七.九；一九三〇年增至百分之八三.一；一九三一年为历年之最高峰，达百分之八六.一。厂丝出口成数之增加之由百分之二八.六（一八九五）至百分之八六.一（一九三一），正所以显示手缫丝成数之低落由百分之七一.四（一八九五）至百分之一三.九（一九三一）。三十七年间竟减五分之四，宁不惊人！

中国制茶业亦为极普遍之乡村工业，但近年来之发展，与棉纺及缫丝二者，同其命运。请再以出口之数字，为其降落之指数。一八八六年为自一八六六至一九三二年出口最多之一年，故可以此年为起点，而测视其降落之情形。一八八六年茶之出口总额凡二，二一七，二九五担，一八九〇年缩至一，六六五，三九六担，当一八八六年之百分之七五.一，而一九〇〇年又减至一，三八四，三二四担，当一八八六年之百分之六二.四。拳匪乱后一年（一九〇一），出口更为缩减，为一，一五七，九九三担；翌年稍呈兴旺，略增至一，五一九，二一一担。此后十三年中，变动较少，至一九一五年而达一，七八二，三五三担，为近三十年来出口最多之数字。自兹以后，出口暴跌，一九二〇年出口为三〇五，九〇六担，为自一八六六至一九三二年间之最低额。一九二〇年以后，逐渐增长，一九二九年而达九四七，七三〇担，自是后又趋减缩，至一九三二年茶之出口为六五三，五五六担，仅当一八八六年之百分之二九.五。

第七表　中国之生丝出口（1895—1932）

年	白丝及黄丝				白丝,黄丝及灰丝			
	厂丝		总额		厂丝		总额	
	担数	百分数	担数	百分数	担数	百分数	担数	百分数
1895	27,056	28.6	94,678	100.0				
1896	27,041	37.5	72,036	100.0				
1897	41,485	42.5	97,564	100.0				
1898	41,050	44.5	92,333	100.0				
1899	49,434	40.1	123,424	100.0				
1900	35,277	45.1	78,267	100.0				
1901	49,937	45.9	108,696	100.0				
1902	50,557	50.3	100,519	100.0				
1903	43,979	60.5	72,695	100.0				
1904	47,287	51.5	91,885	100.0				
1905	45,347	56.4	80,335	100.0				
1906	45,821	54.0	84,931	100.0				
1907	50,296	54.5	92,317	100.0				
1908	49,206	51.8	94,942	100.0				
1909	51,674	54.0	95,773	100.0				
1910	63,969	58.1	110,184	100.0				
1911	55,416	57.7	96,094	100.0				
1912	59,157	48.5	121,877	100.0	74,019	46.8	158,038	100.0
1913	69,541	58.3	119,344	100.0	70,150	47.1	149,006	100.0
1914	56,766	64.9	87,517	100.0	56,860	52.4	108,589	100.0
1915	63,139	57.9	109,093	100.0	87,364	61.1	143,097	100.0
1916	68,286	65.9	103,561	100.0	81,451	66.6	122,243	100.0
1917	73,103	67.9	107,584	100.0	87,413	69.5	125,820	100.0
1918	64,187	66.6	96,366	100.0	87,514	70.0	124,954	100.0
1919	90,038	68.5	131,506	100.0	118,028	71.5	165,187	100.0
1920	56,043	67.9	82,530	100.0	72,917	69.9	104,315	100.0
1921	87,484	76.8	113,980	100.0	118,895	78.7	151,064	100.0
1922	89,248	74.5	119,737	100.0	110,040	76.7	143,478	100.0
1923	77,470	72.2	107,227	100.0	106,827	77.2	138,423	100.0
1924	81,047	75.2	107,766	100.0	101,112	77.6	130,338	100.0
1925	103,290	78.4	131,802	100.0	136,324	81.9	166,416	100.0

（续表）

年	白丝及黄丝				白丝,黄丝及灰丝			
	厂丝		总额		厂丝		总额	
	担数	百分数	担数	百分数	担数	百分数	担数	百分数
1926	107,279	79.2	135,536	100.0	137,493	82.5	166,632	100.0
1927	101,889	76.8	132,656	100.0	126,582	80.3	157,589	100.0
1928	123,170	83.4	147,667	100.0	151,343	86.0	176,039	100.0
1929	123,045	81.7	150,515	100.0	152,360	84.6	180,034	100.0
1930	100,242	83.1	120,664	100.0	126,173	85.9	146,862	100.0
1931	86,736	86.1	100,793	100.0	118,886	89.4	133,047	100.0
1932	45,896	70.4	65,195	100.0	57,334	74.8	76,670	100.0

第八表　中国茶之出口（1866—1938）

（1866 = 100）

年	担数	指数	年	担数	指数
1866	1,192,138	53.8	1883	1,987,324	89.6
1867	1,330,974	60.0	1884	2,016,218	90.9
1868	1,475,210	66.5	1885	2,128,751	96.0
1869	1,528,149	68.9	1886	2,217,295	100.0
1870	1,380,998	62.3	1887	2,153,037	97.1
1871	1,679,643	75.8	1888	2,167,552	97.8
1872	1,774,663	80.0	1889	1,877,331	84.7
1873	1,617,763	73.0	1890	1,665,396	75.1
1874	1,735,379	78.3	1891	1,750,034	78.9
1875	1,818,387	82.0	1892	1,622,681	73.2
1876	1,762,887	79.5	1893	1,820,831	82.1
1877	1,909,700	86.1	1894	1,862,312	84.0
1878	1,898,956	85.6	1895	1,865,680	84.1
1879	1,987,463	89.6	1896	1,712,841	77.2
1880	2,097,118	94.6	1897	1,532,158	69.1
1881	2,137,472	96.4	1898	1,538,600	69.4
1882	2,017,151	91.0	1899	1,630,795	73.5

(续表)

年	担数	指数	年	担数	指数
1900	1,384,324	62.4	1917	1,125,535	50.8
1901	1,157,993	52.2	1918	404,217	18.2
1902	1,519,211	68.5	1919	690,155	31.1
1903	1,677,530	75.7	1920	305,906	13.8
1904	1,451,249	65.5	1921	430,328	19.4
1905	1,369,298	61.8	1922	576,073	26.0
1906	1,404,128	63.3	1923	801,417	36.1
1907	1,610,125	72.6	1924	765,935	34.5
1908	1,576,136	71.1	1925	833,008	37.6
1909	1,498,443	67.6	1926	839,317	37.9
1910	1,560,800	70.4	1927	872,176	39.3
1911	1,462,803	66.0	1928	926,022	41.8
1912	1,481,700	66.8	1929	947,730	42.7
1913	1,442,109	65.0	1930	694,048	31.3
1914	1,495,799	67.5	1931	703,206	31.7
1915	1,782,353	80.4	1932	653,556	29.5
1916	1,542,633	69.6			

除此三种基本乡村之工业外，其他乡村工业，近年来亦有衰落之象。如纸类进口，虽因少数新需要如新闻纸等之增加而激增，显示国内制纸业之式微。一九〇三年时，中国纸类进口不过二一七，七二六担，此后日益增多，一九一〇年为五四九，〇三〇担，一九二〇年为一，〇二六，五一一担，一九三〇年为一，九九二，〇九三担，一九三二年而至最高峰二，〇七五，二八三担，较一九〇三年凡高十倍。面粉业亦然。磨粉业本为乡村工业，自国外面粉及国内粉厂竞争以来，遂日益衰颓。一八八七年以后，外国面粉进口，亦年有增加。一八八七年面粉进口合关银五六四，二一四两，一八九〇年即增至七七五，五四八关两，一九〇〇年又增至三，三二九，八六

八关两,一九一○年三,四四四,四○七关两,一九二○年稍低,为二,三三○,二一五关两,但一九三○年暴增至三一,九二六,二二○关两,一九三二年为三六,一七六,一二七关两,较一八八七年增加六十四倍。纸类与面粉二种乡村工业,皆不但须与外货竞争,且须与国内产品竞争,以面粉为尤甚。尚有用菜子及其他种子榨油以充家庭中燃料之事业,亦因外国煤油之输入,而受排挤。一八八六年,煤油进口不过二三,○三八,一○一加伦,后每年续有增长,一八九○年为三○,八二八,七二四加伦,一九○○年为八三,五八○,○二四加伦,一九一○年为一六三,五二六,八八○加伦,一九二○年为一八九,五八八,五四○加伦,是在三十五年间,已较一八八六年增八倍以上。一九二○年以后进口稍现衰微,一九三○年为一八五,六○八,五九六加伦,一九三一年为一七一,一四○,三八○加伦,一九三二年则又减至一四五,九一八,七九四加伦。

第九表　中国纸类面粉及煤油之进口(1867—1932)

年	纸类		面粉		煤油	
	担+	海关两	担	海关两	加伦	海关两
1870						140,080
1880				564,214*		413,612
1890				775,548	30,828,724	4,092,874
1900	217,726**	2,584,437**		3,329,868	83,580,024	13,955,582
1910	549,030	5,486,764	740,841	3,444,407	163,526,880	22,358,946
1920	1,026,511	14,159,186	511,021	2,330,215	189,588,540	54,318,290
1930	1,992,093	37,384,275	5,413,353	31,926,220	185,608,596	54,864,546
1931	2,042,339	45,404,637	5,204,788	30,920,302	171,140,830	64,549,371
1932	2,075,283	34,445,353	6,705,837	36,176,127	145,918,794	60,439,975

*1887
**1903
+不包括只有价值而无数量之小量纸类。

第十表　中国主要乡村工业产品之出口（1927—1932）

	1932	1931	1930	1929	1928	1927
绸缎及茧绸	18,478,940	24,412,445	19,564,158	21,032,898	23,903,778	25,170,934
绸缎	12,235,992	11,357,734	11,442,517	13,147,808	16,979,891	18,115,194
茧绸	6,242,948	13,054,711	8,121,641	7,885,090	7,223,887	7,055,740
河南茧绸	1,479,913	4,870,880	2,973,080	1,912,712	3,301,882	3,533,640
山东茧绸	3,754,754	6,375,829	3,790,891	4,314,290	2,900,373	3,231,528
其他茧绸	1,008,281	1,808,002	1,357,670	1,658,088	1,021,632	290,572
土布	1,259,938	3,621,703	2,677,644	2,742,758	2,816,626	2,507,510
夏布	1,102,477	4,943,925	2,391,262	4,232,100	5,794,844	5,354,744
粗夏布	209,523	724,097	264,932	492,048	527,052	445,204
细夏布	892,954	4,219,828	2,126,330	3,740,052	5,267,792	4,909,540
绣货	6,146,802	9,012,691	4,122,013	3,457,482	2,402,286	1,815,850
棉麻绣货	3,114,636	3,757,728	—	—	—	—
丝绣货	3,032,166	5,254,963	4,122,013	3,457,482	2,402,286	1,815,850
镂空花边及花边	2,208,124	3,540,265	3,196,062	2,705,697	3,132,355	4,694,127
抽纱品	5,162,114	4,864,388	3,740,194	2,562,880	2,169,333	1,008,202
发网	1,359,902	995,634	1,313,052	1,315,345	1,021,341	1,277,448
草帽辫	2,581,302	1,504,740	1,538,923	2,151,805	2,748,398	2,612,092
花草帽辫	1,273,153	784,091	989,550	1,338,158	1,498,622	1,130,570

(续表)

	1932	1931	1930	1929	1928	1927
白草帽辫	1,308,149	720,649	549,373	813,647	1,249,776	1,481,522
草席及地席	2,291,209	7,248,649	4,907,016	3,871,831	3,680,877	3,754,697
清草席蒲草席	1,662,627	5,805,417	2,646,976	1,944,561	1,808,804	2,162,786
其他席	155,017	879,768	1,547,183	1,317,276	1,249,924	874,554
地席	473,565	563,464	712,857	609,994	622,149	717,357
酒	297,947	468,662	651,362	860,344	837,848	993,842
酒	169,945	246,473	295,257	297,173	249,188	250,952
药酒	128,002	222,189	356,105	563,171	588,760	742,890
粉丝,通心粉	2,253,278	3,138,652	3,974,630	4,225,124	4,313,378	5,378,633
纸	3,119,155	3,643,855	4,927,249	4,803,526	5,103,884	5,263,235
纸箔(锡箔)	970,666	1,518,949	2,393,132	2,423,987	2,237,423	2,182,679
其他纸	2,148,489	2,124,906	2,534,117	2,379,539	2,866,461	3,080,556
爆竹,烟火	1,411,785	2,091,883	3,159,166	3,887,614	3,364,967	3,198,921
桐油	14,866,003	20,416,102	30,546,872	23,519,702	23,302,221	21,970,947
十四种总计	62,538,976	89,903,594	86,709,603	81,369,106	84,592,136	85,001,182
减4,6,7三种	12,668,818	14,872,713	9,175,259	7,335,707	5,592,960	4,101,500
十一种总计	49,870,158	75,030,881	77,534,344	74,033,399	78,999,176	80,899,682
生丝(非厂丝)	7,199,162	6,518,901	11,024,720	15,742,714	14,666,213	17,985,859
茶	24,761,556	33,253,158	26,283,929	41,252,428	37,133,853	31,616,949
十三种总计	81,830,881	114,802,940	114,812,987	131,028,541	130,799,242	131,502,490

上述六种乡村工业,棉纺,缫丝,制茶,造纸,面粉,及榨油或有极锐之削减,或竟全然泯灭。同时外国之出产,乃在国内或国外取而代之。在国内棉纱,纸,面粉,及煤油四种进口,久已喧宾夺主;唯因西方工业化之熏陶,国内之棉纱业及面粉业之出品,尚能供国内大部之需要。至丝茶二者,一八九〇年时,尚当中国全出口之半。但年来因日本之产丝及印度,锡兰,荷属东印度群岛及日本之产茶,我国丝茶之国外市场,半为所夺,故今日丝茶之出口,只占我国全出口之八分之一矣(一九三二年占全出口百分之一二.四)。

除丝茶而外,近年来其他乡村工业产品之出口,亦皆有降低之趋势。如第十表所显示,自一九二七至一九三二年六年间中国十四种乡村工业主要产品之出口中,减低者竟有十一种之多,依一九三二年出口价值之相对重要而为排列,则为绸缎及茧绸,桐油,纸张(以锡箔为主),草帽辫,草席,粉丝及通心粉,镂空花边及花边,爆竹及焰火,土布,夏布,与酒是也。此十一种产品出口总值在一九二七年为八〇,八九九,六八二关两,一九三二年仅为四九,八七〇,一五八关两,减少凡百分之三八.四。至于刺绣品,抽纱品,及发网三种,一九二七年出口值为四,一〇一,五〇〇关两,而一九三二年则为一二,六六八,八一八关两,增加百分之三〇九。

(四) 中国乡村工业之现在情形

中国今日之乡村工业,当仍以手织棉,丝,苎麻,毛业为主。至于棉之手织较机织占优势者,在远东或世界各国中,中国为仅存之最重要国家。一九二五年日本之力织机凡二三八,九九九架,手织机凡一二六,三六〇架;一九二六年印度棉布之生产于力织机者为一,九五〇兆码,生产于手织机者为一,一六〇兆码。在中国,按所消费之纱数计算,力织机仅当手织机之四分之一。第十一表显示一九三〇年纱线总消费量九六一兆磅中,力织机所消费者不过二〇七兆磅,其余之七五四兆磅,则为手织机所消耗,约当总数之五分之四。①

手织业一部在城市,但大部皆在乡村,在后者则为副业。盖农忙以后,农民率从事于织布也。织布只为足一家之用,当属于家族工业之阶段;但农人除为自给之外,每有为贩卖而织造者,与工业革命前欧西各国情形相同,高阳县之农民即其例焉。请于讨论"河北省之乡村工业"时详述之。

第十一表　中国棉纱及棉线之统计(1913 及 1930)

（以磅为单位）

	1913		1930	
	数量	百分数	数量	百分数
国内出产	200,000,000	35.84	982,070,800	102.22
进口	358,000,000	64.16	22,616,000	2.35
减出口			43,987,064	4.57
总消费量	558,000,000	100.00	960,699,736	100.00
力织机用	15,000,000	2.69	206,913,532	21.54
手织机用	543,000,000	97.31	753,786,204	78.46

---

① 方显廷著之 *Cotton Industry and Trade in China*,卷一,230 页。

中国丝织业皆用手织机,且在华中,华东以及华北之河南,山东各省之乡村工业中,占极重要之地位。其程度可由中国生丝消费之统计测之。据大英百科全书之估计,一九二五年中国生丝之消费量为九,九二四,〇〇〇基罗格兰姆,约当世界产额之六分之一。① 而在此九,九二四,〇〇〇基罗格兰姆中,三一,二九五担或一,八三八,〇〇〇基罗格兰姆又以绸缎及茧绸之形式输出国外。如第十二表所显示,此三一,二九五担之输出,近年虽因人造丝之竞争而较为平稳然已较一八六七年之四,〇〇八担增八倍,一八八〇年之八,三九〇担增四倍,一八九二年之一五,八六八担增二倍矣。

第十二表　中国绸缎及茧绸之出口(1867—1932)

年	担数	海关两	年	担数	海关两
1867	4,008	2,172,370	1880	8,390	5,421,721
1868	3,568	1,947,258	1881	7,188	4,612,273
1869	3,383	1,695,259	1882	6,598	3,396,374
1870	3,791	1,896,294	1883	7,731	4,022,749
1871	4,490	2,352,781	1884	8,808	4,426,973
1872	5,302	2,607,052	1885	10,279	4,556,470
1873	5,149	2,203,342	1886	12,495	6,754,708
1874	5,778	2,374,854	1887	14,184	6,723,149
1875	6,468	4,022,538	1888	16,036	7,893,987
1876	5,889	3,986,038	1889	14,682	7,175,038
1877	6,460	4,432,121	1890	11,140	5,320,810
1878	7,440	4,507,047	1891	13,166	6,464,689
1879	6,920	4,498,992	1892	15,868	7,371,850

① 大英百科全书第十四版,卷二十,676 页。

(续表)

年	担数	海关两	年	担数	海关两
1893	17,135	8,253,087	1913	34,500	20,873,778
1894	19,081	8,415,549	1914	26,721	15,562,386
1895	23,122	11,330,697	1915	41,158	21,558,073
1896	20,850	9,723,313	1916	39,121	20,019,966
1897	20,401	10,094,747	1917	30,209	17,229,766
1898	19,319	10,044,578	1918	34,559	18,911,247
1899	18,088	9,892,525	1919	39,464	23,260,228
1900	18,297	9,028,051	1920	37,453	24,317,477
1901	20,695	10,226,778	1921	42,824	30,274,652
1902	20,628	9,651,708	1922	30,946	23,631,284
1903	20,207	13,784,910	1923	28,495	24,548,608
1904	21,567	11,763,368	1924	27,322	22,300,873
1905	15,727	9,938,750	1925	31,295	23,202,322
1906	15,497	9,753,854	1926	38,711	30,857,682
1907	20,496	12,926,152	1927	32,821	25,170,934
1908	22,824	13,727,341	1928	33,125	23,903,778
1909	28,406	17,891,709	1929	29,606	21,032,898
1910	29,996	17,998,679	1930	29,893	19,564,158
1911	28,073	17,050,871	1931	34,154	24,412,445
1912	28,539	16,106,787	1932	22,229	18,478,940

江苏吴江县之盛泽镇，为出丝绸最著之区，然其地并无丝厂及织丝工人。丝之供给，来自邻近，而以此为集散之中心。其制造作坊之规模极小，散于家皆织丝之邻近各村中。在盛泽无生丝之生产，皆为城中丝商由邻近各县运来，以供给农家之需要。织机由城中小进口商处购得，花样亦自城中之设计专家处购来。农人于购买生丝及售出成品间如有拮据，可向城中绸庄或领业请求通融现款。成品织成之后，即直接由绸庄或间接由领业售与当地之绸行。

称量则由绸行之团体即培元公所规定之,一切交易皆以此为准。①

夏布之织造,其重要远亚于棉布及丝绸二者。但在产苎麻之省分中,夏布亦为一极普遍之家庭工业。夏布与棉布及丝绸二者对国内外市场,皆有供给。如在一九二八年夏布出口最盛时,竟达二六,六二三担,值五,七九四,八四四关两。出产最著者为江西,广东,湖南,福建及四川五省;江苏出产亦丰,河北,广西,河南之出产则较少。各省中之夏布,大都由乡村幼女于农闲之时织造,江西省即其例。江西风俗,每届秋令,农家即教幼女以纺麻织布之术。幼女心细手巧,故有时可纺麻纱精密如六十支棉纱者。唯纺绩时多在地窖或阴室中,盖麻纱非常细脆,曝日中每有碎裂之虞。纺绩时期约在八月至十一月间,但因地势之潮湿,幼女鲜能竟日工作其中。夏布织成之后,则售与附近城市之商店。上海,汉口为中国夏布业之中心,每年自此出口运往朝鲜,香港,英属印度,新嘉坡,荷属东印度群岛,安南,缅甸者甚夥。②

除棉,丝,苎麻三种手织业外,其他之编织工业如轧棉,缫丝,纺毛,制绳,针织,花边,抽纱品,发网,草帽辫,缎带,毛巾,袋布,芦席等,在中国乡村工业中亦占有相当之地位。轧棉工业多盛行于初级棉花市场中,为作坊工业之一。农人产棉数量有限,每家置一轧棉机极不经济,故在乡村中有轧棉作坊,棉农去坊轧棉而付与工费。其他乡村工业如花边,抽纱品,绣花等,率为女工制作之家庭工业,今特略述于下:

---

① 《盛泽之绸业》,《经济半月刊》,二卷八期,民一七,四。
② 《中国夏布之产销概况》,《中外经济周刊》125号,民一四,八,一五;*Chinese Economic Bulletin*, Dec. 8, 1928。

手缫丝虽因厂丝之竞争而跌落,但用土法缫丝之区仍多。在嘉兴及其他江浙一带之产丝中心,丝商所贩卖者,皆为农家所缫之丝 大都用于国内之丝织厂。广东亦多用旧法缫丝,其丝不第粗细不等,色泽亦欠光彩,故多为织造绉纱及其他夏日服装之用,国外市场无所需也。①

针织业为近十余年来外货进口后始产生之。但今日在乡村工业中已占有相当地位。如浙江沪杭甬铁路线附近之平湖,嘉兴,石门及硖石等处,针织业皆极兴旺。平湖针织之组织,与其他各乡村相同,皆为商人雇主制度,散处工人自商人雇主处将纱领得后,必须同时租赁商人雇主所购置之针织机器。租赁时须交报名费二元及押款六元。押款于交回机器时退还,报名费则否。此后则工人每月交租金二元,自每月工资中扣除。此种制度,实与商人雇主以莫大利益,盖针织机之原价尚未逮二十五元,而其所收租金,每年已二十四元,至修理保存各项,所费极少。工人方面则多为妇人及幼女,此辈亦蒙此制度相当之利益。因此制未引用之先,贫家妇女除家务外无所谓生产副业,至幼女则并家务亦无之,与其每日消耗时间,不若稍事生产之为愈也。②

花边业与抽纱品及绣花业皆为出口工业,在上海(浦东),无锡,烟台,及汕头等地,极为隆盛。烟台之花边业,有包工者,一方由花边商处赊取纱线,一方将赊得纱线散给散处工人。工人多为乡村妇女,按包工人因时习之好尚而定之式样,在家工作。织成后

---

① 《广东丝业之调查》,《中外经济周刊》146号,民一五,一,一六;*Chinese Economic Journal*, July, 1926, p. 601.

② 《浙江平湖织机工业之状况》,《中外经济周刊》147号,民一五,一,二三。

则由包工人至工人处收取而卖与花边商,自货价中减除纱价及工资,即为包工人之利益。据最近之估计,烟台附近村庄妇女从事于织花边者,凡四万五千人。① 无锡亦为花边业之中心。此业首由某女校输入,其规定亦多不同之处。花边商(商人雇主)设计花样之后,将花样及应用之纱线,交与请求工作之幼女,同时予账本一,以记载纱线发出之数量及应织花边之数量。女童乃将纱线花样携家编织,并将账本保存。织成后仍交与花边商,商店将满意之花边留下,不满意者退还,并在账本上登记所收之数量。工资按码计算。商店收到成品时,即付工资,如织成一半或四分之一,亦可先交与商店而领此做成部分之工资,其余工资日后作成再领。最兴旺之季,无锡南门里一带因与工作幼女居处之接近,有花边商百五十家。一九二六年则缩至五十家。每家皆有代理人十人之谱,负收发之责。最大商店资本为一万元,小商店则为五百元至一千元。一九一七年,无锡花边业者已组织花边业同业公会,所以谋业务之进展而杜竞争也。②

草帽辫不特供国内之需要,且亦输出国外,为我国旧有之工业。山西农人从事于此者已有百年之历史。河北省有铁路以前,草帽辫业已极繁盛,而运诸云南,缅甸等处销售。欧洲之市场则起于二十世纪初叶,德人占青岛后始收集草帽辫以运输国外。此种工业以谷秆为原料,全国农村,皆有出产,而以华北为最。如河北省之南乐县,人民依草帽辫为生者较耕种者为多;山东出口商人有

---

① *Chinese Economic Bulletin*, June 16, 1928.
② 《无锡出口之花边及绣花品》,《中外经济周刊》176号,民一五,八,二一; *Chinese Economic Bulletin*, July 17, 1926.

代理人在此坐庄收买者,不下五十余人。其编制多由乡村妇女于闲暇时以麦秆或其他谷物之秆为之。编成后,束捆以至市场,每捆二十卷(每卷为一尺八寸至二尺三寸),按重量售与出口商或其代理人。①

　　编席业亦须有当地原料之供给,但此工业较有组织,如在出席著名之苏州浒墅关有席行之设立,以收集及分发蒲秆或芦苇并购买编成之席。芦苇之生产,多在车场一带,农人以此为专业,席行代表即与此辈农夫接洽购买。交易既成,乃雇工人将此种芦苇依其秆之长短及质之精粗而束之,每束约三斤,束成后即运至浒墅关之厝行,席行再售与编席者。至编席者皆以耕种为主业,而以编席为副业。且编席者无雇工或学徒之制,盖一家庭即一作坊,成人即工人,儿童即学徒也。故大家庭之中有时有编席机十具以上,小家庭亦有一二具。销售方法亦与花边绣货等不同,而由编席人直接售与席行。席行之数约二十散处于车站附近半英里以内之地,编席人每晨以船运席至此购买中心,各行于是开列席价,编席者如认为满意,则钱货两交。如编席人对价格不满,可携其席至各行推售。但各行皆言无二价,无争价之制。最大之行,每年可做生意三四万元,平均每行生意每年亦有一万五千元之谱,其资本则自五千元至二万元不等。最忙之季为四月,时各处贩席者来此与各行定购,以备夏日之售卖。五月交易数量亦大,但八月除自编席人收买编成之席以备来年四五月之贩卖外,其他交易绝少。席行对批发商招待极周,并供给食宿。各行因席质之精粗及供给之多寡而定

---

① 《草帽辫之产销及制造概况》,《中外经济周刊》50号,民一三,二,二三;《直隶青县之经济状况》,同上,220号,民一六,七,一六。

价格;价格虽不一定,但亦无争价之说。各行竞争较烈,对售价无合作,但有席行公会,由各行组织之,每年开常会二次。①

第二类之中国乡村工业为食品业,如舂米,磨面,粉丝及通心粉,酿酒,榨油,制茶,罐头等业是。米茶等业,多为售卖而制造;其他则半为市场,半为自用,兹择尤略述于下:

粉丝之制造,为乡村之家庭工业或作坊工业,但皆为农闲时农人之副业。粉丝之原料为豆粉,或为豆粉,高粱粉及麦粉之混合物。山东龙口每年之出口由七十至八十万包,每包皆六十斤,可见其重要。农民于农闲时制造,制成后捆以席包,以驴车运至龙口,售与粉丝商人。此辈商人除收买粉丝外,尚自大连进口大豆,以为制粉丝之用。农民每于售粉丝时,自商人处购大豆回乡,且有时与此辈商人定约预购者。然买卖皆根据信用,账目则每月一清。安徽宣城粉丝,则为作坊工业,为富农所经营,另雇五六工人为辅。作坊中重要工具为灶一,锅炉一,缸二及晒粉丝之木架一,规模大者,工具亦多。全县之粉丝作坊约三百,皆位于乡间。夏冬二季,因气候不宜,各作坊皆无工作。此外除阴天及孵蚕之时间外,各作坊极少停工。其成品则售与当地之批发商人,再由批发商人转售与邻近各县。河北大城县,与宣城情形相同,粉丝作坊亦多为暂时之经营,于秋季农忙以后,开始制造。粉之成分为青豆六成,红高粱四成。粉丝多供当地之用,有时亦运至天津及葛沽;糟粕则以饲猪。②

酿酒业与粉丝业同为家庭或作坊之工业。江苏泰兴县视为

---

① *Chinese Economic Bulletin*. Feb. 13,1926.
② 同上 Dec. 27,1924;Oct. 13,1928;*Chinese Economic Journal*,September,1928.

重要之家庭副业,几于家皆酿酒;但其目的,非在售酒而得利(每缸约赔四元至五元),实在利用酿酒所余之糟粕以饲猪。至举国知名之绍兴酒,则多为作坊工业,出浙江之绍兴县。酿酒者凡七百余家,每年出酒约五万缸,每缸十坛,昔者年约出三十万缸或三百万坛,每坛售价二元,总值六百万元。一九二六年出产约五万缸,每坛四元,约值二百万元。今日课税繁重,产量已远不如前矣。

安徽宣城农民,率用小麦,燕麦,高粱,稻米酿酒,以所得之三分之一装木桶运至附近城市销售。亦有用马铃薯及玉蜀黍酿酒者,其质较劣,多农民自供销费。①

制茶亦为乡村工业,昔日极为普遍,今日各乡村制造者仍多,然皆用旧法,不适出口。一九二七年浙江省之报告:"浙江之茶产多为绿茶,方法亦未改良,尤以西北部为然,故不易寻得国外之市场。"②中国茶业之惊人衰落,实株守成规之咎;至小规模之生产,则尤为不进步之主因。

砖茶多在集散之中心如张家口,汉口等处制造,为农工于农闲时至城市觅工之极有趣之例。砖茶工厂每年互有增减,但一九二四年张家口包头镇及归绥之处有砖茶工厂二十八处。"平常每厂雇二百人至四百人;特忙时,有多至千人者。故当工厂全力工作之时,对工人之需要极大,远地农民之来此以应工作者极多。"③此类情形亦可见之湖北。湖北砖茶销于蒙古,新疆一带,多为山西帮

---

① 《中国之酿酒业》,《中外经济周刊》162 号,民一五,五,一五; *Chinese Economic Bulletin*, Oct. 27, 1928; *Chinese Economic Bulletin*, Oct. 1926, pp. 439-441。

② *Chinese Economic Journal*, August, 1927, p. 752.

③ 同上。Nov., 1929, p. 938.

所制造。谓为口庄,盖销场在口外或长城以外也。其工厂及器具皆为临时性质,厂房租自房主,用具则贷自茶业经纪人。工作期间只数月,多在秋季起始。至砖茶制至预定数量时,便停止工作,退雇工人,并还场址及工具于所有人。厂房率多宽敞,公事房,制造室,打包间等应有尽有,最大者能容二千人。十年前房主及茶业经纪人,常为其租客之代理人,以购置茶叶。迩因商业之衰落,经纪人多停止营业,仅存者亦不再作代理人,仅为逆旅主人,经纪人云云,今已名存而实亡矣。①

其他之食品工业,尚有豆油,火腿及罐头等业。沿陇海铁路一带各乡村,旧式油坊极夥,规模较小,为农人所经营。所用原料,即农民所自种之豆。豆油出产,须赖豆之收成如何以为断,故欠收之年,此种油坊大都无事。② 鲜果保藏,亦为副业,如浙江之半山,泰山即其例。其地梅子出产,远过于当地需要,故农人或用甜露或用盐渍,以保藏之而出口。每年总产额约五万担,价值约四十万元,所保藏者则其一部。③ 金华及浙江东部,火腿极为著名,猪之屠宰,或由农人自为之,或卖与当地屠户屠之,前者则由农人制成火腿,后者则将鲜腿售与制腿者制为火腿,然后贩诸市场。④

第三类乡村工业可谓为化学工业,如造纸,陶器,玻璃,爆竹,桐油等。造纸为我国最早工业,中国南部,盛产造纸之原料如竹,如稻秆,故纸业亦集中于华南。浙江与福建,江苏则为最大造纸区。据一九二九年之统计,浙江一省有手工造纸槽户二四,四三七

---

① 《晋商在湖北制造砖茶之现状》,《中外经济周刊》171号,民一五,七,一七。
② *Chinese Economic Journal*, Jan., 1929, p. 54.
③ *Chinese Economic Bulletin*, July, 26, 1930, p. 46.
④ 《金华火腿》,《工商半月刊》,一卷一三号,民一八,七月。

处，分布于四十三县，雇工总数为一二六，八五二人（男工九二，七四三，女工二二，〇一三，童工一二，〇九六），资本总额凡五，〇九〇，〇二八元，出产总值二〇，八五〇，四八七元，平均每户有工人五.二人，资本二〇八.三元，每年出品值八五三.二元。由各县槽户之工作人数，资本额及出品值差异之甚，可证明各户中有以造纸关主业者，有以造纸为副业者。以每户工人而言，最多者为嵊县之一七.二人，最少者为温岭之二人。按等级而分，则每户有工人一〇.二一一七.二者十三县，其余之三十县则为二一八.八人。以资本额而言，最多者为新登之一，四一五元，最少者为平阳之十四元。按等级而分则每户有资本一，〇五〇一一，四一五元者八县，有五二八一九三四元者五县，一〇六一四六九元者十七县，余十三县则每户为一四一九九元。以每年之出品值而言，最多者为武义之七，六〇八元，最少为天台之九一元，以等级而分，则每户出口介一，〇六〇一七，六〇八元间者二十二县，九一一九二八元间者二十一县。①

今试比较各县工人每年出品之价值，即可证明造纸工人工作之断续，盖此职业之本身，即含有"副业"之性质。如最高率遂昌县每工人每年出品值一，〇二五.七七元，最低率松阳县每工人不过九.四八元，但多数之县，为每工人每年出品值在一六四元左右。依等级而分，则在一〇九—三三六元间者为二十五县，高于三三六元者九县，低于一〇九元者亦九县。

---

① 浙江省政府设计科：《浙江之纸业》，民国十九年十二月；*Nankai Weekly Statistical Service*, Mar. 13, 1933。

第十三表　浙江省之手工造纸业（1929）

县	纸槽户数	工人 总数	工人 每户	资本（元）总数	资本（元）每户	工人总数	出产价值 每户	出产价值 每工
安吉	2	12	6.00	400	200.00	2,120	1,060.00	176.67
昌化	85	487	5.73	15,935	187.47	53,248	626.45	109.33
常山	296	4,376	14.78	276,400	933.78	274,800	928.38	62.80
庆元	54	359	6.65	10,368	192.00	71,156	1,317.70	198.21
建德	4	35	8.75	852	213.00	5,400	1,350.00	154.29
衢县	505	7,047	13.95	266,817	528.35	1,034,783	2,049.08	146.84
诸暨	1,110	6,166	5.55	206,123	185.70	724,450	652.66	117.49
奉化	180	1,406	7.81	21,239	117.99	169,050	919.17	120.23
富阳	10,069	40,675	4.04	2,355,082	233.89	8,667,912	860.85	213.10
萧山	510	2,971	5.83	197,350	386.96	1,360,620	2,667.88	457.97
黄岩	579	2,369	4.10	111,976	194.40	518,722	900.56	218.96
瑞安	640	1,920	3.00	17,024	26.60	506,070	790.73	263.58
江山	154	2,490	16.17	168,067	1,091.34	753,336	4,891.79	302.54
金华	422	1,266	3.00	44,648	105.80	308,640	731.37	243.79
临安	786	2,909	3.70	40,973	52.13	548,028	697.24	188.39
临海	234	738	3.15	67,765	289.59	248,040	1,060.00	336.10
龙游	121	1,802	14.89	89,966	743.52	454,910	3,759.59	252.45

(续表)

县	纸槽户数	工人		资本（元）			出产价值		
		总数	每户	总数	每户	总数	每户	每工	
平阳	110	228	2.07	1,493	13.57	48,536	441.23	212.88	
浦江	45	555	12.33	47,242	1,049.82	61,848	1,374.40	114.44	
上虞	54	324	6.00	57,221	1,059.65	127,224	2,356.00	392.67	
绍兴	476	2,939	6.17	63,715	133.85	179,880	177.90	61.20	
寿昌	74	900	12.16	22,796	308.05	158,400	2,140.54	176.00	
嵊县	46	789	17.15	9,065	197.07	87,966	1,912.30	111.49	
孝丰	136	1,018	7.49	94,626	695.78	283,520	2,084.71	276.51	
仙居	36	205	5.69	1,658	46.06	8,988	249.67	43.83	
新昌	60	255	4.25	8,027	133.78	16,836	280.60	66.02	
新登	926	3,831	4.14	131,029	1,415.00	276,307	298.39	72.12	
遂安	179	1,946	11.06	83,920	468.83	239,778	1,339.54	123.22	
遂昌	53	108	2.04	55,784	1,052.53	110,783	2,090.25	1,025.77	
松阳	792	11,488	14.51	13,229	16.70	108,913	137.52	9.48	
泰顺	297	1,945	6.55	19,763	66.54	685,200	2,307.07	352.29	
汤溪	45	720	16.00	23,112	51.36	155,420	2,453.78	215.86	
天台	296	699	2.36	22,348	74.50	27,052	91.39	38.70	
景宁	75	500	6.66	4,837	64.49	202,350	2,698.00	404.70	

(续表)

县	纸槽户数	工人 总数	工人 每户	资本(元) 总数	资本(元) 每户	出产价值 总数	出产价值 每户	出产价值 每工
缙云	122	1,243	10.19	66,794	547.49	274,807	2,252.52	221.08
桐庐	1,135	5,697	5.02	112,275	98.83	405,347	356.82	71.15
温岭	340	680	2.00	5,508	16.20	100,980	297.00	148.50
武义	32	448	14.00	39,068	1,220.88	243,456	7,608.00	543.43
余杭	2,052	8,540	4.16	68,892	26.57	671,100	327.05	78.58
永嘉	1,185	4,244	3.48	218,414	184.32	529,644	446.96	124.80
永康	16	240	15.00	19,647	1,227.94	85,194	5,324.63	354.98
于潜	104	270	2.60	6,092	48.58	54,921	528.09	208.41
余姚	2	12	6.00	2,488	1,244.00	4,752	2,376.00	396.20
总计	24,437	126,852	5.19	5,090,028	208.29	20,850,487	853.23	164.37

其他地方之造纸业亦为乡村工业,可于零散之记录中得之。如关于河北省保定之报告则曰:"各乡村有纸槽极多。"于山东之周村则曰:"在乡村中亦可发现制纸之中心,而制纸则为农人之副业。"关于山东潍县则曰:"安固与辛庄附近之七八村中,草纸,元书纸,及箔纸,制造极多,大率为农家所制,此种家庭除农忙外,几每日从事于造纸工作,每年进款约一二百元之间。"①

第二种乡村化学工业为陶器业,砖瓦业及料器业。江苏之宜兴为陶器最著之区,其制造者皆为宜兴附近之乡人,窑在离宜兴城十余里之鼎山蜀山之间。宜兴交通方便,水路可直达苏州,无锡,常州,陆路距沪宁铁路车站甚近,故陶器多自此运输。陶窑附近三十方里内,皆从事陶业,东之湖滨,西之铜官山,南之南山,北之荆溪皆然。人口之从事陶业者约占百分之六十以上。三分之二为女工,多制"黄货","砂货"及"黑货";三分之一为男工,则从事于"细货"及"粗货"之制造。②

山东博山之料器,亦由乡村中之作坊制造,谓之为小炉房。此种小炉房并不熔化玻璃,其原料由大炉房购买。或自商店中购买已制成之玻璃条,熔化其一部分,而作为玩物,璧画,料珠,或赝造珠宝等物品。当一九二七年调查时,国内情形不定,销路较滞。较大之作坊,在济南皆有售品处。学徒制在此工业中极盛,期约四年。常年工作,惟新年时停工一月。③

每年夏季浙江嘉善县之造砖业,为农民主要之职业。砖窑凡

---

① *Chinese Economic Monthly*, Dec., 1926, p. 532; *Chinese Economic Journal*, June, 1927, p. 548; Aug, 1928, p. 648.
② 《江苏陶业之概况》,《中外经济周刊》72号,民一三,七,二六。
③ *Chinese Economic Journal*, June, 1927, pp. 586-587.

五百余所,在干窑镇者一百,在洪家滩者九十,在下田庙者百五十,在范径者二十,而其邻近各村,亦有窑三五不等。各窑全体工作时,每月可出砖约四万五千万至五万万方。用于上海者百分之七十,其余百分之三十,则用于江浙两省。造砖季起四月迄十一月,十二月至三月则因气候较凉而停工。福州之制瓦,亦为农闲时之副业。土坯为离地面五尺下之黏土,地面之土,则不适用。在福州四乡,有窑约二十余座,工人四五百人。福州附近之各县如将乐及梅江等亦多制造。瓦多售与富家之将兴土木者,或经木匠或瓦匠之手而售与包工者。城市中亦有砖瓦商人,自瓦厂趸来零售。

其他之乡村化学工业为边炮工业,集中于湖南之浏阳。长寸半直径二分五厘之边炮,率来自浏阳,约占全国销路之半,每年出品价值在五百万元以上。销场不只中国,尚多出口,以应华侨及外人之需。边炮纸为浏阳之特产,纸质特佳,浏阳之边炮因以著名。其附近城市及江西省之万载县及萍乡县每年亦有边炮出产,但不若浏阳之盛。边炮之制造,有即在家庭中者,农闲之季,农夫每与其家人,制边炮以搏收入。制成后售与城市中之边炮商人,边炮商人加以彩饰,盖戳及打包后,乃运往销售。① 山东之潍县各村中如南湖住北湖住则尔庄等,亦以制边炮著名,惟规模较小,每家每年收入约百余元。出品或售与当地,或销诸乡村。②

第四类乡村工业为杂项工业,虽不如上述三类之重要,但亦有其地位。山东之博山产煤,瓷器,及料器极富,其四乡居民,大半以掘陶土及采矿为业,而以采煤者为尤多。博山著名之煤矿,多在城

---

① 《浏阳边炮销行汉市状况》,《工商半月刊》,一卷,一九期,民一八,一,一。
② *Chinese Economic Journal*, Aug., 1928, p.649.

市东南之黑山,东北之西河,及正西之城西,农民于其地内发现煤苗时,每用旧法,组织而采掘之。少数石灰窑亦在此。① 河北邯郸县农人于农闲时,多从事采掘陶土,上等之陶土色洁白可代肥皂之用,次等者可掺于煤屑中以制煤球,如北平煤球店之以黄土掺于煤屑中是。该项陶土各村皆产之,每车(一千二百余斤)约值五十铜元。山东龙口之掘陶土,亦为农余副业。② 河北省磁县之彭城产陶土,其出品较细致,亦为副业之一。戴乐仁氏(J. B. Tayler)曰:"作碗之土坯,为软而灰色之物质,在彭城二英里内深六十英尺至百英尺下之地中得之。采掘多在冬季,农民为之,每组约六七人。入土井中者五人,二人凿土,二人推土至井底,一人照料其上运;在地面者二人。采掘时须与土井所在地之地主以赔价金五元,及出品百分之三。……然坑道所在之地主,则应无所得。……此种规定尚有一特点,即为工人分成,而无工资。……陶土用独轮车或骡车运至陶窑。每组每日可掘陶土七吨,运至陶窑则需二日,其价值约每分十斤。故平均每人每日可得五角五分之谱。"③

与陶业异其性质者为硝皮,制胶,马鬃筛,毛笔等工业,此等乡村工业,依动物产品而存在。河北枣强县大营镇之农民,多从事于硝皮工作。此辈农民每结伴赴邻近各乡收买兽皮,如有急需,且可与皮货商人接洽通融。硝皮作坊极多,有为收买兽皮人自己经营者。所硝之皮货于未至市场前,即制成各种皮产品,然后携至市场贩卖。皮货之出口在八月及十月之间,经德州而至天津。普通之

---

① *Chinese Economic Journal*, June, 1927, pp. 579-580, 587.

② 同上 May, 1927, p. 468; *Chinese Economic Bulletin*, July 7, 1928, p. 5.

③ Taylor, J. B.: "The Hopel pottery industry and the problem of modernization", in *Chinese Social and Political Science Review*, April, 1930, pp. 186-187.

皮货商人为出口商之代理人，奔走于硝皮者及出口商之间，实力丰厚者，亦常自作生意。熬胶以山东周村为最有名，将兽皮及蹄角等加以熬炼，亦农民之副业。胶褐色，作长方形，长短不一，在市场销售者极多，但出口商来周村购买者亦不少。每月出口数量约为百五十担。以马鬃作筛者，见于河北安平，工作者多为妇女及儿童。马鬃为皮毛商人自张家口、归绥、包头等处贩来，然后再售与制筛者。成品销于河北、山东、山西、河南各省，以为筛面粉之用。安平县尚有以马鬃制网及面幕者，多销于外国。全国知名之湖笔，出于湖州之善琏镇，原料为羊毛、鼬鼠毛、兔毫、雏鸡毛等。当地居民，皆从事之，除孵蚕时期外，制笔事业几占居民所有之时间。农民于种桑秧稻之余，亦多从事于此。制笔庄所雇工人分二种：一为长工，一为短工。长工供宿，而短工则在家庭工作。长工总计约千三百人，女工占三分之二，短工按件计算，人数亦不定。至湖州城内所有之长工，不过五十人。①

其次为艺术品，如天津迤南之杨柳青及炒米店之彩画。最初不过庙中神像，厥后乃有风景人物及历史上之事迹。工人为乡人，画之种类亦可百十种，依画师之技术而分粗、细、加细三种。工资按件计算，每人每日约二角。每年春季画店将画稿发与工人，使其着色。画稿为一约略图样，以指示大意，普通皆为木板印刷。家庭中人则分工合作，如甲画面孔，乙填五官，丙再加彩色而成画。炒米店十一月至正月间有画市，画店于此时期，多在各旅店中置销售人，或在街头设摊以求售。小贩来此购买者最多，以备新年时沿村

---

① *Chinese Economic Journal*, Dec., 1926, pp. 532-533; Oct., 1927, pp. 905-906; *Chinese Economic Bulletin*, Oct. 9, 1926, p. 215; Nov. 26, 1927, pp. 280-282.

售卖。恒有在七八月间购买,以便运至东三省,热河,蒙古等处销售,至运销于陕西,甘肃,新疆者因程途较远,多于三四月间即起运矣。天津左近画店凡三十余家,资本最多者为十八万元。迩者津市之石印局,亦多经营彩画为副业。总之,在天津范围以内,依绘画为生者,在六千人以上,炒米店居民一五一户中,业画者为百分之八十;古佛寺一四五户中,业画者则为百分之六十;周李吴村一〇五户中业画者为百分之四十以上。①

杂类乡村工业之中,最后可得而述者,为农村所需服务之供给是。河北定县四五三村中,农民除耕稼外,其主要副业尚有为铁匠者一村,木匠者十村,锯木匠者十二村,泥水匠者六村,造车匠者二村,关于次要副业,则为制水车者一村,制辘轳者一村,掘井者二村。② 他如故城农人于农闲之季,几皆为乡间治工。铁铺凡十二座,制造刀叉烹饪器具,及农具等。原料为废铁,自邻村输入,年约二十万块。③

上述之纺织,食品,化学,及杂项四类乡村工业中,吾人愿作进一步之研究,以探讨其存在或引用之因素,地理之分配,组织之方式,及原料,人工,出产各问题。一工业之引用及存在于乡村,常根据一种或数种之因素。第一即乡民之企业性。企业性丰富之人如在他乡工作,习得一种工业技术,如此项工业能辅农业之不足者,为自助助人计,遂携归而介绍于本乡。如河北高阳县之织布工业,即其实例。第二因素为西洋教士之传导,如圣功女士(Miss Nettie

---

① 《杨柳青画业之现状》,《经济半月刊》,一卷三期,民一六,一二。
② 李景汉著,《定县社会调查概况》,中华平民教育促进会出版,民国二十二年二月,149—154 页。
③ *Chinese Economic Journal*, Oct., 1927, p. 903.

Senger)之于锦州华北毛织学校,即其一例。① 第三因素为资本家之商业动机。农闲之时,农人急欲寻工作以增加收入,资本家乃有剥削谋利之机会。如平湖之针织工业,皆雇用女工;但此辈女工虽被剥削,然有额外之收入,亦感觉满足。出口品工业如花边,刺绣,抽纱品等之雇用工资较贱之女工者,亦为其例。第四因素为乡民欲处置其过丰之收获或于农闲时利用农业副产物。如浙江半山及泰山之腌梅及华北之草帽辫工业,可资例证。唯此种工业之引用,技术用具,皆须简单,否则农民得不偿失,定摈而不用。第五因素为农人之欲乘暇制备已收作物,如缫丝,制茶,榨油即其例。最后一因素则为原料之便于就地制造,如博山彭城等处煤及陶土之采掘是也。

乡村工业地理上之分布,亦因各原素而定,如原料之所在,市场之接近,及技术之集中等,皆极重要。原料则又因自然之蕴积及气候之不同而异,依此则乡村工业可约略分为北方工业及南方工业二种。丝,茶,苎麻,竹,稻秆(造纸用),只能产于温带,故缫丝,制茶,夏布及造纸为华南之工业;羊毛及麦秆,出于北方,故毛织及草帽辫为华北之工业。至陶器之在江苏宜兴与河北彭城,则因陶土之自然蕴藏之关系也。以接近市场为重要之因素者,则有砖瓦,编篮等工业。至工业之因技术集中而存在者,则有绍兴之酒,宜兴之陶器及天津之年画等。

乡村工业组织之方式繁多,但多带有过渡性质。同一工业适于主匠制度者,商人雇主制亦优为之。总之,工业化以前曾一度盛

---

① Senger, Nettie M.; *The Chin Chou Wool Project*, 1933.

行于欧西如英国等之工业制度,今日仍可见之于中国。①

　　工业出品成于一家之中者,谓之家庭制度(Household system)。在此制下,一切原料,人工及器具,皆为家庭所供给,出品亦为家庭所消费,如制茶,酿酒,榨油,脯果,火腿等一类工业皆是。惟乡村中此种组织绝少,主匠制则较通行。如绍兴之酒,小部分固为自供消费,大部分则在主匠制度下所生产,以供市场之需要。

　　主匠制又可分为家庭主匠及作坊主匠二种。普通所谓主匠制度者,即指作坊主匠制,匠人自有其器具及作坊,原料则自外购,出品售与消费者及商人。但在家庭主匠制之下,主匠每为家庭中之分子,多为零工而少整工,且技术简单,无须贵重之工具或作坊。通常出品,皆售与贩卖人或在市场销售,直接售与消费者,实不多觏。此种组织之代表为草帽辫,编席,编丝,织夏布等。至于酿酒,陶器料器,造纸,边炮等工业,则为作坊主匠制之绝好例证。

　　商人雇主制以商人雇主为中枢,由商人购买原料,直接自商店或栈房中,或间接经店内代理人或其他中间人,将原料发与散处四乡之工人。平湖之针织业及无锡之花边业,皆其例也。前者由商人雇主在商店中将原料发与工人;后者则聘有代理人以负分发原料及收回成品之责。方法之选择,要以工人之分散程度及距商店之远近而定。商人雇主制独行者甚鲜,多与主匠制并行,例如高阳之手织业。需要盛时,其一切商业上之危险如购料销货等,均为商人雇主一人所负荷。但当营业萧条之季,商人雇主多缩少范围,或停止经营,工人因此无工可做,不得不自行冒险购买原料制成成品而求沽焉。

---

① 方显廷著之 *Triumph of Factory System in Engiand*,1930。

规模较大之乡村工业,亦有采用独力经营之工厂制度者,如造纸,陶业,采煤等是。但此制度,除因特殊之环境,对乡村工业似不适宜。虽因原料供给之富饶及特殊技能之存在之关系,如陶器,酿酒等业,可应用工厂之组织,然工厂需要有规律不间断之进行,与乡村劳工之供给情形,殊相径庭也。

乡村工业应用之原料可依供给来源,生产阶段,所有权及购买方法诸项,加以分析。自供给来源方面言之:则原料有出于农人自种者,如缫丝业之蚕茧,制茶业之茶叶,脯果业之鲜果,草帽辫业之麦秆等;有来自远村者,如榨油业之豆,棉织业之棉纱;有来自国外者,如高阳织布业之人造丝。自制造阶段言之:乡村工业所用原料之中,有为真正之原料者,如酿酒业之米及高粱,榨油业及粉丝业之豆,制茶业之茶叶,缫丝业之蚕茧;其他原料如棉纱,花边,纸(作边炮用),则为已成品或半成品。原料之所有权,则依组织之方式而不同。在主匠制度之下,原料概属于工人,不问其出自田间抑购自他处。至自外方购买之种类有二:一为自商贩处购买,制成成品后仍售与此商贩;一为自市集上购买,例如高阳手织业所用之棉纱。原料由商人雇主所供给者,如针织,花边,刺绣等工业原料,则连同所需花样直接或间接由商人雇主发与工人。

乡村工业之劳工,具有特殊之性质。第一即其季节性,多为农忙以后之工作。第二为其家庭性,家庭中之父母子女及其他分子皆得工作。细巧工作,如花边,刺绣,夏布等多雇用女工,尤以年幼女工为然;需人力及技术工作,则多男工任之。第三为无组织。乡村工人分散各方,极少集合举动,故恒受中间人之剥削。且因管理之缺乏,出品毫无定量,质地低劣,品类亦杂。第四即简单幼稚之技术。此种技术之幼稚,非特影响于中国二大基本工业丝茶之衰落,亦且有关于草帽辫,陶器等工业之衰落也。至技术之简单,本关乡村工业之本色,尤以带副业性质者为然。盖从事于副业者,实无余力且雅不欲作学徒而受严格训练也。以是若干之乡村工业之技术如编席,草帽辫,花边,针织等,咸可于短期内习之,且有设学校以教授者,如花边学校是。

乡村工业之出品,大都供当地之消费,例如砖瓦。但亦多输出区内外者,于前节"中国乡村工业之衰落"中,已可见乡村工业出品对于出口之重要。各种出品有时先由出口商与商贩以信用上之便利,再由此种商贩向农民定货,如烟台之花边业,即其例也。但通常皆系农人将其成品售与商贩,再由商贩售与出口商。博山之料器,制造者设推销处于济南,则属例外之情形。

(五)河北省之乡村工业

因材料之缺乏,故上述之中国乡村工业之情形,仅为一约略之说明。在河北省,则对于乡村家庭工业,已有较详尽之调查,除各乡村中家庭制造工业之含有副业性质者外,并及含有作坊性质之工业之一部分。根据一九二八年之调查,河北省之一二九县中之有家庭工业者为一二七县,工业凡四十四种,亦可依前节中国乡村工业之分类分为纺织,食品,化学,杂项四大类。其详细情形见第十四表。依此表所示,一九二八年河北省家庭工业出品之总值为一〇三,八五六,七五三元,其中纺织类占九一,五五四,二〇七元,当全数之百分之八八.二;食品类为八一四,八一二元,当全数之百分之〇.八;化学类为三,九四三,六二四元,当全数之百分之三.八;杂项类为七,五一七,一〇〇元,当全数之百分之七.二。但在此四十四种工业中,以八种最为重要,价值为一〇〇,三〇三,九〇九元,约当全数百分之九六.六;兹将此八种工业依其相对之重要列表如下:

	总值(元)	百分数
棉布	45,072,427	43.0
棉及人造丝布	31,640,000	30.5
皮袄皮件	6,969,690	6.7
草帽辫	4,766,520	4.6
芦苇席	4,388,848	4.2
爆竹	3,112,960	3.0
棉纱	2,726,870	2.6
荆柳桑编织物	1,626,594	1.6
总　计	100,303,909	96.6

一九二八年河北省一二七县家庭工业之生产总值,凡一〇三,八五六,七五三元。依第十五表所示,则每县生产值皆在百万元以上之二十一县之生产总值凡八一,八一七,六二四元,占全额百分之七八.六。在此二十一县中,以高阳为最多,凡三一,六二〇,〇〇〇元,占全额百分之三〇.四;次为束鹿,出产值七,〇〇五,二八九元,占百分之六.七;玉田出产值四,五八八,三〇〇元,占百分之四.四;任丘为四,四五一,一〇〇元,占百分之四.三;清苑为四,一七〇,〇〇〇元,占百分之四;遵化为三,五六一,〇〇〇元,占百分之三.四;定县为三,一七五,〇五〇元,占百分之三.一;其余逐渐递减。

第十四表　河北省家庭工业出品之价值（1928）

（单位：元）

工业名称	价值	百分比	工业名称	价值	百分比
纺织业	91,554,217	88.2	草帽	28,730	—
缫丝	96,000	0.1	蒲器	162,520	0.2
纺造	2,794,870	2.6	食物类	841,812	0.8
纱线	2,276,870	2.6	熏枣、瓢枣	11,540	—
毛线	50,000	—	绿豆粉	20,844	—
麻绳	18,000	—	饴糖	400	—
编织	82,060,974	79.1	花生油	2,728	—
棉	45,939,557	44.3	烟丝	6,300	—
棉布	45,072,427	43.4	冬菜	800,000	0.8
其他物品	867,130	0.9	化学类	3,943,624	3.8
毛巾	72,940	0.1	粉笔	598	—
棉带	274,990	0.3	爆竹	3,112,960	3.0
口袋	509,200	0.5	纸	830,066	0.8
其他	10,000	—	杂项类	7,517,100	7.2
棉及人造丝布	31,640,000	30.5	宫花	26,000	—
绫绸	27,160	—	竹帘	16,000	—
毛毯	54,609	0.1	笤帚	64,500	0.1
牛毛毯	3,600	—	木炭	1,280	—
苇席	4,388,848	4.2	皮袄,皮件	6,969,690	6.7
秫秸席	7,200	—	石砚	28,500	—
针织	18,009	—	铁器	14,520	—
线袜	17,919	—	香	81,050	0.1
毛织品	90	—	织布穿子	15,000	—
编织	6,584,364	6.4	水笔	90,000	0.1
荆柳桑编织物	1,626,594	1.6	杆	480	—
编草	4,957,770	4.8	罗底	210,000	0.2
草帽辫	4,766,520	4.6	锡器	80	—
			合计	103,856,753	100.0

今试进而一考第十五表所示之每人生产价值，则二十一县中以高阳为最多，每人约二一五.二元；最低者为迁安，为二.一元。其余十九县依其相对之重要排列，则为束鹿之一九.三元，任丘之

一六.七元,玉田之一四.六元,南乐之一三.四元,蠡县之一二.五元,完县之一〇.三元,清苑之一〇.二元。其余依次递减。

第十五表　河北省家庭工业出品之价值(1928)

县	出品 价值	百分数	人口	每人平均出产之价值
高阳	31,620,000	30.4	146,923	215.2
束鹿	7,005,289	6.7	362,558	19.3
玉田	4,588,300	4.4	313,454	14.6
任丘	4,451,100	4.3	266,533	16.7
清苑	4,170,000	4.0	407,312	10.2
遵化	3,561,000	3.4	416,880	8.5
定县	3,175,050	3.1	351,803	9.0
宝坻	3,025,000	2.9	315,065	9.6
南乐	2,480,650	2.8	214,496	13.4
蠡县	2,282,245	2.2	183,286	12.5
濮阳	1,967,690	1.9	364,209	5.4
完县	1,626,500	1.6	157,282	10.3
平乡	1,600,000	1.5	245,387	6.5
丰润	1,530,000	1.5	669,130	2.3
迁安	1,415,000	1.4	687,869	2.1
清丰	1,292,600	1.2	316,051	4.1
藁城	1,248,000	1.2	243,722	5.1
曲周	1,190,000	1.1	209,820	5.7
长垣	1,070,200	1.0	244,264	4.4
肥乡	1,050,000	1.0	135,125	7.8
香河	1,049,000	1.0	148,211	7.1
其他106县	22,039,129	21.4	21,268,824	1.04
总计	103,856,753	100.0	27,668,204*	3.75

*天津之461,388人及涞远之111,830人未包括在内,因此二县对河北省之家庭工业无所贡献也。

如第十六表所示，一九二八年间此二十一重要县分之出产，占河北省之生产值百分之七八.六。其皮毛生产占全省皮毛生产之百分之百，棉及人造丝布则占全省出产百分之九九.九，爆竹占百分之九十，棉纱及棉线占百分之八五.四，草帽辫占百分之七九，棉布占百分之六五.九，芦苇席占百分之四九.二，荆柳桑编织品占百分之四一.五，其他三十六种工业占百分之五〇.七。此表亦表示在此二十一县中，蠡县，平乡，藁城，曲周及肥乡五县之棉布生产占其生产值之百分之百，宝坻则为百分之九九.二，长垣则为百分之九九.一，任丘则为百分九八.九，濮阳则为百分之九六.六，香河则为百分之九五.三，清苑则为百分之九三.五，完县则为百分之九二.二，玉田则为百分之八一.九。至棉及人造丝之织造，高阳占百分之百。其余七县中，皮件集中束鹿县，占其生产值之百分之九九.五；草帽辫之在南乐者占百分之百，在清丰者占百分之八六.二；爆竹在遵化者占分之七五.八；棉纱及棉线在定县者占百分之七三.三。至荆柳桑编织品及芦苇席二种工业，不若上述六种工业之集中而分散于各地。在二十一县中，其百分数最高者，芦苇席为三润之百分之二八.四，荆柳桑编织品则为迁安之百分之十二。①

棉及人造丝布之织造，在河北省家庭工业中最为重要，一九二八年其出产值为七一，七一二，四二七元，当该年河北省四十四种家庭工业之总生产值之百分之七三.九。故南开大学经济学院特选定河北省织布业代表之高阳县，以为调查之对象，自本年之正月

---

① 河北省政府秘书处：《河北省行政统计概要》，民国十七年；*Nankai Weekly Statistical Service*, May 29, 1933；高阳工业方面之材料，为南开大学经济学院吴知君所供给。

起,作一精细之调查。以下各节,即对此生产值三一,六四〇,〇〇〇元之织品,当全省家庭工业出产值百分之三〇.五之高阳县棉织业之较详细之阐述:

高阳为三等县,居河北省之中,面积一,四四〇方里,人口一五四,一三〇人,人口密度为每方里一〇七人(当每方英里七九二人)。交通四达,铁路,航运,汽车皆极方便。西北七十里为保定,为平汉路之重镇;东北三十里为白洋淀;东边之同口镇,经大清河三百里而至华北名都市之天津;此外长途汽车奔驰于天津,高阳间者,每日亦有开行,其距离亦三百里。

高阳乡村工业——棉布及人造丝布织造——之兴起,原因非止一端。其最重要者厥为人口过多而地质贫瘠,仅恃农产不足以维生活。据一九三一年高阳县政府对省府民政厅之报告,高阳有地五一〇,〇〇〇亩,即九四四方里。然收益地不过三五一,三九八亩,仅当百分之六十九;其余一五八,六〇二亩,或百分之三十一之田,地质洼湿,或碱性过甚,皆为无益地。际此情形之下,乃不得不另开蹊径,以辅农业上不足之收入。一九〇六年袁世凯氏在天津设立实习工厂,内设织染一科,实习工厂于一九〇九年停办之后,其继起之高等工业学校,仍分织染二科,高阳人先后在实习工厂及工业学校之织染科受训练者极多,学成之后,感于高阳之需要辅助工业及不堪受天津纺织界竞争之压迫,返乡着手组织,至今遂蔚为大观。他如交通之方便,及欧战期间疋头进口之停止,皆足以促进高阳纺织业之发展。

一九一四年至一九一九年间高阳织布业之进步极速。至一九一九年外货入口竞争复烈,高阳织布者乃改良其设计,并引用由天津制造之提花机,以人造丝为纬,以棉为经,而改良高阳布之织造。

一九二五年人造丝上浆法发明，韧性增高，足供为经之用，昔之以棉为经人造丝为纬者，今改为经纬皆用人造丝，营业益加扩展。但年来因组织，生产，销售各方面之退步，自一九二九年达最高峰后，近日已开始降落，此点当于后文详述之。

高阳手织业之组织，大都为商人雇主制，亦可表示此制在中国最为盛行。工人皆分居于其乡村之家庭中。商人雇主购纱线后，即分散与工人，以易其织成之布，然后再在本人或其他资本家在城内所设之工厂内整理之。较勤奋之工人，工作数年稍有积蓄，亦可引用主匠制，而自设作坊经营，自购纱线，并将其成品在市集或城中售与布商。至织布工厂，因须继续不断工作，且开支较大，颇不多见。现有中等规模之工厂数家，其主人率能在需求不定之市场中控制一部分可靠之顾客。至商人顾主及散处工人以及销售与金融机关等，当于下节再为详述。

高阳之商人雇主有二种，一为布线庄，一为染线厂。南开大学经济学院于一九三三年上半年调查时，该县有布线庄六十一，其职务如下：

（1）向本县线市或由天津，青岛，上海之分行购办纱线（由分行购买纱线之布线庄规模较大，在高阳约有十余家）；

（2）在本县线市或线集上零售一部已购之纱（多数售与乡间之织工）；

（3）散发纱线与所熟识之散处各地之工人，收取织成布疋，按件付以工资；

（4）除约定工人织布外，自市场购取布疋；

（5）将布疋在各工厂中染色，砑光并整理之；

（6）将已整理之布疋，运至外埠分行销售。最大之庄家有分

行九,最少者分行一,平均则有二三分行;

(7) 将售货所得之款,解至天津钱庄,或以款购纱或再汇回高阳。

布线庄之主要功能,第一在发散纱线与散工以织布,及在市场购买已织成之布定。第二为经外埠之分行,以推销其成品。故需大量资本,以供给购纱后及销售前约八阅月之时期之用。以是最大之布线庄有资本一二十万元,最小者亦有数千元,普通则为二三万元。至布线庄所雇佣之人员,因其规模而不同,约在十人至六十人之间,有经理,司账,分庄经理,店员,学徒,差役,衙役等。

染线厂之规模较布线庄为小。一九三三年上半季有厂三十,在城中者十一,其余十九厂中之十一厂,则集中于城西南之于留佐村。此等染线厂之主要功能,亦为在线市购买纱线,然后在其厂中经工人加以染色,再发与四乡之散处织工,以织条纹布及格子布。织成后,染线厂复收集之,以骡车运至市场销售。因其规模较小而周转率较速,资本之需要亦较少,为一千元至万元之间,普通多为三四千元。其组织普通有经理,司账各一人,职员及学徒三四人,染工数人。织工之雇佣,须经机头之介绍。机头率为织布工人之首领,信誉较佳,且与染线厂有较久之关系。不特对所介绍之织工,负道德上之担保,且分发纱线并监督工人,使迅速交工,如工人到期不能交布,则机头助染线厂收回尚未织成之纱线。凡此事务,染线厂每年三节皆有馈赠,其礼物在五元至十元之间,以为报酬。机头所织之布,纵稍有缺点,亦可接收,且于送货时可就餐于染线厂中。此外机头所织之布,多由工人代为运送。每染线厂皆雇机头四五人,每人管理散处织工数十人至百人不等。

乡村织工,大都为商人雇主工作,然自行雇用工匠经营者亦多。有时织工联合租一作坊，一处工作，各人仍自营生产，互不相谋。于留佐村有来自高阳南百余里安平之织工，从事于条纹布及格子布之织造，其组织较为奇特。每组约八人至十人，尚有学徒四五人，购机器五六架，即在于留佐村赁屋数椽以资作坊。染色之纱线系自染线厂赊来，织成布后，复托染线厂代为出售。染线厂每通融款项与此辈织工以应急需，于年终与购纱线及售布疋之款一齐清算。清算之差数即为作坊本届之毛利，减去本年之开销而为纯利。各织工乃按预先之规定，而分成焉。

除商人雇主及织工外，与此手织业有关系之组织及商号如线市，线集，布集，线庄，布商及整理工厂等，应略述之，以冀有整个之了解。当一九三三年南开经济学院调查时，高阳城中有线庄四，其职务为自外埠购得大批纱线，在线市转售本地商人，同时亦贩卖颜料。因经营范围之辽阔，资本最少须十万元。布商则分布庄与布店二者。前者有外埠分行，后者则无之，然其规模均不如布线庄。布庄之功能与布线庄相似，惟不分发纱线与织工以织造。高阳有布庄凡三十一，资本最多者二三万元，平均则为五六千元。布店无外埠分店，其业务多为自乡村织工处贩来布疋，转售布线庄或布庄。高阳有布店三十三，平均资本约千元，最高者三四千元，最低者只数百元。

线市始设于一九一三年，每日有交易时间二：一为上午十时至十二时，一为下午四时至六时。严格言之，此种线市，当纯为棉纱及人造丝之交易，唯因新式银行之阙如，线市实具国内汇兑市场之功能，对天津之汇兑，一如天津之棉纱及人造丝然，亦可自由买卖，且按天津，青岛或上海之电示及市场之涨落为之。此线市之功用，对高阳工商业既如是重要，故城内商人，几皆为此市场之会员，会费不过二元,每日派遣店员一人至数人以参与其交易,交易之规定,口头书面皆有,投机事业亦屡见不鲜。

除线市较有组织外,其他尚有零线市,色线市,麻丝市,白布市,条格布市,麻布市等不同市集。此种市集,于一定之地方举行,或即在街市之上。月凡六次,零线市,色线市,及白布市之集市,为阴历每月之初四,初九,十四,十九,二十四,二十九六日。条格布市及麻布市则于每月之初三日,八日,十三,十八,二十三,二十八六日举行。麻丝之集市则在每月之初二,初七,十二,十七,二十二,二十七六日举行。在线市交易单位为纱线半包(每包四十捆,每捆重十磅零四两),在零线市则以捆或束为交易单位。每捆之束数因纱线之支数而异,十四支纱及十四支以下之纱,其束数倍于支数,十四支以上之纱,则束数与支数同。

高阳他种之附属工业,与织布业亦有联带之关系。如机器整染工厂,杂色染坊,山西蓝缸染房,印花厂,踩坊等皆是。一九三三年上季,高阳有整染工厂十二,经营机器轧光及涂色等工作,其中四场为布线庄或染线厂所经营,资本自数千元至三万元。且因竞争之激烈,此辈已组轧厂同业工会。杂色染坊凡二十二,资本约一二千元,仅能染色,其轧光工作,须倩整染工厂代任。山西蓝缸染坊共九所,以山西土法染色,资本最高不过八百元。印花厂数亦九,为店主携学徒所经营之作坊,资本自数百元至一千元,其所染者多为麻丝被面及被单等。踩坊凡十,规模极小,以手工踩光,资本不过二百元。其他有砸花作坊三,浆麻作坊二,提花机楼子兼代售自行车商一,尚有作坊二,以修理织机及贩卖零件为业。

高阳纺织工业原料为棉纱及麻丝或人造丝,由布线庄及线庄购买,前已言之。布线庄及线庄在天津皆有分庄,以便就当地之纱厂或纱号购买,其办事处或在高阳商会,或在栈中。如分庄与天津纱号之交易由跑合者说成,则先由跑合发给单据,载明商标,支数,包数及每包之价格,此种临时单据,须经纱号认可后,再出一单据,以为交易之凭证。售价之一部可以预付,但其总额则在月终结算。纱号所发之单据,多交与运输公司以船或骡车自天津运至高阳。此辈运输公司多已作业多年,信誉极著,鲜有不能按期运到者。

高阳纱线多自天津购买,每至年终,天津即派收账员赴高阳清算,故根据收账员之报告,即可估计高阳每年购买纱线之数量。高阳织布业一九二九年达最高峰,彼年纱线之购买量为一〇〇,〇〇〇包,其中之二〇,〇〇〇包。则转售与清苑,肃宁,任丘及其他邻县。近年消费量已缩减,一九三二年已降至最低额三〇,〇〇〇包,较一九二九年所消费之八〇,〇〇〇包者,相差一倍半有余。

高阳织布业所用之纱线,百分之七〇至八〇为二十支及三十二支,其余则为十六支及四十二支。昔者多从日本进口,较粗之十二支及十六支纱,方为本国自纺。九·一八东北事变后,高阳对日本纱线亦图抵制,其结果我国自纺之纱,已占百分之三十至四十矣。

人造丝之用为织布原料,一九二五年始为普遍。是年自上海直接购买者不过一家,一九二七增至二家,一九二八增至六家,一九二九乃至十一家。厥后亦有至天津购买者。据一九二九年之估计,购人造丝共二万箱,而销于高阳者凡一万二千箱。每箱合人造丝二百磅,分为二十捆,普通皆为百二十或百五十号。一九三二年人造丝之进口亦锐减,不过八,〇〇〇箱。仅当一九二九年之百分之四〇。

棉布及人造丝布织造所需要之人工,第十七表可予以充分之比较。织长百尺宽二尺五寸之白布八疋或面积二千方尺者,工资成本为六元二角,则每方尺平均之工资成本为三厘一毫。如织长五丈二宽二尺一寸之人造丝布十疋或面积一,〇九二方尺者,其工资成本为七元四角五分,每方尺平均工资成本为六厘八毫。当织白布之工资成本二倍以上。

第十七表　高阳织棉布与织人造丝布工资比较表(1933)

	八日间每架织机织本色布八疋之工资(每疋长百尺宽二尺五寸,重八斤)			十日间每架织机织人造丝布十疋之工资(每疋长五二尺宽二.一尺,经线与纬线皆为一二〇号,并有经线三千)		
	人工(以日计)		工资(元)	人工(以日计)		工资(元)
	男工	女工及童工		男工	女工及童工	
上浆	1		0.40	$\frac{1}{2}$		20
络经		4	0.80		7	1.40
上经	$\frac{1}{2}$		0.20	1		0.40
穿杼	1		0.40	1		0.40
络纬		6	1.20		$3\frac{1}{2}$	1.05
织布	8		3.20	10		4.00
合计	$10\frac{1}{2}$	10	6.20	$12\frac{1}{2}$	$10\frac{1}{2}$	7.45

附注:织人造丝布之花板系自砸花作坊购来,至络纬则须学徒之协助,故工资较高。

依第十七表棉布及人造丝布织造对人工之需要,则高阳乡村织机之数目,可得约略之估计。试以(一)棉织机每日每架可织纱线半捆,人造丝织机每日每架可织人造丝四分之一捆;(二)每年工作三百二十日(减去歇工日及假日)为根据,则当一九二九年所销棉纱之八〇,〇〇〇包或三,二〇〇,〇〇〇捆及人造丝之一二,〇〇〇箱或二四〇,〇〇〇捆,棉织机须有二万架,人造丝织机须有三千架,总计为二万三千架。设当农忙时及其他原因织机之百分之二十无工作,则有工作及无工作织机总数,当为二万七千六百架。惟织工家庭中非每人皆从事织造,尚有家务待理。吾人假设每架织机平均需要四个男人,妇女及儿童以做预备及织造之工作,如是,则高阳有织机二七,六〇〇架,当有织布乡人一一〇,四〇〇人,其中三分之一为男工,从事于上浆上经,穿杼及织布等工作,三分之二则为妇女及儿童,非每日工作者也。

高阳乡村除工人及助手一一〇,四〇〇人外,一九三三年间城中染色,轧光,印花等工厂尚有工人四二三人及学徒三〇五人。此四二三工人中染色工人二四九,轧光工人一六四,印花工人十。

第十八表　高阳织布附业工人之统计

	厂数	染色工人	轧光工人	印花工人	学徒	合计
机器染色及轧花厂	12	153	84		145	382
杂色染坊	22	}96	}50		}132	}278
山西蓝缸染坊	9					
印花厂	9			10	28	38
踩坊	10		30			30
总计	62	249	164	10	305	728

高阳手织业自一九二九达最高峰后,近来日渐凋落。一九二九年高阳销费棉纱八〇,〇〇〇包,人造丝一二,〇〇〇箱者,一九三二年不过销棉纱三〇,〇〇〇包,人造丝八,〇〇〇箱。一九三三年,此业更见零替。据南开大学经济学院之调查,一九三三年上半季有工作之织机,尚不及一九三二年之半。设此种惊人之衰落延续不已,前途实不堪设想,而此曾有繁荣历史之工业将趋于逐渐消灭,其影响于乡村人口之生计方面,实至重且巨。今特推原究

始,查其衰落之原因安在,俾为谋复兴者之张本焉。

高阳织布工业衰落之原因,可分内部及外部两方面加以论列。外部之原因绝非高阳工业本身所可控制,如农村购买力之衰微,日俄疋头在中国市场之倾销,丝织品与人造丝织品之竞争等。高阳布之销场,大率在华北平原,西北及长江流域,不幸年来此等地带,非受内战外患之骚乱,即蒙全世界不景气之影响。如西北各省之陕西,甘肃,宁夏,山西,绥远,察哈尔,热河等省,多赖羊毛,羊皮,牛皮,及其他皮毛之出口,以维持其繁荣。但全世界经济衰落之结果,昔日皮货出口三千七百七十万关两者,今日不过一千八百八十万关两。一九三一年羊毛出口之一千另二十万关两者,一九三二年只三百三十万关两。且中国之经济组织,以战乱频仍,如四川之内哄,湖北,江西,湖南,福建等省战乱之蹂躏,以及十九年声讨阎冯之役,摧残破坏,已达极度。一九三一年九月日本攫夺满洲,一九三二年上海中日之战,一九三三年华北之战,更加促中国经济组织之崩溃。内外战争扩大,乡村人民遂不得不遁入通商区埠以求安全与保障。小康之家率皆变其产业为现金,汇诸城市中以存放,谋保安全。故农村间不独因人民麇集城市,生产能力及富力为之减少,即金钱信用,亦感贫乏。结果,乡村金融枯寂,利率奇高,而城市通货膨涨,过度繁荣。高阳布疋系以内地为市场者,因之不得推销其货物。至俄日疋头在中国市场之倾销,为高阳手织业衰落之另一原因。外国商人既货高价廉,且有严密之商业组织与充实之金融接济,与我国高阳布商之毫无组织者相抗衡,其胜负当无待乎龟蓍。俄日之疋头较高阳者确贱百分之二十至三十,而高阳商不在生产成本上求经济,反减低纱线之质与量,以冀与外货之价格相平,此种自杀之政策,危险殊甚。他如生丝及棉纱价格之暴落,及以银价计算之人造纱价格之增长，亦为高阳手织业衰颓之主因。中国生丝在纽约市场每磅之价格，在一九三二年正月为二.六四金元，至六月乃突降至每磅一.七六金元，相差约三分之一。故对人造丝织品之购买能力之一部，几已转向丝织品。至棉纱价格之降落，亦颇令人惊诧。人钟牌十六支纱在一九三二年第一星期为每包一六八.五〇两，至一九三三年五月末一星期竟落至每包一三三.五〇两，相差凡五分之一。故高阳之布商，均各减少营业范围，不愿多蒙在高价市场买纱而在低价市场卖布之危险。人造丝之价格，亦有跌落之象。但我国为银本位国家，年来银价狂跌，故以银价计算之人造丝之价格乃高涨，是亦为阻滞高阳手织业之要因。

高阳手织业衰落之内部原因，一言以蔽之，为组织之缺乏，或可谓为无组织。近二十年来，高阳织布工业之发展，固未可讳言，如一九二八年生产值已达三千一百万元以上，可为明证。惟如此宏大之工业，对制造，贩卖，及金融等毫无有效率而必需之设备，则亦为不可掩之事实。此种工业最低限度应有相当规模动力厂之设立，虽不用于纺织，亦应为轧光等整理手续之用。惟高阳布商对电力之经济，尚无相当之认识，对此种动力厂之设立，或犹未梦及。于需要机械动力较殷之各种整理手续，虽有十二较大蒸气动力工场之设置，但亦各自为政，对合力而设发电厂以资公用，尚未计及也。对棉纱及布疋储藏必需之仓库，亦付阙如。成品及原料率堆积于工厂或商店后部，火灾之保险，及有系统之排列，以求取用时之方便，则绝未虑及。各种货物既如此堆积，则当商业情形疲敝，或周转太慢时，资本必受束缚。设有一较现代化之货栈之设立，其他利益姑不具论，即已被束缚之资本，亦可利用有流动性之栈单而减轻其束缚。至无现代银行之设备,以供给此规模较大之织布工业,尤为高阳织布工业组织上不完美之明证。金融之周转,皆赖一线市,前已言之。惟此线市组织简陋,实不能应付规模宏大之工业之需要。高阳有拨条之制者,专供市面之流通,格式为高阳商会所规定,流通既广,现款乃极少见,要求现款例须贴水。设甲商自乙商购得纱线,即付拨条一纸以代货款。设乙再向丙处购买,则又将甲之拨条转付于丙,如钱数不同,则乙可更开一拨条与之。设甲商需要现款以付工资,须将拨条按行市贴现,如甲欲避免此项损失,则可另雇跑街就原开拨条人以收款项。设此拨条系乙商发出,则跑街须先至乙处,如乙商尚有丙商之拨条,则乙商不欲付现而以丙之拨条易之,跑街须再至丙处,请求付现,于是由丙而丁,直至最终之债务人止。甲商于此,可以拨条面额请求付现,然雇佣跑街所费当亦不资。高阳较大之商人,每年须追讨拨条五六次,每次需跑街十余人,其损失当可概见。总之,拨条之制,拙钝异常,且因无清算机关,持拨条者实不能避免雇佣跑街之额外开支及因发拨条人不能付款而所蒙损失之危险。

高阳商人之无组织,可再设例明之。一九二八年高阳布出产总值凡三千一百万元,而无一人从事于运销之调查,以考其聚散之迹。各布商对买纱织布,以及销售,亦多固执己见,毫不合作。一旦市场上剧变袭来,则此种无准备无组织之危险更形显著。对需要之性质,来源,大小,既无考量,他处技术上新发展之报告,亦无搜集。换言之,处今日竞争激烈之世,高阳工业之盲目的凭幸运而获利,将不可能。不求织造上之进步,而用偷工减料及模仿以应付竞争,则更危险矣。

（六）中国乡村工业与中国建设

中国乡村工业，近年虽见衰落，但其在中国未来建设上之地位，不能忽视。苟设法将衰落之内部及外部之原因，铲除尽净，乡村工业实有社会的及经济的二大功能，以助长中国之国家生命。经济功能中之最重要者即闲暇人工之利用，此点于中国之农业更为重要。盖我国农民占全人口之百分之七四.五，其劳工皆具有季节性者也。上节引卜凯教授对中国农业经济之研究已可见一斑，客来塞（Cressey）教授之地理的研究亦有同样之结论。满洲西部之兴安岭，每年适于耕稼时期不过百日，而两粤山地，则长年可资稼穑。华北平原之人口密度每方英里为六四七人，已耕地则每方里为九七八人，生长时期亦不过二百日。其他重要之农区，则满洲平原为百五十日，黄土高原为百七十五日，扬子江流域为三百日，四川之红土盆地则为三百二十五日，①凡此皆足以显示中国各部于不能耕稼时期，有人工呆滞之虞也。最近华北工业协进社致罗氏基金团之备忘录中，关于农工之季节性之重要，曾作下述："在华北，因农田之纤小，谷产之性质及严冬之季节，农业已为零工之实业，农村除有副业可工作者，农闲之时间常有五六月之久。经审慎估计之结果，全国十五岁至五十四岁之农民因此而损失之工作机会，几等于五千五百万人之完全失业。且因气候之关系，及雨

---

① Cressey, G. B.: The geographic regions of China. In Annals of the American Academy of Political and Social Science, Nov., 1930 (China number); Nankal Weekly Statistical Service, Peb. 29,1932.

量之不定及不匀,以农业为生,非无危险。凡此情形,皆使现存之乡村工业极形重要,未可因其无科学之指导及健全之组织而厚非之也。"①

第二经济功能,即对本地土产及副产之利用。如上节所述,今日乡村工业之因利用当地原料而存在者甚多,如采矿,造砖,榨油,磨粉,粉丝,酿酒,果品保藏,毛织,夏布织造,缫丝等。农业之副产如芦苇,麦秆等则又为他种乡村工业之原料。印度之乡村中此类因当地原料而成立之工业亦盛,印度皇家农业委员会之结论曰:"工业及农业之关系愈趋密切,则乡村之简陋工厂(如轧棉,舂米,制糖)之数目及种类,愈有较速之增加。是类季节性之职业,实为农民经济之重要原素,如贝哈尔(Bihar)及敖黎萨(Orissa)处十五大糖厂,其工人之百分之七十五为农民。"②

第三经济功能为增加农民进款,使生活略有余裕,以备歉年及匪灾后之不足。据卜凯教授之调查,中国五省之十二县家庭工业之进款,平均仅占农家全收入之百分之二.九,但此成数在江苏江宁为百分之一四.八,在安徽怀远则为百分之一〇.四。③ 然依百朗博士(Dr. Brown)之调查,则四川省峨嵋山之二十五农家家庭工业之收入为十五元四角,占全收入一七六元一角之百分之八.八。④但此种收入,并非每农民皆然,依农田之大小及田制而异。百朗博

---

① 华北工业协进社致罗氏基金委员会驻华代表 Selskar M. Gunn 博士之未出版之备忘录题为 Proposals for industrial research and training, a phase of rural reconstruction, dated June, 1933。

② Report, op cit., p. 576.

③ Buck. op. cit., p. 98.

④ Brown, Harold D.: "A survey of 25 farms on Mount Omel", Szechuen, in *Chinese Economic Journal*, December, 1927, p. 1071.

士于成都平原五十农家之调查时曰："百分之五十八之农家,有育蚕纺织等家庭工业之收入。是项收入,每农家之平均数,为十一元九角;若只在有家庭工业收入之农家上平均之,则为二十元五角一分。对穷困之农人,不无小补。自耕农从事于家庭工业者百之四十,半耕农亦为百分之四十,佃农则为百分之七十九。五英亩之田,九人耕种之,其收入高至七十元。如此则佃农之平均收入为十八元三角五分,半耕农为七元八角,自耕农为六元一角三分。此种事实,足以指示佃农之农田虽小,而致力于家庭工业者甚大,且因较重之胁迫,不能不从事于此,以博收入"。①

其他经济之功能,为供给地方之需要,减少输入或促进输出以增加乡村社会之收入,均平乡村生活之程度,鼓励乡村技术之进步等。最后之功能厥为机器及运输便利对于农业上之利用,此点按中国之情形,最近之将来或难实现。中国农民小农最多,设能利用此种机器为农闲时制造之用,对农民始较为有利,不然则欲益反损也。

乡村工业之社会的功能,与经济的功能同其重要。乡村工业之特质,为小规模或分散之生产,其发展也足以避免近代机械工业过度发展后而产生之种种危害,且可得工人对机器之认识及应用。再者,乡村工业可使乡村人民习于制造事业,使生活更有兴趣,人民更为有机智进取。其教育之价值,亦未容漠视,尤以乡村工业之应用合作组织者为然;盖此种合作运动,能尽若丹麦之乡农学校(Folk High School)之职务。"独立或小组生产,使能参加较大之合

---

① Brown, Harold D.: "A survey of 50 farms on the Chengtu plain", in *Chinese Economic Journal*, Jan., 1928, p. 60.

作社以为社员,则可启发个人之责任心及合作之美德。乡村社会的传统观念,已为此种发展之膏腴;若再利用工业上之新组合,则更能促进大规模之社会合作。吾人闻有不少之领袖,产生于德法之相同组织之下,而终于在合作社及手艺工人联合会中占首要之行政地位也"。[①]

今日中国所两难者,为一方极需乡村工业以助益农民生计,改善乡村社会,他方则乡村工业方日趋于急遽衰落是也。衰落之原因滋多,吾人于前节分析河北省之乡村工业时已言之綦详。中有为非乡村工业本身所能为力者,如大规模生产之较为经济是,棉纺织业为最适于应用大规模机器生产之工业,故近代纺纱业兴,手纺纱业即如晞露之消灭矣。亦有为藉技术组织之改良可自行救济者,如教育与训练便利之供给,合作机关之设立等是。良以欲出品之能获得市场,首须求质地之精良,使能适应市场之需要。故技术之改良,实今日乡村工业之要务,欲求技术之改良,要亦非朝夕所可立致,而须循序渐进焉。调查今日乡村工业之实际情形与技术状况,最急切之需要与最适当之设备,以为改良之根本,一也;聘任专家研究,仿照各处农事试验场成法,设立乡村工业试验所,按实际需要,研究建设与改良之步筹与方法,二也;择试验与研究之结果之有成效者,推行于乡村,使乡农实地应用,三也。实则使研究结果,果有成效,能改良品质,增进效率,减低成本,乡农耳目所濡,自然发生信仰,起而效尤;研究机关所应注意者,予以改良之便利与指导已耳。

技术之改良既须加意进行,组织上之改善亦须因势利导。今

---

① *Proposals for Industrial research and training*, op. cit., p. 4.

日乡村各地农民之从事工业者，受其雇主与中间人之剥削者屡矣。彼辈每以工人无知，生计困难，从中克扣渔利，而工人因收入短少，成本缺乏，遂亦不能求品质上之改良，而致出品销路滞钝。推原其故，今日盛行之主匠制度及商人雇主制度实尸其咎，是以组织上之改良亦至迫切。至未来乡村工业之组织，谓宜利用合作方法，以尽调剂信用，采购原料，推广销售，发展动力，调查商情花样之职。今日江浙河北诸省乡村信用合作社组织已颇著成效。乡村工业之合作组织，亦可先行试办信用合作，范围局于一村，然后同时将职务与范围推广，使成为各地生产者之联合组织，庶小规模工业得有保护，获得信用购买销售之便利，减少被剥削之机会；复可以各业互相内外联络，以免隔膜而促进步。然合作社组织之外，生产与商人间之中介人，无论其为合作社之雇员，抑为独立商人，仍不可或少；所应注意者中介人为数不宜过多，且须能为生产者与消费者克尽厥职也。①

至此种技术与组织改进运动之费用如研究之耗费，合作社之基金，藉借工商界与银行界之投资，顷者上海商业储蓄银行与南京金陵大学农业经济系合作，从事此种运动，可谓良好之先例。而华北合作事业，几全由华洋义赈会经办，亦莫大之援助也。惟吾人以为此种事业不应视作慈善事业，以其有关乎国计民生，必须具有永久基础与长远计划，方得其可，否则，如视为慈善事业，则随慈善机关而存亡，一旦慈善机关消灭，乡村工业亦同归于尽，其危险为何如乎？

---

① 戴乐仁：《发展中国小规模工业的一个建议》，《东方杂志》二八卷九号，民二〇，五，一〇；Woods, op. cit., Part I. Ch. IV。

乡村工业与中国经济建设

一、中国乡村工业之重要

实业的意义,就是一切人类经济活动的总称。是人类为满足各种物质的或非物质的欲望的努力。通常可以分为主要实业、附属实业及自由职业三类。主要实业又可分为采伐业和种植业两类,像渔猎、伐木、采矿等是采伐业,农稼、畜牧等是种植业。附属实业,又可分为制造业及商业两类,属于前者是纺织、钢铁、工程、建筑、造路等工业,属于后者是运输、交通、银行、保险、转运、批发等业。至于自由职业所包括的,则是医药、教育保护、传教、管理、娱乐等各项职业[1]。乡村实业的意义,就是所有在乡村的这些实业的总称。在中国的乡村实业,自然是农业最为重要,根据立法院统计处的统计,中国的农民,占全人口的百分之七十五,或四分之三,因此农业差不多可以代表乡村实业了[2]。不过,乡村的制造工业在

---

[1] Bogart Ernest L. and Landon, Charls : Modern Industry, New York, Longmans, 1927, p. 214。

[2] 国民政府主计处统计局编:《统计月报》,民国二十一年,一二月号合刊。

中国也占一个极重要的地位：第一，因为中国的工业大部分集中在乡村；第二，乡村的制造工业是农闲时候的主要副业。我们说中国的制造工业大部分集中在乡村，大家也许要奇怪，因为在过去数十年中，特别是欧战开始以后，中国工业化进展的迅速，是有目共睹的事实。然而仔细想一想，我们也就会知道，像上海、天津、汉口、无锡等等的工商业区域，只占中国制造业的一小部分。我们试举织布工业为例，布是日常生活必需品之一，棉纺织业也是中国最有历史最大规模的工厂工业，我们常用来表示中国工业化的程度的，然而最近的统计告诉我们，在民国十九年全国共销九六一兆镑，当中力织机的消费量仅二〇七兆镑，而手织机的消费量竟达七五四兆镑。换句话说，也就是中国机织业与手织业的比例，用来棉纱的消费量计算，是一与四的比例，另一方面，乡村制造工业的重要，是由于这是辅助农业的主要农余副业了[①]。中国农业的季节变迁，曾经金陵大学农业经济教授卜凯（J. L. Buck）就安徽、河北、河南、山西、江苏、福建等六省里面的九县研究的结果，发现有七种主要作物——稻、麦、高粱、小米、玉蜀黍、大豆、棉的一年工作，有百分之八十四，是在从五月到十月这六个月中间做的，其余半年便只有剩下来的一年之百分之十六的工作可做[②]。农余时间既然这样的长久，乡村制造工业又是主要的副业，其对于农村经济的重要可以想见了。

---

① Fong, H. D.: *Cotton Industry and Trade in China*, 卷一, 230 页。
② Buck, J. Lossing: *Chinese Farm Economy*, Shanghai, Commercial Press, 1930, pp. 238-244.

二、中国乡村工业之现状及急遽衰落

中国现在的乡村工业,可以大略分为四类:纺织工业、食品工业、化学工业和杂类工业。纺织工业包括棉、丝、苎麻、毛、以及人造丝的手织工业、针织业、花边业、草帽辫业及织席业。棉织业自然是今日中国最普遍的乡村工业,前面已经说过,手织机的生产,占今日全国布产的五分之四。不过近来,因为外商棉布的倾销,特别是日俄的棉布,使得土布工业有急遽的衰落。即在乡间,洋布的消费,也有超过土布而上之的趋势。丝织业集中于江南数省;在从前,土织丝绸出品不但供给国内市场的需要,同时还运销到外洋去,近年因人造丝的竞争,已有衰落的趋势。但就出口而论,从民国十六年到二十一年,六年中间,丝绸与茧绸的出口,逐渐从二五,一七〇,九三四海关两,减到一八,四七八,九四〇海关两。夏布业在中国乡间虽没有棉织业及丝织业那样重要,在产苎麻的行省如江西、广东、湖南、福建、四川等也是一种重要的家庭工业。毛织业集中于华北;人造丝织业则是新近输入的乡村工业,主要的中心是河北高阳、蠡县等县。针织业在中国中部及南部很普遍,在华北的许多乡区还是没有见过。花边业则和刺绣业似的,以几处地方如烟台、汕头及上海浦东等处,特别重要,是当地的主要出口品之一,出口值往往在数百万元以上。织席与草帽辫大概都是生产这些原料的地方的本地工业,也运销到国外去,特别供给海外侨胞的应用。

乡村的食品工业,主要是面粉业、榨油、酿酒、焙茶、干鲜果品的制备等。面粉业本是华北很重要的乡村工业,但自输入外国面粉和国内自用机器磨制面粉以来,已日趋衰落。自一八八七年以后,除了几年是例外,面粉的进口,终是不断地增加。一八八七年的进口值,五六四,二一海关两,到前年,一九三二年的进口值增为三六,一七六,一二七海关两,计增加六十四倍之多。榨油业呢,也和面粉业一样,因为煤油的竞争,已失去从前的重要地位等。煤油的进口在一八八六年为二三,○三八,一○一加仑,到一九二○年则增至一八九,五八八,五四○加仑,在三十五年内增加八倍。一九二○年以后,略为减少,前年的进口量为一四五,九一八,七九四加仑。中国的汽车事业绝不发达,进口煤油的大部分都是用做燃灯的,因此在现在的乡间,无论是怎样的穷乡僻壤,已看不见菜油豆油灯,而完全代以煤油灯。而油茶事业本是南方数省很重要且很普遍的乡村工业,但现在不但失去了外国市场,特别是英俄两国的市场,就是国内市场,也居然被外国茶叶所侵入。茶的出口,在一八八六年到一九三二年的中间,以一八八六年的出口量为最高,计二,二一七,二九五担,以后即一蹶不振,继续低减,到了一九○二年,只三○五,九○六担,为这时期中最低的一年;以后虽逐渐恢复,最高的一年,一九二九年,也不过九四七,七三○担,去年为六五三,五五六担,仅及一八八六年的百分之三十。至于酿酒事业,我们一向知道绍兴酒是极著名的,此外山西汾酒、北方各省的高粱酒也都是名产,然而在宴会场中,饮用明星(München)啤酒与香槟的,总占大多数。蔬菜保藏业的情形也是这样。中国本有许多著名特产,而国外进口的罐头蔬菜很不少,每年的漏卮也极大。

关于乡村化学工业,这里只就造纸、瓷器、砖瓦等项约略加以说明。作为例证,这些门类的工业,都是依原料与技艺的存在而发生的,近年以来,也逐渐衰落了。造纸本是中国旧有工业之一,因为原料——竹,稻秆等的关系,集中于江南数省,而浙江、江苏、福建诸省的造纸事业为尤盛。然而就纸货进口量的增加看来,纸业在近数年来,也迅速的衰落了。一九〇三年我国进口纸张不过二一七,七二六担,但到了去年一九三二年已增至二,〇七五,二八三担,计增加十倍。中国的瓷业也是这样,在过去是一种极大极重要的工业,到现在,则最著名的景德镇瓷业衰落了。宜兴瓷业也衰落了。在化学工业中,唯一没有受外货影响的,是砖瓦业,因其运输成本的重大,远地的出产自然不能来竞争。在杂类工业里面,包括重工业如矿产的开采至轻工业如乡村的彩画,门类极多,不过也可以一言以蔽之,则是由于技术与组织的拙劣,及地方的不靖,灾荒的频仍,许多工业都逐渐衰落了[1]。

所以中国乡村工业的历史,是一部失败的历史,在欧西各国,当工业革命的初期,农业为全国最重要的实业,其为农业主要副业的乡村工业,其主要也和今日的中国乡村工业一样。到现在欧西各国工业革命完成,农业地位逐渐衰落,农业亦逐渐减少,英格兰与威尔士的农民至不过全人口百分之七,美国农民亦只占全人口之百分之二十六,德国占百分之三十,法国占百分之三十八,他们的制造工业的重要,远在农业之上[2]。而在中国,情形是不同的,我们的农业尚占全人口的四分之三,乡村人口的十分之九,城市制造

---

[1] Fong, H. D.: *Rural Industries in China*, *Institute of Pacific Relations*, China Council, Shanghai 1933, pp. 10-39.

[2] League of Nations, *Statistical Yearbook*, 1931-32, pp. 44-45,《日本帝国统计摘要》10—11页。

工业发展很迟缓，因此，乡村工业的衰落，意义实在非常重大，如坐视不救无异是自蹈经济上的自杀。一方面，因为工业生产的低减，国入随之而减少，另一方面，则以前之为乡村工业所供给的生产品，现在得输入外货来替代，即是增加漏卮。一方面减少收入，一方面增加漏卮，这不是经济自杀吗？

三、中国乡村工业与乡村建设

中国现在国计日蹙，民生阽危。是从各方面看，都极显然的事实；就经济方面说，即是政府也理解到趋于破产的危险。本来中国的理想政治是无为而治，最良循的管理只是与民生息，然而现在的政府也竟计议了许多经济建设计划，虽属纸上谈兵，至少也可见政府对于国家经济危机有相当的认识。自民国十六年国民政府奠都南京以来，过去的七年中间，这样的计划之多真是指不胜屈，最早有民十七年孙科的第一十年计划，其次有十八年国民党第三次全国代表大会的训政时期物质建设计划及预算案，民二十年五月有全国国民会议物质建设六年计划，八月有国际联盟中国十年建设计划，以及二十一年十一月组织的全国经济委员会的三年计划。除了这许多以全国为对象的经济建设计划之外，尚有许多经各部长官，特别是孔祥熙、陈公博二实业部长认可的各种地方的及特殊的计划①。在这些计划里面，对全国经济问题的各方面都曾有相当

---

① Chen, Gideon: *Chinese government economic planning and reconstruction since 1927*, Institute of Pacific Relations, China Council Shanghai 1933, pp. 6-25.

的考虑,农业因其关系之重要,自然得到了特殊的关心,不过对于乡村制造工业,却很少予以注意,只有在本年五月汪精卫氏召集的农村复兴会议中,有组织农村副业的提议。自然,一般的漠视这个问题,并不足表示这个问题对于国家经济发展的不重要。事实上,根据作者在过去五年中对中国工业问题的研究,以中国天然富源如煤、铁、石油等的缺乏,中国家庭制度对于个人企业的束缚,以及不安定的政治情形等等的原因,深以为大规模工业的发展,在中国很有问题①。而乡村小规模工业的发展,则是很光明的:因为发展这些乡村工业,并不需要巨额的资本与大批的人才。中国对于资本与人才,和苏俄一样,两感缺乏。如有需要,只有用长时间慢慢的积聚起来,或是完全从外国借入。此外,乡村工业普遍都是小规模的,因为规模小,无论在用人上,在经营上,伸缩性就比较大。普通乡村工业雇佣人工很少,除了农家的家人之外,只间或雇佣几个职工,或学徒帮忙,这样,劳工问题自然不会发生的。经营是可伸缩的,因为乡村工业普遍都是辅助农家的副业,纵使有一种工业不振,其危险是全体乡农所平均负担的,况且他们又都可以以农业为主要职业,而在欧西的工业国家里面,和过去数年内似的一旦有经济倾跌,即可以有百万千万依制造工业为生的失业个人。因为这种衰落的现象与失业问题,屡次发生,现在资本主义国家的经济学家与政治家,都在设法如何使竞争制度下大规模经济的现代工业制度可以稳固,同时也发现了小规模工业的许多优点。伦敦农业经济研究所所长乌尔文氏(C. S. Orwin)在一本近出的书《英威乡村

---

① 方显廷:《中国工业化之统计的分析》,见《经济统计季刊》第一卷第一期,三月,86—92页。

工业》(*Rural Industries in England and Wales*)的序文里,曾经说过几句极有意义的话:"无论从哪一方面考虑发展乡村问题,地方工业在乡村生活中都占一个重要地位。在过去,当村落还是一种自给的经济单位的时候,乡村工业的重要是很显然的。在现在呢,乡村工业的重要功用,是使乡村居民的生活更加充实,免得向城市迁移,许多近代工业的问题,也赖以解决。因此,这是日就显然的,我们应当研究乡村工业现在的情形,研究乡村工业怎样受近代社会经济情形的变迁而至于衰落,研究改进乡村工业之适合这些情形的可能性。在纯真的乡村社会里面,乡村工业因能够供给小田主及农工闲暇时以副业,能够供给一家男女老少以在本家或本村工作的机会,能够供给农业所需的几项要素,乡村工业或者仍然能够继续着辅助农业。现在,许多人随时随地都在进行经济原则与制度上的革命。乡村工业,以其集中人事上的优点,或者也可以用来抵抗货品的大量生产与大规模的城市工业单位。小规模的工业还有一种好处,就是可以使一个人明了一件物品的制造与应用中间的全部连带关系,使一人的工作,不但与他一人的生命有关系,同时与他所处的社会,也发生关系。"[①]

四、中国乡村工业所急需的救济

现在中国所两难的问题,是一方面乡村工业在经济建设上极

[①] *Rural Industries of England and wales*: II, by Helen E. Fitzrandolph and M. Doriel Hay Clarendon Press, Oxford, See Preface by C. S. Orwin of the Agriculural Economics Research Institute, 1926.

为重要,另一方面则是已有的乡村工业方在日趋衰落与毁灭。然则,这些工业现在所遭遇的究竟是什么困难呢?有许多困难,像大规模机器生产的比较经济的地方,是乡村工业所无法克服的。比如棉纺业,以大规模机器生产最为适宜,小规模纺纱工业便只有日趋消灭。其余的困难,则是可以藉技术与组织的改良去设法消灭的。乡村工业现在缺少应有的征信、教育与训练的便利,因为要使工业出品能上市场,获得市场上的地位,必定得适应市场的需要,生产质地良好的货品。因此,技术上的改良,实是首要的工作。第一,我们应当先调查现在乡村工业的实际情形,与生产技术状况,最急切的需要与最适当的设备,以谋介绍创办新工业与改良旧工业的办法。第二,聘请专门工程师研究,仿照已有成效的农事试验场办法,就乡村设立工业试验所,按乡村实际的需要,研究建设与改良的步骤和方法。第三是推广,即是把已有成效的实验与研究的结果,介绍给乡村工人去实地应用。事实上,如果研究的结果确有效验,能够改良质地,增进生产效率,减低成本,乡民耳目所濡,自会发生信仰,起而效尤,研究机关所应注意的是给以种种的改良便利与指导。

另一方面,现在分散各地的乡村工人,常受他们的雇主及中间人的欺骗。雇主及中间人以工人们的无知,茫然于市场情形和价格,又以他们生活上的急需,常常尅减价格,趁火打劫,从中渔利。因此,工人收入短少,出品质地往往不良,在现代工业化之社会中,乡村工业本是以质地见长的,这样,便一无可取了。推其原因,便是由于主匠制度与商人雇主制度等组织不良的缘故。不过在将来的发展上,可以用一种新的制度——合作社来代替这种组织。这种合作社组织,现在河北、江苏、浙江数省的信用合作社已开其端,以后很可以应用到乡村工业这方面来，以解决农村信用，采购原料，推广销售，发展原动力，调查商情及花样等问题。不过在组织上，我们主张先从最简单的办起，先办信用合作，范围限于一村，然后一方面把工作逐渐推广到购买销售工作上去，另一方面，把范围由一村推广到一区，一县，一省，成为各地生产者的职业组织；这样，小规模工业可以得到保护，取得信用购买销售等等的便利，减少高利贷者中间人种种的剥削；同时各业对内对外可以保持适当的联络，而不至于彼此隔膜，缺少进步。至于这种运动的费用，如研究的耗费及合作社的资本，我们希望能得国内银行界与工商界的投资。上海商业储蓄银行曾经拨款捐助金陵大学农业经济系从事这方面的事业。可谓很好的先驱，现在华北的合作事业，差不多是华洋义赈会经办的，这种帮助，我们希望继续进行下去。不过我们不希望把这种事业当做慈善事业办理，因为这是关系于国计民生的事业，必须有永久的基础与长久的计划，如果视作慈善事业，随慈善机关以存亡，则一旦慈善机关覆灭，乡村工业也要同归于尽，岂不是很危险？其次，虽有合作社的组织，同时生产者与商人间的中间人，不论他是合作社的社员，或是独立的商人，仍旧是不可缺少的。只是为数不能太多，而且一定要替生产者与消费者克尽厥职。①

我们相信，如果乡村工业的技术与组织能够双管齐下，同时改进，前途发展，实是很有希望，全国经济问题的解决，农村复兴的出路，或者都要求之于是吧。

---

① Taylor, J. B: A policy for small scale industry in China, in China Critic. March 16, 1931, Woods, Rural Industries Round Oxford, Part I. Ch. IV.

中国之工业化与乡村工业

一　中国工业化之特征

自瓦特发明汽机以来,西欧各国,类以"工业化"为经济发展必经之常轨,在远东方面,赖政府之提倡与资助,类似之演变亦已发轫,然以言自由经营或独创事业之成熟发展,则相距甚远也。日本自明治维新,俄国自解放农奴以后,莫不如此;至言中国,设非赖一二眼光远大之辅政大臣,如曾国藩、张之洞、李鸿章辈之倡导,则所谓"工业化"之实现为期必当较晚,此可断言。"工业化"进程之缓速,固系于各种重要因素之关联,尤以外力之袭击为著;但政府当局,至少亦应负其哺育成长之责,此无需讳言者也。近年苏俄于政府策划之下,排除一切困难,推进"工业化",极尽指挥自如之效,可为显例。

轻工业之片面发展,为各国"工业化"所同有之现象,西欧各国,如英国在工业化之初期,即以纺织业为最发达;法比两国,亦复如是。今日之日本,因缺乏大量煤铁之故,重工业之较可称者,仅军火之制造,而著称于世者,亦适为纺织工业也。革命初期之苏俄,其主要进口货,仍多为生产品而非消费品。中国之钢铁工厂,系创始于十九世纪末叶,但时至今日,经营最早规模最大之汉冶萍公司,仅余其惨落之陈迹,点缀于中国工业一中心区之武汉而已。

新式工业之集中沿海港埠,为东西工业化不同之点,而以中国为尤甚。诸如棉织业、缫丝业、面粉业、榨油业、制烟业、印刷业、机器业及其他次要工业等,多集中于沿海数大城市之内,即广州、上海、青岛、天津、大连等地是也。其同为工业主要中心区,而位于长江流域之腹地者,仅有武昌、汉口及汉阳三处,成鼎立之武汉三镇。此等集中趋势,其理甚明。盖工业集中之各区域内,为中外接触最早之地,外人于此,即可借鸦片战争以来历次修订之商约,推行其商务;复可援一八九五年日人作俑之例,从事制造业之经营,而外资工业乃益进。外资工业既如是兴起,国人乃相继仿效设立工厂。至各埠租界,无形予工业以投资稳固之保障,优越之环境,遂迥非国内其他各地在同一时期所能有者。租界在各工业国家法律统辖之下,关于交通运输事宜,及适应商业上金融上之各种机关,先后继起,在在均有助于工业之发展。且埠际劳工,既多且廉,各项事业,皆不缺乏人才,足供利用;即技术专家,亦可求之于海外各国,朝聘夕至。所有私营商行或公司之经济来源,类可敷适量设备之用,借收分工利器,及优遇得力人员之益。迨租界人口日增,其自身对此等制造品之消耗量亦随之增加,因本地出品,辄较舶来品成本稍低也。

二 阻滞中国工业化之主因

中国为一农业国家,工业化程度,甚属有限。试以中国今日最前进之新式工业,即棉纺织业为例。按照人口数字与纺棉锭数之比较,中国在世界各国中,居于末位。英国每千人有纺锭一,一九九枚,中国则仅得九枚,尚不及其百分之一。即与世界两大农业国相较,印度每千人尚可得二六枚,俄国可得四八枚,中国对之,宁无愧色?然则阻滞中国工业之前进者,其故何在?

新式工业在中国之不能长足发展,其因首在所处之环境。自社会政治经济各方面言之,均未脱离中古时代之本质。中国之社会组织,始终拘泥于终古不变之家族制度,此足使力能造成世界新工业地位之私人企业为之濡滞不前。盖徒知崇法先贤之顽固思想,而不顾人类进化之自然法则;奖进财产之集团消耗,而不事私人资本之积储。遂至新式工业无由发荣滋长。复次,中国之农业经济,原不利于新工业之发展,政府虽欲以任何助力,重定一左袒工业之新均势,然动遭失败。盖此等计划中所需动量之钜,实非人类历史经验所能为力。中国国民,大都以工业为农暇之副业,凡工业能以光荣之职业树其一帜者,仅若干城市中少数部门而已。中国历史中,向不知大规模工业为何物。有之,亦为餍足皇室欲壑之用,丝业磁业,皆其明例。且中国政府,自身即不能积极图强,俾有利于工业之长足发展,近百年来,复因政权衰落,而引起工业先进国家之统治热,致所有工业化可走之途径,悉遭杜绝。中国之工业,非惟不能享受保护关税之益,且须与本国领土内之外籍同业相竞争。就事实言,外人在中国经营之各种工业,恃条约之惠许,关于繁苛之地方税捐如厘金等,已蠲除殆尽,而中国之厂主,即在国府通令严禁厘金制度之今日,而有数地点尚未能普遍豁去该项致命之剥削也。

三　小规模工业在中国之盛行

今日之中国工业,仍濡滞于半现代化之境,大规模工业为数虽极有限,但无往而不遭剧烈竞争之打击。既须与国内之外籍同业相角逐,复不得不与漏税跌价之舶来品相抗衡。在中国走私之风,司空见惯,始仅见于汕头、大连等处,近复遍及华北各埠,由是倾销益烈,而规模较大之中国工业,胥受威胁而苦难支持矣。反观小规模工业,则获利较易,散播亦较广。欧美大规模工业之因技术或成本限制而不能以小规模经营者,在中国固不得不以大规模经营之,其可大可小者,则悉属之于小规模。诸如棉纺业、钢铁业、造船业、面粉业及水泥业等,均为前者之例;缫丝业、丝棉织造业、针织业、火柴业、印刷业、机器业及卷烟业等,则均属于后者,后者所以优于前者之故,或可作如下之解释:一、小规模工业需要资本较少,凡稍具进取心及相当经验者,恒易向亲戚及其他关系人方面筹得之;二、小本工业实际上无需固定成本之支出,较普通需要较完善之设备,而不能收大量生产之益者,售价可较廉。然以减低生产成本之机器代替人工者,自又当别论;三、"价""质"完全一致之大量生产品,中国社会并不需要;四、所有无须技巧之工役,皆可以家中闲居人员充之;五、厂主于厂务弛缓时,可暂使工作停顿,受雇于其他获利较多之工作;六、名义上独立之厂主,实则不啻一长于顾客之雇工,或为一种散工,专为商人雇主生产而已。

小规模工业在今日之中国,殊与工业革命初期之西欧各国情形相似。其微有不同者,即中国工业化为时较晚,故所处之环境稍异,而其工业化之途径,固亦难免异趣也。今日中国与小规模工业之竞争者,原非国人自营羽翼未丰之大规模工业,而为国内之外人企业,及舶来之制造品;但后述二者,至今仍与我国小工业之领域,无何冲突,纵或有之,亦皆与其本身有损无益,致此之由,其最著者,即过多之劳工,足使生存竞争愈趋剧烈;欧美各国工业化之发轫,恒以机械节省人工,需要既殷,成功自易;反观我国,凡企图以机械替代人工者,每遇经济恐慌期中,辄为经常固定开支所累,以致周转不灵,或于此人口过剩之国度中,无法抵制其廉价之劳工,结果辄遭失败。外人初至中国,乍观上海埠际脱卸重载时,多舍去机械不用,而代以浪费之苦力,往往惊诧莫名,若一旦深知两者真正耗费差数时,则将禁口不谈所谓革新建议矣。中国工业化显著之特征,固属多端,但以重人力而轻机械之利用为尤著。论者或谓工业化运动,加强劳工之需要,足使人口压迫,为之稍苏,殊不知人口之增加,有赖于生活程度之提高。在最近期间,中国人民生活程度,恐仍无提高之望,节言之,横死于水旱灾荒及长期"剿共"军事之下者年以数万或数十万计,其生活程度之低,益可知矣。

四 中国乡村工业对城市工业形势之优越

吾人曾于前述各节,论及中国盛行各大城市之新工业,规模均甚狭小;其技术上经济上,非小规模经营所能胜任者,始以大规模经营之。至世代相传之手工业,及农民主要副业之乡村工业,则均未论及。以生产数量言,此种工业——尤以乡村工业为甚,——其地位实较新工业为重要，此极易以简单数字表明之。试以主要衣料棉布为例：棉布工业为中国较为可称之工厂工业，援以为例，足见中国工业之进步，究至若何程度；惟据最近之统计数字，曾载明民国十九年一年间，全国织布工业之棉纱消耗量，达九六一兆磅，其中力织机制成者为二〇七兆磅，手织机制成者，竟得七五四兆磅。易言之，即中国机织业与手织业之比，以棉纱消耗量言，仅得一对四而已。

乡村工业之优于城市工业，本为农业国——工业前期之中国——之特色。其所恃以自存且能较新工业为更有利者，其因正与城市小规模工业相仿，即工力之低廉是也。因农季之短促，乡村工业之与农民，实不容分离。金大教授卜克（J. L. Buck）研究华北及华中东部之农业经济，曾宣称各该地带之农民，每年直接用于农产事业之时间，仅约四分之一。沪大教授克莱塞（G. E. Cressey）之地理研究，更说明中国之农季，因地不同，如满洲西部兴安岭附近，每年仅约百日左右，而两广境内之丘峦，则全年三百六十五日，均宜种植；至华北平原之农季则在二百日左右也。

乡村工业特盛之另一原因，为交通之闭塞。运货昂贵，故新工业之销售市场，亦囿于少数交通便利区域。其能担负昂贵之运费以致远者，惟绸缎磁器等量轻值高之货物耳。前任我国交通部会计统计顾问被誉为中国运输问题权威之贝克（J. E. Baker）氏，曾作如下之假定，谓："一搬运夫运米赴市；若往返各需六日半，则米之售价，仅能维持搬运夫在同时期内之生活及其家属，设每日行十七公里时，则售米市场将不得超过一一一公里，即二二五华里或七五英里之距离。"盖乡村工业，需借地方富源或副产物，地方商场及农暇劳工之利用，始获存在也。就事实言，中国之乡村工业，十之八九均赖利用地方富源以图生存,诸如采矿业、制砖业、榨油业、面粉业、酿酒业、面条制造业、果品饯制业以及麻系、羊毛之织造业等,皆其显例。至农业副产品,如庐苇、草帽辫等,又为芦苇、草帽等乡村工业立一基础,此与印度早年情形,约略相似;其从事乡村修葺及其制造事宜之手艺工人,如车匠、木匠、泥水匠、铁匠、成衣匠等,亦与地方商场不可分离者也。

五　中国乡村工业之没落

乡村工业之盛,实非经常不变之现象,中国工业化之尺进寸展均须牺牲若干小规模工业,乡村城市,如出一辙。此类情形,在其他各国初受工业化之影响时,已数见不鲜,工业化之英国如此,农业化之印度亦莫不如此。盖各地情形虽异,然终难与经济发展之常轨背道而驰也。今日之中国乡村工业虽尚有多处因农暇劳工之丰裕,地方富源及地方商场之利用,获有微利;但广大之内地,一旦受新式运输方法之启发,地方经济,有退让国家经济之倾向时,则所有乡村工业寄托之脆弱基础,设非积极早图改进,必将立遭严重之打击。盖中国非若其他经历工业化过程之国家,既无关税壁垒,可资屏障,复未能垄断设厂主权,归己独有,所谓自由商场,实已名副其实,焉能与世界各工业先进国相颉颃?益以政治之昧弱,偕经济之颠顿以俱来,又已陷中国为世界工业国家之奴隶地位矣。

中国之乡村工业,早现普遍衰落之景象;若非因其关系农民日常生活过于密切之故而被视为农业之一部,则其没落程度当更见显露。新工业剥蚀之反映,亦必愈形刻骨。今则乡村工业最后全部扑灭之趋势，亦已昭然若揭。目前中国乡村工业如纺织、食品、化学、杂组等四项，均一致惨遭渐次崩溃之厄运。纺织业中之主要者，如棉、丝、麻、羊毛及人造丝之手机纺织业、针织业、花边业、草帽辫业、织席业等，莫不呈一致之衰落。手织棉布业，为中国流行最广之乡村工业，自价廉物美之棉布，可自中外各大纱厂购得后，其没落之程度实足惊人。根据统计之数字，自民国二年至十九年间，虽因机纱产量之激增，影响手工纺纱业之衰落，致手织棉布业之纱线消耗量，增加百分之三十九；但在同一期间内，机织业方面，竟陡增十三倍左右。手工缫丝业，多设于华东华南各部，中外各埠，原多于兹取给；但因机器缫丝业之竞争，最近亦呈十分衰落之象。一八九五年间，我国出口之人工缫丝，仍达八三、五六五担，占生丝全部出口量百分之七十五，自后比数，逐年递减，计一九〇〇年为百分之六十四，一九一〇年为百分之五十四，一九二〇年为百分之三十，一九三〇年为百分之十七，迨至一九三一年间，竟降至一七.三〇〇担之最低数，约占全额百分之十三，相距仅三十七年，衰落之数量，已达原额五分之四。至手机织丝业之没落，亦大致相同。中国丝织物之出口，因机械织丝业尚在草创时期，故仍多出自手机，但于一九一五年一度登四一，一五八担最高峰之后，复递减至一九三二年之二二，二二九担，开历来未有之最低纪录。夏布之织造，虽在出产原料之各省区内，如江西、广东、湖南、福建、四川等省，尚不失为农民主要之家庭职业，但不若棉丝织业之重要；手机织毛业，多设于华北各地，尤以西北部产毛地带为最盛；人造丝手机织造业，新近始见倡行，为河北省若干区域内之主要乡村工业，其最著者，当推高阳区域。此等工业，均已显江河日下之势，如高阳专织人造丝之提花机，曾自一九二九年之四，三二四架，递减至一九三〇年之三,〇八九架,一九三一年之二,三五五架,一九三二年之一,一一八架,至一九三三年四月间,仅余二〇九架而已。其他关系较小之纺织业,当以花边制造业之没落情形为最可注目,自一九二七至一九三二年数年之间,出口货价,自四百七十万关两,跌至二百二十万关两,竟减少过半矣。

饮食品工业中主要之乡村工业,包括面粉业、酿酒业、制茶业及蔬菜果品之干制业等。华北之主要食粮,厥为小麦,故其主要乡村工业,亦即为面粉业,惟以国外面粉不断输入,及国内粉厂生产增加之故,该业亦呈衰靡不振之象。一九一〇年面粉之进口,为七四〇.八四一担,至一九三二年时,竟增至六,七〇五,八三七担,二十三年之间几增九倍,与国人利用机械磨粉业之增加数量,堪称并驾齐驱。至华中各地之制茶业,没落尤为惨烈,试以出口数字,作为没落之指数观之,一八八六年之输出额,最高时达二,二二〇,〇〇〇担,至一九三二年竟减至六五〇,〇〇〇担,仅及前者三分之一。

化学工业中,可择榨油业、制纸业、玻璃陶器业、砖瓦业数项言之,此类乡村工业之发生,恒视其当地原料或技术之供给而定,但其中之多数,亦已大见减色。菜油业所产油质,原足供华南各地烹燃之用,自煤油采作燃料后,不啻横遭劲敌:一八九〇年煤油进口之总量,仅为三一兆加仑,至一九三二年,竟达一四六兆加仑,四十三年之内,陡增五倍。我国发轫最早之制纸工业,因便于就地取材——竹料与稻秸——之故,多集中于华南浙赣闽等省,近年因洋纸之竞争,竟亦一落千丈。洋纸之进口,固为适应新兴事业,如新闻事业等之需要而来;但其源源不断之输入,仍为瓜代一度垄断市面之国产纸张,自亦毫无疑义。一九〇三年间,洋纸之进口,尚不过二一七，七二六担，嗣后逐年递增，计一九一〇年为五四九，〇三〇担，一九二〇年为一，〇二六，五一一担，一九三〇年为一，九九二，〇九三担，至一九三二年，竟增至二，〇七五，二八三担，达最高之纪录。该年输入数字，几及一九〇三年时之十倍，殊值吾人注意。至言陶磁工业，曩为江西景德镇——我国四大名镇之一——之主要工业，十余年前之生产总值，恒在一千万元以上。今日则尚不及盛时之半，此亦因……致陶业中心所在，受其影响也。

乡区杂组工业中，包罗极广，自土法采矿以至美术画片之制造，无所不有。试就河北省定县作一研究，该县四五三乡村中，农民农暇期间主要副业之工业，计业铁匠者一村，业木匠者十村，业锯木匠者十二村，业泥水匠者六村，业造车匠者二村；就次要副业之工业言之，计业制水车者一村，制辘轳者一村，掘井者二村。上述各种杂组工业，无往而不濒于没落之惨境，是否因技术上组织上之落后，抑因天灾人祸之迭来，则殊难断言也。

六　乡村工业之组织制度

中国乡村工业并无固定之组织制度，如某项工业，既可于主匠制度下组织之，复可于商人雇主制度下，施行无阻，即此一端，可知其屈伸自如之一斑。就大体言之，工业前期之组织制度，曾一度风行于欧西各国者，尚可求之于今日之中国。

家庭工业之组织制度，系于一家之内，以自有之原料、劳力、器具等，从事制造而供一家之消费，此可以农产为原料之饮食品及制造业为证，如茶、酒、菜油等。惟在一乡区内，欲求一绝对家庭化之工业,其例綦难,吾人所习见者,必同时搀用他种制度,尤以主匠制度为甚。如绍兴酒之制造,一部原定为自身之消耗,但其中之大部,仍于主匠制度下制造之,以谋推销市场之用。

工匠制度,复可分为主匠制与家庭工匠制两种,所谓主匠制者,系以一己之工具及工作场所,将购入之原料,制成各种精美物品,售之于买主,或商人;至所谓家庭工匠制,则恒以一己之家属,执工匠之役,其工作期间,时作时辍,技术方面,亦甚简陋,既无需成本过昂之设备,复不需多数房屋,充作工场之用,所有出品非售于小本商人,即送往集市,其直接售于买主者,可谓罕见,如上述草帽辫业、织席业、缫丝业及夏布织造业等,均可为家庭工匠制之例,而酿酒业、陶器业、制纸业等则属主匠制焉。

商人雇主制,系以商人雇主为中枢之工业制度,于购入大批原料后,或直接由其公事房、堆栈等处,或间接由其代理人,将原料分给散工,制成各级物品,粗细不一。浙江平湖之织袜业,江苏无锡之花边业,均属于此项制度。前者之原料,系商人雇主,直接由其公事房供给,后者则委之于代理人,其制造品之收集,亦须假手于该项代理人,其所以如此者,殆因工人分散各处,距离过远之故,惟此项制度,仍不能单独施行,正如高阳之棉麻手织业,非借助于主匠制不可。当需要殷切时,经营制造业之一切危险,将由商人雇主完全自负,但至市况呆滞期间,所有雇工,均陷于失业或半失业状态,其购入原料售出生产品等一切事宜,遂不得不以自身作孤注之一掷。简言之,即不得不就自身若干财力,冒险作小本企业之经营也。

工厂制度能于集中场所内,在统一管理下,求得大量生产。乡村工业中,如制纸业、陶器业,及采煤业等均属此例。惟此项制度除在少数特殊环境之下，对乡区不尽适合，虽以原料及人工方面，皆可就地取材，如陶器制造业，即为一例，但工厂制度，恒需有规定不断之工作，与农村社会之劳工情形，颇多扞格之处，江苏南通产棉区，曾有一纱厂，其开办时，闻专为农民暇时谋工作而设，惟自邻近各厂，相率踵起，与之抗衡后，该厂经理人，鉴于农暇农忙期间雇工之不时更迭，殊多烦费，为提高效率起见，卒毅然改弦更张，停工半年，俾就业工人，深知该厂最近不再开工，可转谋他业也。

七　中国乡村工业之前途

乡村工业在中国国民经济中所占地位之重要，如上所述。吾人深知中国之工业生产品，来自乡村家庭或乡村工场者，当在四分之三以上，惟根据西欧工业国家之先例，及最近中国工业之发展历程观之，乡村工业能否历长时间之存在。或作进一步之发展，尚属疑问。西欧各国之乡村工业，均为工场制度下之机械制造品，逐一扫荡无余。远在一八四四年时，工厂制度之权威柯克泰诺(Cooke-Taylor)氏曾作如下大胆之说明，谓："英国所有工业，以至遍及欧美各国之工业，其组织被工厂化之程度，日深一日，虽以人类之远识与其立法精神，对此等伟大变迁，亦如风向潮流，殊有无法控制之感，因此，吾人运用法律智慧之适当范围，乃在谋该项制度之如何完成，决非制止其进展也。"(*Factories and the Factory System*, p.111)

讵料自是以后，柯氏之预言，竟未见实现。此可分两点论之：

其一为工业本身之日趋分散化,其二则为工业组织中,合作制度已代替资本制度而兴起。近年以来,工业分散化之趋势,就各种新发展之能改变工业机构者观之,已由纯粹理论时期,进为实际需要时期。诸如新原料及其代替品之发现;自动或半自动机械之巧代人工;电力运用之增广与汽力之挫退,大量资本之分散城乡以从事于有利可图之企业;各大消费区左近制造工场之林立,及乡村生活有裨于劳工之认识等,凡此种种,均足促进工业之分散化,即在工业化程度较深之国家,亦无不如是,以言英国,则目前因电力传递普遍化之结果,工业亦随之有分散化趋势,如素以农业著称之东盎格里亚(East Anglia)、肯德(Kent)等州,新式工场,大小踵起,备极星罗棋布之致;其原已存在者,更无不力求扩展。为防止次要工业中心之逐渐衰败,复有进谋农业方面连带发展之势。以言美国,则最富兴趣之实例,莫如田纳西河流域(Tennessee Valley)之电汽化工程,该项工程,设一旦蒇功时,将为侧重地方工业化一切工程中之翘楚,欧西各国经济专家及来华游历者,如唐莱(R. H. Tawney)、沙尔德(Sir Arthur Salter)、戴乐仁(J. B. Tayler)诸氏,均着眼于小规模工业及乡村工业之发展,唐氏曾谓:"常人之误见,在默认如下之假定,以为'大量生产,既为若干重要工业有效发展之应有现象,则所有工业,当莫不如此。因之,欲谋经济进化惟一可能之方法,即在加紧提倡大量生产而已。'曩时欧洲各部,多不免为此等误解所蒙蔽,今则大部觉悟矣。中国自不应重踏西欧诸国之覆辙,盖中国将永为农民及手艺工人组成之国家,吾人如忽视其传统经济制度之改良而另倡异说,必致陷于重大之错误也。"(*Land and Labor in China*, p. 145)

就大体言,小规模工业之发展,在中国当较为有利。中国素乏铁、铜、煤油等主要矿产,故重工业无从发展。其家族制度"反资本"之倾向,与其纯粹不适时宜之运输方法,徒使地方色彩愈益浓厚,于城市工业文明之进步妨碍极大。且中国农民生产力超过消费力之限度,本极轻微,故其购买力及资产积储力,亦甚薄弱,此尤足阻滞大规模工业之发展焉。

工业组织中,合作制度代替资本制度之崛兴,显为有利于小本工人之另一助力,彼等恃以为生之乡村工业,亦多方受其庇护。当工业革命正盛时,合作组织即已开始演化。吾人深知构成城市工业战胜乡村工业之主要因素,厥为大规模经济物质上之实益,但在合作组织之下,资力薄弱之小生产者,亦可享受大规模经营之实益。此种组织之发轫,远在一八四四年,藉罗虚戴尔手织工人之提倡,其后发展颇为顺利,今已风行世界矣。由此不仅使耕地为生之佃农,得逃出地主商人高利贷主三重无情之剥削,即乡村手工业者,亦得同样脱离厄运而恢复自由。一九二九年杪,德国所有休氏式(Schulz Delitzsch)合作社共一,三八七所,其中之一,二五四所有社员一,〇一七,一九三人,社员中业工匠者竟达四分之一以上。苏俄于一九三〇年十月一日时共有工匠合作社一八,三六三所,社员二,〇〇二,〇〇〇人,其中约五分之三均来自乡间。至言印度,则所有漂染工人、皮业工人、木器工人、五金工人、印刷工人以及手织工人等,均有合作社之组织。美国名教授格拉斯氏(N. S. B. Gras)曾于分析手工业批发制度或商人雇主制度时,得如下之结论:"合作组织,现正赋与手工业以强有力之生命,为小本工人力求解脱。吾人舍此不由,则所谓手工业批发制度,及其一切剥削方法,将随之俱来矣。"(*Industrial Evolution*, p. 250)

中国之合作运动,已有十七年之历史,迄二十四年止,全国已有合作社二六,一二八所,社员一,〇〇〇,八〇九人,其中四,五九六社(或百分之一七.六)社员二二三,三九〇人(或百分之二二.三)均属生产运销性质;从事乡村工业者,虽无确数可查,但其比数之小,则毫无疑义。工业合作之不能扩大发展,虽与组织合作社时技术常识之需要及经营危险程度之过大有密切之关系,惟设能假以充分发展之助力,则合作组织,未始不可用以维持并促进中国现存之乡村工业,而追步印度、日本、德国胜利之后尘也。

八 复兴中国乡村工业之实施与建议

迩来乡村复兴运动虽已弥漫全国,但对乡村工业之复兴,则殊为官方所忽视。迄二十二年五月间,前行政院长汪精卫氏,始有就农村复兴委员会中,组织农村副业组之提议。自是以后,国府及其隶属各机关,对乡村工业,渐加注意。是年十二月,前国防设计委员会,即今之资源委员会,始就江苏省南通、南汇、溧阳三县作手工业之初步调查。此项工作,具有四种目的:一、明了手工业在国家资源上之重要性及其与国防之关系;二、考查手工业在国民职业上及所得上之地位;三、观察手工业本身之存在及其发展之可能性;四、依据调查所得之现状作为今后设施之准备(见蔡正雅编"手工业试查报告")。至二十三年一月间,全国经济委员会,复特遣工作人员,由国联专家沙尔德氏领导,考查浙江省之经济财政情形,该省之乡村工业,由是始辟作专题之研究。同年六月,全国经济委员会江西农村服务区成立,该省举办农村服务事业之十大中心区,亦随同设立,除原定农业、合作、卫生、教育及村政等工作范围外,复从事乡村副业之改进。是年秋间，实业部中央农业实验所，特辟一乡村工业组，以专责成，该所前此曾作赣省乡村工业之调查，其最大使命，为襄助各机关搜集材料，筹划一切方策，各省省政府及其他机关团体等，凡深觉其领域内，有此种必要或可能，并欲见诸实行者，可以之为顾问机关焉。

政府机关以外，对于中国乡村工业，注意较早者，私人如戴乐仁氏，曾于十七年在其短著《中国之农场与工场》(Farm and Factory in China)一书中，为中国乡村小规模工业反复辩护，吾人谓为此项倡议之第一声，实无不可。彼所持之意见，在"改进中国小规模工业之方策"一文中，言之更为具体，此文系贡献于全国青年协会所主办之民生会议（二十年二月间在上海开会）。即二十一年十一月间成立之华北工业改进社，戴氏倡导之功，亦不可没。改进社之目的：在"以研究、训练及合作组织等方法，促进乡村工业及小工业，以期改善人民之生活情形"（见该社社章），但该社工作，迄今仍限于下列三项之研究，即山西省之炼铁业、华北之毛织业，及河北省之棉花运销是也。

至乡村工业之实地调查，发动极晚，至二十二年一月间，始有南开大学经济研究所，应太平洋国际学会之请，着手河北省高阳区手工织布业之调查工作。高阳——中国乡村工业区之巨擘——于十七年一年间，所产棉织品及人造丝织品之总额，共值国币三千万元以上，实为中国工业化之乡区绝无仅有者。二十三年，该所复从事宝坻县手工织布业之调查工作。此两项研究报告现均编竣出版。（高阳报告见本所出版拙著《华北织布工业与商人雇主制度》及吴知著《乡村织布工业的一个研究》，宝坻报告见本所出版拙著《由宝坻手织工业观察工业制度之演变》。）他如中华平民教育促进

会之定县乡村工业调查工作，最近亦已分析完竣，刊行问世矣。（见张世文著《定县农村工业调查》）

综上所述，中国最近复兴乡村工业之实施工作，仍未迈出研究提倡等工作范围之外。虽因乡村工业，在国民经济中位置之重要，及其近年日趋没落之现象，均已引起社会人士之充分注意；但从事实际工作之领导人才及政府助力，均感极度缺乏，故乡村工业之没落，恐非短期所能挽救也。从事乡村工业者，当具有生产方式之常识，故教育与训练，极为重要。盖欲于商场中，取得地位，非借助于适合优良产品之生产方式不可，此而不谋，则失败无疑。此项阻难之解除方法，惟有多设专谋推广事宜之乡村模范工场，如改进农业，非先从设立农业试验场入手不可，其理正复无异，所望中枢行政机关中，有关工业发展之最高当局，如实业部，全国经济委员会等，亟起与各省省政府、各学术机关，及各业代表，善谋合作，以共挽此颓势耳。抑尤有进者，劳工群众，因不谙交易方法及市价，且因需款迫切之故，往往为商人雇主等减低货价，任意剥削。每逢经济恐慌，恒不免减低成本，使作物之品质，更趋低劣，而农村制造品所恃以畅销市面之惟一优点，亦坐是丧失。此种流弊，系由盛行各地之工业组织制度，如工匠制、商人雇主制等因袭而来；但就乡村工业未来之发展观之，新式之合作制度，即将代之而起。今日之中国，实与半世纪前之丹麦处境相若，当时之丹麦，既遭重辱于普鲁士人之手；复因美、俄、印等国成本极低之农产品，垄断市面，形成极度严重之农业恐慌，故不得不乞灵于农业合作制度，先后数十年间，竟一跃而居世界农业生产之首位，且以世界农业合作之模范国著称。中国之乡村工业复兴，果能勇往迈进，则假以时日，或亦不难有荣膺世界工匠合作制度首席之一日欤！

总之，中国工业化之未来，系于乡村工业之复兴者至钜，是项复兴工作，基于下列两大要点，即一面以科学的研究及教育方法，谋技术上之改进；一面须速谋以合作的组织方式，以代替资本组织是也。

一九三六年五月二十日

第三编
部门工业概览

我国钢铁工业之鸟瞰

方显廷　谷源田

一　导言

　　实业部与德商喜望公司合作，由该公司投资六千五百万元，兴办钢铁厂各节，业已志诸报端。对于厂址问题，实业部颇费斟酌，曾派员分赴各地调查，为时已达二年，盖铁矿蕴藏之贫富，矿质含铁之多寡，运输之难易，制炼成本之轻重，附近地方焦煤、石灰、水力等之供给是否充足，皆有关于将来厂务之兴衰，宜乎该部对厂址之决定审慎从事也。闻最近据调查及研究之结果，拟将厂址设于当涂附近之马鞍山，而合同条文业已详细厘订，签字手续，静待经济委员会审查后，始可举行。若此计划果能成功，且能经营得当，则烟囱凸起，屋脊纵横，蔚然大观，足为我国重工业发展之基础。此不特年可塞六七千万关两之漏卮，且有助于国防者实多也。

　　然我国国营事业，证诸以往，率皆有始无终，"议而不决，决而不行"，为政府之惯技。计划叠出，实行无期，堆积案头，徒壮观瞻。即幸"议而决，决而行者"，亦多以事业为位置冗员之所，以公款为徇情济贫之用，经营者乏责任心，凡事敷衍，一旦资金困绌，不谋久远之计,辄举债以苟延,饮鸩止渴,养痈贻患,终必至关闭而后已。实业部此次之计划,是否能见诸实行,实行后是否能经营得当,愿国人拭目以俟之,愿国人尽国民之责以监督之。

兴言及此,吾人有不能已于言者,我国已粗俱规模而停闭之钢铁厂,除汉阳及大冶外,尚有石景山之龙烟铁厂。汉阳、大冶二厂,或以机炉陈旧不堪再用,或以日债关系,无法整理,然龙烟公司之铁厂,设备完善,据云除印度外,置有东亚最佳之化铁炉。政府何不予以援助,何不就原厂加以整理?而重行举债,另建铁厂,虽为倬越之谋,然亦难免令人有大惑不解之处。

夫煤铁为近代文化之基础,亦为一国国防之先决条件。盖公理须以武备为后盾,国防不固,存亡堪虞,观夫去春一二八淞沪之战,及本年春间日军侵扰华北之役,飞机炸弹之凶狠,坦克大炮之坚利,可以审矣。月来太平洋风云紧急,各国急于军备之扩充,设一旦大战爆发,我国将何以自卫?钢铁既为发展工业及国防之本,则我国铁矿之蕴藏若干,钢铁工业之概况若何,是不可不知者也。吾人愿书所知,以为国人参考焉。

二 吾国铁工业发展历史

我国用铁之始,当在春秋以前(722—481 B.C.)。左传载:"禹使九牧贡金,乃铸九鼎",此处所谓"金"者,当系青铜,故至春秋战国时用铜甚广,兵器多用铜,然农具则用铁。历五百余年至秦汉之间,兵器多用铁,铁业始盛。铁用既广,政府渐加注意。秦汉时盐铁为政府之专利事业。汉武帝时桓宽以铁为制造农具之必需品,曾著《盐铁论》，反对当时之铁政。唐宋仍以铁归政府专办，金元亦厉行铁政，且招工或强迫开采，并禁铁输出，盖东征西伐，干戈扰攘无已时，需多量之铁以制军器也。明开铁禁，清亦不禁采铁，于是土法冶炼之炉，几遍全国，民间农具及其他家用器具，悉取给于土法冶炼之铁。然墨守旧规，技术上毫无进步之可言。截至海禁大开，舶来之钢铁输入，旧式铁业因之日见衰落。是为我国旧式铁工业发展之概略。

清光绪元年曾谕派李鸿章试办磁州煤铁等矿，后以订购之熔铁机器未能成交而中止，是为政府注重新式矿业之开端。光绪十六年鄂督张之洞创办之汉阳铁厂兴工，于十九年告成，采大冶之铁砂，从事冶炼，此为我国新法采铁炼铁之先导。汉阳铁厂，初系官办，以办理不善，资本告罄，乃改为官商合办，由盛宣怀主其事，后复合并汉阳、萍乡、大冶三处改组为"汉冶萍煤铁有限公司"，卒以经营不当，借债苟延（自民国二年起至十三年止，举债二十二次，共计借款达日金五七，〇〇〇，〇〇〇元之多）。钢铁炉早已熄火，矿区虽未停工，然系代人谋，采砂以供日本钢铁厂之冶炼也！

欧战期中，铁价暴涨，我国新式铁业亦因之而勃兴。民国四年奉天本溪湖公司冶炼庙儿沟之铁矿，民国六年和兴公司设化铁炉于上海之浦东，民国七年官商合办之龙烟公司成立，民国八年山东金岭镇铁矿为日人攫去，积极开采（民国十年改由中日合办之鲁大公司采掘），安徽繁昌之裕繁公司亦正式出矿，中日合办之振兴公司采掘鞍山铁矿，化铁炉亦正式出铁，同年扬子机器公司在汉口谌家矶建设化铁炉一座，翌年正式出铁，民国九年，湖北官矿局成立，开采象鼻山铁矿，至此我国新式钢铁工业，颇盛极一时。迨欧战告终,铁价暴跌,各矿厂以不堪赔累,纷纷停工。民国十年本溪湖铁矿停工,十一年本溪湖铁厂及汉阳钢厂停工,十二年扬子机器厂停工,十三年鲁大公司停工,十五年汉阳铁厂停工,十八年起福利民益华等公司亦相继停工。我国之新式钢铁工业,至是遂一蹶不振。

三 我国铁矿之储量

据实业部地质调查所之估计,我国重要铁矿之储量逾一,〇〇〇兆吨,分配如下:

省　　别	储量(单位千吨)	百分比(%)
辽宁	752,000	75.2
察哈尔	91,645	9.2
湖北	46,640	4.7
河北	32,424	3.2
安徽	19,818	2.0
山东	13,700	1.4
热河	11,340	1.1
浙江	7,154	0.7
广东	4,000	0.4
江苏	2,000	0.2
河南	1,019	0.1
其他(江西等)	18,454	1.8
合计	1,000,194,292 吨	100.0

据此吾人所知,我国铁矿蕴量四分之三系在辽宁一省,今辽宁已非我有;热河储量为百分之一.一,多于浙江、江苏及河南三省储量之和,而今亦沦亡,谋国事者其何以对吾民?

以上系专指其重要者言,至矿层过薄,仅适于土法开采者(如山西等)概未列入,盖土法开采,出产有限,不足以列入近世工业之林也。

四 我国重要铁矿之概况及其产量

I 重要铁矿概况

自清光绪十六年鄂督张之洞创办汉阳钢铁厂开采大冶铁矿起,至今日止,已领办之重要矿区,已采未采,采而复停,及仍继续开采之铁矿,共计有十余矿之多,略为分述于下:

(一) 湖北大冶铁矿 自唐代起即行采冶,历宋明而冶业不衰。光绪二年,由盛宣怀雇用之英矿师觅得,光绪十七年售与汉冶萍公司,同年开始采掘。矿局面积周围约计二百方里,储量达一七,三〇〇,〇〇〇吨,铁质甚佳,含铁成份在百分之六十左右,露天开采,成本极低。光绪二十五年,汉冶萍公司向日人预借砂款,订立合同,年给矿石十万吨及汉阳生铁若干吨。民国二年举借日债复与日人订立四十年内,除前次合同规定外,应售与日本头等铁矿砂一千五百万吨,生铁八百万吨。以二吨铁砂冶一吨生铁计,则须供给日本之矿砂综合为三千万吨左右,倾大冶储量之所有,尚不敷日人要求之三分之二,饮鸩止渴,愚昧至极。开采迄未停止,所出矿砂,输销日本,藉以履行契约之规定,为人作嫁,失却自给之本旨,殊可叹也。去年日本停止运砂,该矿遂濒于停顿。

（二）湖北象鼻山铁矿　距大冶铁矿不远,储量约计八,五三八,〇〇〇吨。含铁亦在百分之六十左右,于民国九年起,由湖北象鼻山官矿局开采,年约产矿砂四万五千余吨,一部份扬子机器公司冶炼,一部份则输销日本。

（三）辽宁庙儿沟铁矿　在辽宁本溪县东,矿区纯为山地,约高出海面一千公尺。二百余年前,即以产铁煤著称,日俄战后,遂归日人大仓氏之手,后经叠次交涉,始于宣统三年组织奉天本溪湖中日合办煤铁有限公司。全矿蕴量约计七〇,〇〇〇,〇〇〇吨,矿砂含铁成分不等,约自百分之三七至六六。民国四年正式出矿并炼铁,产铁多运销日本。民十一年因铁价暴落停工,民十二年十月复工。辽宁失陷,此矿久已为日人之囊中物矣！

（四）辽宁弓长岭铁矿　在辽宁辽阳县东,矿区亦为山地,高距平原四百五十公尺。本地居民久以土法开采。民国八年奉天省政府与日人饭田延太郎合组之弓长岭铁矿公司成立。全矿蕴量约为二七〇,〇〇〇,〇〇〇吨,矿质成份亦佳,富矿含铁达百分之六八。据第三次矿业纪要所载,迄未开采也。

（五）辽宁鞍山铁矿　在辽宁辽阳县之南,为民国四年日本二十一条件关于日本开采南满十处矿山之一；民国五年起,归中日合办之振兴铁矿公司开采。所采之铁,悉供给南满铁道株式会社所经营之鞍山铁厂冶炼。全矿储量达四一二,〇〇〇,〇〇〇吨。大部分矿石含铁太少,佳矿蕴量不多,但可采选矿法精选矿砂,以供提炼。

（六）安徽繁昌铁矿　在安徽繁昌县。初系国人与日本三井物产公司合组裕繁公司，后复将全矿转让与中日实业公司，民国五年农商部乃批准将全矿归裕繁公司开采，矿砂输销日本。全矿蕴量约计四,六四五,〇〇〇吨,矿质含铁平均为百分之六十左右。

（七）安徽当涂铁矿　又称太平铁矿。铁矿可分为南北二区,储量约计六,一七三,〇〇〇吨。矿质多燐,含铁最低为百分之三〇.五一,最高为百分之六三.三六。现归宝兴、昌华、福利民等公司开采。与日本订有借款售砂合同,故所产矿砂多输销日本。

（八）安徽铜官山铁矿　在铜陵县东南,唐时已开采,唐宋并设官以督采炼。光绪三十一年,英人凯约翰,垂涎该矿,与政府交涉成功,组织伦中理事公司,以备开采,同时又有日人组织之安裕公司,亦拟开采,签约一年后未开工,且交涉叠起,皖民激于爱国热忱,督促政府于宣统二年以英金五万镑赎回矿权,由皖省官矿局组织一纯粹华资之泾铜公司,拟采铜官山铁矿及泾县煤矿,然迄未开工。后皖省府以财政困绌,乃以之作抵,举借日债。全矿蕴量约计五,〇〇〇,〇〇〇吨,矿砂硫分稍高,含铁成份约在百分之五五左右。

（九）江苏凤凰山铁矿　在江宁县南,距南京水路约五十里,铁矿多在山顶,高出平原约百公尺。全矿储量约计二,〇〇〇,〇〇〇吨,矿质佳者含铁在百分之五五左右,民国五年华人与日人有组织中日合资公司之议,苏省士绅反对,政府未允,而呈请开采权者又纷至沓来,纠纷甚多,迄今未曾开采。

（十）山东金岭镇铁矿　此矿位于益都、临淄、长山、桓台四县之间。山岭高出海面约二百六十公尺。该矿之开采,系肇端于十三世纪,终止于十八世纪之中叶。光绪二十四年中德胶州条约许德人建筑铁路并开采铁路旁三十里路内矿产权,翌年该矿为德人发现,民国二年德华矿务公司与山东铁路公司合并增加资本,拟在沧口设厂炼铁。民国三年十一月日人据青岛,该矿遂为日人攫去,惨淡经营,于民国八年五月正式采矿,铁砂输销日本。民国十年华府会议后,青岛由日本交还吾国,金岭镇铁矿亦依中日协定,由中日合办之鲁大公司经营。民十三年起停工,至今尚未复工。全矿蕴量约计一三,七〇〇,〇〇〇吨,矿质甚佳,佳矿含铁在百分之六十以上。

（十一）河北滦县铁矿　光绪三十四年政府批准滦州矿地公司章程时,即已许该公司以滦州境内之煤铁开采权,但政府对核准该公司之铁矿权并未履行。宣统三年,复有华人组织永平铁矿公司,获得采掘永平境内之铁矿权,然迄未开采。全矿蕴量约计三二,四二四,〇〇〇吨,矿砂虽含铁不高,但可采选矿法,提佳者以供冶炼,交通便利,熔剂及焦炭之供给亦便。

（十二）察哈尔宣龙铁矿　此矿位于浑河流域之中部,在宣化、龙关、怀来三县之间,经政府所雇用之西籍矿师探测后,始知蕴藏甚丰。全矿蕴量约计九一,六四五,〇〇〇吨。欧战时铁价暴涨,官商合办之龙关铁矿公司乃于民国七年应运而生,后发现烟筒山蕴有极佳矿层,该公司乃增加资本,改名为龙烟铁矿公司,民国七年冬起始开采烟筒山铁矿,运至汉阳铁厂试炼,民国八年因欧战告终,铁价暴跌而停止。民国九年该公司又于北平西之石景山建筑冶铁厂,工程将竣,而资金用罄,遂行停工。

（十三）河南修武铁矿　矿质不甚佳,佳矿含铁只百分之四八.六六,全矿储量约计一,〇一九,〇〇〇吨,由宏豫公司开采;数月即停。

（十四）其他主要矿区　尚未经用新法开采者,列表如下,藉供参考：

矿 区	储量(单位:千吨)	矿 区	储量(单位:千吨)
湖北灵乡	6,340	湖北鄂城西山雷山	10,200
山东益都	4,262	安徽鸡冠山	4,000
热河滦平隆化	11,340	广东廉江仰塘	4,000
浙江长兴李家港	5,130	浙江建德淳安	2,024
其他(江西等省)	18,454		

II 铁矿产量

国内采矿之法,可分为旧法与新法。旧法采矿规模简陋,可称为小矿,多散漫各处,无法统计,只可作约略之估计。新法采矿,则悉系大矿,统计较易。兹将民国十六至民国二十年,五年来国内大小矿之产量列表于下:

年 份	大矿共产(吨)	小矿共产(吨)	合 计(吨)
民国十六年	1,181,235	528,900	1,710,135
民国十七年	1,474,900	528,900	2,003,800
民国十八年	2,046,996	583,180	2,630,176
民国十九年	1,773,536	478,950	2,252,486
民国二十年	1,950,920	496,100	2,447,020
合 计	8,427,587	2,616,030	11,043,617

据此吾人可知国内大矿五年内铁砂之产量为八百四十余万

吨。然欲知何矿产量最多,何矿产量最少,则请阅下表:

矿　　区	五年之总产额(吨)	百分比(%)
辽宁鞍山	3,424,766	41
辽宁本溪湖	642,267	7
湖北大冶	1,942,345	23
湖北象鼻山	662,617	8
安徽繁昌(裕繁公司)	961,533	11
安徽当涂(宝兴福利民等)	750,338	10
山西保晋公司	43,721	
合　　计	8,427,587	100

据此可知,国内铁矿产量,以鞍山为最多,大冶次之。鞍山本溪湖固无论矣,大冶、繁昌、当涂等矿皆与日本有借款售砂契约,故除象鼻山及保晋公司所产之微量外(约估总产量十分之一),国内铁砂产量,几尽入日人之手矣。外人谋我铁矿的详情,容另节论之。

五　我国重要钢铁厂之概况及其产量

国内制铁炼钢之法,亦有土法与新式之别,土法制炼及其他规模较小之厂不计外,兹将国内各重要新式钢铁厂概况,略述于下:

(一)汉阳钢铁厂　隶属于汉冶萍公司,在汉阳龟山之南,共有化铁炉四座,计一百吨者两座,二百五十吨者两座,每年最高产量可出铁二三〇,〇〇〇吨。炼钢厂计有炼钢炉七座,年可出钢七〇,〇〇〇吨,并轧钢厂等设备,规模宏大,惜以办理不善,民国五年起停工，至今尚未复工。

（二）大冶铁厂　亦系隶属于汉冶萍公司，厂设大冶袁家湖，民国三年借日债建筑者。以欧战影响，定购之机炉未到，民国五年始克兴工，十一年夏，开始出铁。共有化铁炉二座，年可出铁三二〇，〇〇〇吨，民国十二年起，以铁价低落，因而停工，今尚未复工。

（三）本溪湖炼厂　共有化铁炉四座，年可产铁九〇，〇〇〇吨。民国三年开始出铁，十一年因铁价大跌停工，翌年复工，现仍继续制炼。

（四）鞍山铁厂　炼厂纯属于南满铁路株式会社，计有化铁炉二座，年可出铁一八〇，〇〇〇吨。民国九年开始化炼，至今未停，且产量日增。

（五）扬子机器公司　位于汉口附近之谌家矶，建有化铁炉一座，年可出铁三六，〇〇〇吨，民国九年开工，十二年归六河沟公司接办，时开时停，二十年冬季，复行开炉出铁。

（六）龙烟公司　共有化铁炉一座，最高产量，预定年可出铁九〇，〇〇〇吨，化铁炉为纽约贝林马萧公司所计划，说者谓除印度外为亚洲最佳之化铁炉，惜资金告罄，未开炉即歇业，至今音息沉寂，复工无期。

（七）和兴铁工厂　民国六年成立，初设十二吨化铁炉一座，该时适值欧战，铁价暴涨，获利颇丰，乃复增设三十五吨化铁炉一座，欧战后曾一时停滞，后停止化铁设开心炉二座炼钢，每月可出钢一千三百吨，资本一百万元，纯系华资。

（八）阳泉铁厂　属于山西保晋公司，民国六年开办，设有化铁炉一座，于十年竣工，每昼夜可出铁十五至二十吨。欧战后曾停炼生铁,十五年起又继续冶炼,每日可出铁十二吨,规模虽小,经营尚得其道。

(九)其他 太原则有育才钢厂设有炼炉一座,上海高昌庙上海炼钢厂有炼炉一座等,详情不悉,故从略焉。

对于国内钢铁厂既有一概念,进而论国内钢铁之产量,兹将近五年钢铁之产量分列于下:

民国十六年至二十年生铁产额表

年 份	新式化铁炉产额(吨)	土法产额(吨)
民国十六年	232,278	178,870
民国十七年	254,973	178,870
民国十八年	308,090	135,368
民国十九年	350,641	122,226
民国二十年	351,905	126,130
合 计	1,497,887	741,464

新式化铁炉五年内之产量几近一百五十余万吨,按产厂细加分析,则可知产量百分之九七系出自鞍山及本溪湖铁厂,兹列表于下:

铁 厂	五年生铁产量(吨)	百分比(%)
鞍山	1,082,556	72
本溪湖	274,549	25
扬子	20,980	3
保晋	19,802	
合计	1,497,887	100

至于钢之产量，为数亦微，约略估计于下：

民国十六年	30,000 吨	民国十九年	15,000 吨
民国十七年	30,000 吨	民国二十年	15,000 吨
民国十八年	20,000 吨		

六　我国铁矿及钢铁业在世界上之地位

（一）矿砂储量　据最近估计，世界铁矿蕴量约计二二五，四七四兆吨，我国之蕴量为一，〇〇〇兆吨。占世界总量百分之〇.六。以国别论，美国居首，拥有铁矿九四，三二四兆吨，占世界总储量百分之四一.八；其次为加拿大，计二八，二四四兆吨，占百分之一二.五；再次为印度，计二三，八二六兆吨，占百分之一〇.六；再次为法国、英国……日本为八五兆吨不及千分之一，我国与西班牙同列居第十五位。我国储量若与他国相较，则当美国九十四分之一，加拿大二十八分之一，印度二十三分之一，英、法各十二分之一，德国四分之一。以每人之平均储量论，我国每人约可得矿砂二吨余，美国则为七八六吨，法国为二九九吨，英国二六七吨，瑞典四七九吨，日本则为一吨。然吾人须知，我国铁矿储量，辽宁占其四分之三，内地储量，仅及四分之一，即此四分之一，亦多为日资所缚，今辽宁陷落，矿不我存，贫而益贫，殊可慨也。

（二）生铁及钢　国内各厂生铁及钢之产量，已详本文第五节。民国十六年世界生铁之产量约计八四，七七六，〇〇〇吨，我国之产量仅占百分之〇.四四，民国二十年世界之总产量为五五，五五三,〇〇〇吨,我国之产量仅占百分之〇.六八。钢之产量,则更为微小,民国十六年世界之总产量为九〇,九三一,〇〇〇吨,我国之产量仅占百分之〇.〇三,民国二十年世界之总产量为七〇,〇〇一,〇〇〇吨,我国仅占百分之〇.〇二。我国产钢甚少,然需钢则甚多,据海关报告,每年输入之钢铁约在四十至七十万吨之间,产额与输入之和,减输出之差,则为国内消费量,据地质调查所之统计我国每人每年之钢铁消费量,计民国二年为一公斤,当美国三七二分之一,英国二三六分之一,日本九分之一;民国十九年为二公斤,当美国二八五分之一,英国一四一分之一,日本二三.五分之一。

七 我国铁矿与列强之关系

考外人之投资于我国铁矿业也,其方法有四:

(一)敷设铁路而要求路旁若干里内之矿山开采权,如依光绪二十四年中德胶州条约之规定,开采金岭镇之铁矿是也。

(二)与政府直接交涉,取其全省或一部分之矿权,如英商福公司获得山西若干县煤铁矿之采取权是也。

(三)指定矿地得政府之特许者,如凯约翰之于铜官山铁矿是也。

(四)以武力为后盾,提出条款,迫政府答应者,例辽宁鞍山铁矿迫于民国四年日本二十一条之让与是也。

以此四法,我国铁矿被侵殆尽,篇幅有限,仅将国内各铁矿按其性质列表于下,以供参考:

（甲）中日合办者：

矿　区	公　　司	储量(%)	备　考
鞍山等处	振兴公司	四一.二	采
庙儿沟	本溪湖公司	七.〇	采
金岭镇	鲁大公司	一.四	停
弓长岭	弓长岭铁矿公司	二七.〇	未采

（乙）向日本借款定有售砂合同者：

大冶	汉冶萍公司	一.七	采
繁昌	繁昌公司	〇.五	采
当涂	宝兴益华振冶福利民公司等	〇.六	采

（丙）中国独资创办者：

象鼻山	湖北官矿局（省办）	〇.九	采
修武	宏豫公司（商办）	〇.一	停
铜官山	泾铜公司（官商合办）	〇.五	未采
凤凰山	秣陵公司	〇.二	未采
滦县	永平公司（商办）	三.二	未采
宣化龙关	龙烟公司（官商合办）	九.二	未采

（丁）其他：

政府赎回者——英商福公司之山西煤铁矿权。凯约翰之铜官山铁矿。英商立德约之四川江北县煤铁矿。

外人自动取消者——粤商于光绪二十五年开采贵州铜仁县之煤铁水银矿，经营失败而自动取消。

八 我国钢铁工业失败之原因

国内新式钢铁工业虽已有四十余年之历史,然时至今日,委靡不振,停歇者比比皆是,其幸存而未歇闭者,亦多苟延残喘,是以国内钢铁之需,除土法出产之微量外,悉仰给于外人,长此以往,非但漏卮过钜,即以国防计,亦非久远之道。实业部有国营钢铁厂之企图,实为倬越之谋。然钢铁工业,经营非易,设处理不当,则失败堪虞,吾人愿将国内以往钢铁工业失败之原因,简述于下,以供国人参考,冀能知症结之所在,庶不致故辙复蹈,则吾国之钢铁工业,有厚望焉。

(一)缺乏常识　张之洞之创办钢铁厂也,对于铁矿之所在,矿砂之性质若何,及冶炼所需焦煤之有无,尽皆茫然,即以"中国之大,何处无煤铁佳矿"之豪语,遽行定购机炉。复以"大冶照料不便"及"见铁厂之烟囱",遽将铁厂建于汉阳。结果须以大冶之砂,搬运至汉阳,运费足以增加铁之成本,弊之一也;贝色麻酸性炼炉所出之铁,含磷太多,性脆弱,不适宜于制造钢轨,弊之二也,炼铁乏焦炭,乃向德国购买,成本倍增,弊之三也,此皆缺乏常识有以致之也。

(二)缺乏资本　钢铁工业,需资较多,国人对于公司组织,向无信仰,故铁厂每每以资本告罄而停业,其不停业者,亦须别谋补救之策,饥不择食,以苛刻之条件,募借外债,债多而利息重,息重而复举债,正如负草行于大雨中,愈行而负担愈重,饮鸩止渴,作茧自缚,良可慨也。

(三)经营不当　历来官办及官商合办之企业,多带官场习气,内部乏有系统之组织,不能收指臂之效;冗员多而且系门外汉,尸位素餐，徒靡公款，至于工作乏效率，会计无制度，营私舞弊，又其余事也。

（四）成本过高　我国人工价廉，产品成本，似宜足与外人竞争，然事竟大谬不然，人工虽廉，然其他则所费不赀。炼铁一吨，需煤二吨，故世界之制铁事业多集中于煤矿产地，德人有言曰："铁追煤而行，"诚不诬也。盖如此，始可减轻铁之成本，然国内之铁厂，除大冶外，多建于距煤铁矿甚远之地，成本随运费而增高，此外利息负担之奇重，经营不当之虚耗，皆为制铁成本过钜之原因也。

（五）缺乏专门人材　张之洞之创办钢铁厂也，虽有远识，但缺乏专门人材，冒然设厂，致使阻碍横生；不特此也，当大冶铁厂之设也，以借款合同关系，雇用日人为技师，计划不周，工程上缺点甚多，阻碍叠起，所费不赀。美国钢铁大王堪纳奇有言曰："使我之钢厂成为灰烬而留我钢厂所有之人才，我于六个月内即可建设同式之钢厂，"信哉是言，盖不特一人须能尽一人之功用，而又须有专门之技术也。

（六）时局影响　年来国内干戈扰攘，战争频仍，凡百工业，鲜不受其影响者，故钢铁工业亦不能例外。内乱一起，交通梗阻，原料及制成品之运输，发生困难，营业停滞，赔累立至，其甚者遭炮火之毁击，则损失尤钜。

统观以上，吾人可知钢铁工业之成败，端在经营之是否得当，若能人尽其事，地尽其利处理得方，则成功自在意中。语云："前车之覆，后车之鉴，"愿从事于钢铁工业之企业家，注意及之。

一九三三年十二月三十日

中国水泥工业之鸟瞰

方显廷　谷源田

一　水泥之种类用途及其重要

水泥系一种青灰色之粉末，着水后即能在水中或空气中凝固如石，为建筑工程之重要材料。"洋灰"，"红毛人泥"，"士敏土"，"水门汀"，"塞门德"皆其名称也。前二者盖以其来自外洋而命名，后三者则悉系英文 Cement 一字之译音。其种类大别有三：一为天然产水泥，一为火山灰水泥，一为扑特兰水泥（Portland Cement）。前二者，或系就天然岩石，加以煅炼，或系就火山灰磨碎，拌以熟石灰，制法颇为简单。扑特兰水泥则系将灰石、粘土研细，按比例调均，入窑烧炼，炼后冷却，再加入少许石膏磨碎，即成。以其着水凝固后如英国扑特兰岛所产之石，故名之曰扑特兰水泥。我国各厂所产，皆扑特兰水泥也。

水泥之特性，遇水即凝固如坚石，为近世建筑工程之主要材料。水泥未发明前，人皆用石灰及泥沙以为建筑材料，然用于运河及口岸等被水之处，鲜能持久。迨水泥之制兴，世界建筑术为之一变，昔之叠石砌砖，今则采用水泥矣。高楼、大厦、通路、桥梁、码头、船坞、水池、灯塔、炮台、地道、堤防、水道管等，凡百建筑工程，无不惟水泥是赖。无水泥，则今日世界之各大城市，决难有如是之辉煌，运输亦决难有如是之便利。钢铁、玻璃与水泥合作，则建筑界另放异彩，纽约数十层之摩天高楼，其一例也，是水泥之重要可知。水泥非特坚固任重，且形色美观，性能耐久，工作时颇经济便利，又无潮湿穿窬火患之虞。有水泥，然后可言建设，有建设，然后始需水泥。说者谓：一国工业之发达与否，视乎三酸消耗量之多寡，而建设事业之进步如何，则可卜之于该国国内水泥销路之畅滞，其重要概可想见。我国政府年来高唱建设，若果真锐意建设，则水泥之用途必广，用量必钜，而国内产厂之供给必不足，是则我国水泥业前途之发展，固未可限量也。

二　我国水泥业之沿革与分布

我国国人自办之水泥工业，始于逊清光绪二十四年开平矿务局就其煤矿附近设立之水泥厂。该厂初系延聘英人为技师，用旧式直窑烧制，旋以管理不善，销路未广，致亏耗停工。光绪三十二年乃将原厂让归华商经营，更名为启新洋灰公司。继启新而起者，为光绪三十三年清政府于广州附近设立之广东士敏土厂。宣统二年湖北大冶水泥厂成立，后以经营不善，民国三年归并于启新洋灰公司，更名"华记湖北水泥公司"。迨欧战兴起，向由欧西输入之水泥来源断绝，国内水泥业因以勃兴。九年上海华商水泥公司成立，设厂于上海附近龙华江边。十年中国水泥公司成立，设厂于江苏句容县属之龙潭。十二年无锡太湖水泥公司告成，迄未开工，十七年复将机器售与中国水泥公司。十八年广东省府应铁道部之请,于广州附近创设"西村士敏土厂",制泥以为建筑粤汉铁路之需。此外济南附近有致敬水泥公司,沿革不详;吉林省垣有筹备未竟因九一八事变而中止之众志洋灰公司。

外人在我国设厂制造水泥,最早者为英商青洲水泥公司,据云该公司系于一八八六年(光绪十二年)成立于香港,设制造厂于澳门及九龙。一九〇八年日本小野田水门汀会社设分厂于大连之周水子地方。民国六年日人设山东水泥会社于青岛。二十二年日人复筹设吉林洋灰公司于吉林。统计三十余年间,国内先后已设及筹设之华洋水泥厂,合计为十四厂,属于华商者九,日商者三,英商者二,此我国水泥工业沿革之概略也。

若以地理上分布之情形观之,则位于辽宁、吉林、湖北及河北省者各一厂,山东者二厂,江苏者三厂,广东者二厂,九龙及澳门租借地各一厂。此我国水泥工业地域上分布之概况也。

兹将各厂概况列表如下,以资参考:

第一表 华洋水泥厂一览表

国别	工厂名称	厂址	资本额	成立年	商标	包袋	每年出产能力
华商	启新洋灰公司	河北唐山	国币1200万元	1898	马牌	桶,袋	160(万桶)
华商	广东士敏土厂	广州	国币1200万元	1907	狮球牌	桶,袋	20(万桶)
华商	华记湖北水泥公司	湖北大冶	银100万两	1910	塔牌	桶,袋	18(万桶)
华商	上海华商水泥公司	江苏龙华	国币163万余元	1920	象牌	桶,袋	64(万桶)

（续表）

国别	工厂名称	厂址	资本额	成立年	商标	包袋	每年出产能力
华商	中国水泥公司	江苏龙潭	国币200万元	1921	泰山牌	桶,袋	90（万桶）
华商	西村士敏土厂	广州	港币200万元	1929	五羊牌	桶,袋	50（万桶）
华商	致敬水泥公司	山东济南	国币20万元				9（万桶）
英商	青洲水泥公司	澳门九龙	港币300万元	1886	黑驴牌 青洲牌	桶	120余（万桶）
日商	小野田水门汀会社	大连	日币650万元	1908	龙牌	桶,袋	150（万桶）
日商	山东水泥会社	青岛	日币100万元	1917	虎头牌	桶	10（万桶）
日商	吉林洋灰公司	吉林	日币300万元	1933	未出品		

三　水泥之生产贸易及消费

我国国内之水泥厂，为数不多，故产量有限。据本文第一表所示，以各厂每年之出产能力论，华资厂七，每年之出产能力合计为四百十一万桶；外资厂四，每年之出产能力合计为二百九十万桶。中外十一厂每年之出产能力合计为七百万桶。然每年实有之产量，则远在此数之下。据各方面之调查与估计，自民十一至民二十，十年来，国内华洋各厂之产量，约略如下：

年　份	华厂产量(桶)	外厂产量(桶)	中外合计(桶)
民国 11 年	1,564,892	235,370	1,800,262
民国 12 年	1,753,063	297,680	2,050,743
民国 13 年	1,494,315	601,088	2,095,403
民国 14 年	1,623,125	518,083	2,141,208
民国 15 年	2,284,444	632,411	2,916,855
民国 16 年	2,268,513	661,039	2,929,552
民国 17 年	2,535,076	1,041,651	3,576,727
民国 18 年	3,043,644	1,394,735	4,438,879
民国 19 年	2,736,311	1,323,500	4,059,811
民国 20 年	2,959,840	1,085,467	4,045,307

上列产量,虽未可据为详尽,但至少可作吾人之参考也。

国内水泥产量,既如上述,请进而论水泥贸易。水泥为近代之新工业,我国初无出产,故国内所需,悉仰给于外人。降及逊清光绪中叶,国人始自办水泥厂。事属初创,信誉未孚,且规模甚小,终难与舶来品相颉颃,是故洋产水泥,源源而入。欧战期中,洋产水泥输入锐减,国内水泥业因而勃兴。欧战结束后,洋产水泥贬价竞销,复行涌来。此我国水泥输入之概况也。以言输出,据海关贸易统计册所载,则始自民国元年(一九一二)。兹将历年输入之洋产水泥,及输出之国产水泥统计列表如下,以资参考:

第二表　中国历年水泥进出口统计

(单位:千担)

年份	进口	出口	年份	进口	出口
1894	165		1898	303	
1895	110		1899	238	
1896	——		1900	——	
1897	——		1901	——	

（续表）

年份	进口	出口	年份	进口	出口
1902	——		1918	862	503
1903	347		1919	1,515	170
1904	262		1920	1,752	174
1905	554		1921	2,534	87
1906	913		1922	3,179	7
1907	1,592		1923	2,655	267
1908	1,411		1924	1,788	408
1909	1,656		1925	1,761	397
1910	1,704		1926	2,417	464
1911	780		1927	1,916	503
1912	489	220	1928	2,281	1,048
1913	618	396	1929	2,833	1,065
1914	890	472	1930	3,045	1,009
1915	701	518	1931*	3,289	444
1916	827	239	1932**	3,670	329
1917	706	395	1933**	2,279	19

* 只包括东三省上半年之统计。

** 东三省除外。

若以水泥输入之国别论，则以输自日本及朝鲜、（中国）台湾者为最多，香港及安南次之，澳门更次之。日本、朝鲜、（中国）台湾，与我国一水相隔，海运极便，故可源源而来。自台湾输入之水泥，系日商浅野水泥会社台湾支社之出品；自香港及澳门输入者，多为英商青洲水泥公司之出品，自安南输入者，当系法商海防水泥公司之出品。水泥之为物，值低而体重，远道运输，运费过钜，故只适于短程之贩运，是以自其他各国输入之水泥，为量甚微，无足轻重。洋产水泥之输入，以经上海、安东、大连、广州海关入口者为最多。

以论输出，须察输出之水泥皆为国内何厂之产品，及出口水泥，多系运往何处。试分别论之：

（一）欲知历年输出之水泥皆系何厂之出品，则须先考察水泥究系经何处海关出口。以数量论，水泥输出，以经天津关者为最多，次为大连，再次为秦皇岛，再次为镇江、上海、汉口、广州、南京等。自天津及秦皇岛输出者，悉为启新洋灰公司之出品；自大连出口者，为小野田大连支社之出品，自上海出口者，为上海华商水泥公司之出品，自镇江及南京出口者，则为中国龙潭水泥公司之出品，汉口为华记湖北水泥公司之产品，广州则为广东及西村二厂之出品无疑。

（二）国产水泥之出口，以运往香港者为最多，历年皆占水泥总输出半数以上。香港系一无税口岸，水泥运往香港，非为香港当地所消费，及经由香港而转口也。输往南洋一带（安南、印度、新嘉坡、爪哇等处），为次多；日本、朝鲜、（中国）台湾更次之。至输往其他国家，时有时无，为最殊微，无足道及。

关于国内之水泥生产，输入及输出等，业已论及，请进而论国内之水泥消费量。国内产量加输入量，减输出量，即可窥知消费之概数。爰就十年来之统计，列表于下，以资参考：

第三表　民国十一年至二十年中国水泥消费统计表

（单位：桶）

年份	国内产量	输入量*	输出量*	消费量
民国 11 年	1,800,262	931,509	2,383	2,729,388
民国 12 年	2,050,743	627,298	93,851	2,584,190
民国 13 年	2,095,403	617,914	143,063	2,590,254
民国 14 年	2,141,208	848,031	139,307	2,849,932
民国 15 年	2,916,855	672,100	162,950	3,426,005
民国 16 年	2,929,552	800,159	176,333	3,553,378
民国 17 年	3,576,727	993,960	367,581	4,203,106
民国 18 年	4,438,379	1,068,338	373,635	5,133,082
民国 19 年	4,059,811	1,153,927	354,047	4,859,691
民国 20 年	4,045,307	1,287,758	155,815	5,177,250

* 按每担合 133 1/3 磅，每桶合 380 磅计算而得。

据上表所示，国内每年之水泥消费量最近约五百二十万桶。统计不完，此数或失之太低。据外人之估计，国内每年之水泥消费量约七百万桶或二十六兆磅，若姑以此数为准，则每一国民年消费之水泥约为六磅，与安南、（中国）台湾之每一国民消费量等。朝鲜为七磅半，菲律滨为十五磅，日本为一三一.六磅，当中国之二十二倍，美国为四五〇磅，当中国之七十五倍。国内水泥消费量之微，与夫建设事业之亟待发展，于此可见一斑。

四　衰落原因及改革建议

我国之水泥工业，自创始迄今，已有三十余年之历史，虽有相当之发展，然自国内水泥消费量增加之速度观之，发展似过濡缓。即现有之厂，每年之销售量，亦只当其产量十分之九。旧厂产品销路不振，新厂自不易增设。我国水泥业之不克发展，厥因甚多，试摘要述之。

（一）一般原因　我国水泥工业不克发展之一般原因可分数端述之于下：

（甲）国民之迷信愚昧及守旧　我国教育不普及，人民缺乏科学知识，性富保守，对于矿山开发，以其与风水有关，每疾首痛心，出而阻止。制造水泥，则非开采灰石及粘土不可。且水泥系一种新工业，人民以未晓其用度，故多踟蹰不肯采用。既采用矣，亦每对国人之出品，发生怀疑。此我国水泥工业不克迅速发展一般原因之一也。

（乙）政府乏建设政策　逊清之末，政治窳败，固无足论，即鼎革后，军人政客，徒忙于政争，无暇注意国内之经济建设。堤防失修，水道不整，洪水泛滥不问也；道路冲坏，桥梁倾塌，不问也。设当时政府，实施建设工程，则我国之水泥工业，因需要增加，自必大为发展也。

（丙）国内工商业发展迟缓之影响　建筑事业，每可为工商业发展之风雨表。盖工业发达，建工厂，筑堆栈，修房屋，整道路，建筑事业，与以俱兴。建筑事业兴，则采用水泥为量自钜，水泥事业，因以发展。惜我国生产落后，缺乏资本组织与技术人员，且关税不得自主，对国内实业，无法实施保护之策，致使国内实业发展迟缓，而水泥工业亦直接间接受其影响。此我国水泥工业不克迅速发展一般原因之三也。

（二）特殊原因

（甲）成本过高　制造水泥所需之原料为灰石、粘土、石膏及煤炭。原料笨重，搬运费高，故创办水泥事业，厂址地点，须择原料丰产之区。然厂址是否接近水道铁路，运输上是否便利，是否接近市场，皆须加以注意。我国已有之水泥厂，对于上述各点，诸多顾到，惟增加成本者，乃在燃料所用之煤。我国既乏天然之煤气，又乏煤油之供给，故煤为制造水泥之惟一燃料。据云在消耗烟煤最多之工业中，水泥占第四位。故制造水泥所需之煤，其重量为制成水泥之半数，例如所制之水泥为四百吨，所需之煤则为二百吨。故煤愈廉，则水泥之成本愈低。而所需之煤，则须为烟煤，而非无烟白煤。且煤须有恒久不断之供给，否则甚为危险，菲律滨水泥公司之失败，即原于此，可为殷鉴。考我国之水泥厂，除启新洋灰公司及致敬水泥公司设于煤矿附近外，余者如湖北华记、上海华商、龙潭、广东、西村等厂，所需之煤，非购自开滦矿务局，即购自日本、

(中国)台湾或安南,路途遥远,运费过钜,致使水泥之成本大增,难与舶来品相抗衡。综此数因,国内水泥之消费量,虽远在国内各厂出产能力之上,然各厂每年之实有产量,则远在生产能力之下,且水泥销额,仅及实有产额十分之九,而外国水泥却源源而来。成本过高,以致运销不便,事甚显然。

(乙)外厂与外货之倾销　外商在我国内设立之水泥厂,其产量之钜,与夫经营之得宜,远非我国各厂所能及。故外厂出品之减价倾销,势所难免。我国关税自主权丧失历数十年之久,权不我存,无法增筑关税壁垒,以杜外货之倾销,而施行国内水泥业保护之策,致使外货潮涌,国产水泥,大受压迫。

(丙)内乱之影响　我国年来,政变叠兴,军阀割据,内乱频仍,交通阻断,凡百工商,莫不大受影响,而水泥业亦不能例外。如民十一年奉直之战,奉军大扣京奉路之车辆,致唐山启新洋灰公司之水泥运输大受影响。民国十六年北伐之役,龙潭水泥厂曾受战事影响而停工,此又一例也。

以上所述,概为我国水泥业发展迟缓之原因。请进而论补救方策。

(1)政府明令提倡　政府年来,高唱经济建设,若果真锐意建设,则需用之水泥为量必钜。政府不妨明令规定,一切政府建筑,非至万不得已,概须采用国产水泥。对舶来之水泥,若果悉其确系贬价倾销,则无妨酌量情形,提高关税或加征倾销税,借以保护国内华商各厂。

(2)改良并扩充旧有之厂,并酌增办新厂　国内已有之厂,应设法改良,使一切合理化,提高利用程度,减低出品成本,改善推销方法。旧厂更应扩充,新厂亦应酌量添增,总期国内所产水泥,足够国内之需求。

其他如国内石膏矿之亟应开发,运输上之亟应谋求便利,以广销场等,皆为发展国内水泥业之要务也。

一九三四年十二月五日

# 第四编
## 中国区域与战时工业论丛

西南经济建设与工业化

一、西南经济概况

西南一词,恒指粤、桂、川、康、滇、黔等省。自军兴以来,我国最高当局,采取以空间战胜时间之抗战政策,西南各省,遂一跃而为全国军事政治经济及交通之重心,开发西南运动,遂为朝野上下所注目。最近,闻行营有西南经济建设委员会之设,划川、康、滇、黔四省为该会工作对象,于是西南一词,包括范围较狭,然含义则更见肯定。良以战区日广,即位居西南之粤、桂等省,从经济建设立场言,自宜另划为外卫区域,而以川、康、滇、黔四省为建设之中心。本文所指之西南亦照行营定义,庶免混淆。

川、康、滇、黔四省之面积为一,四五一千方公里,占全国面积(一一,一七四千方公里)八分之一,内康四七三千方公里居首,川四〇四千方公里,滇三九九千方公里,黔一七六千方公里次之。四省人口为七九,八八八,〇〇〇人,占全国人口(四四一,八四九,〇〇〇)六分之一强。内川五四,〇一〇,〇〇〇人居首,黔一二,六九二,〇〇〇人,滇一二,六六五,〇〇〇人,康五二一,〇〇〇人次之。人口密度，若以每平方公里计，则以川之一三四人为最高，黔之七二人，滇之三二人，及康之一人次之。四省人口平均密度每方公里为五五人，较全国平均四〇人约高出四分之一。

西南四省之面积及人口，各占全国面积与人口八分之一及六分之一，其重要概可想见。至于四省之物产，亦极富饶，试就农林畜牧与矿，逐一述之如下：

就农产言，据中央农业实验所二十五年之二十一省（东四省，西康、广西、新疆、西藏，蒙古除外）调查川滇黔三省各种农产量占全国农产量之百分比，蚕豆为四四，油菜为三八，烟叶为三四，豌豆为三二，玉米为二七，大麦为二四，稻为一九，大豆及花生各为一二，小麦为一一，高粱为八，棉花为四，小米为二（见表一）。可知三省—特别四川——之粮食生产，尚堪自给；而油菜烟叶之属，产

表一 民国二十五年西南各省主要作物产量统计

（单位：千市担）

	四川	云南	贵州	三省合计数量	占全国之%	中国
冬季作物						
小麦	38,395	7,195	5,854	51,444	11	461,555
大麦	30,633	3,884	4,808	39,325	24	162,748
豌豆	17,968	2,789	1,621	22,378	32	69,096
蚕豆	16,319	9,615	1,791	27,725	44	62,253
油菜	14,877	1,518	2,396	18,791	38	49,572
夏季作物						
稻	119,402	30,970	18,999	169,371	19	871,002
高粱	11,179	664	661	12,504	8	153,532

（续表）

	四川	云南	贵州	三省合计数量	占全国之%	中国
小米	1,866	490	425	2,781	2	135,487
玉米	20,220	7,350	5,519	33,089	27	122,602
大豆	8,169	3,785	2,512	14,466	12	118,220
棉花	755	40	78	873	4	20,639
花生	4,946	294	911	6,151	12	52,622
烟叶	2,763	354	1,178	4,295	34	12,673

量甚丰，如能设法就地加工，则自给之余，尚可外销。至衣料如棉花之类，三省产量只占全国产量百分之四，其不能自给而必须取诸邻省以资调剂，则又灼然可见。他如桐油、茶叶、丝茧及蔗糖之生产，虽无确切统计，然为量必甚可观，若能善加提倡，力求改进，则自给外可供外销者，为量当不在少也。

表二　西南各省林作面积统计

（面积单位：百万公亩）

	贵州	云南	四川	西康	四省合计	全国
总面积	1,765	3,986	4,036	4,727	14,514	111,736
林地面积	882	1,993	1,978	2,364	7,217	43,958
占总面积(%)	50	50	49	50	50	39
森林地面积	159	917	1,372	95	2,543	9,109
% 总面积	9	23	34	2	17	9
% 林作面积	18	46	69	4	35	21
宜林地面积	723	1,076	606	2,269	4,674	34,849
% 总面积	41	27	15	48	33	30
% 林作面积	82	54	31	96	64	79

西南各省，崇山峻岭，最宜林牧事业。川康滇黔四省一如东北四省及闽、湘、青海，其林地面积，均占全面积二分之一。四省合计，有林地七，二一七兆公亩，占全国林地面积（四三，九五八兆公亩）六分之一。惜人谋不臧，造林事业，未能积极进行，致有林地面积远在宜林地面积之下。四省林地面积占全面积百分之五十，然有林地面积，仅占全面积百分之一七，其余百分之三三，为宜林地。若按省计，则有林地面积，占全面积之百分比，以四川之三四居首，云南之二三，贵州之九，及西康之二次之。至畜牧事业，多为农业之附庸，单独经营者，尚属罕见。川、滇、黔三省——特别四川——均产耕作用之水牛及农家副产如猪及家禽（包括鸭鹅鸡）之属，至供运输用之骡驴及供衣料用之绵羊、山羊等，则为数有限。如表三所示，全国二十一省中，川、滇、黔三省所占之百分比，水牛为三六，猪为二六，家禽为一四，马为二○，骡驴为三，山羊及绵羊为一一。

表三　西南各省牲畜统计　（单位：千头）

	四川	云南	贵州	三省合计	全国	三省占全国之(%)
牛						
水牛	2,767	714	694	4,175	11,603	36
牛	986	805	546	2,337	22,647	10
猪	11,738	2,696	1,652	16,086	62,639	26
马	158	471	200	829	4,080	20
骡驴						
骡	98	314	23	435	4,666	9
驴	40	50	6	96	10,547	1
羊						
山羊	3,427	501	415	4,343	21,933	20

（续表）

	四川	云南	贵州	三省合计	全国	三省占全国之(%)
绵羊	234	111	120	465	20,957	2
家畜						
鸭	7,995	1,478	1,146	10,619	56,724	19
鹅	1,279	129	215	1,623	10,538	15
鸡	22,355	5,315	5,201	33,871	246,688	13

西南各省之矿藏，种类虽多，为量则甚有限，煤铁之类尤甚。全国二十七省煤储量（西康、西藏、蒙古除外）估计为二四三，六六九兆公吨，川滇黔三省仅一三，〇五〇兆公吨，占全国煤储量百分之五强，内川为九，八七四兆公吨，滇为一，六二七兆公吨，黔为一，五四九兆公吨。铁矿储量，四川较富，估计为一百万吨，不及全国（东四省在内）储量（一，二〇六兆吨）千分之一。其他矿产之较著者，厥为川滇之岩盐，川康之砂金，川省之石油，滇省之锡，及黔省之汞等。至铜锌铝等，则三省均有发现，而以云南为尤夥。

由上所述，西南各省除四川外，其他三省之人口密度，均甚微小，而西康尤甚。盖西南诸省受地理及人事之限制，与外界殊少往来，类多闭关自守，呈十足之中古时代地方经济色彩。复以烟祸蔓延，居民体质横被削弱，驯致懒惰成性，绝鲜现代社会所具之进取精神。在重庆、成都、昆明、贵阳等大都市中，虽不乏电灯、电话、自来水、轮船、汽车等现代经济产物，以及一切供给有闲阶级消费之奢侈用品与设备，然不过少数人之享受而已，与一般人民之生活及现代生产之促进，要无重大关系。抗战以来，西南各省，一跃而为抗战胜利民族复兴之基础，迩者广州、武汉相继失守，地位更臻重要。究应如何急起直追建设新西南,俾得完成其新膺之重大使命,实为吾人目前所最宜注意之问题。

二、西南经济建设应以工业化为方针

经济建设,经纬万端,诸农业之改进、工矿之开发、交通之促进、贸易之增加、金融之流通,与夫财政之革新,不过其荦荦大者。然建设之道,首宜认清目标,目标既明,则方针可以确定,然后一切建设,均得循序以进,卒底于成。经济建设之目标无他,求一国之富强而已。富强之道,舍工业化莫属,盖一国之富强与否,胥视其工业化程度之高下以为断,此乃百年来世界经济发展史所昭示吾人之铁证也。我国提倡工业化,几与暴日同时,而收效悬殊,不啻霄壤,推原其故,不外国人对于工业化之认识未能彻底,对于工业化之实行,未能尽力耳。夫欲一国之工业化,非徒事现代工业之提倡与建立,可达目的也,必也其国之社会、政治、经济、军事、教育诸端,均已循现代工业发展所取之途径,利用科学技术,采取大规模组织,以适应现代国家生存之需要而后可。即就经济一端言,亦必须工业以外之一切经济活动如农、矿、交通、贸易、金融、以及财政等,均已循工业发展之途径,引用新式技术与大规模组织,始得谓为已臻工业化之境。返观我国以往之经济建设,往往与此背道而驰。第一,我国工业本身,尚未能完全工业化:手工业遍布城乡,在生产上仍占重要地位,其生产方式,凭借人工而不用动力,组织规模,多属家庭作坊之类。第二,工业以外之经济活动(尤以农业为甚),一如大部分之工业,亦尚未臻工业化之境,胥以个人经营为原则,即合作组织,亦最近始渐萌芽,集团经营,更无论矣。第三,各种经济事业间,缺少必要之联系与调整,此于工业化之促进,颇多阻碍。如农业与工业间之关系,即其一例:我国现代工业所必需之原料,虽不乏国产可资利用,然大部分仍须仰给海外,如小麦、棉花、丝茧等,不过其尤著者耳。此盖由于经营农业者不知适应工业方面之需要,自绝销路,而从事工业者对农业生产亦绝鲜提携,只知求一时之方便。一旦国际局势恶化,国外原料供给中断时,惟有出诸减工停厂之一途。年来农业工业化之声浪,始渐有所闻,其重要诚如邹树文氏所言:"农业不顾及工业,而狭义的改进农业,是改进不了的;所有农业的改进出于工业需要之迫切而发展的甚多;农业工业应该互相顾及,中国农业的衰落,应该是农业与工业同负其责任。"(《新民族》一卷十九期七页)

西南经济建设之目标在求西南各省之富强,近以充实后方经济,增强抗战力量;远以促进边省建设,巩固国家防务。其应以工业化为进行之唯一方针,可无疑义。至于实施工业化之途径,容于次节中申讨之。

三、西南经济建设之途径

西南经济建设,应以工业化为进行之唯一方策,以跻西南诸省于富强之域,上节之甚详。值此抗战期间,因粤汉之不守,西南地位,更臻重要,不久将来,或将由后方而转变为前线,故求西南之强较求西南之富,尤为迫切。自经济建设立场言,欲求西南之强,应以建立国防工业为目前最迫切之中心工作,而其他一切经济建设事业,如农业之改良,矿藏之开发,交通之促进,贸易之增加,金融之维持,与夫财政之健全,均宜以促成国防工业之早日建立为鹄的。本文限于篇幅,未遑一一申述,兹仅就国防工业之树立一项,略加探讨。

国防工业,广义言之,包括一切有利于战事进行之工业,诸凡有关(一)给养士兵如衣食及医药等工业,(二)供给器械如钢铁及军器及化学等工业,(三)维持交通如制车、制轨、炼油等工业,及(四)输出国外藉以换取外汇俾得购置国内无法自给之军需用品等工业如钨、锑、锡、汞之采冶及农产品如茶、丝、桐油等之制造与加工等均属之。第一,关于给养士兵工业如衣食及医药等业之促进,在西南各省中应积极进行。西南以气候关系,棉产颇感不足,过去川、滇、黔、康等省进口品中,以棉纱、棉布为大宗,此后应力求自给,择适宜地点,如四川之遂宁,云南之开远,及贵州之罗甸等区,种植优良棉种,以补繁殖。此外,西南多山,本宜畜牧,应提倡羊毛生产,以补棉产之不足。其次,西南粮食生产,仅足自给,复以交通闭塞,甲地即略有盈余,亦难运销乙地,以资调剂。故此后除尽力发展交通外,更宜就交通中心如渝、筑、蓉、昆等市提倡粮食作物之加工与制造,庶小麦可磨成面粉,稻米可制成膨胀米,以利运输而便军用。复次,我国药料生产丰富,积数千年经验所保存之中药,量质俱有足称者,如麻黄一药,一经加以科学的分析,西医即视同珍宝,西南各省(特别四川),药材生产,素称丰富,此后宜在重庆成都等市设立药厂,采用科学方法,详加分析与研究,制成各种药剂,以应战时之需,庶前方将士之裹创扶病者,不致因西药之供给困难,而徒唤奈何。第二,供给器械如铜铁军器及化学等工业之举办,虽非一蹴可几,然亦宜早日着手筹备。年来政府对重工业之建设,不遗余力,惜以为时太促,多数厂矿,未及开工而敌骑已深入或迫近,遂使机器与人员不得不辗转播迁。此后一方自宜从速将邻近湘桂鄂赣等省之厂矿设备,移置西南各省重要市县,一方更宜选择交通与资源适宜地点,采冶西南各省煤铁铜铅锌等矿藏,以为工业树必要之基础。至一切工业——特别军器工业——所必需之动力工业,尤宜于西南各省中择适宜地点如重庆、昆明、贵阳、万县、长寿、东川、富民等处,利用煤藏及天然水力,装置发电之设备。第三,维持交通如制车制轨及炼油等工业,亦甚重要。西南各省交通,向称闭塞,滇越铁路而外,其他干线——如沟通国际路线之川滇及滇缅,贯彻国防要道之湘黔及成渝等铁路,虽早在中央擘划之中,惜抗战突起,未能实施。此后宜设法进行,将迫近战区如浙赣及粤汉等路之设备移用兴修。西南宜林地甚多,几占全面积二分之一,但荒芜已久,迄今童山濯濯,绝少利用。当局宜广辟林区,择宜林要地如成都、毕节、贵阳等区,建立锯木厂,庶铺轨用之枕木,得源源接济。西南公路,年来兴修甚为积极,以贵阳为中心之四大干线,东可至湘,西可至滇,南可至桂,北可至川。近以军事关系,复有川滇及滇缅两公路线之开辟,闻不日即可通车,此后问题重养路及用路而不重修路。如何而使车辆及车油,不断供给,俾现有公路得发挥其最高功用,实为关心国防工业者所煞费筹虑之问题。自制汽车,一时尚不可能,退而求其次,惟有大量制造轻而易举之手推车,在类似驿站制之组织下,尽量利用现有之公路,作运输方面最后之努力。军需急用品,仍用汽车输送,次要者则可利用此项手推车。汽车供给,将日感困难,汽油供给亦然。川省富石油,自宜急谋提取。而汽油代用品如植物油及酒精等之提炼,尤应赶速进行。西南各省,素以产植物油——特别桐油——著名;同时,可资提炼酒精之玉蜀黍、甘薯及甘蔗等,尤触目皆是,原料供给,当无问题。至成本是否过高,值此抗战期间,自难兼顾,在政府经营或津贴之原则下,当可获得适当之解决。第四,输出国外藉以换取外汇购置国内无法自给之军需用品等工业,亟宜设法促进。西南四省矿产如川康之砂金,云南箇旧之锡,贵州铜仁省溪八寨之汞,均宜大量开采与冶炼,以为换取外汇之用。其尚未开采者,应由资源委员会火速探勘经营,其已经开采而经营不善者如箇旧之锡,亦应仿赣钨及湘锑旧例,由资委员会接收管理,庶产销两方得收最高成效。农产品如茶丝桐油之加工,亟应设法改进,以利外销。至该项农产品加工以前原有之缺点,宜由政府指定生产中心区域如嘉定、南充之于川丝,雅安、名山及灌县之于川茶,蒙自、思茅之于滇茶,万县、贵阳之于桐油,实施改进,如选种及划一标准等等。

以上略述国防工业建立之途径。夫经济建设,经纬万端,且其相互之间,有密切关系,国防工业,不过其一端耳。必也各个经济部门均已充分发达,然后整个国家经济始克臻于健全。且甲部门之建设成功,往往有赖于乙丙丁诸部门之同时并举,就乙丙丁诸部门分别言之亦然。故欲谋国防工业之树立有成,必须谋国防工业以外之有关系经济建设同时并进,而供给原料之农矿林牧,输送原料与成品之交通运输,流动资金之金融机构,殆其尤要者也。农矿林牧之开发,按诸西南各省之经济情形与国防工业原料方面之需要,应注重给养士兵所需之粮食,衣料及药材,供给军用器械所需之煤铁与钢,维持交通工业所需之木材与提炼植物油所需之原料如桐、玉蜀黍、甘薯与甘蔗,及换取外汇之出口品如金、锡、汞、茶、丝、桐油、皮毛、猪鬃等。交通路线之开辟,第一注重铁路与南干线如川滇与滇缅之早日完成。第二注重水陆交通路线之联系。第三注重现有公路利用程度之提高。金融机械之调整,如桂币与滇币之取缔,西南金融网之布置,及法币之稳定与外汇之维持,中央与地方当局,均已有适当措施,兹不复赘。

四、结论

大体言之,西南四省人口繁衍,物产富饶,四川自昔有"天府之国"之称,云南亦富农矿产品,惟贵州比较贫瘠,西康尚待开发。诸省过去以地处边陲及交通不便,外界未及注意,且因政治黑暗,烟毒蔓延,民众受苛捐杂税之剥削与黑祸之摧残,进取精神,丧失殆尽,经济建设,一无可言。近年来中央当局秉承总理遗志,锐意倡导经济建设,复以军事关系,内地各省,亦积极兴建公路,西南省外界接触之机会,于以增多,现代政治经济设施,遂逐渐普及于西南各省。自去年七七抗战以来,战线日广,国土日蹙,西北西南,同为支持抗战之后方,今则西南诸省竟自后方一跃而为前线,地位愈形重要,促进经济建设,以巩固国防,增强实力,更觉刻不容缓矣。

西南经济建设,值此抗战期间,其目的在增强抗战实力,其方针则在求西南诸省之工业化,盖旷观近二百年来世界经济发展之趋势,一国国势之强弱,莫不视其工业化程度之高下以为断也。工业化之要义,在以现代工业所实施之科学技术及大规模组织,普遍引用于一切经济部门中,举凡农矿、交通、贸易、金融、财政等等,均应追随现代工业之后,采取同样之技术与组织,而加以适当之改进或改造。西南经济建设之目标,既在求国防之巩固,而其方针又在求工业化之实施,则在现阶段之过程中,自应以建立国防工业为中心工作,而其他一切经济建设之举办,胥当以促进或协助国防工业之早日完成为鹄的。此项建设,举其要者,约分三端,即(一)促进农矿林牧等业,俾国防工业所必须之原料,有所取给而不致中断。(二)建设水陆交通路线,俾不能自给之机器原料或成品而为国防工业所必需者,得由国外源源输入,而换取外汇藉以购置上项机器原料与成品之出口物品,亦得由西南源源输出。(三)调整金融制度与机构,庶币制得告统一而法币价格亦得藉外汇之维持而更趋稳定。

西南经济建设,困难滋多,而国防工业之建立,尤非旦夕可冀,必须假以时日,始有可观之成绩。然凡事困难愈多,则意志愈宜坚强,成功自愈有把握。且自抗战以来,外资竞争失却作用,外货输入已受限制,消极裨补于民族工业之发展者已属不鲜,而战区人口与资金之大量集中向内,金融重心之渐由长江口岸移至内地各埠,更予民族工业之建立以有利条件。此外,国内政治之空前稳定,各党各派之坚强团结,民族意识之普遍觉醒,国际援助之逐日增进,以及政府统制力量之日益加强,更无一不利于工业化之进行,好自为之,必有成功。

二十七年十月卅一日于贵阳

抗战期间中国工业之没落及其复兴途径

一、抗战期间中国工业之没落

我国自七七抗战以来,转瞬一载有半。土地人民之先后沦陷者,几达二分之一,数十年来历尽艰辛而仅得之些许民族工业根基亦随之化归乌有。盖我国现代工业,多位置于沿海及沿江沿铁路地带。前者因缺乏海防,暴日遂得唾手攫取,后者因沿路沿江,类多平地,暴日藉机械化部队之助,竟直入无阻。时至今日,一等工业中心如上海、天津、青岛、武汉;二等工业中心如北平、无锡、广州、济南;三等工业中心如塘沽、唐山、通州等等,均已沦陷敌手。其仅存之工业城市,或已迫近战区如华中之郑州、长沙、宜昌、沙市,或僻处后方交通闭塞之区如西南之重庆、成都、昆明、贵阳、箇旧、自井及西北之西安、兰州,若与已沦陷之工业城市比较,无论就生产设备及能力言,或就未来发展之前途言,实不逮远甚。抗战建国,端赖工业建设之能否积极推进。今工业区域,泰半沦陷敌手,抗战前途之日见艰难,不言而喻矣。

诚然,工业区域之沦陷,在以消耗敌人实力为目的之长期抗战国策下,自属无法避免之预期结果,他日战事告终,最后胜利,若仍我属,则沦陷之工业区域,不难一一收复。然暴日所予我国工业之打击,不仅工业区域之暂时沦陷已也,其尤足痛心者,则为已陷工业区域中过去所有之工业设备,在有计划的破坏与掠夺之下,均已不复存在。以上海一地言,上海为我国工业中心,其生产占全国工业生产二分之一以上。八一三战事以前,华商工厂集中其地者,达五千二百余家,因沪战而全部被毁者,闸北一带约有百分之三十五,浦东、南市一带各约百分之二十,合计被毁工厂,当在总数百分之七十左右。据前上海市社会局估计,此次战争,上海被毁工厂约二千家,损失额在五亿元以上,此犹系南市华军尚未撤退以前之估计,若并合南市被毁者计算之,则损失总额当在八亿元以上(见二十七年十月二十五日贵州《革命日报》)。上海较大之工业区原在闸北、浦东、曹家渡、南市、龙华等处,而不在租界。但据上海公共租界工部局之报告,即租界内之被毁工厂,亦达九〇五家,此九〇五家工厂平时共雇用工人三〇,八六八人。此外,约有一千家左右之大小工厂及工场,蒙受严重之损害。该报告称:"这些工厂和工场的情形究竟如何,不能详述,但确实知道若干规模较大的工厂所有机器,已不能再用,必须加以改换……侵扰和劫掠工厂的证据,甚为普遍,恐怕所有工厂都不能够复工了。"(田伯烈:《外人目睹中之日军暴行》,一五九页。)

或谓暴日对于上海工业之横加摧残,系为报复我国自动退出青岛前毁灭日商纱厂而发,此诚无稽之谈,不可置信。实则上海工业之被毁,早在暴日预定计划之中,其主要目的,在根本铲除我国之新兴工业,使我历尽千辛万苦所仅得之民族工业基础,无复遗存,然后彼可充分发展其工商业,尽量利用我之丰富原料与广大市场。其所采手段,则焚毁与劫掠兼而行之。焚毁之结果,已如上述。劫掠之例,观于暴日在沪搜括十万吨钢铁时所采取之手段,亦可窥见一斑。二十七年二月四日《字林西报》载称:"日方从汇山杨树浦一带搬取的,并非限于铣铁,他们还拆卸中国人的机器,运往日本。所有各种机件铁器,从汽锅到马达,都在罗掘之列。他们剥夺了上海的复兴工具,中国人回到荒凉的故居时,一切须从头做起,白手创业。事实胜于强辩,无从掩饰。日方剥夺复兴上海的一部分工具,到底是为了什么目标呢?是否要使上海永远陷入万劫不复之境呢?"据中立之外国观察家曾赴日军所占扬子江下游三角地带作旅行视察者之报告,吾人知上述破坏劫掠情形,决非只限于上海及其附近,一切沦陷之较大城市如南京、无锡、苏州、镇江等处,均同罹浩劫。此等城市中,财产——包括工业投资在内——之毁灭,与上海无异,大多并非由于战争之直接结果,而系日军占领后有计划的造成。据二十七年三月十九日《密勒士评论》周报增刊之记载:上海是扬子江三角地带最重要的一个都市。上海损毁的情形,异常惨重,上海以外无数的城市村镇,其损毁的情形,却也如出一辙。在上海周围的一百英里内,不下十二个大城市,五千万以上的人口。这些城市都受到绝大的破坏,至于较小的市镇和村舍,其损坏的情形,更无从统计。距上海约一百英里的无锡,本来是一个工业区,有人口九十万。所有工厂建筑,因日机的猛烈轰炸,或损失甚钜,或全部被毁,其中最重要的有几家面粉厂,一家纱厂,一家电厂和一家设备非常新式的丝厂。嘉兴是浙江省的一个丝业中心,原有人口四十五万,现已变成为死城,二十万人口的松江,差不多仅余灰烬。古老而殷富的苏州,原有人口三十五万,日军占领该城时,只剩五百人了。

暴日对于我国工业之摧残,除在各工业区沦陷以后所施之焚毁与劫掠外，其于沦陷以前藉飞机之轰炸而施之破坏，亦极巨大。据上海文化界国际宣传委员会之统计，自去年七月至本年六月之一年中，日机轰炸我国不设防城市之范围，遍及苏浙皖赣闽粤冀鲁晋湘鄂甘桂豫川陕等十六省，共达二，一二七次，投弹二〇，八六六枚，受伤人数二一，一九八，死亡人数一五，九六一，内以工业荟萃之粤苏浙三省所受损失尤为惨重，计被炸至一，五〇五次或百分之七〇，投弹一〇，四七六枚或百分之五〇，受伤人一六，二一八或百分之七六，死亡人一一，五一二或百分之七二。（见《贵州晨报》二十七年月二十七日）

二、抗战期间中国工业复兴之途径

抗战以来我国工业什九被毁，所受损失，诚属不赀，然因抗战之故，我国工业已呈新的发展姿态，为工业之复兴，树远大而不可限量之基础。语云，塞翁失马，焉知非福。我国新工业复兴之进程与结果，其将因抗战而加速与增大乎？兹就有关各点，逐一探讨，以就正于关心战时工业建设之人士。

（一）发展国防工业：经济建设应以发展工业为中心，进而求一切经济组织之工业化，此近二百年来世界各国经济发展之共同趋势也。良以一国之工业发达，则其人民之生活程度可以提高，国防之力量可以增强，既富且强，然后可以屹立世界。我国提倡新工业，垂九十年，为时不可谓短，惜外受帝国主义列强不平等条约之束缚，内受政治紊乱与内战频仍之影响，工业之发展，至为有限，且偏于民生工业而忽于国防工业，至于一切经济部门之工业化，更谈不到矣。迄抗战爆发,国人目睹脆弱之民族工业基础,在暴日有计划的摧毁之下,已化归乌有,同时战事方激烈进行,更迫切等待工业生产之源源接济,然后憬然觉悟,深信工业建设为目前抗战建国大业中极重要之纲目,迫切等待全国上下之努力进行,而国防工业,尤为重要。故《抗战建国纲领》第十九条规定"开发矿产,树立重工业的基础,鼓励轻工业的经营,并发展各地之手工业,"明定此后发展我国工业应采之政策,以国防工业之树立为首要,民生工业之发展次之。当此强敌压境,国运垂危之际,吾人如欲坚持抗战,自非积极实行此种政策不可。

（二）统制工业建设：自鸦片战争以来,列强先后迫我签订之不平等条件,不下数十起。其主要之点不外以经济侵略之方式,陷我于半殖民地之地位,使永远不能自拔,然后彼可尽量利用我丰富之原料,广大之市场,以及贱价之劳力。统制大权,尽操外人之手。结果,关系民生之轻工业虽得相当发展,然有关国防之重工业,则甚鲜发展机会,即已有之厂家,其营业亦日就衰落,如汉冶萍公司之类,即因无法维持而不得不宣告停顿,曷胜浩叹。此后工业建设,自应由政府全盘计划,统筹办理,不再因循泄沓,一唯他人之马首是瞻。所幸经济部新制之"非常时期农矿工商管理条例",自去年十二月二十二日公布后,已于本年十月六日经府令修正公布,对于全国农矿工商业之发展,作全盘之统制。其包括之企业及物品,分下列四类：（一）棉、丝、麻、羊毛及其制品,（二）金、银、钢、铁、铜、锡、铝、镍、铅、锌、钨、锑、锰、汞及其制品,（三）食粮、植物油、茶、糖、皮革、木材、盐、煤及焦炭、煤油、汽油、柴油、润滑油、纸、漆、酒精、水泥、石灰、酸碱、火柴、交通器材、电工器材、电汽机器工具、教育用品、药品、人造肥料、陶器、砖瓦、玻璃,（四）其他经经济部呈准行政院指定者。此项条例，共计二十六条，其中心原则有二，一曰适应军事需要，二曰促进战时生产。为适应军事需要计，对于工业之种类、分布、生产、价格、输出入以及消费，均有扼要之规定。

甲、种类：（一）所用原料为军用所必需及制造非必需品而所用原料供给缺乏之企业，经济部得令其停业。前项停业之企业，经济部得将其土地、房屋、机器、动力、材料、工具等移作其他用途，（二）经济部对于制造奢侈品或其他非必要之企业得分别限制或禁止之，（三）企业之原有设备足以改制军用有关之物品者，经济部得令其改制。

乙、分布：在战区或邻近战区之指定各企业，经济部得因必要分别令其迁移。

丙、生产：各指定企业及物品，其生产者或经营者（一）非经经济部核准不得歇业停业或停工，其已歇业停业或停工者经济部得限期令其复业复工；（二）不得有投机垄断或其他操纵行为。

丁、输出入：经济部对于指定物品之输入输出，得因必要分别限制或禁止之。

戊、价格：经济部对于指定之物品，（一）得因必要分别为禁售或平价之处分；（二）为适应非常时期之需要，得依公平价格分别收买其全部或一部。

己、消费：经济部对于指定之物品，（一）得依供求实况分别调节其消费，（二）得因必要令生产者或经营者储藏或移置之。

关于促进战时生产方面，该条例对于经营方式、劳资关系，及政府指导监督与协助等项，均有规定：

甲、经营方式：（一）经济部为适应非常时期之需要经行政院核准，得将左列各企业分别收归政府办理或由政府投资合办；子、关于战事必需之各矿业，丑、关于制造军用品之各工业，寅、关于电汽事业；（二）指定之企业或物品为生活日用所必需者，经济部应各地方之需要，得随时分别种类地域直接经营之；（三）关于指定之企业技术上或管理上有改善之必要经令其改善而不改善时，经济部得代管之；（四）经济部对于指定之企业，得因必要分别令其增资合并或缩减范围。

乙、劳资关系：指定各企业之员工，不得罢市罢工或怠工。

丙、政府指导，监督与协助：（一）经济部对于指定之企业或物品，得就生产或经营之方法，原料之种类及存量，工作时间及劳工待遇，品质及产量存量，生产费用，运销方法，价格及利润，明定适当之标准；（二）对于指定之企业或物品有特殊发明或专利者，经济部得因必要令其报告试验或禁止其公布或泄漏，并得收归政府利用或由政府投资合办，（三）经济部对于指定之企业依下列各款予以协助：资金之扩充，材料之供给，建设之规划，设备之补充，技术之指导，动力之供给调剂，出品之运销调剂，劳工之供给调剂；（四）由战区或邻近战区自动迁移之企业或物品经济部应随时予以协助并得予以保障。

（三）兼重大小工业：产业革命以来，大工业有取小工业而代之之势，世界各国小工业之衰落，无论在城市或在乡村，均为普遍之现象。其在我国，产业革命虽已有九十余年之历史，然以社会政治经济条件之未臻完备，大工业之兴起，仅限于通商口岸及外力较易伸入之交通中心，就全国工业生产量言，在抗战以前小工业仍占优胜地位。抗战以来，大工业中心，先后沦入敌区，小工业在我国工业生产上所占之地位，尤见重要。党政当轴，鉴于小工业之不容忽视，故"抗战建国纲领"中，有"发展各地之手工业"之规定。最近经济、教育、内政三部，复于八月十二日会同公布"推广小工业设计委员会章程"，组织推广小工业设计委员会，以为普遍振兴小工业，增加生产能力之张本。该委员会所办理之事项，有：（一）关于各种小工业推广程序之厘订，（二）关于各种小工业采用完全手工业半手工半机械或主要部份用机械之设计，（三）关于普遍设立小型工厂地点分配之规定，（四）关于实施某县区地方基本职业教育之计划，（五）关于小工业人才之介绍及训练，（六）关于小工业之奖励及资金借贷之协助，（七）关于政府自行举办小型模范工厂之筹拟。

在此二十世纪大工业遍及世界之时而欲提倡树立小工业，不免迹近复古或开倒车。然就此时此地之中国言，实有其客观上之需要。且吾人所欲提倡之小工业，非指一般之小工业而言。其性质、技术及组织，均与以往之小工业有异。就性质言，吾人所欲提倡之小工业。第一，须为属于军需品及生活必需品之范围者，如棉布、纱布、线毯、药棉、皮革、木材、糖、盐之类；第二，属于与机器生产无直接冲突而在相当时间内可以同时存在者，如织布之类；第三，属于有特殊海外市场的工艺品之范围者，如花边、丝绸之类（见吴半农：《战时手工业问题》一文，载《时事类编》特刊第十六号）。就技术言，吾人所欲提倡之小工业，须在可能范围内，能尽量引用现代科学所发明之新工具或新器械者。由政府负技术指导之责，在适中地点，设置示范工场或工业指导员，一如农业之有示范农场或农业指导员。就组织言，吾人所欲提倡之小工业，应摹仿农业先例，组织合作社，以经营之。自原料之购置与加工，以至成品之出售，一唯合作社是赖，使家庭工业制（又称包工制、散活制或商人雇主制）下商人雇主对于家庭或外勤工人之劳力，所施之剥削与榨取,得以免除,此点作者于三年前调查河北省高阳县手工织布业时,已力加提倡(见拙著《华北乡村织布工业与商人雇主制度》,二十四年七月),本年夏间中外人士,亦有同样主张,拟以五百万元资本组织三万个工业合作社,以为抗战期间我国工业生产之主体。闻现已开始进行。

(四)发展内地工业:我国自与西洋通商以来,因内乱外患之频仍,新工业之发展,大多集中于通商口岸及交通便利之点,倚赖外力之保护,苟且偷安。九一八事变,东北与沪滨之工业,首当其冲。上海一隅,抗战未及一月,损失达十五亿元。于是工商各界,始渐感有海岸而无海防之威胁,纷向内地作工业之投资。不幸未及五载,而七七变起,曾不一年,工商重镇齐陷敌手。战区厂矿之内迁者,截止本年十月底止,已达三四一家,有机器六万三千吨,然与沦陷区之厂矿比较,尚不及什一,杯水车薪,殊无补于大局!迩者,广州沦陷,海岸几尽被封锁,后方重镇如川之重庆、成都,滇之昆明、简旧、黔之贵阳、遵义,桂之桂林、南宁,与陕甘之西安、兰州,遂一跃而为工商要区,行见内地工业之发展,将因战事之转移,由理想而成为事实,要亦不幸中之一幸也。

随抗战军事之进展,国土日益削弱,所谓内地,仅西南西北各省,尚能保持领土完整,至如湘鄂豫赣,则已局部沦入敌手,只得视同外卫区域,不能划入内地工业建设之范围。故内地工业建设,应暂从西南之川滇黔桂及西北之陕甘等省入手。其应行发展之工业,自以适应抗战需要之国防工业为限。惟国防工业一辞,应作广义之解释,而不仅限于军用工业。广义的国防工业,似应包括一切有利于战事进行之工业,诸凡有关(一)给养士兵如衣食及医药等工业,(二)供给器械如钢铁、军器及化学等工业,(三)维持交通如制车、制轨、炼油等工业,及(四)输出国外藉以换取外汇俾得购买国内无法自给之军需用品等工业如钨、锑、锡、汞之采冶及农产品如茶、丝、桐油等之制造与加工等均属之。

(五)利用民族资本:工业之发展,端赖资本之筹集。我国工业资本,向以外国政府与商人之投资占主要成份,本国资本,仅居附庸地位。是以工业政策,一由外人操纵,驯致反客为主,其害之大,可以想见。今后自宜革除以往积弊,努力于民族资本之积聚与利用,以为我国民族工业,树必要之基础。筹集民族资本,要须从促进生产与节省消费二方面着手。其方法,不外外汇之取得及国内资金之筹集二端,前者为购置我国尚难自行制造之机器所必需,后者则为建筑厂屋,购入原料,发付工资及利息等所不可或少者。取得外汇之方法有四:即(一)输出国内农林渔牧产品如桐油、猪鬃、鸡蛋及蛋制品、生丝、茶、牛皮、羊皮、羊毛、肠衣、芝麻、棉花、杂粮等物;(二)输出钨、锑、锡等矿砂;(三)吸收华侨投资(本年十一月一日经济部曾公布"非常时期华侨投资国内经济事业奖助办法");及(四)出售金银及古物。对于国内资金之筹集方法,约有五种:(一)税制之改良如实行征收所得税,遗产税与战时利得税等;(二)建国公债之发行,强制国内各种金融机关,须就其吸收得来或代为保存之现款提取百分之几购买之;(三)由政府控制私人投资,仿照德国先例,由国家将应行举办之事业,酌量轻重缓急,指定投资之次序;(四)推行节约运动;(五)增加各种经济事业之生产。(见吴景超:《中国工业化的途径》,商务,二七)

(六)联系农工生产:工业乃加工于自然物体以变其形质而增高其效用之行为,所谓自然物体,包括农林渔牧矿产之类,而以农产为尤要。农业无工业,则人类经济,当仍滞留于原始之茹毛饮血时代,工业无农业,则原料既无法取给,加工更无从实施。农工二业关系之密切,可以概见。我国自新工业发轫以来,对于农业之改进,向未深加注意,农业生产,在质量二方面均不能符合工业生产之需求,驯致新兴之棉毛、缫丝、面粉等工业,以本国原料质量俱逊,竟弃之不顾,转而倚赖外国原料之供给。此种办法,若仅就工业之经营言,固不无些许裨补,然自整个国家经济之立场观之,实为极端危险之现象。盖一方面农产将因缺乏销路而日趋衰落,一方面倘一旦战事爆发,国外原料供给中断,工厂即将随之停闭,此种事实,固已一度实现于欧战期间矣。我国农业不振之原因虽多,以工农二业之未能密切连系为最要。我国产棉,但如"甘肃宜棉之地,而大姑娘没有布裤蔽体,何以兰州纺造厂不做棉的纺织呢"?我国产麻,"但是麻袋恐怕是印度来的占最大多数,吾国麻袋工业或者是绝无仅有"。我国盛产丝茶,但丝茶业之衰落,当以我国为最甚。我国产木,但"洋木充斥,所有建木西木的销路,都被夺去"。我国产米,但"洋米囤得起,本国米囤不起。……洋米耐久。本国米不耐久"。上述诸例,触目皆是,诚如邹树文氏所言,"农业不顾及工业,而狭义的改进农业,是改进不了的;所有农业改进的出于工业需要之迫切而发展的甚多;农业工业应该互相顾及,中国农业的衰落,应该是农业与工业同负其责任。"(以上引语均见《新民族》一卷十九期)

(七)统一工业行政:我国工业行政,在抗战以前,由行政院及军事委员会分别执掌。行政院所属者有实业部之工业司及中央工业试验所;全国经济委员会之棉业统制委员会及蚕丝改良委员会;建设委员会所经办之国营电汽车业如电机制造厂、戚墅堰电厂及首都电厂。军事委员会所属者,有资源委员会,负国防工业建树之责。抗战发生后,为适应战时需要起见,复于军事委员会之下设工矿调整委员会,第三部(重工业)及第四部(国民经济)之轻工业组。行政机构重复,事权尤不集中。今春政府改组,上述工业行政机关,均经先后合并于经济部,由该部分设工业司,资源委员会,工矿调整处,及中央工业试验所等四机关分司其事。工业司之职掌,根据一月十四日府令公布及七月三十日府令修正公布之"经济部组织法",有下列各项:(一)国营工业之筹设,(二)民营工业之保护奖进及监督,(三)制造品之征集,试验及检定,(四)工业之专利及特许,(五)国货之证明及奖励,(六)工厂之登记及考核,(七)工业技师之登记及考核,(八)工业及劳工团体之登记及监督,(九)工业标准之规定,(十)度量衡之制造检定及进行,(十一)劳工生活之改良及保障,(十二)工人与雇主间纠纷之调解及劳资协作之指导,(十三)工人与工会相互间之关系,(十四)工业或劳工之调查,及(十五)其他关于工业及劳工等事项。资源委员会按照八月一日府令修正公布之"组织条例",分设工业,矿业,电业,技术,经济研究及购料等处室,司掌(一)创办及管理经营基本工业,(二)开发及管理经营重要矿业,(三)创办及管理经营动力事业,及(四)办理政府指定之其他事业等事项。工矿调整处按照九月七日部令公布之"办事细则",分总力、业务、财务、秘书及会计等五组室。业务组司掌(一)工矿设备之迁移补充,(二)工矿动力之调剂供应,(三)工矿材料之供需调剂,(四)工矿物品之运输分配,(五)工矿建设之规划协助,(六)工矿事业之合作互动,(七)工矿技术人员之征集训调,及(八)工矿调整之设计审议考核督导等事项。财务组司掌(一)工厂资金之筹措协助,(二)营运资金之保管出纳,(三)工矿借款之审核订约,(四)工矿借款抵押品之保管稽核,

(五)工矿借款本息之收回,(六)工矿投资之调查审议,及(七)工矿资金运用之其他事项。中央工业试验所按照六月十三日府令公布之"组织条例",司掌考验工业原料,改良制造方法及鉴定工业制品之责,分设酿造、纤维、胶体、油脂、制糖、盐碱、纺织染、材料、动力及电汽等试验室,及化学分析室。此外,因试验上之必要,复得附设实验工厂。上述四机关工作之性质及其主管工业之种类,各不相同。就工作之性质言,工业司为行政机关,资源委员会为事业机关,调整处为促进机关、试验所为技术机关。就其主管工业之种类言,工业司及试验所兼顾轻重两种工业,资委会与调整处则分管重工业与轻工业。工业行政,经此次之合并与改组,已焕然一新。组织系统既臻健全,实施权责自可专一,行见此后我国之工业行政,益将蒸蒸日上矣。

三、结论

以上就我国在抗战中民族工业之没落,以及目前工业建设之新途径,如发展国防工业,统制工业建设,兼重大小工业,发展内地工业,利用民族资本,联系农工生产,及统一工业行政诸端,略陈梗概。过去我国工业之发展,因受帝国主义列强不平等条约之束缚,呈现十足之殖民经济色彩。抗战发生,为时不逮一年有半,而主要工业区域,什九沦陷敌手,言之良用痛心。然自另一方面观之,则塞翁失马,安知非福。我国工业,经此莫大打击后,当能纠正以往之种种错误,另循正当之途径发展矣。

工业建设,为经济建设之一端。工业建设之成功,有赖于其他经济部门建设之同时并举，故欲求工业之树立有成，必须谋工业以外其他有关经济部门建设之同时并进，而供给原料之农林渔牧，输送原料与成品之交通运输，流动资金之金融机构，殆其尤要者也。

工业建设，本非旦夕可冀，在此抗战时期，困难尤多。然苟能抱定坚强之意志，以坚苦卓绝之努力赴之，自能克服一切困难，而底于成功。且自抗战以来，外资竞争已失作用，外货输入亦受限制，消极裨补于民族工业之发展者已多，而战区人口与资金之大量集中向内，金融重心之渐由长江口岸移至内地各埠，尤予民族工业之建立以有利之条件。更加国内政治之空前稳定，各党各派之坚强团结，民族意识之普遍觉醒，国际援助之逐日增进，以及政府统制力量之日夜加强，更无一不利于工业建设之进行，语云，事在人为，愿我国人勉力图之！

中国小工业之衰落及其复兴途径

一、小工业之意义

　　小工业与大工业虽为对立之名词，然小大之别为相对的而非绝对的，故时人对于小工业一辞，迄未有肯定之说明。或有以手工之引用为小工业最显著之特征，因而谓小工业即手工业者。然手工业亦有采大规模组织者，如秦汉以来之皇室工业——特别瓷业与丝织等业，发展甚速，颇为宏大。唐时昌南——即今之景德镇，为瓷业之中心，成都产蜀锦，尤负盛名，清乾隆年间，于南京、苏州、杭州三处，设立织造衙门，各置提督织造太监一人，监制各式衣类及制帛、诰敕、彩缯之类，以供御用，及宫廷祭祀颁赏之需。民国以来，平津手织地毯业，闻名全国，每家雇工至五百人之多，资本亦在十万元以上。上述各种工业，虽采用手工进行，而未尝引用机械，然若称之为小工业，则不合事实。英国在产业革命以前所盛行之手织厂（Handloomfactories），时人恒称为工厂，即不以作坊呼之，马克思且谓此种组织为由手工（Handicraft）到机械制造之过渡，而特名为手工制造（Manufacture）。故小工业之特质，决非手工业一点可以概括。

小工业与大工业之又一区别,为组织或经营方式之不同。工业组织,分主匠制(或手工制),商人雇主制(即家庭制或散活制)及工场制三种;前二种为小工业组织之方式,第三种则为大工业组织之方式,此中外所同。惟商人雇主制下之工业,可大可小,其组织之规模,介乎主匠制与工场制之间,而盛行于产业革命之前期。我国产业革命虽早,惟发展萦缓,故时至今日,商人雇主制仍盛行于各种可大可小之工业,如地毯、针织、织布等。然大工业之组织,则莫不以工场制为典型,商人雇主制不过其过渡阶段耳。

大工业与小工业之第三区别,为分布区域之不同。大工业多位置于交通便利之通商大邑以便于资金、劳力与原料之取给,以及市场之容纳,而小工业则散布于交通不甚便利之城市或乡村,藉当地之原料与劳力,从事于小规模之生产,其所制成品,亦以供给当地市场之消费为主,而以外销为例外。

综上三点,吾人对于大工业与小工业,专作作如下之定义:大工业多应用机械,在工场制度下,于城市交通便利之处,从事大规模之生产。小工业多应用手工,在主匠制或商人雇主制下,于城市或乡村,作小规模之生产。

二、小工业之重要

产业革命以来,大工业勃兴,小工业日趋衰落。英美德法等工业先进国家之工业生产,莫不惟大工业是赖,小工业早已退居附庸地位。惟在我国则反是。我国大工业之兴起,为时虽逾九十年,然以内乱外患之纷至杳来,列强帝国主义之侵略压迫,其发展至形缓滞,是以全国工业生产,仍以小工业为主干。如棉布为日用必需品之一。我国棉布生产,按消费之纱数计,力织机仅当手织机之四分之一。十九年纱线的消费量九六一兆磅中,力织机所消费者不过一〇七兆磅,其余之七五四兆磅,则为手织机所消耗,约当总数之五分之四。小工业在中国工业生产中地位之重要,于此可见。工业之大小诚不宜仅凭力织机与手织机之引用以为分野,然手工之引用为小工业最显著之特征,固为不争之事实也。

在小工业方面,吾人尚缺乏精确之统计,故不得不引用手工业统计,以说明小工业在国民经济中所占地位之重要。手工制品在吾国日常生活上之重要,夫人能言之。每日开门七事,柴米油盐酱醋茶,无一非手工艺品,有人谓中国日常生活品中,至少有五分之四为手工艺品,若以上述之棉布为例,或非过论。手工业之生产统计,迄今尚付阙如,惟国际贸易方面,对于手工制品输出之统计,尚称完备,堪资参考。手工艺品输出总值,据罗敦伟氏之估计(《十年来的中国》,一五〇页)民二十一年为二二七兆元,占全体输出总值百分之三〇;民二十二年为一八五兆元,占百分之三〇;民二十三年为一七五兆元,占百分之三三;民二十四年为一八九兆元,占百分之三三;民二十年为二二八兆元,占百分之三二。综观五年来手工制品输出总值,占全体输出总值三分之一弱,其重要概可想见。

我国之大工业,类多位置于沿海沿铁路及沿江之通商口岸与城市,七七抗战以来,迄今一载有半,上述之通商口岸与城市,大多沦陷敌手,九十年来历尽艰辛所创造之大工业,在敌人破坏掠夺之下,化归乌有,他日失地收复之时,必须从头做起。故小工业在我国工业所占之地位,在抗战期间以及抗战胜利以后,愈见重要。且小工业因设备较简,易于移动,不若大工业之设备笨重,每随国土之沦陷而落入敌手，其在抗战期间，更具有类似游击队之功用焉。

三、小工业之衰落及其原因

因产业革命之进展，大工业遂有渐取小工业而代之之势，此在欧美各国，因已司空见惯，我国亦未能例外。盖需要既集中于工商中心，以手艺制度下之小规模生产以应供给，殊不经济。大工业如工程及造船等，因技术及资本之限制，不得不引用大规模组织以从事生产，为促进小工业消灭之重要因素。出品之统一化，为近世机械工业之先决条件，须能在大规模之工厂生产下，始能实行。是以我国小工业之衰落，实为必然之趋势。至其衰落情形，试取棉纺、缫丝及制茶三种较为普遍之小工业稍加检讨，便可了然。洋纱进口之增长，显示国内手工棉纺业之衰落。当一八二一年吾国首先输入英国机制纱时，进口额不过三十八担，至一八六七年猛涨至三四千担，自此以后，年有增涨，直至一八九〇年中国纱厂兴起，其势始杀。但一八六七年之三四千担之进口，已为一八二一年之九百倍。一八六九年为一三二千担，一八八七年为五九四千担，一八九九年之二，七四九千担，则为历年来之最高峰，已当一八六七年之进口额八十二倍矣。一八九九年以后，洋纱进口始见缩减，至一九三一年，已为七五千担，但此种棉纱进口量之缩减，非因手纺业之复兴，实为国内新式纱厂勃兴之结果。中国纱厂之棉纺锤，一八九〇年初设时，凡一一五千锭，至一九三六年暴进至五，五四六千锭，增五十倍。在国外机纺纱及国内机纺纱之双层竞争下，手纺纱渐受淘汰。吾人于此，愿引一八三三年英国民众对纱厂兴起之呼吁，以作比观,其言曰:"纺轮竿及棉纺锤竟在何处?……妇人儿童昔日能在家庭度其舒适独立之生活,今也彼辈之雇佣安在?——皆为机器所兼并而为'贱'的呼声所牺牲。"(见拙著《中国之乡村工业》,《经济统计季刊》二卷,五六九页)

手工缫丝业之衰落,非若手工棉纺业之显著。一八九五年海关对厂丝之出口始列有统计时,手缫黄白丝之出口量为六八千担,占生丝全出口量百分之七一。嗣后厂丝出口之百分数逐年增加,一九〇〇年为百分之四五,一九一〇年为百分之五八,一九二〇年为百分之六八,一九三〇年增至百分之八三。一九三一年厂丝出口占生丝出口总量百分之八六,为历年之最高峰。厂丝出口成数之增加,由一八九五年之百分之二九至一九三一年之百分之八六,正显示手缫丝成数之低落,——由一八九五年之百分之七一至一九三一年之百分之一四。三十七年间,竟减五分之四,宁不惊人!

制茶亦为我国极普遍之小工业,尤盛行于乡村,但近年来之发展,与纺棉及缫丝二者,同其命运。请再以出口之数字,为其降落之指数。自一八八六至一九三五年中,一八八六年为出口最多之一年,故可以此年为起点,而测示其降落之情形。一八八六年茶之出口总额凡二,二一七千担,一八九〇年减至一,六六五千担,当一八八六年之百分之七五,而一九〇〇年又减至一,三八四千担,当一八八六年之百分之六二。拳匪乱后一年(一九〇一),出口更为缩减,为一,一五八千担;翌年稍见兴旺,略增至一,五一九千担。此后十三年中,变动较少,至一九一五年而达一,七八二千担,为近四十年来出口最多之数字。自兹以后,出口暴跌,一九二〇年出口为三〇六千担,为自一八八六至一九三五年期间之最低额。一九二〇年以后,逐渐增长,一九二九年又达九四八千担,自是以后又趋缩减，至一九三五年茶之出口为六三九千担，仅当一八八六年之百分之二九。

除上述三种较为普遍之小工业外，其他小工业近年来亦均有衰落之势。如纸类进口之激增。虽因新需要如报纸杂志等之增加及现代教育之普及等之影响。同时亦显示国内手工制纸业之式微。一九〇三年时，中国纸类进口不过二一八千担，此后日益增多，一九一〇年为五四九千担，一九二〇年为一，〇二七千担，一九三〇年为一，九九二千担，一九三二年而至最高峰二，〇七五千担，较一九〇三年高十倍。面粉业亦然。磨粉业本为小工业，自受国外面粉及国内粉厂竞争之影响后，遂日益衰减。一八八七年以后，外国面粉进口，年有增加。一八八七年面粉进口仅关银五六四千两，一八九〇年即增至七七五千两，一九〇〇年又增至三，三三〇千两，一九一〇年三，四四四千两，一九二〇年稍低，为二，三三〇千两，一九三〇年暴增至三，九二六千两，一九三二年为三六，〇七六千两，较一八八七年增加六十四倍。纸与面粉两种手工业，不但须与外货竞争，且须与国内机器产品竞争，面粉业所受影响为尤甚。此外，用菜子及其他植物种子榨油以充家庭中燃料之小工业，亦因外国煤油之输入，而受排挤。一八八六年煤油进口不过二三兆加伦，此后年有增加，一八九〇年有三一兆加伦，一九〇〇年为八四兆加伦，一九一〇年为一六四兆加伦，一九二〇年为一九〇兆加伦，在三十五年间已较一八八六年增加八倍以上。一九一〇年以后进口稍减，一九三〇年为一八六兆加伦，一九三二年则减至一四六兆加伦。

上述棉纺，缲丝，制茶，造纸，面粉，榨油六种小工业，自受外货及国内机械产品之竞争后，或则生产锐减，或竟全然消灭。同时外国之产品,则取其在中国国内或海外之市场而代之,棉纱、纸、面粉及煤油四种进口,久已喧宾夺主;可幸国内新兴棉纱业及面粉业之出口,尚能供国内大部之需要。至丝茶二者,一八九〇年时,尚当我国全出口之半。迨后日本之丝及印度、锡兰、荷属东印度及日本之茶,遂畅销欧美,我国丝茶之国外市场,半为所夺,故今日丝茶之出口,只占我国全出口之八分之一矣(一九三二年占全出口百分之一二)。

四、小工业存在之可能

我国之小工业,虽已呈迅速衰落之象,然其在我国工业生产中所占之地位,仍较大工业为重要。此固由于我国大工业因受种种限制未能积极发展,然小工业之于中国经济组织尚有其存在之必要。实不可否认。我国自海禁开放以来,为时虽近一个世纪,然整个国家经济组织,迄未脱离中古农业经济之范畴。农业经济之特征,即为生活之自足自给,是以我国农民,不仅从事于土地耕种而获得粮食,还须自造非由土地生产之日用品,以维持自足自给之经济生活,此种日用品之制造,端赖手工之运用,而以小规模之组织经营之。农业经济与小规模之手工业,有不可分离之关系,此证之产业革命以前之欧西各国,及产业革命尚在进展中之我国,无一不然。其原因:第一,农业劳动富于季节性,其在华北,农闲时间,有长至半年之久者,农民正可藉此余暇,以从事于乡村手工业之经营。第二,农民不仅有剩余劳力,且有制造原料如棉花、蚕丝、小麦、菜子等等,以为纺纱、缫丝、磨粉、榨油等等之用。第三,农民若仅能以谷物或某种原料换取一切日用制成品，则极不经济，棉花与棉纱交换，麦子与面粉交换，价值相差数倍；农民为自身利益计，不得不从事手工业。基上述三因，手工业在农业经济盛行之我国，尚有其存在之经济上的必要。

小规模之手工业，在农业经济盛行之我国，不惟在农村有其存在之必要，即在城市，一时亦难全部消灭。此不仅指内地的中小都市而言，即首屈一指之工商中心上海，亦难例外。据上海市社会局二十四年调查，上海市商店（特别区除外）之兼有手工业性质者有二六，一二八家，纯粹手工业工厂有五，八七四家（见《新经济》二期，四六页）。夷考其故，不外：一、中国新工业不发达，不能供给社会普遍的需要，必须藉手工业制品为之补充。二、中国劳力过贱，资本缺乏，不做手工业，亦难找到其他生活途径。三、中国机器制品之价格，当较手工艺品为高，社会购买力薄弱，常思舍贵就贱。

小工业之存在，在中国有其必要，即在高度工业化之国家，亦有加以提倡者。盖自一九二九年世界经济恐慌以来，欧美高度工业化之国家，特别英美两国，咸感大工业每因生产之剧烈变动而引起生产过剩与劳工失业，对于小工业之存在，认为有提倡之必要。其于小工业之分散化或乡村化，尤为注意。如在英国，一派之主张，以为工业应分散于乡村，盖如此可减轻城市人口过多及居住拥挤之程度；另一派之主张，认为工业分散化，可使农村居民生活更加丰裕，可遏止自乡村迁至城市之人口移动，并可为近代工业化所产生之劳资问题作部分之解决焉。（见拙著《华北乡村织布工业与商人雇主制度》，《政治经济学报》四卷，一一八页）。

五、小工业复兴之途径

小工业之重要及其存在之可能,上节已略加申述,然小工业之日趋衰落,亦为不可讳言之事实。究应采取何种方策以谋其复兴,实值得吾人之探讨,小工业之亟宜复兴,党政当轴,早已注意及之。故三月二十九日中国国民党临时全国代表大会所定之"抗战建国纲领"中,有"发展各地之手工业"之规定。最近经济、教育、内政三部,复于八月十二日会同公布,"推广小工业设计委员会章程",组织推广小工业设计委员会,以为普遍振兴小工业,增加生产能力之张本。该委员会所办理之事项,有:(一)关于各种小工业推广程序之厘订,(二)关于各种小工业采用完全手工业半手工业机械或主要部份用机械之设计,(三)关于普遍设立小型工厂地点分散之规定,(四)关于实施某县区地方基本职业教育之计划,(五)关于小工业人才之介绍及训练,(六)关于小工业之奖励及资金借贷之协助;(七)关于政府自行举办小型模范工厂之筹拟。

吾人在此时此地之中国提倡小工业,实有其客观环境上之需要。吾人所欲提倡之小工业,亦非仅指一般之小工业而言。在性质、技术及组织,均与以往之小工业有异。就性质言,吾人所欲提倡之小工业,第一:须为属于军需品及生活必需品之范围者,如棉布、纱布、线毯、药棉、皮革、木料、糖、盐之类;第二,属于与机器生产无直接冲突而在相当时间内可以同时存在者,如织布之类,第三,属于有特殊海外市场的工业品之范围者,如花边、丝绸之类(见吴半农,《战时手工业问题》一文,载《时事类编》特刊第十六号)。

就技术言，吾人所欲提倡之小工业，须在可能范围内，能尽量引用现代科学所发明之新器械者。由政府负技术指导之责，在适中地点，设置示范工场或工业指导员，一如农业之有示范农场或农业指导员。就组织言，吾人所欲提倡之小工业，应摹仿农业先例，组织合作社，以经营之。自原料之购置与加工，以至成品之出售，一惟合作社是赖，使商人雇主制（又称包工制、散活制或家庭工业制）下商人雇主对于家庭或外勤工人之劳力所施之剥削与榨取，得以免除。此点作者于三年前调查河北省高阳县手工织布业时，已力加提倡（见拙著《华北乡村织布工业与商人雇主制度》，二十四年十月）。本年夏间中外人士，亦有同样主张，拟以五百万元资本组织三万个工业合作社，以为抗战期间我国工业生产之主体。惜未蒙当轴采纳，故迄未实现（见英文《中国之工业合作》一书）。

六、结论

大小工业，恒视引用技术、组织制度及地理分布之不同而分野。小工业多引用手工，在主匠制及商人雇主制下，从事小规模之生产，大工业则引用机械，在工匠制度下，从事大规模之生产。自产业革命以来，大工业之排除小工业之势，然因农业经济之盛行与夫大工业生产之不能满足需要，小工业仍有存在之必要与可能。我国以工业生产之数量言，则小工业远较大工业为重要。以棉布为例，则五分之四之产量仰给于小规模生产之手工业，而机织工业所供给者，仅五分之一而已。况在抗战期间，大工业什九均随国土之沦陷而丢失，可见此后工业生产，多数将惟小工业是赖，小工业在我国经济组织上所占地位之重要,盖昭然若揭矣。

虽然自九十年前大工业输入我国以来,我国之小工业,已有日趋衰落之势,而如棉纺业一类之小工业,且已全被淘汰,若不急起直追,早图改进与复兴之道,则此后工业生产,将一惟舶来品是赖,而在抗战期间,因交通梗阻,舶来品亦无法输入,工业产品之供给,即将宣告断绝,影响抗战前途,至为重大!良以近代战争,端赖工业生产之源源供给,决非仅赖农业生产所可支持也。

党政当轴,对于小工业之复兴,已渐加注意,"抗战建国纲领"首有发展各地手工业之规定,经济部近复组织小工业推广委员会,以从事小工业之推广及改良。此后小工业之复兴,一方利用科学方法,作技术之改良,一方采用合作组织,藉收大规模经营之利益,其进展自当较抗战以前更为迅速矣。

川康纺织工业建设之途径

方显廷　毕相辉

吾国纺织工业,在战前为民族工业之一重镇,自敌寇侵入,原有工厂设备,或遭破坏,或被掠夺,内迁复业者,为量殊微,重谋建造,刻不容缓。而论其建设地点,又以川康为最宜。盖西南为民族复兴根据地,川康尤为后方经济建设之重心,一般工矿动力资源,蕴藏较富,其于纺织农产原料,则或已有相当产量,或具有推广前途,故于川康奠立新兴纺织工业之始基,不仅有此迫需,抑且切合环境。顾今日建立纺织工业,正犹之建立其他工业,一方面须急谋生产量之提高,而另一方面尤须顾及生产本身之质的改善;一方面须迎头赶上旧日之水准,而另方面尤须超越此水准,使发展其应有之民族性与独立性。以今日川康物资开发之仅具端倪,基础工业之未及见效,交通运输,尚多逆境,其欲达成此项任务,事非简易,不言可知。兹有关要点,略抒管见,刍荛之议,冀有一得耳。

川康棉毛麻织品,平时产量匪丰,供应民用,多赖输入。抗战已还,人口较增,军需尤钜,而产量有限,输入频断,遂致供需失调,形势严重。是故川康纺织工业之建设,首要急务,厥惟增产。今请略论各种纺织品供需失调之概况,籍见其需要增产之缓急。首言棉纺织品。川康平年自外埠输入棉纱十二万包,棉布二百万匹,加计川康土纺手织自产数额,始足以维持平年川康五千四百余万人口之衣被需求,而每人平均耗布量且不过六.四码。抗战以来,棉纱布输入减少，川康两省棉纱布总供给量降至平年百分之五〇，除去军需消耗，则民用额仅占平年消耗量之百分之三〇。棉纺织品战时供给悬殊如此，毛麻亦然。按毛织工业，西南素无基础，所产手工纺织物，品质极低，远不合今日消费之水准，而产量尤微，平素即不能供给需求，当地消费概赖外埠外国之输入。抗战以来，输入停顿，虽有军呢厂自北平内迁，章华厂亦正于四川从事建设新厂，但规模有限，对于军需呢绒及军毯之供给且不足适应，更无余剩以供民用。至于麻纺织，川省虽有夏布为著名麻织特产，然以织造技术落后之故，仅能供夏服之需，销售有限，并无若何调剂作用。同时麻纺工业更为幼稚，军民急需之麻袋布及粗帆布，均绝无供给。综而观之，需供关系之亟待调整，棉纱布为最，毛麻次之，而建立西南纺织工业之首应以增产为急图，由此可具见矣。

既言增产，则首要又需注意增产之速率，易言之，即增产计划必须以最大速率促其完成。就棉纺织业为例而言，以今日外汇暴涨之烈，运输能力之缩减之剧，设使按照纺织技术最高水准为标的以从事建设，则因购机资金过钜，机件输入维艰，结果建厂规模遂必不能过大，而经过购运装置，或须在若干年后始可完工出货。此于将来之纺织事业，未必能厚奠根基，而对目前急需，亦复无所裨益。但吾人苟舍此途径而自另一方面观之，则川康棉纺织业之旧有技术，具有悠久之历史，设能加以利用，对于增产实可大有补助。如川康共有三十余县从事于纺棉纱，近八十县从事手工制造棉布，如按现有纺机数量逐年推广百分之三〇，则于三年后即能增产棉纱十七万包；如按照现有布机生产率逐年提高百分之一四，则于三年后即能增产八百七十余万疋。此项棉纱棉布，若设置机械工厂以事生产，须设纱锭二十五万枚及动力布机一万架，处在今日，办此实属戛乎其难。至于消费水准方面,则吾人可将起略予降低,以适应土产供给,如川康需求棉布以八百万疋论,设全部以机纱制造,约需棉纱三十余万包,此在事实上,难于办到;若将布疋改以土纱交织,则能节减机纱约二分之一,而土纱供给固比较不成问题,如此增产目的短期内即可达到。此可见吾人若图以最大速率完成增产,以解决当前需要,则于建设之手段与步骤,实不能不有所选择。毛麻纺织,虽与棉纺织情形不一,但其增产之途径,亦有赖于从事设计者之详加审察,可以此例推。

本乎上述,则关于工业近代化与技术化之问题,吾人亦应取特殊之观点。此观点为何,即问题之重心应在生产组织,而不在技术本身是也。易言之,即今日建立川康纺织工业,主要须建立合理之生产组织,使足以逐渐推进技术化及近代化之水准,而非必立即建立高度之技术是也。按生产之技术化与近代化,因为吾人对于中国经济建设所抱之信念,亦为建立新中国民族工业之唯一前途。然设使生产组织合理,设使此组织不妨碍技术运用之进步,则无论其用动力,用手工,仅为运用技术之程度上的不同而无本质上的差别。易言之,即设使生产组织合理,即令迫于环境而不得不大规模利用手工,但随生产事业之推进,仍可渐跻于高度技术化之地位,此种手工生产,不能视其本质为落后。就纺织工业而言,毛麻纺织旧有技术太劣,远不足以适应近代消费之水准与范围,故建立毛麻纺织工业,自以建立新型机械工厂为宜。但棉纺织则不然。棉纺织为旧时代手工生产之一巨大营垒;已有技术(尤其手织技术),略足以与近代产品骈肩。此种技术之利用,第一可以急速增加生产,第二对于乡村既有工业不但可予维持,并能从而改进,同时即为改善农村经济之助力。若使此种技术与合作社之组织相配合，并使成立联合社以统筹其产销，并与国家金融机关联合，则在渐进之程序中，此种旧有技术，将自能脱离其固有之封建性，且不难逐渐蜕变为动力机械，或竟能自行建立其机械工场，其所具之进步性及进步速率或较一般私营工厂为大。要之，生产组织问题实为问题之重心，必须有健全之组织，然后对于技术自能为合理之运用。即就毛麻纺织工业而言，纵使所建立之新型工厂在技术设备上已渐臻高度，但组织管理等问题，实仍处于较重要地位也。

工业建设，有赖于原料供给之畅利。欲建立川康纺织工业，则纺织工业原料问题必须同时解决，并使农业与工业之发展相互衔接。按川省产棉素丰，然大部系以供给人民日常絮棉之消耗，其用于手纺工业之消耗者为数仅达二十万市担。而所输入十二万包棉纱及二百万疋棉布，计其棉花数量，则约达八十万市担之钜。故为建立健全之棉纺织工业，一方面须急速于川康境内推广棉作，而另方面则尤须急谋川康与西北交通运输之改善，使能自邻省产棉区输入适量棉花以供纺造。至于原毛，川康毛产，数量达七万市担。抗战以来，因外输之减少，尚有三万市担，可供西南自用。顾西南毛纺织品需求，为量亦钜，即使取足此三万市担充量应用，对于今日军需尚不能全部满足，遑论民用。是故川康原毛之有待增产，与棉花情形正同。惟川康毛产，品质粗短，仅足供纺粗纱之用，哔叽等类零用细纱之织物，设使不从外国输入细毛，则其生产势不得不陷于停顿。故增产原毛，对于品质改良，在今日实尤迫要。复次，今日川康虽尚有三万市担原毛可资利用，然设使不从商业制度上、运销方式上以及交通设备上妥为设法，三万市担是否可能集中，极成问题。此则纺织工业之建设不仅须与农业取得联系，且关于原料收购运销之属于商业部分者亦宜有所统筹办理者也。至于麻纺织工业,川省素以麻产著称,苎麻大麻,产量均钜。其中苎麻为夏布原料,且亦为输出麻产之主要品类,加以推广,产量尚可大增,以供细麻布原料之用。大麻为织造粗麻布如粗帆布麻袋布之原料,单就温江一县,产量已达五万余市担,温江毗邻如崇庆、崇宁、郫县等县,均宜种植大麻,故大麻推广之希望亦无限量。同时川省宜于种植黄麻之土地,亦属广大。黄麻推广,较其他麻类较为便易,生产成本,亦较其他麻类为低,以此供粗麻布之织造,且较大麻为经济。故建立四川麻纺织工业,对于原料取给,殊不成为困难问题。但麻纺织工业之旧有技术既不足以广泛采用,而新型工业亦绝无基础,从头建设,进度必不甚速,若一味推广植麻,超出工业部分所能容纳之程度以外,则匪特于建立麻纺织工业无助,于农业经济反有损。要之,工业部分之建设,须以原料之供给程度为标准,此在今日交通运输困难之情形中尤然。同时,农业部分之推广(除输出农产外),亦须视工业生产率之大小定其限度。此就原料一点上所涉农工间联系言之,其他联系性为建立纺织工业所不可忽者尚多,可以类推,故不具述。

建立川康纺织工业之主要途径,略如上述。此外关于资本问题,亦有须附带一言者。纺织工业之宜归民营,已毋待论;毛麻纺织工厂之资金,应由民营者自筹,亦无疑义。至于工业资本之供给与周转问题,则大抵工业银行之筹立,与乎金融市场之兴建,乃一般工业所亟需,民营纺织工业自亦有所利赖。惟今日环境特殊,私人工业投资,一时难期踊跃,势所必然。故于利用金融机构、统制游资、驱使资金流入工业用途外,政府对于民营工业,实仍有率先投资倡导,或尽量协助,或使民营工业获有安全保证之必要。此则政府已树有政策，于此亦无待赘言，至关于棉纺织业之建立，设使循合作途径进行，则合作经营之资金问题，尚须于工商农各专业银行之外另筹办法，盖今日合作事业银行在中国尚未正式建立，而合作事业则进展甚速，为适应合作事业之发展，似应设立合作事业银行专负推进合作事业及合作今日之责。在专门金融机关提携之下，益以合作社本身资金之累集，则合作形式之资本将不难汇为民族资本之一巨大渊泉，而棉纺织业合作资本亦将占其主要地位焉。

方显廷　毕相辉
原刊载于《新经济》半月刊
1940年第3卷第11期

论农业与工业之关系

农业与工业之关系各为经济活动之一部门，前者生产食粮与原料，后者则就粮食与原料加工制造，变换形式，增加效用，农工两方互相联系，农业对工业供给食粮与原料，工业对农业供给制造品。一业进步，对于他业恒有良好之影响。农业进步，则工业所需之原料食粮价格低廉；工业进步，农民亦能获得廉价之制造品。生产事业，农工分立，各专一业，可收分工之利。

我国经济，以农业为主，工业发展，至为有限。近百年来，新式工业渐见兴起，但进展甚缓，成效不著。于是遂致农业所生产之原料如蚕丝、棉花、皮革、猪鬃、桐油、花生、大豆及豆油等，本国工业无力充分吸收，往往大宗输出，以资外国工业之需要。同时，国内有限之新式工业，恒赖国外农业供给原料，以资调剂。如新式面粉业之购用美、加、澳等地之小麦，新式纺纱业之购用美、印等之棉花等皆是。我国工业何以利用外国原料，其主要原因在乎质量之不足。我国原料品质比较外国粗劣，如棉花可供纺粗纱之用，纺细纱则不相宜，纱厂采购细纱原料，自不能不拣选品质较优之外棉。面粉业及毛纺业亦常嫌本国小麦、羊毛品质低劣而采购洋麦、洋毛。次则本国原料种类繁多，而每种产量，均极为有限，亦为不能不利用外国原料的原因之一。故上海、汉口等地之面粉厂，每因市上本国小麦品质不一，且每种小麦产量有限，不能适应大规模制造之需要,而订购洋麦。

我国工业发展,尚属有限,而此仅有之工业生产,又未能与农业生产取得密切联系,致农业与工业往往脱节而均遭受莫大之损失。盖国内农业生产,赖国外工业界之吸收,而国内工业所需之原料,又不得不取给于国外之农业生产,结果,农工两业之兴衰,悉以国外之供给与需要为转移,其在承平时期,固已沦为他人之附庸;一旦战事发生,交通断绝,农业原料无法脱售,工业原料无法取给,则农工两业,势将同时陷入停顿状态,对于经济自给打击之严重,自不难设想。

如上所述,我国农工关系之失调,在于农工两业之未能平行发展,以收农工分工之效。至于如何促进我国农工两业之平行发展,以求自给自足,举其荦荦大者,不外下列数端:一、确定农工业之种类,二、配合农工业之分布,三、调整农工业之组织。

何种农业应谋发展,何种工业应予奖励,庶农业所生产之原料得为工业所吸收,工业所需要之原料可以自给而毋须求诸国外,此为农工两业平行发展之第一要着。其决定之权,不在惟利是图之企业家或商人,而有赖于统筹民生福利之政府当轴。抗战以来,对于选择亟宜发展之农工两业部门,不乏精密之研讨,惟以求效过急,难免贻只图治标而不图治本之讥。如在西南提倡毛纺织业,若羊种不予积极改良,则设厂制造,不啻先车后马。又如向西南迁移之纱厂,其在重庆附近者,已不下十余万锭,川省原棉产量,原属有限,欲图大量增产,自非一蹴可成,此时若盛倡增加棉纺纱锭,从农工平行发展观点言,亦非所宜也。

次之,欲求农工两业之平行发展,则在交通梗阻之我国,尤宜力求农工两业生产地域之接近,以便节省运费,降低成本。我国主要手工业如棉织、丝织、磨粉、碾米、榨油、造纸等类,多位置于原料出产地带,农工两业在地域上之联系,尚称密切。新式机器工业选择生产地点,需要考虑之条件较多,如动力与劳力之供给,交通形势之优劣,商业与金融设备之有无等。在手工业每毋庸顾及,新式工业则悉须加以注意。因此,欲使农工两业在地域上发生密切联系,自较手工业为困难。但谋国是者,必以民生福利为前提,其于规定发展农工两业之区域时,自宜力求其接近与联系。至农工两业区域不能密切联系者,当建设两地间交通以沟通之。抗战以来,倡言分区建设国防论者,尤感农工两业生产地域之应力求接近。盖生产一定物品之农工两业如分处相距甚远之两地,则战时一地陷落,他处顿失依赖,或成仅有工业而无原料如棉纺织业,或成仅有原料而不能制造如缫丝业之布局,其于自给,仍无补也。

最后,农工两业之组织,应力求沟通。农业生产规模小,工业生产规模大,规模不同,组织自异。结果,农工两业之距离亦愈远。盖小规模组织所生产之原料,恒假手于无数中间人,始由田场输入诸工厂。如是,不惟成本加高,而中间人复从中弄弊,掺伪掺杂,无所不出,驯致原料由田场送至工场时,往往鱼目混珠,品质不一。若不慎加选择、分级、与整理,即无法加以制造。因此,唯利是图之企业家,多视国产原料为畏途,而竟向外商直接订购原料,以济其需要。是以我国农工两业之未能平行发展,组织之未能调整与沟通,亦为主因之一。农业生产之组织,欲由小规模而运行改为大规模,自非旦夕间事。然自十九世纪中叶以来,农业合作运动风行一时,自德而丹而英而美而俄、日、印等国,行之均颇著成效。小规模生产之农民,籍生产、运销、信用等合作社之组织,亦得享受大规模组织之便利。自农业生产——包括种子改良、农田水利、农具肥料及种子之购置等——以至农产分级、包装、堆栈、运销等等,合作社均取中间人之地位而代之,与工厂发生直接关系。工厂方面,籍农业合作机器之运用,质高量富之原料,亦可垂手而得,双方均有裨益,而农工关系,亦复日见密切。我国农业合作运动,自国民政府成立以来,推进不遗余力,迄今乃如雨后春笋,方兴未艾,若能质量并进,则农业组织之改善指日可待,而农工组织之沟通,为期或亦不远矣。

注:刊载于《西南实业通讯》1940年第1卷第3期

论工业建设

一

　　工业建设,为经济设立之中心,盖自工业革命以还,一国之富强或贫弱,莫不以工业进展程度之高下为断。此在欧美工业先进国家,已成老生常谈,无庸置辩。其在我国,虽尚有主张以农立国者,然只能哄动于一时,不值识者之攻讦而自破。抗战以还,我国工业区域,先后沦陷,通商口岸,逐一封锁,战时工业用品之供给,遂致中断,欲谋补救,端赖后方工业建设之推进。于是工业建设遂一跃而为战时经济建设之中心,朝野上下,群致力于工业建设之设计与推进。考工业建设,分工业环境建设与工业本身建设二部门。前者受整个社会政治经济发展之限制,后者赖个别工业之努力。本文限于篇幅,仅就后者加以分析如次。

二

　　工业本身之建设,分资金之筹集,厂基、房屋、机器、原料及服务之获得,成品之制造,及成品之销售四步骤。工业资金分固定资金及流动资金二种,前者如厂基、房屋及机器等,后者如原料及半成品。筹集资金之方法,按上述用途之不同而互异。固定资金,多采用公司股票或公债方式而筹得,而原料之购置与劳工及其他服务如管理与技术人才,水电与保险等之获得,则恒取给于银行贷款及卖主放款。前者为长期放款,属投资银行之范围,后者为短期放款,属商业银行之范围。我国工业落后,从事于工业者,对工商两业恒多不分轩轾,只求近益,不谋远利,故工业金融为商业金融之附庸,触目皆是之商业银行,虽有游资充斥之虞,然投资银行,则初未见有成立者。此于工业建设之进展,阻碍实多,而亟宜早日设法予以纠正者也。

厂基房屋机器原料及服务之获得,为工业建设之第二步骤。厂基之经济觅得,亦即工业之地域的合理分布,其先决条件甚多,如交通便利,劳力、原料与水电供给,市场距离,地价高低,租税轻重等皆是。西南资源,素称丰富,但以交通闭塞,致工业发展有限。西南乏棉,故棉纺织业不发达。抗战以来,棉纺织业自东南及华中移向西南者,不及二十万锭,然已呈棉荒之象者,则原棉受封锁而不克内输外,当以棉产不足为主因。水电对于工业之重要,不亚于交通与原料。抗战以来,敌人不惜屡次以水电厂为轰炸之目标者,其故不外此。工业生产,必规模宏大,始能获利,故工业建设,恒荟萃于人口稠密及交通便利之区。吾人试列举西南目前之工业中心,如重庆、成都、昆明、贵阳、桂林等处,盖莫不受惠于上述数因之有利的存在也。

厂基、房屋、机器之获得,得取给于固定资金,原料与劳力之获得,则取给于流动资金。固定资金与流动资金间之比例,各业不一。

此种比例之决定，则为从事工业者所不可忽视。如第一次欧战告终，我国因欧战而赢利独厚之纱厂，莫不因此种比例措置之不当，固定资金与流动资金恒成四与一之畸形比例，而竟告失败，可为前车之鉴。

厂基、房屋、机器、原料与服务之获得，应以减低成本至最低限度为原则。如由甲工程师负责设计及修建之工厂，因配置合理，能将生产效率提高至预期标准如百分之百，而由乙工程师负责设计及修建之工厂，因配置不合理，致其产生效率，仅及百分之八十，则予甲以每年万元之待遇不为高，予乙以每年五千元之待遇不为低。他如机器虽贵而效用大，原料虽昂而成品高，工价虽涨而成绩优，均与经济原则不相背驰，而为从事工业者所必守之原则也。

成品之制造，为工业建设之第三步骤。成品制造问题虽多，要以科学管理原则之合法运用为最要。十九世纪末叶美哲泰楼氏对就于是项原则之阐明，不遗余力，继起者更不乏人，于是凡从事于工业者，莫不奉科学管理为经营工业之圭臬。考科学管理原则，不外厂基、房屋、原料及服务之有效运用及其成本之精密计算，务以最低量成本，制成最高量成品。迩来是学进展甚速，科学管理而外，另倡人事管理一学。前者指物的方面，后者指人的方面。如原料与成品之标准化，属科学管理；雇主与雇工间关系之调整，属人事管理。上述两学，对于工业贡献甚大。就工业进展较速之国家如美国而言，据一九二九年美国商部标准局所发表之统计言，各业因未能将原料或成品标准化而遭受之浪费，最高如男子服装业达百分之六十四，最低如五金业达百分之二十九，诚属惊人。我国工业落后，小工业占优势，其因标准不一而遭受之浪费，若与美国比较，自更难言喻矣。即以大工业论，标准化运动，亦在萌芽，而成本会计制度之设立，亦未加注意，欲求制造成本之减低，更非易事矣。

成品之销售,为工业建设之第四步骤。各业对于成品销售之手续,繁简互异,如日报日出日发,手续简单。汽车种类既多,价值又昂,手续繁琐。故汽车一业,必也广告新奇动人,售价按期缴付,则推销始易普遍,大规模生产,方克进行。考销售(广义的)包括广告、仓储、保险、运输及销售(狭义的)等手续。如何而使各手续所应有之费用,减至最低限度,同时,其所得之效用,增至最高限度,实为合理销售(广义的)之鹄的。若就我国情形而论,则销售之不合理,触目皆然。第一,国货次于洋货之心理,深入人心,此就一般情形及我国工业发展落后而言,虽具有相当理由,然亦不乏例外。为我国工业前途计,一方固宜竞谋国货品质之改良,以与洋货相拮抗,一方尤须造成民众爱护国货之心理,为民族工业树立广大而可靠之市场。今后广告术之发展,要当注重此点。第二,我国工业组织,规模狭小,制造如此,销售亦莫不然。多数工厂,仅从事于制造,而以销售假手于商号。此种商号,百货兼售,甚少以全副精神,从事于某一商品之销售者。结果,力量薄弱,收效有限。诸如顾主对于商品是否满意,商品价格是否适宜等问题,厂主一概无法探悉而谋适应。制造与销售,既未能密切联系,驯致市场日狭,而成本亦日高,我国工业之一蹶不振,此亦原因之一也。

三

工业建设,分资金之筹集、厂基、房屋、机器、原料及服务之获得,成品之制造及成品之销售四步骤。就我国工业现状言,此四步骤均有亟待改进之处。第一,工业金融宜脱离商业金融之束缚而另谋自立之途径。工业或投资银行及工业证券(股票或公债)市场,尤须早日成立。第二,工厂之设立,诸如厂基、房屋、机器、原料及服务之获得,应有统盘之筹划。固定资金与流动资金之分配,应求得一合理之比例。第三,制造方面,应力求合于科学管理,而于人事之调整,成本之计算,则须合于人事管理及成本会计之原则。第四,销售机构与制造机构应求联系,以免两者间之脱节而提高最后之成本。上述四点,均为当前工业建设之要着,若能一一予以实施,则我国工业建设之前途其有望乎?

二十九年八月十八日,贵阳《中央日报》

工业建设之商榷

一

我国工业发展,虽近百年,而成效不著,举凡轻重工业,其基础之脆弱,为众所周知。兹者,抗战已近三载,工业建设,言效果虽尚乏显著进展;言方向则此短期中所收获之经验认识,诚属未可限量。此对于我国未来之工业建设,实足以树植正确而积固之宏基。因就管见所及,按工业种类、区域、及经营三问题逐一臆述如次,以求正于建设当轴。

二

工业种类之确定,为工业建设之第一问题。处今日军事第一之世界,国防工业握军事胜负之枢纽,工业建设,应以国防工业为首要,自无待言。抗战以还,我政府在经济部资源委员会主持之下,对国防工业之建树,已有深远之计划及长足之进展,至可欣幸。

此种工业,耗时费财,决非一蹴可就,诚如该会负责人所言,"平地起楼台,诚哉不易,但是有个开始,将来总有成功的一天。……我们应该不顾毁誉,不计成败,不敷衍,不迁就,以坚毅不拔的精神,来建设光明灿烂的中国"。(《新经济》二卷一期,五至六页)

国防工业,固属首要,民生工业,亦须兼顾。惟民生工业,种类繁夥,何者宜先予发展,何者宜暂缓举办,窃以为应以谋我国商品农产之尽量加工为先决条件。俾农工两业,有适当之联系,而均得平行发展,不致再蹈昔日本国原料大量输出,而同时复需输入小麦、棉花等农业原料之矛盾政策。抗战以来,时人对于农工两业亟宜发展之各部门之选择,虽不乏精密之研讨,惟以求效过急,难免贻图标忘本之义。如在西南提倡毛纺织业,若羊种不予积极改良,则设厂制造,不啻先车后马。又如向西南迁移之纱厂,其在重庆附近者,已不下十余万锭,川省原棉产额,欲图大量增产,即属一时可能,亦非久长之计(西南棉价,因交通不便,已高涨至饱和程度,而棉产增加,仍难如预期之大。一旦抗战结束,水陆交通开放,陕鄂棉产侵入,则川棉必被压倒无疑),此时若盛倡增加机纺纱锭,促农工平行发展,亦非所宜也。

三

工业区域之选择,为工业建设之第二问题。选择之标准必需兼顾交通、资源及国防地位三端。抗战以前,工业建设区域之选择,偏重交通与资源两端。

抗战以来,鉴于有工业而无国防屏障之危险,内地工业建设之声浪,遂甚嚣尘上。西南一区,尤为朝野上下所注目之工业建设中心。良以西南位处后方,有崇山峻岭为之保障,交通虽感不便,而国防地位,则极巩固。且资源蕴藏丰富,极宜于积极开发。是故倡言西南工业建设者颇不乏人。资源委员会且派员赴川西南区作三月之切实调查,备为工业区域建设之张本。该区包括乐山、夹江、犍为、宜宾、南溪、江安、纳溪、泸县、富顺、自贡井、内江、威远、荣县、资中等十四县市及岷江支流各重要地方。按此虽非一截然划分之天然区域,然以交通形势而论,大部位于岷、沱、扬子三江之间,颇形成一单位。就农业言,四川省府曾划此为甜薯、稻、棉区;就工矿业言,不独四川之三大盐场集中于此,且为糖业之中心,其他如煤、纸、丝等业,亦荟萃于此区以内。其在战前,工业已较川中其他各区为发达,战事发生后,因工厂之西迁,与外货来源之缺乏,实与此区以发展之最大机会。若就国防地位而言,此区远离前方战线,尤大可从长计划。

虽然,划西南为此后工业建设区之议,自国防地位资源富饶两点而言,固未可厚非,然自交通便利及其他方面言,则战后尚难免受其他区域竞争之影响。抗战以来,东南及华中工业之向西南迁移者,为数甚多,政府协助不遗余力,奖诱有加,然困难所在,仍有不易一时解除者。诚如杨端六氏所言:"下江人的生活与内地人很多不同。他们如果不把家室与财产移到内地来,则偶然到内地经营事业仍然是做客一样,一有机会,还是来得迟,去得快。其难一也。内地气候水土和下江不同,下江的人在国难期间勉强忍受,不啻受苦,战事结束,就不能再忍了。其难二也。西南西北各省,除广西以外,地方治安常要发生问题。若地方政府不予保护,下江人到此每每感觉生命财产的危险。其难三也。内地工业幼稚,技术低弱,下江人一来,难免不感觉一种压迫,甚或引起反抗之举动。

下江人舍本乡土顺利之环境而来与内地人争不可必得之利益,非有坚忍之毅力与和婉之手段不成功。其难四也。有此数难,故即令政府多方奖诱,还不易得到结果。在抗战继续时期,有许多人,一则因占领区域之不易经营,一则因爱国心理之易于激发,倒不难冒万难而从事内地工业之建设。一旦战事停止,自由经济的心理恐不免要战胜统制经济的心理,使正在萌芽的内地工业趋于崩溃。"(《今日评论》二卷六期,八五页)

顾上述困难,非尽绝无解除办法,政府若抱有开发西南工业之决心,不妨利用差别待遇办法,奖诱内地特别西南工业之进展。此种办法。可分差别关税、差别运营、差别利率、及差别工资四种是也。

四

工业经营,为工业建设之第三问题。各种工业中,何者应归国营,何者应归民营。民营工业之经营,或经营或联营。均为工业经营之切要问题,兹请逐一商榷如后:

国营工业与民营工业之分野,必须理论事实兼顾,始获适当之解决。例如煤铁与酸碱工业,均为国防工业之母,就实际而言,在此抗战期间,煤铁资源之取给于私人企业经营者,亦不在少数。至酸碱工业,则战前之南吴北范,现均移厂西南,重整旗鼓,以供应国家目前基本之需要。此种事实颇难一笔抹杀。惟按诸理论,此后工业上之新建设,凡于国防有关之工业,自应归由国营也。是以经济部部长翁文灏氏,对于国营事业之用意,有如下之说明:"政府的工作,重在推动与领导全国的人力财力,在一定方针之下,去努力开发内地。其用意乃是为国生产,而非与民争利。所以举办的事业,都以下列原则为范围:(一)国防的急需应当特别经营的,(二)有统筹或统制之必要的,(三)规模宏大,设备艰巨,非寻常财力所能举办的,(四)为国防民生所亟需,而盈亏无甚把握的,(五)为民营工业供给动力或燃料的。政府所办的事业都要合乎上列几个标准,而且并不独占,除有特别理由者外,政府不因办了某种事业,便禁止或妨碍人民举办同类的事业。就是法令上规定是应该国营的,政府也可用合办或出租的方法,委托人民经营。"

民营工业之应否单营或联营,非绝对的而为相对的问题。我国经济落后,民营工业恒多单独经营,重复浪费,不可胜计,值此抗战期间,物资匮乏,各业间尤应取得适当联系,冀以最低成本,促成最高产量。是以联营办法,尤值得提倡与促进,以求我国早日自力更生。此种办法,在经济部工矿调整处积极推进之下,幸已见诸实施,日渐推广。内迁数百厂矿之联营办法,若按联合动机为分类之标准,约可分为下列五种:一、由于机器之利用而形成之联合;二、由于承揽工活而形成的联合;三、由于求原料自给而形成的联合;四、为解决运输困难而形成的联合;五、为新建工业区而形成的联合。

五

工业建设,为经济建设之中心,抗战以来,我国工业,什九被毁,所受损失,诚属不赀。然因抗战之故,我国工业建设因战事之迫切需要,得重奠新基,向前猛进,不可谓非幸事。语云,塞翁失马,安知非福,其此之谓乎?

中国工业上的几个问题

方显廷 讲　顾浚泉 记

中国应以工业立国,注重工业建设,现在已成为天经地义的一个原则。第一,利用机械,增进生产;第二,用大规模组织,节省费用。不过,工业问题很多,自欧西发生产业革命以来,至今已有一百七十年,举其要者,不外资本、土地(即自然资本)、劳工与管理四端,今请逐一简单分析如后:

(一)资本问题　中国资本缺乏,可怜万分,全国所有的近代工业资本,据估计在战前约为四十万万元,以四万万五千万人平均,每人不足十元,与美国每人的平均几千元相较,简直不能比拟。中国境内的纱厂、煤矿、纸烟厂等,都是外国人占优势。国人创办的工厂,资本短少,而又集中于沿海一带,以资金论,约占全国总额的四分之一,其余四分之三的工业资金,都在外人手中。试以棉纺织业一项为例,战前全国各纱厂连正在计划中的在内,共有六百万锭,中日各占一半。其已开工者,共有五百万锭,中国工厂占二百四十万锭。但是抗战以后,其中六十万锭被日本人强占,其中三十万锭被毁,又有五六十万锭在他们统制之下,剩下的只有六七十万锭还在中国人手里,可是将来迟早恐怕还要被日本人夺去。这是中国最大的一种近代民族工业被摧残的情形。至于在西南各地的工业,战前只占全国十分之一,战后虽有沿海一带工厂内迁,但除去被摧毁者外,连战时在后方新建设的工业在内,至多仍不足战前全国工业资本问题的十分之二。所以中国的工业要想发展,很不容易。近年推行工业合作社,很得外人称赞;但是这实在是开倒车,由近代的机器工业退到手工业,只能算是无办法中之办法而已。

关于资本方面,将来有三条路可走:(1)外国资本,(2)华侨资本,(3)本国资本。

(A) 外国资本　今后利用外资有两个问题:(1)政治问题。我们要利用外资,不要再被外人利用,应尽力维持我们主权的独立。(2)经济问题。这次世界战争,范围广泛,结束以后,英美是不是能有大量资本供我们利用,现在很难预料。

(B) 华侨资本　华侨的资本,在国际眼光看来,是很有限的。即如新加坡等地的华侨,过去因受种种排斥,现在人数很有限,政府又不去鼓励他们,所以他们的资金不多出来,并且当地政府对于资金外流都有相当限制,汇出也很困难。

(C) 本国资本　生产超过消费,才能有资本,放眼看去,中国有钱的人太少,一般人的消费能力,都很有限;因之生活到相当阶段,就不容易再行降低。至生产能力若不欲图工业化,也很难设法增加。战后能否有进步,很成问题。

从上面的分析看来我觉得中国资本的来源太悲观——这是从大处着想。

(二) 自然资源问题　中国号称地大物博,一般人很觉得自豪;但是我们试一研究农业与矿业的资源,便觉得不尽准确。

中国的煤铁矿藏很多;但是煤矿中五分之四是在山西、陕西两省,交通不便,现在一部分已在日人的手中。抚顺煤矿每年出产五百万吨,而山西的煤矿则可取之无尽,以前同蒲路只有窄轨,运输不便,陇海路亦未完工,陕西的煤产无法外运。至于铁矿,十分之七实是在辽宁、察哈尔两省,质地不佳,约合纯铁百分之三十左右。此外以西康、四川两省最多。但皆尚未大规模开发。所以中国要有钢铁工业,非收复东北不可。现代的工业文明,完全是机器文明,现在外国因为受战争影响,不能供给我们机器,我们便无办法。除非能把东四省和山西开发,才有希望;否则中国便只能做外国的附庸。

讲到农产物,如棉花、羊毛等类,应该要标准化,并且大量生产;而中国的农业,还未能达到这种地步。今后要想发展农业,必须(1)标准化,(2)农业与工业密切合作。以前这两方面漠不相关,工厂是大规模的,农业是小规模的,工业需要大宗原料,不便分向各农家单独采购,以致宁愿购买外国原料,所以农业要有合作社的组织,利用大规模经营,集中销售,以适应工厂的需要。

(三)劳工问题 英国在十四世纪以前,大陆上的邻人,北部有德、法、比利时,南部有意大利和他竞争,于是英国首要工业即毛纺织业向比国(当时的法荣明①)移入技工,设法振兴,十六世纪英国的毛纺业、丝业二次复兴,亦归功于外国即法国工人的参加工作。不过他们几国文化相近,生活类同,可以利用别国工人;而我们的文化生活程度与他们完全不同,不能招致他们的工人来。中国以前所请的外国工程师,大都是三四等人物,本国的留学生,又大都没有实际经验,不知道应该怎样做。本问题又可分析为两项:

(1)技术问题 技术的训练很费时间,技工是不是短时间所

---

① 即佛拉芒(Flamade)。曾为法国北部和荷兰南部的一部分,后为比利时北部的一个地区。——编者注

能大量产生的；不过从前上海、天津、广州等地熟练工人很多，共计有一百万人，战后到内地去的大约只有数万人，很不够用。可知战前没有把这批熟练技工移到内地去，实在是大错误。

（2）纪律问题　中国西南各省人民，大都生长农村，不肯放弃家庭到工厂去，不习惯工厂的有纪律生活，所以中国的劳工不是适于工厂工作的劳工，这也是一个大问题。

（四）管理人才　以前曾国藩、李鸿章、左宗棠等人创办工厂，可以称为衙门式，官吏资本主义，聘用少数外国工程师，其后有买办阶级参加，再后又加入一批留学生，以及国联所派的专家。最近内地一般流亡难民中之具有企业性者，也在开办小工厂。工厂方面最得用的管理人员，还要以中国自己训练的大学生为好。战前每年大学毕业生有四千人，其中投入工业界的为数想亦太少，希望此后能有增加。

总之，农工商业要有密切联系，金融交通贸易必须联贯，才能发展。美国自一八六五年南北议和时起，即修筑横贯东西的大铁路，交通便利，货物畅通，所以工商业大大发达。中国的西南铁路网以前如已完成，内地的工业不至于没有办法。又如苏联在一九二一年实行新经济政策后，将西伯利亚铁路铺设双轨，东西各地的货物可以运输便利，工业进步甚速。所以交通是工业的生命线，必须设法使他发达起来。

以上所演的大都很悲观，最后要说的一点，是痛心的，但是乐观的。中国过去可以说是保护外人工业，外国工厂出品，无须缴纳苛捐杂税，机器都是很新式，生产速率快，工人多不罢工，规模又都很大，资本雄厚。例如日本人在上海办的纱厂，八九个工厂隶属于一个大公司之下，所以他们很容易发达。而中国工厂往往自相残杀，不知合作，以致无法与他们竞争。抗战以来，中国经济重心，移到内地，他们外人都不进去，中国可以自主；最近英美又表示过将来战争结束以后，准备放弃领事裁判权，与中国自更有利。中国过去是跟外国人跑的，将来不平等条约取消之后，一切工业，都可以有光明的前途。此外还可以报告诸位一些好的消息，最近经济部编制一种统计，表明自一九三七——九四〇年各种工业生产量的增进，多者增加至十三倍，普通均增加一至五倍，在这国难严重、日机大肆轰炸、对于工作效能大有影响的情势下，还能有如此良好的成绩，实在是很可庆幸的，也是我国工业将来的出路。

第五编
工业文献及述评

中国之工业讲义大纲

方显廷 谷源田　合编

纲　目

教科书及参考书表
每课教科书留课页数表
中国之工业讲议纲要
　第一讲　导论
　第二讲　大工业与小工业
　第三讲　中国工业发展之背境——资本主义
　第四讲　中国新工业之发展
　第五讲　中国工业发展之因子
　第六讲　中国之钢铁工业
　第七讲　中国之机器制造业及造船业
　第八讲　中国之棉纺织工业
　第九讲　中国之缫丝及丝织业
　第十讲　中国之毛纺织业
　第十一讲　中国之面粉业
　第十二讲　中国之榨油业
　第十三讲　中国之卷烟业
　第十四讲　中国之精盐业
　第十五讲　中国之造纸业
　第十六讲　中国之水泥工业
　第十七讲　中国之火柴工业

教科书及参考书表

教科书：

龚俊：《中国新工业发展史大纲》，商务，民二二

朱新繁：《中国资本主义之发展》，联合，民一八

吴承洛：《今世中国实业通志》（上下二册），商务，民一八

* 陈铭勋：《经济改造中之中国工业问题》，商务，民一七

* Lieu, D. K.: *China's industries and finance*, Peking, 1927

* Nieh, C. L.: *China's industrial development: its problems and prospect*, Shanghai, 1933

*（1）Fong, H. D.: *Rural Industries in China*, 1933

*（2）方显廷：《中国工业化之统计的分析》，《经济统计季刊》第一卷，第一期，80—127 页

*（3）方显廷：《中国棉纺织业及棉纺织品贸易》，《经济统计季刊》第一卷，第三期，395—486 页

*（4）方显廷：《天津地毯工业》，民一九

*（5）方显廷：《天津针织工业》，民二〇

参考书：

宋应星：《天工开物》，崇祯一〇（1637），上中下卷

马扎亚尔著，徐公达译，《中国经济大纲》，新生命，民二二

《中国实业志》（江苏省），国际贸易局，民二二

许衍灼:《中国工业史略》,新学会社,民一二

安原美佐雄:《支那の工业と原料》,上下二卷,大正八(1919)

上海特别市社会局编,《上海之工业》,中华,民一九

何躬行:《上海之小工业》,生活,民二一

《天津工商业》,天津特别市社会局,民一九

《中国矿业纪要》第四次(民一八至二〇),北平地质调查所,民二一

黄著勋:《中国矿产》,商务,民一五

《盐务年鉴》(民一八),财政部盐务署,民一九

尹良莹:《中国蚕业史》,商务

曾同春:《中国丝业》,商务,民一八

赵烈:《中国茶业问题》,大东,民二〇

《浙江之纸业》,浙江省政府设计会,民一九

China Yearbook, 1933

Breton, M.: *China, its costume, arts, manufactures etc.* 2 vols., London, 1812

Tawney, R. H.: *Land and labor in China*, London, 1932

Nagano, Akira: *Development of capitalism in China*, 1931

Willoughby, W. W.: *Foreign rights and interests in China*, 2 vols., revised and enlarged edition, 1927, Baltimore

Clark, Grover: *Economic rivalries in China*, New Haven, 1932

Vinacke, Harold M.: *Problems of industrial development in China*, Princeton, 1926

Morse, H. B.: *The gilds of China*, New York, 1909

Lamb, Jefferson D. H.: *The origin and development of social legislation in China*, Yenching, 1930

Bain, H. Foster: *Ores and industry in the Far East*, New York, 1927

Tegengren, F. R.: *The iron ores and industry of China*, 2 parts, Peking, 1923-24

Torgasheff, Boris P.: *Mining labor in China*, Shanghai, 1930

Fong, H. D.: *Cotton industry and trade in China*, 2 vols., Tientsin, 1932

（注：凡有星号之教科书每种三册可向木斋图书室借书柜借阅。）

每课教科书留课页数表

1 Fong(1)	1-44, 63-68		大小工业之比较
2 ,,	44-63,	方(4), 11-23 Lieu 1-19	工业制度之比较
3 龚	1-5,	朱 79-106	中国工业史
4 ,,	6-48,		,,
5 ,,	49-91,		,,
6 ,,	93-120		,,
7 方(2)	80-127		,,
8 Nieh	1-53		工业发展之因子
9 陈	68-96		,, ,, ,, ,, ,, 政治
10 ,,	97-119		,, ,, ,, ,, ,, 社会经济
11 ,,	120-146	朱 47-77	,, ,, ,, ,, ,, 帝国主义
12 朱	107-170		,, ,, ,, ,, ,, 农
13 ,,	171-211		,, ,, ,, ,, ,, 关税
14 ,,	213-283		,, ,, ,, ,, ,, 航业
15 ,,	283-397		,, ,, ,, ,, ,, 铁路
16 ,,	399-450		,, ,, ,, ,, ,, 工业金融
17 ,,	45?-476	陈 147-202	,, ,, ,, ,, ,, 结论

(续表)

18 吴上	4-36	龚 208-213	煤
19 ,,	37-64		,,
20 ,,	65-102	龚 214-217	铁
21 ,,	102-120	Lieu 197-219	,,
22 吴下	263-272	龚 232-236	机械
23 ,,	87-105,118-125	,, 121-150,264-267	棉
24 方(3)	395-442		,,
25 ,,	442-486		,,
26 吴下	126-148	龚 105-167,267-269	丝
27 Lieu	220-238		,,
28 吴下	149-161	龚 168-175	毛
29 方(4)	89-100		,,
30 吴下	162-170,180-188	龚 176-182	麻及其他
31 方(5)	1-23,77-85		针织
32 吴下	4-18	龚 183-96,270	面粉
33 ,,	19-43	,, 220,227-232	榨油,碾米,制糖
34 ,,	44-57	,, 245-246	酒及其他
35 ,,	58-76	,, 221-224	茶烟
36 吴上	203-225		盐
37 吴下	194-207	龚 224-227,242	纸及文具印刷
38 ,,	208-224	,, 218-220,244	水泥,陶瓷,砖瓦,玻璃
39 ,,	250-252	,, 197-207	火柴
40 ,,	225-246,259-262	,, 242,244-245	其他化学

中国之工业讲义纲要

第一讲　导论

一、Industries 之定义

广义的——包括一切满足人类欲望之经济活动,物质的或劳役的。

狭义的——制造及建筑工业

二、实业之分类

甲,各国分类不同之原因

1. 经济组织不同
2. 所有之富源不同
3. 分类之目的不同

乙,分类标准化之尝试

1. 1893 Bertillon
2. 1903 国际统计局(International Statistical Institute)
3. 1920 大英帝国统计会议(British Empire Statistical Conference)
4. 1921 国际联盟劳工局之失业问题研究委员会

5. 1923 国际劳工统计专家会议

丙, 分类方法——将实业分为三大类

1. 基本的(Primary)
   a. 农业上的(牧畜,渔猎,森林,耕种)——生产的(genetic)
   b. 矿业上的,——采取的(extractive)
2. 附从的(Secondary)——制造及建筑
   a. 改形的(Transforming)——如织布
   b. 改质的(Chemical)——如炼钢
   c. 集合的(Assembling)——如汽车,钟表,建筑等。
3. 劳役的(Services)
   a. 商业及金融
   b. 交通及运输
   c. 公务行政
   d. 自由职业
   e. 家庭及私人服务

丁, 制造工业之分类

1. 分类之原则:——最好原则:将 a. b. 二原则联合为一。
   a. 按所用之原料分——实用于工业幼稚之国家
   b. 按出品分——实用于工业发达之国家
   c. 按制造手续分
2. 分类系统
   a. 1923 国际劳工统计专家会议议决之分类——共分十六大类

  b. 1912 农商部之分类——共分六大类

  c. 1929 立法院统计处之分类——共分十一大类

  d. 1930 工商部分类——共分十二大类

参考书

  International Labor Office: *Systems of classification of industries and occupations*, In *Studies and Series* N, No:1, Geneva, 1923.

  童家埏:《我国职业分类之商榷》,《统计月报》,一卷二期,50—55页,南京立法院统计处出版,民十八年四月;中国农商统计第一次至第九次(民一至民九),北京农商部出版。

  《全国工人生活及工业生产调查统计报告书》,工商部出版,民十九。

  何廉、方显廷:《中国工业化之程度及其影响》,《工商丛刊》之五,工商访问局出版,上海,民十九。

  《民国十八年上海特别市工资和工作时间》,上海特别市政府社会局出版,民十九。

  Nankai Weekly Statistical Service, Feb. 16, 1931, article on "Industrial workers in China, 1930".

  Bogart, Brnest L. and Landon, Charles E.: *Modern industry*, New York, 1927, Ch. XVII on "Classification of industries".

第二讲　大工业与小工业

一、工业进化之时期

　　甲，家庭工业（Household System）——自给之生产，盛行于前期中古时代（家庭经济）。

　　乙，主匠工业（Craftsman System）——以主匠为生产之主体，所产品直接由主匠售与顾主，盛行于中古时代（城市经济），主匠有二种：

　　　　a. 家庭主匠（Family craftsman）——居乡间

　　　　b. 师傅主匠（Master craftsman）——居城市

　　丙，商人雇主工业（Merchant Employer System）——商人雇主供原料，任销售，手艺工人任生产，互相合作之制度。盛行于十六、十七、十八世纪（国家经济）。

　　丁，工厂工业（Factory System）——生产集中，盛行于十九世纪后（世界经济）。

二、大工业与小工业之不同点

　　甲，组织

　　　　1. 大工业——工厂工业

　　　　2. 小工业——家庭工业，主匠工业及商人雇主工业。

　　乙，地域

　　　　1. 大工业——多在城市

　　　　2. 小工业——多在乡村

三、大工业

　　甲,欧美发展之情形——英,法,德,美,俄,印,日。

　　乙,中国发展之情形——1930工厂统计

四、小工业——按所在地分

　　甲,城市与乡村之区别

　　乙,城市小工业——主匠或行会工业

　1. 中西行会之不同点

　　　a. 起源

　　　　中国——较早,独立的发展起来,与政治毫无关系。

　　　　西洋——较迟,其成立须获得封建郡主,诸侯或国王之特许并领有特许证书。

　　　b. 会员

　　　　中国——自由入会,但有着入会之限制极严。

　　　　西洋——初强迫同业入会,后则限制加严。

　　　c. 会内行政

　　　　中国——较民主的(democratic)

　　　　西洋——为少数人所操纵(oligarchical)

　　　d. 行会之收入

　　　　中国——会费,营业税。

　　　　西洋——会费,自由认捐。

　　　e. 对于会员之管辖权(Jurisdiction over members)

　　　　中国——在法律上无地位,但有绝对的管辖权。

　　　　西洋——合法的,载于特许证书上。

　　　f. 功用——行业之专利

中国——权较大。

西洋——其权初则颇大,后为政府所限制。

2. 行会工业衰落之原因

a. 需要集中。

b. 工业之生产范围扩大,小工业被淘汰。

c. 商品趋于标准化。

d. 预制备需品(ready-made goods)之推销。

3. 工业生产集中之方式

a. 手工业出品被同类之工厂出品所排挤——如布袜等

b. 手工业之制造范围被工厂工业所限定

（1）若干手工业镕合一处成为另一工业——如家具工厂

（2）夺取适合大量生产而复有利可图之手工业出品之制造——如糖刷子等

（3）商品之初步制造需重力者则非大工业莫办——如冶金等

（4）新原料之发现大量制造较优于手工制造——如钉(Wire Nail)

c. 手工业被包括于大企业之中而成为大企业之一部,如大工厂之木工部

d. 手工业由于消费者对需要物品性质之改变而趋衰落——如旅行用具等

e. 行会工业因商人雇主制之兴起而趋衰落——如制鞋等

丙，乡村工业
1. 占有特殊重要地位之主因——利用当地人工,当地原料,当地市场。
2. 中国乡村工业之种类
    a. 纺织类——棉,丝,麻,毛,针织,花边,草帽辫,织席等。
    b. 食物类——粉丝,酿酒,制茶,榨油,火腿,贮藏果类等。
    c. 建筑类——造房,筑堤,浚河等。
    d. 化学类——造纸,陶器,造玻璃,砖窑,爆竹等。
    e. 其他
3. 中国乡村工业衰落之范围颇大,例:土布,缫丝,制茶,造纸,磨粉,榨油等。
4. 中国乡村工业衰落之原因
    a. 技术之忽视,机制品及舶来品之竞争。
    b. 组织不良,中间人从中剥削。
5. 挽救中国乡村工业衰落之方法
    a. 广立乡村模范工场,从事乡村工业技术改良上之推广。
    b. 组织合作社,以铲除中间人之剥削。

参考书

Buecher, Carl: *Industrial evolution*, tr. from 3rd German edition by S. Morley Wickett, Holt, 1901, Ch. IV.

Fong, H. D.: *Triumph of factory system in England*, Tientsin,

1930, Ch. I.

Fong, H. D.: *Rural industries in China*, Tientsin, 1933.

Woods, K. S.: *The rural industries round Oxford*, Oxford, 1921, Ch. I.

Tayler, J. B.: *A policy for small scale industry in China*, in *China Critic*, Mar. 16, 1931. (戴乐仁:《发展中国小规模工业的一个建议》,《东方杂志》,二八,九,民二〇,五,一〇)

Kropotkin, Prince: *Fields, factories and workshops*, New, revised and enlarged edition, London, 1912. (克鲁泡特金著,汉南译:《田园工厂手工场》,上海自由书店,一九二九)

Nankai Weekly Statistical Service, May 29, 1933, article on the "Home industries in Hopei".

马扎亚尔著,徐公达译:《中国经济大纲》,上海,新生命,民二二,第三,四,五章。

《小工业及手工艺奖励规则》(二〇年一五日),《工商半月刊》三卷十一期,法令栏三页,民二〇,六,一。

Morse, H. B.: *The gilds of China*, Longmans, 1909.

第三讲　中国工业发展之背境——资本主义

一、资本主义之定义——投资以营利为目的者,谓之资本主义。

二、资本主义发展之历程——欧洲

甲,商业资本主义——中古末页至1750年

乙,工业资本主义——约自1750年至1870年

丙,金融资本主义——1870年以后

三、中国资本主义发展之主因

甲,帝国主义之侵入

乙,帝国主义在华发展之范围——比较英,日,美,法,德,俄等在华之投资额。

丙,帝国主义在华之侵略方式

1. 普通的——以经济侵略为目的,政治及文化侵略为手段。

2. 特别的

   a. 开商埠——1842南京条约,开上海,广州,福州,厦门,宁波五口为商埠,此后或为自动或受条约强迫,所开之商埠与年俱增,至民22年24省内,共有商埠105处。

   b. 投资于交通事业

   （1）铁路——铁路借款,区划势力范围(Spheres of interest)。

(2) 航运——操纵沿海,内河及大洋航运。

(3) 电报(有线及无线)及电话

c. 开租界

(1) 各国在华占有之租界——日8(皆未收回),英7(已收回4),法5(皆未收回),德2(皆收回),俄2(皆收回),奥,比,匈各1(皆已收回),意,美各1(皆未收回) 公共租界2(皆未收回)。

(2) 租界内资本主义发展之利益——政治上之安全;交通,金融,销售,劳工及技术人员之便利。

d. 创办文化事业——教堂,学校,医院等。为外国资本主义侵入中国之先锋,训练专门人材为其爪牙。

e. 投资于矿业,工业及金融事业等。

(1) 矿业——自1898后开发煤矿等,获得发动力之充分燃料及铁苗以为重工业之基本原料。

(2) 工业——自1895起外人有在华设立工厂之权利。

(3) 金融事业——设立银行,吸收国人之资金,存放政府之关余盐余并发行钞票,定订外汇率,操纵金融市场。

四、中国资本主义之种类

甲,军阀资本主义——军阀资本家

1. 致富之道：——横征暴敛，发公债，库券，及不兑现之军用票，造轻币，售鸦片等不法行为，肥己以祸民。
2. 统制经济机关：——卖买不动产，开矿，办纱厂，设银行，把持交通工具。

乙，官吏资本主义——官吏资本家
1. 昔为大地主，今为企业家。
2. 国营企业，徒肥官吏。

丙，外国资本主义
1. 势力雄厚之原因——有租借地，航运，关税，铁路，矿业，通商口岸设厂制造等之特权。
2. 发展之过程——中国闭关时代，南京条约后，马关条约，日俄战争，民国成立，欧战及欧战后反抗帝国主义运动。
3. 侵略之范围——铁路，航运，进出口，制造业，田产，金融，矿业等。
4. 最近之趋势——多为商业之投资，集中于上海，天津，青岛及东三省等处。国内政治稳定，外资有增加之趋势。

丁，华侨资本主义
1. 华侨之经济发展多在安南，暹罗，爪哇等处。
2. 若国内政治稳定，华侨必多回国投资。

五、中国资本家之特点
甲，多为中小资本家
乙，无托辣斯(Trust)一类之大企业组织丙,地方色彩甚浓,浙江财阀(Chekiang Plutocracy)操纵中国经济生活。

参考书

Nagano, Akira: *Development of capitalism in China*, 1931.

朱新繁:《中国资本主义之发展》,联合,民一八,第一,二章。

李达:《中国产业革命概观》,昆仑,民一八,第六章。

潘肃编:《中国经济论战》,长城,民二一。

Willoughby, W. W.: *Foreign rights and interests in China*, second ed., 2 vols., 1927.

Remer, C. F.: *Foreign investments in China*, New York, 1913.

Clark, Grover: *Economic rivalries in China*, New Haven, 1932.

Overlach, T. W.: *Foreign financial control in China*, New York, 1919.

漆树芬:《经济侵略下之中国》,民一四。

第四讲　中国新工业之发展

一、发展之特点

　　1. 非自动的,乃被动的——受列强之影响。

　　2. 首创军用工业。

　　3. 官厅办理。

二、发展之时期

　　甲,比较各家划分之工业时期:东亚同文会1907,许衍灼1917,安原美佐雄1919,杨铨1922,龚仲皋1929,李达1929,朱新繁1929,龚俊1933。

　　乙,吾人暂拟之工业时期

　　1. 第一时期1862—1881 官办。

　　2. 第二时期1882—1894 官督商办。

　　3. 第三时期1895—1902 外资侵入与民业萌芽。

　　4. 第四时期1903—1913 收回利权与保护民业。

　　5. 第五时期1914—1922 战时华资日资工业焕发。

　　6. 第六时期1923以后,战后华资工业衰落。

三、第一时期1862—1881——官办时期

　　甲,兴起之原因

　　1. 武力思想——深知列强军械之精良。

　　2. 曾国藩,李鸿章等极力提倡。

　　乙,特点——军用工业为主要,聘用外国技师多不学无识之流,企业官办。

丙，重要工业——军械制造业，造船业，机器制造业。

四、第二时期 1882—1894 官督商办时期

　　甲，兴起之原因

　　　　1．民智幼稚，故须政府监督。

　　　　2．各省财政困难，须吸收商人资本。

　　　　3．李鸿章张之洞，极力提倡。

　　乙，特点

　　　　1．商品之制造兴起。

　　　　2．官督商办。

　　丙，重要工业——棉纺织业，毛织业，开铁矿及炼钢，采金矿等。

五、第三时期 1895—1902——外资侵入与民业萌芽时期。

　　甲，兴起之原因

　　　　1．1895 马关条约，允许外商在中国口岸自由设厂制造。

　　　　2．华人工厂内所聘用之外国技师，获得不少经验，故一旦允许外人自由设厂制造，驾轻就熟，成就自易。

　　乙，特点

　　　　1．外商投资实业。

　　　　2．政府觉悟提倡工业。

　　丙，重要工业

　　　　1．外人所经营者——棉纺织，面粉，榨油，火柴，铁，造船，机器等；棉纺织，面粉及铁投资较多，尤以铁为最，外商投资之数额，英籍最多，德次之，俄法美日又次之。

2. 国人所经营者——除上列者外,尚有缫丝,造纸,印刷等,棉纺织缫丝颇见发展,面粉尤为后起之秀。

六、第四时期1903—1913——收回利权与保护民业时期

甲,兴起之原因

1. 武力竞争到经济竞争。
2. 政府觉悟到人民觉悟。

乙,特点

1. 收回失权
2. 政府之提携,如组织商部,办理公司注册,设工厂学校,开展览会,立陈列所,颁布各种商法及奖励工商业法。
3. 私人企业兴起。
4. 开始抵制外货(美货)。
5. 外货日增,日资为尤甚,英俄德法等次之。

丙,重要工业

1. 主要的:棉纺织业,缫丝业,毛织业,面粉业。
2. 次要的:铁,造船,火柴,水泥,卷烟。
3. 尚在发展中的:造纸,砖,陶瓷,玻璃,制糖,制茶,罐头,榨油,针钉,电气等。
4. 外资工业有棉纺织,面粉,榨油,制糖,砖茶,烟草,铁,机器,造船等,以棉织,面粉,铁为最。

七、第五时期1914—1922——战时华资与日资工业焕发时期

甲,兴起之原因

1. 欧战方酣,舶来品之输入断绝。
2. 二十一条之刺激。

3. 日本对华之经济侵略日厉。

4. 官吏政客企业之增加。

乙，特点

1. 私人企业，发展迅速。

2. 日本在华之投资剧增，尤以棉纺织，面粉，榨油及铁业为最。

3. 受二十一条之刺激抵制日货之举兴。

4. 工业逐渐机械化。

5. 工业集中化，以上海，武汉，天津，广州，无锡，青岛，大连，哈尔滨等处为中心。

6. 劳资争议之恒久化。

丙，重要工业

1. 主要的：棉纺织，缫丝，针织，面粉，火柴，铁。

2. 次要的：制糖，榨油，烟草，水泥，玻璃，造纸，印刷，机器，造船。

3. 外资工业：日资工业之主要者，有棉纺织，缫丝，毛织，针钉，电气业等，面粉，制糖，铁等；英资工业之主要者有烟草，电气，蛋粉等。

八、第六时期1923—1933——战后工业衰落时期

甲，特点

1. 重要工业之衰落，由于外货输入与竞争。

2. 内战频仍。

3. 世界经济状况萧条。

乙，衰落之重要工业：棉纺织，缫丝，面粉等业。

九、中国新工业之现状

甲, 按工业之类别分
1. 按工人统计分——以衣, 食, 住, 及化学为最重要。
   a. 以工业类别分——纺织, 饮食品, 衣服, 建筑, 化学, 机械, 教育, 器具, 美术品, 公用, 交通, 其他。
   b. 以各个工业分——棉纺织, 缫丝及丝织, 印刷, 烟叶, 成衣, 机械制造, 木器, 五金器具制造, 针织, 制鞋, 火柴等。(以每种工业占工人总数百分之一以上者为限)
2. 按注册公司资本统计分——亦以衣, 食, 住及化学为最重要。

乙, 按工业之所在地分
1. 按省分
   a. 以工人统计分——江苏, 广东, 湖北, 安徽, 浙江, 山东, 福建, 江西, 广西。
   b. 以棉纺织, 缫丝, 榨油, 电气工业之分配分——江苏, 辽宁, 河北, 广东, 山东, 湖北, 其他。
   c. 以注册公司之资本统计分——江苏, 河北, 山东, 辽宁, 湖北, 四川, 浙江, 河南, 广东, 其他。
2. 按城市分
   a. 以工人统计分——上海, 广州, 武汉, 无锡, 苏州, 顺德, 青岛, 南京, 佛山, 武进, 杭州, 福州, 芜湖等。
   b. 以雇有30人以上之工厂数目分——上海, 无锡, 大连, 汉口, 广州, 哈尔滨, 杭州, 青岛, 安东, 南京, 南通等。

c. 以煤之消费额分——上海,武阳夏,天津,沈阳,北平,哈尔滨,广州,大连,长沙,营口,长春,重庆,济南,福州,南京,汕头,青岛,杭州,苏州等。

丙,各重要城市之工业按工业投资额分

1. 上海:按民十六年资本额分——棉纺织,卷烟,自来水,及印刷,面粉,缫丝及丝织,机械,制革,造纸,针织,榨油等。
2. 天津:按民十七年资本额分——棉纺织,面粉,精盐,制碱,火柴,人造丝织品,酿造等。
3. 无锡:按民十九年资本额分——棉纺织,缫丝,面粉,电气,榨油等。
4. 杭州:按民十九年资本额分——丝织,电气,火柴,棉织等。

丁,工业集中各地之原因

1. 原料
   a. 凡制造笨重而不适于运输原料之工业多集中于原料出产地,例:水泥,造砖业。
   b. 以南北原料生产之不同,故有南北工业之分——例:棉纺织,缫丝及丝织为南方工业,面粉,榨油及毛织为北方工业。
2. 气候——以气候关系只宜于某项工业一例:气候潮湿之地宜于棉纺织。
3. 劳工——大城市内雇佣机会较多,故工人集中。
4. 技术——例:景德镇之陶瓷业,天津北平之地毯业,京苏杭之绸缎业。

5. 动力——大城市内易得原动力之供给——例：上海易租电力，无需自设电厂发电。故纱厂甚多；将来或在水力丰富之处，利用水力，开设需用大量电力之工厂，如造纸厂，锯木厂，人造丝厂。
6. 运输——运输便利，则原料之采购，成品之分销，皆感便利。

    例——石家庄及郑州昔为荒芜之区，自正太，陇海，平汉等路通行后，已渐为工商要镇矣。
7. 金融——大城市利息低，内地利息高。
8. 市场——笨重出品如钢铁，及日用必须品如火柴等工业，皆须接近市场，以便畅销。
9. 历史的背景——昔之皇室工业也，或其他有特殊历史关系者，今仍保持其已有之势力。例：北平之宫灯，及景泰蓝器制造业，景德镇之陶瓷业。

参考书

龚俊：《中国新工业发展史大纲》，商务，民二十二。

安原美佐雄：《支那之工业及原料》，卷上，第二章，大正八（1919）。

杨铨：《五十年来中国之工业》，见最近之五十年，1872—1922（申报馆五十周年纪念册），上海，民一一，一五页。

李达：《中国产业革命概观》，昆仑，民一八，第四章。

马扎亚尔：《中国经济大纲》，新生命，民二二，第六章。

许衍灼：《中国工艺沿革史略》，商务，民六，第四章。

龚仲皋：《中国近代工业发展论》，太平洋，民一八，第三章。

东亚同文会:《支那经济全书》,明治四一。

Ho, Franklin L. and Fong, H. D.: *Extent and effects of industrialization in China*, Tientsin, 1929.

Fong, H. D.: *China's industrialization, a statistical survey*, Shanghai, 1931.

Ho, Franklin L.: *Industries*, Shanghai, 1931.

Lieu, D. K.: *A preliminary report on Shanghai industrialization*, Shanghai, 1933.

Nankai Weekly Statistical Service:

  "Shanghai industries", 1928 (Ⅲ:29) July 21, 1930.

  "Wusih industries", 1929 (Ⅲ:50) Dec. 15, 1930.

  "Tientsin industries", 1928 (Ⅲ:17), Apr. 28, 1930.

  "Hangchow industries", 1928 (Ⅲ:23), June 9, 1930.

  "Industrial workers in China", 1930 (Ⅳ:7), Feb. 16, 1931.

  "Factory labor in Shanghai", 1929 (Ⅵ:39), Sep. 25, 1933.

Tawney, R. H.: *Land and labor in China*, London, 1932, Ch. V.

Huang, K. C.: "Factories determining the choice of the site for the port of Shanghai", in *Transactions of the Science Society of China*, Vol. VI, pp. 63-68, 1930.

第五讲　中国工业发展之因子

一、普通的——政治的,经济的,社会的,自然的。

二、政治的

　　甲,内乱

　　　1. 民元以来之内战史

　　　　a. 1911 辛亥革命——满清退位,举袁世凯为大总统,定都北京,国民党正式成立。

　　　　b. 1913 二次革命——袁世凯向英法俄德日五国大借款,又饬人刺宋教仁,故孙文黄兴等出兵讨袁,是为二次革命,结果失败。

　　　　　1914——五月立新约法

　　　　c. 1915 护国之役——袁世凯改约法称帝,蔡锷起义云南。

　　　　　1916——袁世凯死,国会恢复,按新约法举黎元洪为总统。

　　　　d. 1917 复辟之战——段祺瑞以参战案,被免职,张勋被召入京,意在防段,然竟酝酿复辟,段氏起,出兵讨平之。

　　　　e. 1917 及以后——护法之役——1917 复辟之战平定后,同段为国务总理,冯国璋为代理总统,孙中山在粤组织军政府。

　　　　　1918 冯国璋去位,徐世昌继任。

1919——南北和会毫无结果,南北复成僵局。

1920——吴佩孚,曹锟,张作霖,联合倒段,致演直皖之战。

1921——南方军政府瓦解,孙文重回广州建立大元帅府。

1922——第一次直奉之战——吴佩孚出兵逐张作霖出关,黎元洪复为总统。

1923——曹锟以贿选被举为总统。

f. 1924——第二次直奉之战——冯玉祥倒戈致吴佩孚败退。张作霖入关,段祺瑞主临时执政政府。

1925——奉浙(孙传芳)之战——国(国民军)奉之战,奉军败退出关。

g. 1926——北伐之役——奉直结合与国民军对抗之争,北伐军由蒋介石帅领,抵武汉。

1927——孙传芳败走,北伐军入南京,宁汉分立,阎冯出兵,张作霖败退出关,在皇姑屯遇炸。

1928——蒋介石得阎冯之助进入北京,迁都南京,是年十二月末,张学良易帜归化国民政府。

h. 1929——湘桂之叛

i. 1930——阎冯之叛

j. 1931——剿共之役

2. 内乱之影响

   a. 阻碍生产

     (1) 比较 1919—1932 年间棉花生产量。

(2) 1912—1933 年间入超与年俱增。

(3) 1912—1928 年间输入之原料及半制成品为量日增。

(4) 1928—1932 年间我国主要输入品为数日增,而主要输出品则为数日减。

b. 阻滞交通

(1) 铁路——民 13 年秋:江浙(或齐卢)之战时,沪杭二路自九月初起,停止通车几及二月,沪杭路桥梁被毁,损失尤钜。民 14 年:国奉之战时,京奉间火车交通,漫无准期,达二月之久,即京津间之铁路交通亦断绝十日。

(2) 水运——民 14 年奉浙战时,招商局长江班内之江裕,江靖,江大等轮,行经宁镇,悉被军队扣留将搭客驱逐上岸,江大稍拒,军队即炮击毁其后舱,江北各内河之小轮被扣留者达 120 只,民 15 年孙军与北伐军战于江西。招商局长江班之轮船供孙军驱策者达九艘,江永轮且被毁。

c. 捐税之繁重

(1) 直接的——厘金——关卡重重,舞弊病商。

杂税——为一切货物税,22 省合计 147 种。

杂捐——为一切劳役及货物捐,22 省合计 357 种。

　　　　　　　　兵差——银钱,实物,与力役之
　　　　　　　　征发。
　　　（2）间接的——币制之繁乱:
　　　　　　　　银两——北平一地有公平等七
　　　　　　　　种,上海有九八规元等六种。
　　　　　　　　银圆——袁头,龙洋,鹰洋,北
　　　　　　　　洋等。
　　　　　　　　辅币——袁头,龙头,广东双毫,
　　　　　　　　轻质铜元等。
　　　　　　　　发公债——举债充军费,以便
　　　　　　　　内战。
　d. 战区损失及兵匪之摧残
　　（1）政府举债度日。
　　（2）军费占政府支出之百分比,与年俱增。
　　（3）土匪之抢劫——河南之白狼,山东之孙美
　　　　瑶,河北之老洋人,河南及皖北之红枪会,
　　　　大刀会等。
　e. 政府之工业保护政策——政府对工业行政之支
　　　出。为数极微,且一切奖励实业计划,决而不
　　　行,尽系纸上谈兵。
乙,外患
　1. 列强之侵华史略——可分为三大时期
　　a. 1842—1894 为门户开放时期
　　b. 1895—1918 为列强瓜分中国时期
　　c. 1919—1930 为中国收回失权时期

2. 1842—1894 门户开放时期

   a. 1842——鸦片战争失败,订中英《江宁条约》,开五口通商,割香港,开协定关税恶例。(1844《中美五口贸易章程》载明关税为值百抽五)。

   1843——《中英五口通商章程》,载明"最惠国"条款。

   b. 1858—1860——英法联军之役,订天津北京条约,允各国设公使馆区域于北京,割九龙半岛与英,开天津等处商埠,并允许领事裁判权。

   c. 1876——中英《烟台条约》,又开商埠。

   1885——中法天津条约,认越南为法之保护国。

   1886——英并缅甸。

3. 1895—1918 列强瓜分中国时期

   a. 1895——甲午战败,与日订《马关条约》,允朝鲜独立,割辽东台湾及澎湖,赔兵费二万万两,并开重庆,沙市,长沙,苏州,杭州五口通商,后俄约德法,使日本归我辽东,因而增偿日本三千万两,为偿日本赔款,清政府因而借外债;是为中国举外债之始。

   b. 1898——列强攘夺中国领土权,政治权,经济权。

   德——租胶州湾,租期九十九年,并获胶济铁路之建筑权,及铁道附近左右各三十里之矿产开采权。

   俄——租旅顺口大连湾及其附近一带之地,租期二十五年,俄定名为关东省,设总督治之,并获自哈尔滨至旅大之铁路（即南满铁路）筑造权。1896中俄密约，许俄筑中东铁路，并设华俄道胜银行，以资接济。

法——租广州湾九十九年，并获自安南至云南省城之铁路（或名滇越铁路）筑造权。

英——租威海卫，租期二十五年，扩展九龙之租借地，租期九十九年。

日——向清廷要求福建省及其沿岸不得割让或租借与他国，以免危及台湾，澎湖。

c. 1899——美国提议，经英德俄法日意之承认，保全中国，开放门户，机会均等，中国免得瓜分，各国得免冲突，中国一变而为世界之公共市场。

d. 1901——八国联军之役，订《辛丑条约》，赔款四万万五千万两，分三十九年偿清，为谋整理国家岁入以偿赔款计，立税务署管理关税收入。昔由总理衙门管；各海关三十里的内之常关亦归外人管理；修正1858征收关税之物价表，以谋切实值百抽五。

1902——列强间对中国在华所获各种权利之协约。

(1) 英德协约以防俄

(2) 日英同盟以防俄

(3) 俄法同盟，抵制英日同盟。

(4) 中俄满洲撤兵条约

e. 1905——满洲不撤兵，日俄开战，日俄媾和后，中日订满洲协约,将俄国在辽东半岛之一切利益,让与日本。

　　1905以后,英日二次同盟,日本承认英国对西藏有必要处分权。

　　1907——英俄西藏协约,以保全西藏为中国之领土。

　　1907—1908——日本与法,俄,美订协约,皆以保全中国为口号,保全中国之盟主,由美国而改为日本。

　　1909——日俄协约,共同拒绝美国之满洲铁路中立提议。

　　1911——英日第三次同盟,规定若日本与他国(暗指美国)开战时,英国不负共同开战之义务。(此约要点为英日第一次第二次同盟所约定之共向防御责任之卸除)

f. 1912 英日俄三国密约,约定俄国扶外蒙独立,英国扶西藏独立,东部内蒙划归日本势力范围。

　　1916——五国银行团成立,我国政府举善后大借款二千五百万金镑,以盐余为担保,盐务税收机关,遂为外人所掌管。

g. 1915——二十一条之要求,共分五项

　　(1) 关于山东日本特殊权利之件(四条)

　　(2) 关于满蒙日本特殊地位之件(七条)

　　(3) 关于汉冶萍日本特殊权利之件(二条)

　　(4) 关于中国全国领土之件(一条)

(5) 预备中日合并之件（此项共七条后删去）山东协约，及南满东内蒙协约，南满租期延长九十九年，南满及东内蒙建造铁路借款之优先权及商租权，南满开矿权，汉冶萍中日合办，福建无设施，交还胶州湾等。

1916——日本灭中国之日俄协约与日俄密约

1917——日本与英法俄意订山东密约

1917——日本认中国为日本保护国之日美协定（以领土相接近，承认日本在华有特殊权利）。

1917—1918——西原借款，约计三万万六千万元，其目的在助长中国内乱，以便日本从中渔利。

1919——巴黎和会中国大失败——德人在山东一切权利划归日本。

4. 1920—1930 中国收回失权时期

 a. 1921——平等条约之订定

  1921——中德协约——为中国第一次所结之平等条约

  1924——中俄协定——以平等为原则

  1925——中奥协定——以平等为原则

  1928——中比，中义，中丹，中葡，中西友好通商条约。

 b. 1922——华盛顿会议对中国之协定

  (1) 五国间对中国事件适用各原则及政策之条约。

(2) 关于中国关税税则之条约——允开特别会议，于厘金末废除前征值百抽二五至五之附加税。

(3) 关于各国在中国之领事裁判权议决案。

(4) 关于各国在中国之邮局议决案——议决英美日法四国在华之邮局1923年前撤消之。

(5) 关于中国及有关中国之现有成约议决案。

c. 1922——由英美两国之调停，山东问题得由中日间直接交涉在华府会议时解决之，胶州租借地及胶济铁路均由中国收回。

d. 1925以及后：收回关税自主权

1925——五卅惨案，关税会议，法权调查。

1928——关税自主——第一次中国颁布国定税则于1929年2月1日施行。

1929—1930——与美德挪比义丹葡英瑞法西和日订立关税协定

e. 1927——收回租界及租借地

1927——汉浔镇英租界之收回

1930——天津比租界及厦门英租界之收回，威海卫租借地之收回。

f. 1929——与比义丹西葡签订友好通商条约收回关税自主权及治外法权

5. 经济方面之损失

a. 外人获有通商及居住权

(1) 商埠之种类

由条约所许而开放之商埠——多在沿海及长江流域。

自动开辟之商埠——商埠内之行政权及警察权,概在我国地方行政长官之手。

长江内非通商口岸——按长江统共章程应不准洋商私自起下货物,1876中英《烟台条约》议定:通融办法,轮船准暂停泊,上下客商货物,皆用民船起卸,照章定税。

(2) 通商口岸外人之权利

外人得在通商港口久居或暂住,均准其租赁民房(1858中美条约)或"永租地基自行建造"。(1903中美续议通商行船条约)外人得"从事商业",并得"任便从事各项工艺制造,又得将各项机器任便装运进口,只交所定进口税"。(1895中日《马关条约》)

(3) 内地杂居——只限于传教士,1903中美条约谓"美国教会准在中国各处租赁及永租房屋地基,作为教会公产,以备传教之用……"

b. 关税税率固定;各通商口岸,划一办理——由于"最惠国"条款,各国皆援利益均沾之例。

(1) 税率之种类:

进口及出口税——值百抽五(1842天津条约,从价税),1902增改各国通商进口税则,进口货增至切实值百抽五,一部改为按件抽税。

复进口税——1861年规定为值百抽二.五

子口税——1858年规定为值百二.五

(2) 海关行政

海关——1858《中英天津条约》附属通商章程第十条谓:"现已议定各口划一办理,是由总理外国通商事宜大臣或随时亲诣巡历或委员代办,任凭总理大臣邀请英人帮办税务……"此已承认外人管理上海以外其他各关税权矣,(按上海税关管理权失于1854年)嗣后复规定,以对华贸易占首位之国,中国海关得任用该国人民为总税务司,该时历年英国对华贸易为各国之冠,故总税务司一职,历在英人之手。

内地常关——各国为担保1901《辛丑和约》赔款四百五十兆两计,立约将"所有常关各进款在各通商口岸之常关,均归新关管理……"

(3) 关税税率之修改——1858《中英天津条约》第27款载明:

"此次新定税则……日后彼此两国再欲重修以十年为限……"然只1858,1902,1918及1922修改四次耳。

(4) 关税权之收回——1925北京关税特别会议,1929国定税则,1930国定税则。

c. 沿海航行权

(1) 1863《中丹天津条约》第44款:"丹国商民沿海议定通商各口载运土货约准出口先纳正税,复进他口再纳半税。后复运往他口,以一年为期,准向该关取给半税存票,不复更纳正税。嗣到改运之口,再行照纳半税"。此款已允许外人以沿海各通商航行口岸及运载货物权,但只限于通商口岸。此种权利,在他国只限于其本国人民。

(2) 外货入口交纳进口税后,原封不动,复行运至其他通商口岸时,不复交纳进口税。(1896中日条约),然本国货物由甲口岸运至乙口岸时须交纳复进口税。

(3) 船钞——1858《中英天津条约》:"英国商船应纳钞课,一百五十吨以上,每吨纳钞银四钱;一百五十正吨及一百五十吨以下。每吨纳钞银一钱……"每四月征收一次。

d. 内河航行权——1858《中英天津条约》第十款:"长江一带各口,英商船只俱可通商。"我国之内河航行权,自是拱手外人矣。得寸进尺,侵略日厉,今日我国之内河航行大都操诸外人之手。1902中英续议内港行轮修改章程谓"英国轮船东可向中国人民在河道两岸租栈房及码头,不逾二十五年租期……租满之后亦可续租"。是英人复有起卸及堆存货物之地矣。

e. 内地贸易及旅行权——1876《中英烟台条约》对"内地"二字之解释谓:"洋货运入内地及内地置买土货等语,系指沿海沿江沿河陆路各处不通商口岸,皆为内地。……"换言之:凡非通商口岸皆谓之内地,外人有营商及居住权利。

f. 购买土地权——外人得向当地人民租地建屋。此权以外人职业与居地之不同而有差异,例:商人只限于各通商口岸,传教士及其他人士则无何限制。

g. 铁路建筑权——1898 为外人攘夺中国领土权,政治权及经济权之时期,获得铁路建筑优先权者有二。(1)外国政府(2)外国商号或私人。各含有军事上重要性之铁路建筑权尽落外人之手:1895 允俄筑中东路,1898 允俄筑南满路,1898 允法筑滇越路。铁路之所至,各国之势力范围由是而划分焉。

h. 矿产开采权——外人获得矿权者有二类
  (1) 铁路沿线左右若干里内之矿产开采权;
  (2) 只以开矿为目的者——以其纯利四分之一缴付地方官厅。此外出产税均为 5%,以纯利 6% 偿付借来之资本,以 10% 为积金,以为还本及付息之准备。

三、经济的——中古式之经济

　　甲,农业方面

　　　　1. 农民占 80%

2. 小营业

3. 耕种悉用人工,无新式农具。

4. 永佃制,甚似西洋之佃奴制度。

乙,工业方面

1. 盛行手艺工业——新工业不发达。

2. 地方色彩甚浓——例:行会,公会,帮。

3. 组织多系私人经营或合伙经营,无大公司。

丙,劳工方面

1. 劳工多来自田间,半农半工,有季节性。

2. 未受教育。

3. 工作效率低。

丁,商业方面——国外贸易操诸外国商人之手,此与中古时代英国之情形相仿。

戊,交通方面——铁路,公路,轮船皆少,铁路当美国4.4%,公路当美国3.8%,航运吨位当美国2.2%,电报线当美国6.6%。

己,金融方面

1. 钱庄之势力较银行之势力大。

2. 币制紊乱,各自为政,全国不能划一。

庚,财政

1. 地方与中央各自为政。

2. 出口税及厘金等皆为中古时代之税收制度。

辛,度量衡方面——各地自有其制度,全国不能划一。

四、社会的

甲,家族制度之影响

1. 乏进取精神——例：东三省移民，多归返乡里。
2. 均产制度之结果，无大资本集中。
3. 家族经济上之共产化——养子防老无业者依有业者为生。

乙，社会心理——悉以舶来品为时尚。

五、自然的

甲，灾害频仍——水灾，旱灾，蝗灾等，损失之大当以民二〇江淮之水灾为最，达二十万万元。

乙，富源之不足

1. 农业方面——农作物之出产，为最不足供国内之消费，为质不及舶来品。
   a. 民 17 年饮食品，烟草，原料及半制成品之输入值占总输入值 46.6%。（当 557 兆海关两）
   b. 民 21 年，米，麦，及面粉之进口值为 207 兆海关两，当该年进口总值⅙，棉花之进口值为 120 兆海关两，当该年进口总值⅑。
   c. 国产麦一担可出粉 87 磅，舶来麦一担可出粉 100 磅。
2. 矿产方面
   a. 按贮藏量计：铁之贮藏量为 1,000 兆吨当世界贮藏量 2.3%。
   b. 按出产额计：铁矿砂当世界产量 0.5%，铜当世界产量 0.02%，铅当世界产量 0.09%，锡当世界产量 6%，锌当世界产量 0.09%，钨当世界产量 64.3%，锑当世界产量 77%。

3. 动力方面

    a. 水力——可发展的水力,约有二千万匹马力,占世界第四位,然今日所已开发之水力,只一千匹马力。

    b. 煤——贮藏有限;占全世界4%,且交通不便;产量有限,占全世界1.6%。

    c. 石油——贮藏量占世界1/15,其中半数为油页岩,尽在辽宁一省。

参考书

《申报年刊》,民二二。

朱新繁:《中国资本主义之发展》,民八。

陈铭勋:《经济改造中之中国工业问题》,民一七。

Vinacke, Harold M. : *Problems of industrial development in China*, Princeton, 1926.

Vinacke, Harold M. : "Obstacles to the industrial development in China", in *Annals of the American Academy of Political and Social Science*, November, 1930. (China number) pp. 173-180.

Nieh, C. L. : *China's industrial development: its problems and prospect*, 1933.

Lieu, D. K. : *China's industries and finance*, 1927, Chs. I, IV, V.

《上海之工业》,上海特别市社会局编,民一九。

《中国工业现有困难的分析》,《大公报·经济周刊》第二十六期,民22,8,23。

《中国工业发展的前途》,《大公报·经济周刊》第三十四及三十六期,民 22,10,13 及 11,2。

李剑农:《最近三十年中国政治史》,上海,太平洋,民一九。

刘彦:《最近三十年中国外交史》,上海,太平洋,民一九。

Morse, H. B. and MacNair, H. F. : *Far eastern international relations*, Boston, 1931.

Tyau, M. T. Z. : *The legal obligations arising out of treaty relations between China and other states*, Shanghai, Commercial Press, 1917.

漆树芬:《经济侵略下之中国》,民一四。

陈翰笙:《中国农民担负的赋税》,《东方杂志》,二十五卷十九号,民一七,一○,一○,九至二八页。

王寅生等:《中国北部的兵差与农民》,国立中央研究院社会科学研究所,专刊第五号,上海,民二○。

Chen, Gideon: *Chinese government economic planning and reconstruction since 1927*, Shanghai, 1933.

Tsai, Chien and Chan, Kwan-Wai: *Trend and character of China's foreign trade*, Shanghai, 1933.

《中国工业的流动资本的问题》,《大公报·经济周刊》第十四期。民 22,5,31。

陈翰笙:《亩的差异》,中央研究院专刊第一号,南京。

安原美佐雄:《支那之工业及原料》上卷第二章第五节,大正八年。

第六讲　中国之钢铁工业

一、钢铁之采冶

　　甲，铁矿砂之化学成分——氧化铁及杂质

　　乙，生铁之铸冶

　　　1. 冶铁之化学作用

　　　　a. 使铁矿与焦炭共热以除氧气。

　　　　b. 以石灰共热使其中混合之土质与石质与铁质分开。

　　　　c. 生铁中合有炭,矽,硫,燐,锰等杂质。

　　　2. 熔铁方法之进步

　　　　a. 旧式风箱与其炉

　　　　b. 鼓风炉(Blast furnace, 1340)

　　　　c. 用焦炭代木炭法(Coking process, 1735)

　　　　d. 新式鼓风炉——大者每炉可容原料 1,500 吨——昼夜可出铁 400 至 600 吨。

　　丙,炼钢方法之进步

　　　1. 锻炼法(Comentation process)

　　　2. 贝色麻法(Bessemer process, 1856)——酸性法提炼含燐较少之生铁。

　　　3. 敞炉法(Open hearth process, 1865)或名 Siemeus-Martin Process。

　　　　a. 节制温度。

  b. 节制炭之成分,产钢之种类多。

  c. 容量大,消耗小。

  d. 所产之钢含燐少。

 4. 盐基法(Basic or Thomas process,1876)——提炼燐铁矿。

 5. 电炉法(Electric furnace)——将已由他法炼成之钢再炼成质地较高之钢。

二、铁业发展之历史

甲,旧式铁业

 1. 中国用铁之始,约在722—481 B.C.与各国用铁始期相同。

 2. 春秋(722—481 B.C.)之前,已用铁器,但彼时用铜犹甚广。粗制之农具及家具用铁,兵器则犹多用铜。

 3. 周秦之间,铁器渐盛;秦始皇广收天下之兵器,铸为金人十二,嗣后以铜不足用,铁器渐多,故秦始皇十八年(219 B.C.)可作为铜兵铁兵过渡之时。

 4. 秦汉时铁兵始盛

  a. 东汉以降(25 A.D.):兵器已完全用铁,制作之法亦日渐完美。

  b. 秦汉时代已以盐铁二者为政府专利事业。

  c. 汉武帝时(119 B.C.)桓宽著盐铁之论,尝以铁为制造农具必需之原料,反对当时政府之铁政而卒无效,顺帝时(126—144 A.D.)曾以风水之说施禁。

  d. 东汉后,四方纷如,铁政亦宽严不一。

5. 唐代(618—907 A.D.)仍以铁归政府专办,闻有铁矿数处。

6. 五代(907—959 A.D.)时铁禁渐驰,后唐明宗(926 A.D.)尝招官铁厂出售余铁,较市价低售一成,越七年又令百姓自由买卖,制造农具。

7. 宋(960—1276 A.D.)神宗(1068—)又复铁政,其时北敌契丹,南御交趾,用兵既多,铁供不足,故有此举,而私卖私制者迄难禁止,徽宗时(1101—)复下令民间,除作农具外禁止买铁。金亦厉行铁政;往往强迫开采,1236年迁760户于大同,1000年迁千户于山西,皆为采铁制铁之用。

8. 元代(1273—1367 A.D.)用兵既广,用铁亦多。忽必烈朝于1263年于1月间招集铁工11,800户,次月复招4,000户。1291年复派3,000户开采济南(即今金岭镇铁矿),犹以为不足,复于1293年禁止金铁输出,其后1309年重申此禁,同时准许民间采制,以一二成归其私有。

9. 明(1368—1644 A.D.)初虽无私采之禁,而犹动以细故,封禁铁矿。永乐时(1403—)尽开铁禁,其后则旋禁旋开,铁税亦往往极重。

10. 清(1644—1911 A.D.),亦不禁采铁,产铁之地渐为集中,集中之地产量颇多,例:山西。

乙,新式铁业——其发展可分为三大时期:

1. 1891—1913 汉冶萍公司成立及发展

1890 张之洞筹办汉阳铁厂,资本5,000,000两,机器购自英国,但对煤铁之质,未加考验,即贸然购买机器。

1894 汉阳铁厂开工。

1897 由盛宣怀承办,招股 2,000,000 两,改为官商合办。

1902 借德款 4,000,000 马克,聘用德籍工程师 G. Leinung 在萍乡煤矿制炼焦炭。

1903—1924 向日举债 22 次共借日金 57,000,000 元,已付清者计 12,000,000 元。

1904 李惟格偕同 Thomas Bunt 及 G. Leinung 携冶砂萍煤及汉厂炼出之钢出洋考察,英伦钢铁化学专家,J. E. Soad 化验之结果。知宜用马丁炉,盖大冶铁矿砂内含有燐质。遂借日金三百万元,购置机器。

1907 新建炼钢厂落成,开始炼钢。

1908 盛氏合并汉阳、萍乡、大冶三处而成一汉冶萍煤铁有限公司,呈部注册,完全改归商办,资本定为 20,000,000 两,招收股本 13,000,000 元。但汉冶萍三处用款已达 32,000,000 两。

1911—1912 辛亥革命,因而停工,损失达 3,720,000 两。

1913 复工向日本八幡制铁所及横滨正金银行借日金 15,000,000 元,条件苛刻,供给八幡制铁所矿石生铁以其价值陆续抵还 40 年为止,共须供给头等铁矿砂 15,000,000 吨,生铁 8,000,000 吨,其价值以制铁所通告时所购入价值为标准。

1913 筹办大冶新铁厂，1922 始正式开工。
2. 1914—1919 欧战中迅速发展时期
　　a. 汉冶萍公司之发展
　　　　1915"二十一条"中关于汉冶萍者大意谓不得收归国有，许中日合办，借外资时须借日资。
　　　　1916—1919 欧战时，获利颇厚。
　　　　1917 与日本合办九州安川制钢厂，生铁由汉冶萍供给，年须 60,000 吨。
　　b. 其他公司之兴起
　　　　1915 奉天本溪湖公司在本溪湖煤矿附近新建铁厂，以炼庙儿沟之铁矿。资本 7,000,000 元。中日各半。1915 正式出矿并炼铁，产铁多数运销日本。1922 因铁价跌落停工，1923 七月复工。
　　　　1917 和兴公司在上海浦东建设化铁炉，1918 出钢，时值欧战，销路大畅，获利甚厚。
　　　　1918 官商合办龙烟公司成立，以直隶省宣化龙关之铁矿为基础，炼厂于北平三家店附近之石景山，但该公司向未出矿或铁。
　　　　1918 鲁大公司——山东金岭镇铁矿，昔属德人，战后由日本接收办理，竭力经营，1919 正式采矿，1922 遵华府会议时中日直接交涉之规定，改组中日合办鲁大公司。
　　　　1919 裕繁公司于 1913 成立，但于 1919 年始正式出矿。

1919 鞍山铁矿,在奉天辽阳安山站一带,由中日合办之振兴公司开采,1919 正式出铁。

1920 扬子机器公司 1919 在汉口附近建化铁炉一座,1920 开始出铁,1925 因铁价暴落停工。

1920 象鼻山铁矿,由湖北官矿局承办,1920 春开始采掘。

3. 欧战后衰落时期

  a. 铁铁砂——

    1921—1922 本溪湖铁矿停工。

    1924 起鲁大公司停工。

    1929 福利民公司停工。

    1930 起益华公司停工。

  b. 生铁——

    1922 本溪湖铁厂停工。

    1923—1925,1927,1930 扬子机器厂停工。

    1926 起 汉阳铁厂停工。

  c. 钢——

    1922 起 汉阳钢厂停工。

    1932 中德合办钢铁厂,计划规定日出钢 500 吨,资本定为美金 16,000,000 至 20,000,000 元由德垫付,管理权完全在中国政府手中,但得聘用德籍专家为顾问,地点在浦口或芜湖中择定,自开工起第四年开始还本,十年分摊还完,周息七厘。

  d. 汉冶萍公司之衰落与停工

1920 战后钢铁跌价,汉冶萍自本年起逐年损失甚钜。

1922 大冶新铁厂成立,同年汉阳钢厂停工。

1926 汉阳铁厂停工。

1927—1929 交通部,设整理汉冶萍公司委员会

1929 接管未成,遂沉寂无闻。

三、铁矿砂

甲,储量:辽宁,察哈尔,湖北,河北,安徽,山东,热河,浙江,广东,江苏,河南及其他共计1,000兆吨。辽宁省占752兆吨。

乙,产量

1. 按各矿成立年计

1918 汉冶萍,本溪湖(1920—1922停工后复开工),宝兴公司,振兴公司。

1919 鲁大公司(1923起停工),裕繁公司。

1920 象鼻山官矿。

1926 福利民公司(1929停工翌年复开工),保晋公司。

1929 昌华公司,益华公司(1929开工以后即停工)。

2. 按1920年之产量多寡排列:汉冶萍公司,振兴公司,鲁大公司,本溪湖公司,裕繁公司,象鼻山官矿,宝兴公司。

3. 按1931年产量之多寡排列:振兴公司,汉冶萍公司,裕繁公司,本溪湖公司,宝兴公司,象鼻山官矿,福利民公司,昌华公司,保晋公司。

丙,中外合办及外人经管之铁矿

1. 日本完全管理者——振兴(鞍山)
2. 中日合办者——本溪湖(庙儿沟),弓长岭,鲁大(金岭镇,已停工)
3. 中英合办者——开平(滦州)
4. 借有外债之铁矿——汉冶萍公司,泾铜公司。
5. 与日资有售砂合同者——裕繁公司,宝兴公司,福利民公司。

四、生铁

甲,产量

1. 按各厂成立年计:

1900 汉阳铁厂(1926 起停工)

1916 本溪湖公司(1922 停工,翌年复工)

1919 鞍山铁厂

1920 扬子机器厂(1923—1925,1927,1930,停工)

1926 保晋公司

2. 按 1920 年产量多寡计:汉阳铁厂,鞍山铁厂,本溪湖公司,扬子机器厂。
3. 按 1931 年产量多寡计:鞍山铁厂,本溪湖公司,保晋公司,扬子机器厂。

乙,成本

1. 细目:原料(焦炭,铁砂,石灰,锰矿等),工资,制造费,办事费,经济费。
2. 按成本之高低计:鞍山厂,汉阳厂,本溪湖厂,扬子厂。

五、钢

甲,炼钢厂:汉阳厂 1907—1921,和兴厂 1918 迄今未停。

乙，成本——以汉阳厂之成本为最高，原因焦炭及生铁价昂，运费不资。

六、钢铁业发展中之因子：原料（煤，铁矿），厂址，运输，资本，管理，技术等。

七、中国钢铁业在世界上之地位：

甲，铁矿储量（1,000 兆吨）当世界总储量（225,000 兆吨）百分之 0.4，只够美国钢铁业九年之用。

乙，生铁之产量（478,000 吨）当世界各国总产量（1931 年为 55.6 兆吨）百分之 0.09 弱。

丙，钢之产量（15,000 吨）当世界各国钢产量（70 兆吨）百分之 0.002 强。

丁，钢铁之消费量 1930 年平均每人为：美 570 公斤，法 388 公斤，英 282 公斤，德 289 公斤，日 47 公斤，中国 2 公斤。

参考书

《中国矿业纪要》，地质调查所，北平

第一次（民五），民一。

第二次（民七至一四），民一五。

第三次（民一四至一七），民一八。

第四次（民一八至二〇），民二一。

丁格兰：《中国铁矿志》，地质调查所，民一二。

顾石臣：《中国十大矿厂调查记》，商务，民五。

黄著勋：《中国矿产》，商务，民五。

翊陶：《日人行将提出交涉之汉冶萍公司》，《国闻周报》，四卷四八期,一至八页,民 16,12,11。

Collins, William F. : Mineral enterprise in China, Revised edition, 1922, Chap. V on the "Hanyang-Tayeh-P'inghsiang iron and steel enterprise".

Voskuil, Walter: "The iron and steel industry of China", in *Annals*, November, 1930, pp. 191-195.

Hsueh, K. L. : "The iron and steel industry in China", in *Chinese Economic Journal*, January, 1928, pp. 1-6.

Bain, H. Foster: *Ores and industry in the Far East*, 1927, Chap. III on "Iron".

梁宗鼎:《中国铁矿权之丧失》,《国闻周报》,四卷四六期,一至五页,民 16,11,27。

谢家荣:《外人在华矿业之投资》,民二一。

吴半农:《铁煤及石油》,北平社会调查所,民二一。

Torgasheff, Boris P. : *Coal, iron and oil in the Far East*, 1929.

Smith, Wilfred: *A geographical study of coal and iron in China*, 1916.

刘基磐:《汉冶萍煤铁矿厂整理及复工计划书》,《建设》第八期,计划 1—14 页,民一九,七,第九期,计划 49—70,民一九,一〇。

胡博渊:《汉冶萍公司调查报告》,《建设》第九期,调查 26—32,民一九,一〇。

Lieu, D. K. : *Cost of iron and steel production in China, Far Eastern Review*, 1921.

第七讲　中国之机器制造业及造船业

一、发动力与机器之重要——比较各国之每人工作产量（per capita work output）

二、中国之机器制造工业

　　甲，机器之分类

　　　　1. 实业部之分类：原动机，矿冶机，农业机，工业机（纺织，化学，工作，其他）
　　　　2. 海关之分类：纺织机，推进机，发电机，农业机，缝纫针织及刺绣机，印书订书切纸机，抽水机及装置品，打字机及其配件，酿酒蒸溜及炼糖机，其他机器及机器零件

　　乙，机器进口

　　　　1. 机器进口

　　　　　　a. 进口机器之种类——详海关之分类。
　　　　　　b. 进口之数量以百万海关两计，1887 为 0.4，1894 为 1.1，1905 为 5.5，1913 为 4.3，1919 为 15.9，1921 为 56.9，1925 为 16.8，1931 为 45.4。
　　　　　　c. 进口之国别——以 1919 至 1930 论，英，日，美，德等国为最要。以 1928—1930 三年间各种机器。进口国别而分别：

　　　　　　　纺织机——英，日，美，德，意。
　　　　　　　推进机——英，德，□，比，捷，日。

    发电机——美,英,日,德,意。

    农业机——美,德,英,日。

    印书机——日,德,英,加拿大。

    抽水机——美,英,日,德,意。

   d. 进口之埠别——上海,大连,天津,汉口,胶州（青岛）,哈尔滨,广州,南京等。

 2. 输入机器之危险

  a. 增加入超。

  b. 所购进者多系旧式机器。

  c. 战时之危险——交通断绝,购求不易。

丙,国内自造

 1. 自造机器之种类——以上海为例:纺织（只摇纱机,打包机,纺机另件及手织机）,卷烟制造机（只供小工厂用）,电器（电动机,变压器等）,印刷机（只初步简单之印机）,缫丝及织丝机（丝织机只限于手织者）,针织机（只手摇机）

 2. 机器制造厂之特点

  a. 出品之性质——修理机器,配置零件,用舶来机件配合成机。

  b. 依靠舶来之原料——进口钢铁等之比较。

 3. 机器厂之种类

  a. 铁路机厂——例:津浦路之浦镇机厂。

  b. 工业学校附设机厂——例:昔日东北大学之机器厂。

  c. 私人设立之机厂——例:上海之求新机厂。

(1) 上海各机器厂之现状

(2) 天津各机器厂之现状

4. 机器业衰落之原因：

　　a. 国内原料缺乏，须向外国购买——例：钢，铁，铜。

　　b. 工人无相当之机械知识及训练。

　　c. 设备不完备，多为修理机器之用。

　　d. 管理无方，工作效率低微。

　　e. 机器之标准不同，各地不能划一，适于甲地者往往不适于乙地——例：以各地电灯公司所发出电力之 Voltage 不同，因而家用电器不能移地使用。

　　f. 资本缺乏。

5. 改良之方法——实业部四年计划中之一，为机械工业计划。实部拟办中央机器厂，已与英庚款董事会签约，借款十二万金镑，用以购办机器，厂址拟设南京城外，制造原动机，工作机，及零件等。

三、中国之造船业

甲，历史

1862 江南制造局成立

　　外人在沪设立耶松船坞

1865 江南制造局设立造船部于高昌庙

1866 福州马尾设立船政局

1871—1872 马尾船政局感于外籍工程师之不可靠，先后奏遣学生赴英法学习造船及驾驶之术，但未实行，1876 复奏派闽广学生赴英法学习。

1880 李鸿章奏设天津水师学堂。

1900 外商在沪设立瑞镕机器厂制造机器及船舶等。

1903 求新制造厂成立,开商办造船厂之先例。

1905 江南制造局之造船部,经周馥之奏请改为江南船坞,并特派海军人员管理。

1907 汉口设立商办扬子机器厂。

　　马尾船政局停止造船,此后只从事于修理工程。

1909 日人在沪设中日合办之东华造船株式会社。

1912 江南船坞改为江南造船所。

1918 江南造船所承造美政府万吨运舰四艘计值美金 7,800,000 元。

1926 江南造船所承造美政府军舰六艘。

乙,现状

1. 中国造船厂之分配

　a. 按地域分:上海,广州,厦门,福州,汉口,天津,大连,旅顺。

　b. 按资本国籍分

　　（1）华资:官办——江南,马尾,大沽,厦门,黄浦。

　　　　　　商办——求新,扬子,及其他。

　　（2）外资:英商——耶松,瑞镕。

　　　　　　日资——东华,川崎,海军。

2. 中国造船厂之现状

　a. 海军部江南造船厂——能造长 450 呎,载重 14,000 吨之船。

　b. 恒昌祥机器造船厂——能造长 220 呎,载重

1,200 吨之船。

c. 大中华造船厂——能造长 300 呎，载重 3,000 吨之船。

d. 合兴机器造船厂——能造长 220 呎，载重 1,000 吨之船。

e. 汇昌机器造船厂——能造长 120 呎，载重 500 吨之船。

f. 远大铁工厂——能造载重 500 吨钢壳船。

g. 鸿翔兴船厂——能造长 130 吨船只。

h. 明锠机器厂——能造长 120 呎船只。

i. 南洋制造机器船厂——能造长 150 呎，载重 500 吨船只。

j. 海军马尾造船所——能造载重 5,000 吨船只，但已停止造船。

k. 海军厦门造船所——能造载重 600 吨船只。

l. 其他

参考书

龚俊：《中国新工业发展史大纲》，商务，民二二，232—236 页。

吴承洛：《今世中国实业通志》，下册，263—272 页，商务，民一八。

《上海之工业》，上海特别市社会局，第一编第五章，第二编第五章，民一九。

《天津工商业》，天津特别市社会局，民一九，第六章。

《上海机器制造厂之发达观》，《钱业月刊》二卷七期，调查栏

18—29 页,民 11,8,15。

魏如:《中国机械工业振兴之途径》,《社会月刊》一卷九号,1—7 页,民 18,9。

《实业部创办中央机器制造厂计划书》,《工商半月刊》三卷一五期专载 1-10 页,一六期 1—11 页,民 20,8。

《福州马尾船政局近况调查》,《中外经济周刊》213 期 48-50 页,民 16,5,28。

"Foochow Naval Dockyard", in *Chinese Economic Journal*, Vol. V, No. 6, pp. 1037-1079, Dec., 1929.

"Shipbuilding industry", in *Chinese Economic Journal*, Vol. IV, no. 6, pp. 489-510, June, 1929.

延仲:《我国之机械入口贸易》,《国际贸易导报》,四卷六号,97-113 页,民 21,11。

交通部编:《中华民国十九年交通部统计年报》,民二二,六。

第八讲　中国之棉纺织工业

一、历史

甲, 旧式棉纺织工业

1. 为中国最早之手工业, 传说夏禹之时(2197—2205)民间以棉布进贡。
2. 一说棉花系于唐时(618—907 A.D.)随佛教传入中国。

乙, 新式棉纺织工业

1. 1821 英人输入机制棉纱, 鸦片战争后, 输入之数目尤盛。
2. 新式棉纺织工业发展之四时期

   a. 1890—1904 草创时期

   1890 李鸿章于 1882 奏设之机器织布局于本年在上海开始筹备, 为我国机器织布业之始。

   张之洞于 1889 在粤奏设之织布局于本年移鄂开办。

   1898 机器织布局毁于火, 盛宣怀于 1894 接办, 招募商股, 更名华盛纱厂, 后改又新, 再改集成。

   李鸿章设纺织新局于上海, 由官商合办, 后改为复泰, 再改为恒丰。

   1895《中日马关条约》, 允外人在华设厂制造, 开外厂竞争之恶端,于是英,德,美,日商人之新厂次第成立。

国人鉴于外商设厂之热烈,除上海外在内地如无锡,常州,苏州,南通(均在江苏省),杭州,萧山(均在浙江省)等处设厂。

b. 1905—1913 渐兴时期

1905 受日俄战争之刺激,政府保护并奖励工业,棉纺织业由是渐兴,江苏之常熟,江阴及太仓,浙江之宁波及河南之安阳均相继设立纱厂,本期内日商开始设厂制纱,德美二国商人所开办之厂,则先后出售于英商,日商及华商。

c. 1914—1925 勃兴时期

欧战期间,欧美棉纺织品之输入断绝,华日棉纺织厂因而勃兴,1918 修改关税税率,日人为避免关税起见,纷纷来华设厂。

本期内日商纱厂之增加率较华商纱厂者大一倍。

d. 1926—1930 衰落时期

衰落之原因:

(1) 欧战终止,各国之工业复兴,棉纺品之输入,恢复战前状态,与国产品相竞争。

(2) 年来内战频仍,兵祸连结,人民之购买力,异常低微。

(3) 五卅惨案与工潮勃兴(上海纱厂罢工统针; 1925:38, 1926:78, 1927:55 起),厂方损失甚重。

二、地理上之分布

甲，中心点——上海，青岛，武汉，天津，无锡，通崇海。

乙，地理上分布之原因

1. 原料易得
   a. 棉花产地——江苏，湖北，山东，河北四省产棉最多。
   b. 通商口岸——由上海及胶州（青岛）入口之棉花为最多。
2. 有煤及电力之便
   a. 煤——以产量论，河北及山东产煤最多，以进口量论，以上海及汉口为最多。
   b. 电力——以市论上海居首，以省论江苏居首。
3. 运输便利——铁路与航运。
4. 市场与销路——试比较各省之人口密度。
5. 商业及金融上之便利——进出口商，银行，交易所，保险公司，商品检验局等多集中各大商埠。
6. 纱厂发达较早。

三、组织

甲，规模——按纺锤与织机之多寡计，按资本额之大小计。

乙，纱厂联合会

1. 华商纱厂联合会
   a. 全国组织——1918 成立。
   b. 各地组织——武汉 1921，无锡 1922，天津 1922。
2. 日商纱厂联合会——在上海
3. 中外纱厂联合会——在上海

四、出产

甲，因子

1. 原棉

    a. 来源——国内生产与国外输入。

    b. 困难问题

    （1）量的方面——棉花入超，与年俱增。

    （2）质的方面——绒短；掺假与潮湿；棉种繁多，无一定标准。

2. 劳工

    a. 来源——多自乡间募来，包身制度(Contract System)。

    b. 特点——女工多于男工，采昼夜两班制。

    c. 劳工状况与工厂法之关系——领事裁判权与租界为实施工厂法之最大障碍。

3. 资本

    a. 资金多投于固定资产，无公积金及折旧准备金。

    b. 缺乏流动资金，将纱棉抵押于银行，以高利率借款维持。

4. 管理

    a. 重要职员悉系股东之亲友，无经营之能力，且弊窦丛生。

    b. 缺乏技术人员。

乙，制造手续及机器

1. 制造手续：预备，纺纱，织布，整理。

2. 机器——悉自外国购来，以英国及日本之机器为最多,美国次之,国内自制之棉纺织机器,业已萌芽。

丙,成本与效率

1. 成本——纺纱之支数愈多,则原棉之成本愈低。原棉成本普通占总成本十分之七以上,其他十分之三则为工资,利息,物料,动力,营业开支,捐税等。

2. 效率
   a. 比较每工人掌管纺锤之多寡。
   b. 比较每工人掌管织布机之多寡。
   c. 比较每工人之纱布产量。
   d. 比较之结果:日商纱厂工人之工作效率,高于华商纱厂,但后者工人之效率,逐年增加。

丁,出品——历年纱与布出产之种类及数量。

五、棉纺织品贸易

甲,舶来棉纺织品,足为国产纱布之劲敌。

1. 1790年即有棉织品输入。
2. 日本后起,代替英美出品输入之优势。
3. 近数年来国内出品与输入之舶来品之比例约为四与一之比。

乙,棉纱多为乡间之布机所消费,纱厂所消费者,仅占全产额五分之一耳。

丙,国产纱布额:华商纱厂及外商(多日商)纱厂各占其中,外商纱厂,产品之倾销,为华商纱厂产品滞销之主因。

丁,现货与期货交易之异同——交易所为期货交易之市场——交易所上之买卖以避免因棉或纱市价之涨落所受之损失为目的者名之曰 Hedging；凡各纱厂多利用是法。

六、棉纺织业之将来

甲，地位——发展虽速，然在世界上所占之地位则极低微。

乙，民二十年以来衰落之原因

　　1. 外因——内乱与中日纠纷

　　2. 内因

　　　　a. 资金缺乏

　　　　b. 技术人材缺乏

　　　　c. 管理不良

　　　　d. 劳工效率低微

丙，救济之方策——设立棉业统制委员会

　　1. 组织——分经济，原料，制造，运销，统计等股。

　　2. 功用与事业

　　　　a. 暂时的——编制业观等

　　　　b. 久远的——原料，制造及运销方面之改良

参考书

Fong, H. D.: *Cotton industry and trade in China*, 2 Vols., Tientsin, 1932.

Rearse, Arno S.: *The cotton industry of Japan and China*, 1929.

King, Miss S. T. and Lieu, D. K.: *China's. cotton industry*, 1923.

"British Economic Mission to the Far East, 1930—31": *Report of the Mission*, London, 1931.

方显廷：《中国棉纺织业及棉纺织品贸易》，《经济统计季刊》，

第一卷第三期,395—486 页。

井村薰雄:《中国之纺织业及其出品》,周培兰译,上海,商务,民一七。

江苏实业厅第三科:《江苏省纺织业状况》,上海,商务,民九。

佐藤贞次郎:《支那纺织业之发达及将来》,东亚经济调查局,1932(日文)。

上海商业储蓄银行调查部
 棉,商品调查丛刊第二编,1931
 布,商品调查丛刊第五编,1932

方显廷:《中国棉纺织之危机》,《大公报经济周刊》,民 22,4,19。

方显廷:《我国工厂法与纱厂业之关系》,《大公报经济周刊》,民 22,11,15。

顾毓琮:《中国棉织业之危机及其自救》,《纺织周刊》,121 期,民 22,8,18。

朱仙舫:《中国纺织业之将来》,《纺织时报》,998 期,民 22,6,26。

王子建:《美棉借款问题之检讨》,《纺织周刊》,117 期,民 22,3,21,118 期,民 22,7,28。

棉业统制委员会:《纺织周刊》,136 期,民 22,10,20。

第九讲　中国之缫丝及织丝业

一、缫丝业

　　甲, 历史

　　　　1. 旧法缫丝——四千余年前黄帝时即已有之, 至今仍存。今浙江杭州之七里丝, 即为民间旧法缫丝之一种。
　　　　2. 新法缫丝
　　　　　　a. 1789 年法国第一个新式蒸汽缫丝厂开工。
　　　　　　b. 国内新式丝厂业简史

　　　　　　　　1860 粤人陈启源创办国内第一个新式蒸汽缫丝厂于广东南海, 后遭人反对乃迁至澳门, 后复迁回。顺德亦崛起而为广东之丝业中心。

　　　　　　　　1880 意大利人设新式丝厂于上海, 是为外人在沪设立丝厂之肇始。

　　　　　　　　1881 华人黄佐卿设新式丝厂于上海, 名"公和永", 为上海华商设立新式丝厂之开端。

　　　　　　　　1909 日本之生丝出口量第一次超过我国。

　　　　　　　　1914 因欧洲失却法国生丝市场。

　　　　　　　　1917 中国合众蚕丝改良会成立, 每月经费为关银 4,000 两, 1923 增至 8,000 两, 由海关按月拨交, 广州与芝罘亦设有万国蚕桑改良会, 广州岭南大学与南京金陵大学亦创办蚕桑专课。

1924 上海万国生丝检验所成立。

1927 国人自动改良。

 （1）江苏开放茧行，取消往昔茧行之种种限制。

 （2）无锡设立蚕桑试验场。

 （3）浙江省政府采购日本最新式机器，设立模范缫丝厂于杭州。

 （4）浙江各县创设蚕种及生丝产销合作社，而以萧山一带为尤著名。

 （5）各厂有设立分行于国外，所产生丝，自行出口。

1930 起国内丝业日趋衰落。十一月时上海共有丝厂107家，闭厂停工者达106家，衰落之原因：

 （1）江浙二省该年春茧歉收，故茧价高涨。

 （2）因受世界经济衰落之影响各国之生丝消费量减少而以美国为尤甚。

 （3）日本之生丝生产过剩。

1934 上半年

 （1）开年以来，情况似佳，盖金贵银贱，国外之需要或可增加。但因日本以其积存于海外市场现货，贬价倾销，且因上年春茧歉收，茧价暴涨，丝厂赔累不堪。

 （2）政府颁布丝业公债8,000,000元条例，丝业以干茧向银行抵押借款。

（3）常年时上海租出之丝厂可占上海丝厂总数 80—90%，本年则仅及其半。

（4）本年六月生丝出口减少,七月复增加。

1931 下半年

（1）丝业公债发行 4,000,000 元,以生丝出口附加税为担保(生丝出口每担收银 30 元),受惠丝厂,只限江浙二省,该二省之丝厂多复工。

（2）九一八事变后,反日空气正浓,丝业之副产品(废丝,废茧),不能复售诸日人,而国内之购买力亦降低,丝厂业复遭打击。

1932 情形更为严重

（1）上海丝厂正月份开工者只十家,(一)因日商竞争颇厉,(二)茧价高涨,(三)国内市场人造丝起而与天然丝相竞争。

（2）一二八淞沪之役,闸北丝厂 31 家,毁于日军炮火者计 15 家。三月份开工者只二家。

（3）四月时上海积存之丝达 20,000 包,积存之茧亦可缫丝 17—20,000 包,其严重性可想而知。

（4）五月十八日起,政府取消生丝出口税及出口附加税,为奖励丝茧出口计,每出口生丝一担,补助银100两,每脱售干茧一担补助银二〇两。

(5) 五月至七月,开工者计45厂。

(6) 秋茧丰收,茧价因而跌落,丝厂业渐见起色,惟以内地土丝外销,丝厂业复遭打击。

乙,丝厂地理上之分布:广东,四川,江苏,浙江,辽宁,山东等。

丙,组织

1. 上海丝厂多系租来,其他如顺德等,则情形迥异。
2. 普通多系合伙经营。
3. 厂之大小,依其所投资本之多寡而定。

丁,生产

1. 原料

   a. 来源:江,浙,两粤,鲁,皖,川,鄂等。

   b. 茧有春夏秋之别。

   c. 茧行(有烘茧灶,租赁性质,昔时茧行之设立限制颇严,操纵市场,鱼肉乡民,十六年起,政府已取消其专利权)。

   d. 每厂每月所需原料之量。

   e. 原料之成本——茧价占十分之七以上。

2. 劳工

   a. 职工分:内帐房,外帐房及工帐房。

   b. 工帐房工人之工作分:剥茧,选茧,缫丝,检查,及扯吐。

c. 男工及女工

男工做笨重工作，旧有"武官"之称。

女工之工作分上列五部，缫丝部工人有正车，替车，打盆等之别。

d. 工人数目按每100丝车计，按每一丝厂计。

e. 工作情形：工资与花红（下脚），工作时间。

f. 老鬼及二鬼掌管厂内之蒸汽动力。

3. 资金——由银行钱庄及丝业经纪人予以接济。

4. 丝厂生产能率及生产量。

戊，贸易

1. 中间人之种类：丝厂，丝商或丝经纪人，丝通事，买办，洋行。

2. 洋行之组织：大板室，丝楼，公事室，货仓，再摇室。

3. 交易有现货及期货之别。

4. 包装及复行包装——一包生丝之重量，本地丝商与出口丝商不同。

5. 检验

量的方面——以公量为准则。凡出口丝均需受政府强迫检验。

质的方面——均匀，整洁，拉力等。

6. 等级：共分七级

7. 价格之变迁

8. 出口：近年之衰落。出口丝货之种类，出口目的地之分析。

己，最近之衰落

1. 衰落之原因
   a. 外因
   （1）日本生丝产量过剩，起而竞争。
      （一）出产——比较中日丝产在世界上所占之地位，日本植桑，制种，育蚕，缫丝，及出口贸易，皆有长足进步。
      （二）出口贸易——日本崛起，代替中国在世界市场上之地位。
   （2）人造丝与天然丝竞争——世界人造丝之产量及我国人造丝之进口量，与年俱增。
   （3）世界经济萧条——丝为奢侈品，故丝价跌落，大有一泻千里之势。
   （4）内乱与外患之影响。
      （一）捐税繁重——厘金（已取消），营业税，出口税，出口附加税（抵偿丝业公债）
      （二）人民之购买力降低
   （5）栽桑育蚕之方法陈旧
      （一）制种：
         饲育不合法
         用烈火促进蚕儿之发育
         蚕蛾交配后不待其自己产卵，将卵迫出，附诸纸上
         对蚕种不加选择
      （二）育蚕：

蚕室蚕具之缺乏及简陋

茧未熟即采摘（俗谓摇青头）

b. 内因

(1) 蚕茧

(一) 茧汛特大量收买以便烘干,故所需多量之流动资金,悉以重利向银行借贷,加之茧价之涨落无定,风险特多。

(二) 烘茧之方法不良,温度难匀。

(三) 存茧无适宜货栈,潮湿盗窃之事时生。

(2) 劳工

(一) 包工制——工人之召募,由工头包办。

(二) 对召来之工人,不加训练,打盆升替车,替车升正车。

(三) 工资除剥茧工人外,悉为按时计资制,无改良之奋兴剂。

(四) 工作时间过长,中间无休息时,故工人之工作效率低微。

(五) 无惠工事业：

无工人餐室——工人可随时离厂进餐

不讲卫生之道——工人易罹疾病。

工人教育,概不过问,故工人多文盲

(3) 设备

厂屋分配不当,空气污浊,光线不足。

　　　　　机器——多用意大利机器,但以日本机器为优,无需打盆工人。

　　（4）职员——多系经理亲信,无专家。

　　（5）租赁制度之不良——设厂与租厂者,皆乏责任心。

　　（6）生丝出口,多为外商所操纵。

　　（7）生产——质劣,量微,出品又不划一。

庚,补救方策

　1. 有挽救之可能

　　　a. 以世界论

　　　　（1）人造丝有其缺点。

　　　　（2）生丝消费在服饰纤维中为量甚微,有增加之可能。

　　　b. 以中国论

　　　　（1）近年来国人努力改良蚕种。

　　　　（2）创办蚕茧产销合作社。

　　　　（3）采用新式缫丝机器。

　　　　（4）设立生丝检验所。

　　　　（5）自行办理生丝出口。

辛,挽救方法

　　　a. 政府颁布蚕丝业法,设立督察及改良机关,明定奖罚条例。

　　　b. 蠲免或减轻捐税。

　　　c. 提倡蚕丝产销合作。

　　　d. 丝厂团结与组织。

e. 发展生丝直接出口机关。

f. 设立生丝交易所,规定生丝标准。

二、丝织业

甲,历史——黄帝时(2697—2596B.C.)即已有之。周(1122—220B.C.)已有绢帛之类,自汉以后,多用以赠遗赏赉,西欧各国多遣使以求之,唐时已有手拉提花机之发明,后于1801年法人(Jacquard)亦发明提花机,洎乎光绪中叶,江浙二省,始有日本式之纹针提花机及手拉铁木合制机之输入。民元以来复采用电力织机织造铁机缎等,尤以民九创办之美亚为首创一格,输入最新机械,织造各种丝织品。

乙,组织——为家庭工业,晚近来亦有新式织厂。

丙,地理上之分布

1. 江苏:上海,南京,苏州,盛泽,丹阳,镇江。

2. 浙江:杭州,湖州,绍兴,嘉兴。

3. 广东:顺德,南海,番禺,新会。

4. 四川:成都,嘉定,顺庆,保宁,泸川,重庆。

5. 山东:昌益,栖霞,牟平。

丁,原料

1. 天然丝——家蚕丝与野蚕丝。

2. 人造丝——消费最多之地:上海,天津,胶州(周村)等。

3. 棉纱——为交织品之原料。

戊,劳工——工厂工人与家庭工人。

己,技术——织造手续,分经纬,织造,整理等——雅克提花机(Jacguard)之重要及性质。

庚,出品:绸,缎,绉,纱,绫,纺,罗,绒,锦。

辛,丝织业衰落之原因

1. 舶来丝毛及人造丝织品之竞争。
2. 外国提高关税,阻碍我国丝织品输入。
3. 其他(参阅缫丝业衰落之原因)。

参考书

(一) 书籍

吴承洛:《今世中国实业通志》,下卷,商务,民一八。

《中国实业志》(江苏省),实业部国际贸易局,民二二。

尹良莹:《中国蚕业史》,国立中央大学蚕桑学会,南京,民二〇。

曾同春:《中国丝业》,商务,民一八(万有文库之一)。

佐田弘治郎:《满洲柞蚕》,南满洲铁道株式会社,昭和五。

《首都丝织业调查记》,工商部技术厅,南京,民一九。

杭州市经济调查:丝绸篇,建设委员会调查浙江经济所统计课,民二一。

方显廷:《天津织布工业》,民二〇。

蚕丝专号(《新建设》第三期),广东建设厅编辑处,民一八,一〇,一五。

蚕丝救济号 (《浙江省建设月刊》六卷八期),浙江省政府建设厅,民二二,二。

丝业问题专号(《国际贸易导报》四卷一号),上海商品检验局,民二,六。

生丝检验专号(《国际贸易导报》一卷七号),上海商品检验局,民一九,一〇。

《历年输出各国丝类统计表》,民元至一七年,工商部,民一八年。

Lieu, D. K.: *Silk reeling industry in Shanghai, China Economic and Statistical Research Institute*, Shanghai, 1933.

China Maritime Customs: Silk, 1st ed. 1881, 2nd ed. 1917 (*With a new chapter on Manchurian Tussore Silk by Norman Shaw*).

(二)杂志论文

吴孟炎:《振兴丝业为发展我国经济之要素》,《国际贸易导报》四卷二期,专论 1—58 页,民二一,七月。

侯厚培:《从统计上观察历年来之华丝贸易》,《国际贸易导报》一卷一号,撰著 1—20 页,民一九,四月。

缪锺秀:《上海丝厂业概况》,《国际贸易导报》一卷三号,撰著 1—20 页,民一九,六月。

缪锺秀:《发展中国蚕丝业计划》,《国际贸易导报》二卷十号,特载 1—3 页,民二〇,一〇。

景岳:《中国旧式丝厂的批评》,《钱业月报》十二卷,六,八,九期,业载栏,民二一年,六,八及九月。

陆国香:《上海市之电机织绸厂业》,《国际贸易导报》四卷四期,专论 7-37 页,民二二,九月。

沈九如:《从改良丝业谈到提倡合作制丝》,《国际贸易导报》二卷六期,撰著 1—8 页,民二〇,六月。

蒋逸霄译:《无锡丝厂女工的生活状况》,《国闻周报》七卷 49—50 期,民一九,一二,一五及二二。

《野蚕丝之产销及其贸易状况》,《工商半月刊》二卷20—21期,调查栏,民19,10月。

赵昇元:《辑里湖丝调查记》,《工商半月刊》四卷二三期,调查栏15—25,民21,12,1。

李安:《我国今日丝业问题之性质及其解决之方法》,《国际贸易导报》四卷一号1—16页,民二一,六月。

第十讲　中国之毛纺织业

一、毛纺织品之种类：毛线，呢绒，毛毯，地毯，驼绒，及针织品等。

二、毛纺织品之输入及输出

　　甲，输入

　　　　1. 种类——以毛线，哔叽，花薄呢，直贡呢等为大宗。

　　　　2. 来源——英，德，日本，（中国）香港，法国。

　　　　3. 输入港口——大连，天津，上海，汉口，广州，胶州，汕头。

　　乙，输出——以地毯为大宗。

　　　　1. 输出港口——天津，上海。

　　　　2. 输往国别——以输往美国者为最多。

三、毛纺织业之原料——羊毛

　　甲，种类——按剪期，剪法及产地之分类。

　　乙，产地——内外蒙古，新疆及陕甘，青海，冀鲁晋，东北等地。

　　丙，贸易

　　　　1. 羊毛之集散市场——天津，张家口，归化等。

　　　　2. 贸易之方法——例：包头之毛店。

　　　　3. 羊毛输出

　　　　　　a. 输出口岸——天津，胶州，大连，镇江，安东等。

　　　　　　b. 输往国别——美，英，日等。

丁，中国羊毛之缺点

1. 纤维粗短，缺乏弹性。
2. 掺杂死毛，秽沙太多，并故意使毛潮湿，以增重量。
3. 羊毛选择不精，优劣混杂，毫无标准。

戊，补救之方法

1. 改良羊种——晋省之成绩。
2. 对于出口羊毛施行检验。
3. 羊毛出口，自行办理，不假手外商。

四，毛纺织业

甲，历史

1. 土法毛纺织——毛织物，古谓之褐，周时已盛行。唐来自西域传织绒褐之方法，其后兰州独盛，以兰绒最著名，明清以来，陕西织羊绒为进贡之品。
2. 新式毛纺织。

    a. 1876 左宗棠创设甘肃兰州织呢总局。

    b. 1897 北京清河之溥利呢革公司成立（即今之陆军部织呢厂）。

    c. 1906 上海日辉织呢厂成立（即今之章华）。

    d. 1908 湖北毡呢厂成立于武昌。

    e. 1918 日人设满蒙织绒厂于沈阳。

    f. 欧战时起，毛纺织业勃兴，新厂叠起。

3. 毛纺织厂地理上之分布——天津，上海，北平，及其他（武汉，大同，兰州，沈阳，哈尔滨）
4. 组织——资本，设备，工人。
5. 制造手续——预备，纺毛，织毛，整理。

6. 出产——毛线,呢绒,毛毯,驼绒等。

7. 毛纺织业衰落之原因

    a. 官办企业,经营不当。

    b. 资本不足。

    c. 缺乏专门人材。

    d. 舶来品之压迫。

    e. 国产羊毛之品质不良。

8. 发展之方策——西北有发展之可能。

五、地毯工业

甲,历史——古谓之氍,细者谓之毹(覆小榻之上)毾(施大床之前),1860 北平报国寺之喇嘛传地毯织造法于平民。拳匪乱后,联军兵士载其劫得之地毯而归,我国之地毯始名闻于世,欧洲时勃兴。民一五后复行衰落。

乙,地理上之分布

    新疆——由腾越,司茅输出。

    河北——天津,北平。

    江苏——上海

    山东——济南

    西藏——拉萨

    甘肃——宁夏

    陕西——榆林

    山西——大同

    绥远——包头,归化。

丙,组织——多小规模工厂,原料及花样由洋行及出口商供给。

丁，制造手续——挂经，画经，打底，拴头，过纬，平活，剪花，下活。

戊，劳工——多为学徒制

己，出产

1. 分类之标准——重量，大小，形状，道数，毛高，花样，商业习惯。
2. 销售方法——打包，运输，及税捐。

庚，地毯工业衰落之原因——世界经济萧条，输出不振为最大原因。

参考书

（一）书籍

吴承洛：《今世中国实业通志》，下卷十四章，民一八。

龚俊：《中国新工业发展史大纲》，第八章第三节，民二二。

野中时雄：《支那羊毛》，资料第三十三编，南满洲铁道株式会社，昭和五。

方显廷：《天津地毯工业》，天津，民一九。

朱积权，鲍立德：《北京地毯业调查记》，民一三。

Report of the British Economic Mission to the Far East, 1930-31, London, Stationery Office, 1931, pp. 91-100.

Leith, Gordon B.: *Chinese rugs*, New York, 1929.

Hackmack, Adolf: *Chinese carpets and rugs*, Tientsin, 1924.

（二）杂志论文

唐文起：《中国羊毛之研究》，《农商公报》八卷93期选载9—18，民11，4，15。

允方:《吾国羊毛出产之概况及今后振兴改良方法》,《中东经济月刊》四卷七号,论著17—25,民17,7,15。

李锐才:《包头之羊毛》,《国货研究月刊》一卷一期,53—66,民21,6。

《晋省改良羊种经过情形》,《中外经济周刊》133号7—13,民14,10,10。

彭文和:《振兴吾国毛织工业刍议》,《社会杂志》二卷一二合期,1—10,民20,8,15。

黄叔培:《西北毛织工业初步计划》,《建设》第十一期,F—11,民20,4。

黄叔培:《热察外蒙毛织工业初步计划》,《建设》第十二期,D245—266,民20。

《上海之毛织工业》,《工商半月刊》三卷二十期,调查23—28,民20,10,15。

《北平清和制呢厂参观记》,《工商半月刊》四卷23期,国内经济3—4,民21,12,1。

《湖北毡呢厂之调查及恢复意见》,《工商半月刊》二卷21期,调查13—21,民19,1,1。

《满蒙毛织公司之整理》,《中东经济半月刊》三卷17—18号30—33,民21,10,1。

《东亚毛呢纺织工厂调查记》,《国货研究月刊》一卷二期。147—148,民21,7。

《章华毛绒纺织公司视察记》,《工商半月刊》三卷21期,调查71—73,民20,11,1。

"Methods of trading in China-wool", *Chinese Economic Monthly*,

Oct., 1924, pp. 13-18.

"The wool trade in Paotow", *Chinese Economic Journal*, January, 1938, pp. 33-43.

"Woolen and hosiery mills", *Chinese Economic Bulletin*, Dec. 26, 1925, pp. 262-264.

"Shanghai woolen textile factories", *Chinese Economic Journal*, Dec., 1932, pp. 436-450.

"The manufacture of woolen blankets in Harbin", *Chinese Economic Bulletin*, June 29, 1929, pp. 328-329.

"China's export of sheep and sheep products, 1867-1930", *Nankai Weekly Statistical Service*, Mar. 28, 1932.

"China's import of woolen goods, 1868-1930", *Nankai Weekly Statistical Service*, April 4, 1932.

第十一讲　中国之面粉业

一、历史

甲,土法磨麦——磨麦之具,始于周世公输般所作之碨。晋王戎发明水磨,制粉之器稍进,汉之汤官主饼饵,麦面之制渐盛,元巧工□氏造磨楼,制粉之法益精。

乙,新式粉厂——发展可分为三个时期

1. 1896—1911 草创时期
2. 1912—1921 勃兴时期
3. 1922—1931 衰落时期

丙,日商在东三省势力之锐进

二、地理上之分布——上海,无锡,汉口,济南,天津,长春,哈尔滨。

三、组织

1. 规模——公司组织,大规模,大资本。全国规模宏大之面粉公司有二:

    a. 满洲制粉会社,资本为日金 5,750,000 元。
    b. 荣氏之福新与茂新,计共有粉厂十四。

2. 分部——批发,总务,会计,物料,麦务,机器,运输,粉栈等部。

四、生产

甲,资金

1. 比较各粉厂之资本额。
2. 粉厂流动资金抬注之方法。

a. 将小麦或面粉向银行抵押借款。

　　　b. 信用透支。

乙，原料——小麦

　1. 小麦之种类

　　　a. 按颜色分：赤皮小麦，白色小麦。

　　　b. 按播种时期分：春麦，冬麦。

　　　c. 依麦粒之组成分：软麦，硬麦。

　2. 出产

　　　a. 中国麦产在世界上之地位——产量占第二位。

　　　b. 产麦省份

　　　　（1）春麦区：黑，吉，辽，热。

　　　　（2）冬麦区：晋，冀，鲁，苏，皖，豫，鄂，浙。

　3. 输入及输出——趋势，来源（澳洲及北美）

　4. 交易——粉厂收买小麦之方法

　　　a. 派人至乡间自行收买

　　　b. 向粮行购买

　　　c. 向交易所定购——上海杂粮油饼交易所

　5. 价格——时有变动，使其变动之因子

　　　a. 海外麦市

　　　b. 本国粉销

　　　c. 金价或汇兑

　　　d. 天时

　　　e. 政府设施——例：美麦运华，征收进出口税。

　　　f. 时局

　　　g. 投机

丙,劳工——用机器之处多,故所雇之工人少。
  1. 工人种类(按其职务分):下麦,值机,打包,粉栈,修理,杂务。
  2. 工作情形——工资,工时(日夜班)。
丁,制粉手续:清麦,湿润,去皮,磨粉。
戊,粉厂之可能产量与实有产量之比较——多以原料不足,未能充分发挥其可能产量。

五、面粉之交易
  甲,粉之种类——有顶上粉,本色粉,次粉,及元粉之别。
  乙,交易——粉厂推销面粉之方法。
    1. 粉厂自设批发处。
    2. 客帮——例:上海之南洋帮与北洋帮。
    3. 米店
    4. 交易所——上海机制面粉交易所。
  丙,输入及输出
    1. 输出——欧战期间国外输出最盛,年来则以输往国内各埠为大宗。
      a. 输出口岸:上海
      b. 输入口岸:北方如天津,秦皇岛,烟台,牛庄等处,南方如福州,厦门,汕头,广州等处。
    2. 输入——欧战期后国外输入年有增加。
      a. 输出国家:美,加,日,(中国)香港等处。
      b. 输往口岸:北方如天津,大连,牛庄等处,南方如广州,厦门,上海等处。

六、粉业之衰落与补救

甲，衰落之原因

1. 小麦
    a. 质——掺假，潮湿，含粉成份太少
    b. 量——国内产量不足，每亩产量较诸美国及澳洲皆有逊色。
2. 运输——运费过高，迟延时日，途中损耗。
3. 销售
    a. 洋粉倾销。
    b. 捐税奇重——例：统税及营业税。
4. 资金——缺乏流动资金。

乙，补救之方策

1. 小麦——设立麦种改良试验场，实行小麦检验，推广麦植。
2. 改善运输。
3. 销售——征收外麦外粉进口税及倾销税，减免统税及营业税。
4. 资金——流动资金之调剂。

参考书

(一) 书籍

龚俊：《中国新工业发展史大纲》第八章第五节，民二二。

《中国实业志》(江苏省)，国际贸易局，上海。民二二，331—360。

《小麦及面纷》，《商品调查丛刊》第七编，上海商业储蓄银行调查部，民二一。

《天津面粉业调查报告》，天津市社会局，民二一。

《天津面粉工业状况》(民国二十一年),天津,河北省立工业学院工业经济学会。

《满洲制粉业》(日文),满蒙文化协会,大正一三。

(二) 杂志论文

麦叔度:《河北省小麦之贩运》,《社会科学杂志》一卷一期,73—107,民19,3。

包伯度:《麦作实施计划大纲》,《社会月刊》二卷六号,1—20,民19,12。

张水淇:《中国之面粉业》,《人文月刊》二卷四号,1—9,民20,5。

顾鹤年:《中国面粉业概况》,《国际贸易导报》一卷五期,撰著1—16,民19,8。

威一:《农产落价声中哈尔滨及中东路沿线之面粉业》,《中东半月刊》一卷十一号,1—21,民19,7,16。

王子建:《天津面粉工人及工资的一个研究》,《社会科学杂志》二卷四期,445—472,民20,12。

Fong, H. D.: "Grain trade and milling in Tientsin", in *Chinese Social and Political Science Review*, October 1933, January 1934.

Li, Y. and Tayler, J. B.: "Grain marketing in Hopei Province", in *Chinese Social and Political Science Review*, April, 1933.

"Flour mills in China", in *Chinese Economic Journal*, June, 1928, pp. 533-542.

"Flour industry in Kiangsu", in *Chinese Economic Journal*, July, 1933, pp. 32-48.

Flour mills in Peking, in *Chinese Economic Journal*, January, 1927, pp. 97-100.

第十二讲　中国之榨油业

一、榨油之原料

甲,种类:亚麻子,落花生,棉花子,大豆,椰子,芝麻子等。

乙,生产:产量,主要产国。

丙,含油成分

1. 以世界之产量论:棉花子,落花生,大豆,椰子,亚麻子等。

2. 贸易

   a. 以世界之出口额论:椰子,亚麻子,落花生,大豆,棉子等。

   b. 1909—13 至 1923—27 世界出口额之增减情形。

二、大豆

甲,简史——二十世纪初叶,英人为抵制德人在南非采办棕实榨油计,乃采用大豆制油。1908 大连三井洋行运大豆至英,是为我国大豆出口之肇端,欧战时需油量增,大豆需要剧增,欧战后销路虽呈停滞之象,然德国失去其非洲产棕实之属地,乃改用我国之大豆制油。

乙,生产

1. 生产地带——中国本部,东三省,日本,朝鲜,(中国)台湾,美国,荷属及英属印度。

2. 东三省适植大豆之原因——气候适宜,土地膏腴,沃野千里。

丙，输出

    a. 以北满为最多。

    b. 多运往欧洲。

丁，大豆之用途——食料，饲料，肥田，榨油。

三、大豆榨油

  甲，历史——油坊首在长春及铁岭成立。中日战争后，豆饼始输日。大连之有油坊，始于1906之双和栈。1908因满铁采取特别运费制，油坊勃兴。欧战时因国外需要剧增，油坊之成立者更多，近年以来，则复呈衰落之象矣。

  乙，油坊之分布——大连，安东，牛庄，哈尔滨等处。

  丙，榨油

    1. 榨抽之手续——碎豆，蒸豆，装豆，榨油。

    2. 榨油之方法

      a. 机械的——楔子式，螺旋式，及水压式三种（水压式所出豆饼之形状有圆形及板形二种）。

      b. 化学的——掺合偏苏油（Benzine）及火酒提炼。

      c. 试比较各法榨油之优劣——化学法之优点，在出油多，豆饼含水少，且产碎饼。

  丁，出产——有季节性，实有产量与可能产量之比较（以昼夜计）。

  戊，交易

    1. 方法——买卖成交，在交易所内或交易所外，豆油输出，多假手外人，而以日人经营此业者为尤多。

    2. 输出

a. 输出趋势——日见衰败。

b. 输出口岸

（1）豆油——大连,哈尔滨,牛庄,安东。

（2）豆饼——大连,哈尔滨,安东,牛庄。

c. 输往地带

（1）豆油——国内:上海,国外:荷,英,俄。

（2）豆饼——国内:汕头,厦门,上海,广州,福州。

国外:日本,台湾,俄国,朝鲜,美国。

己,衰落原因

1. 日人改用自制之肥田粉(Ammonia Sulphate),故豆饼之输出大减。

2. 化学抽油法之发明。

3. 关税政策之错误。

4. 欧战停后,各国豆油豆饼之需求减少。

庚,救济方策

1. 直接出口。

2. 保护关税。

3. 实施大豆检验。

4. 组织油业银行。

5. 利用化学抽油法。

参考书

（一）书籍

谢特尼次基(Setnitzsky):《世界市场之黄豆》,中东铁路经济调查局,民一九。

《大豆之加工》,南满洲铁道会社农务课,大正一三(日文)。

佐田弘治郎:《昭和四年满洲油坊现势》,大连,1930。

《历年输出各国豆类统计表》,民元至一七,工商部,民一八。

The soya bean of Manchuria, Shanghai, China Maritime Customs, 1911.

Soya beans in Manchuria, Agricultural Office, South Manchuria Railway Co., Dairen, 1926.

Horvath, A. A.: *The soybean oil of China and its manifold uses*, Booklet Series No. 13, Bureau of Industrial and Commercial Information, Shanghai.

(二) 杂志论文

《东省大豆实况》,《工商半月刊》二十三及二十四期合刊,调查33—56,民20,12,15。

罗锦澄:《中国豆类事业之过去与将来》,《社会杂志》一卷六期,1—21,民20,6,15。

《大豆销路危机对于东三省农民经济与变化》,《中东经济月刊》六卷11号,论著7—15,民19,11,15,12号33—40,民19,12,15。

《东省豆坊之现势》,《中东经济月刊》六卷11号,专载35—40,民19,11,15,12号41—50,民19,12,15。

《大连之油坊业》,《中外经济周刊》134号,6—19,民14,10,17。

《最近三年大连各油坊之制饼情形及其消长原因》,《中东经济月刊》八卷五号7—19,民21,5,15。

《最近数年大连油坊之制饼情形及去年特别减少之原因》,《中东经济月刊》七卷七期23—32,民20,7,15。

《大豆落价声中中东路沿线之油坊业》,《中东半月刊》一卷九号1—10,民19,11,16。

《最近五年间哈尔滨之油坊业》,《中东半月刊》二卷八号20—22,民20,5,1。

《一九三一年中东铁路哈尔滨油坊之工作概况》,《中东半月刊》三卷七号10—12,民21,4,16。

《论东省油业之救济策》,《东三省官银行经济月刊》一卷二期1—8,民18,6,15。

Tsao, Lien-En: "Soya beans and bean oil industry in Manchuria", in *Chinese Economic Journal*, Sep. 1930, pp. 793-805.

Tsao, Lien-En: "The marketing of soya bean and bean oil", *Chinese Economic Journal*, Sep. 1930, pp. 941-971.

第十三讲　中国之卷烟业

一、简述

甲，烟叶——烟叶为美洲之产物，1492 Columbus 发现美洲后其部下将烟叶带至西班牙。1560 驻西法使，Jean Nicot 传之于法，1565 Sir John Hawkins 传之于英，西班牙商舰传之于吕宋（Philippines），再由吕宋传至中国及日本。

乙，土烟业——水烟，旱烟二种。

丙，卷烟业——1902 英美烟公司及北洋烟公司成立，是为我国卷烟业之创始，1906 南洋公司亦在香港成立，1925 五卅事件引起抵制英货运动，华商卷烟公司因而勃兴。

二、地理上之分布——卷烟公司多集中于舶来烟叶输入口岸如上海，汉口，天津，青岛，大连等。

三、组织

甲，上海卷烟公司之种类

　　1. 代卷烟厂——代人制造，不以自己之商标销售。

　　2. 烟业商号——仅有商标托人代卷。

　　3. 自设烟厂制造本牌卷烟者。

乙，重要卷烟公司

　　1. 华商——南洋，华成等。

　　2. 外商——英美烟公司等。

四、出产

甲，原料

1. 种类——烟叶，烟纸，蜡纸，纸板，画片，锡纸，香料等。

2. 烟叶

　　a. 我国烟叶产额在世界上之地位——美国，印度，中国，俄国等。

　　b. 产烟叶之省份——四川，湖北，云南，山东，浙江，河南，湖南，广东等。

3. 烟叶输入

　　a. 近年来输入量，叶多于烟。

　　b. 来源——十之九取给美国。

　　c. 到达口岸：上海，汉口，天津，青岛，大连。

4. 采购之方法——进口烟叶多向洋行采购，国产烟叶则多就产地设办事处向农民直接采办。

乙，资本——额定资本与实交资本之比较。华商公司与外商公司资本之比较。

丙，劳工

1. 制造方法——烤叶，还潮，拣叶，拆骨，加香，切叶，焙叶，卷烟，烘烟，包烟，入盒，装箱。

2. 种类——长工占四分之一，散工件工占四分之三。

3. 工作情形——工资，工时。

丁，机器

1. 种类

2. 来源——美，德，本国自造者。

五、交易

　　甲，卷烟种类——统税旧为七级制,后因原料成本受汇兑影响而抬高,故始改为三级制,再改为二级制,卷烟之商标繁多。

　　乙,销售地带——江苏,浙江,广东、湖北等。

　　丙,输出

　　　　1．趋势——五卅后增加颇速,民一七起则年有减少。

　　　　2．输出口岸——以上海为最重要。

　　　　3．输往国家——新嘉坡等处,日本,香港等。

　　丁,税捐

　　　　1．沿革

　　　　2．近况

六、卷烟业失败之原因。

　　甲,资本不足。

　　乙,原料缺乏,仰仗舶来品。

　　丙,外商烟厂之竞争。

　　丁,舶来品之竞销。

　　戊,内战勒捐等影响。

参考书

（一）书籍

Thomas, James A.: *A pioneer tobacco merchant in the Orient*, Duke Univ. Press, Durham, North Carolina, 1928.

Thomas, James A.: *Trailing trade a million miles*, Durbam, 1931.

《中国实业通志》(江苏省),国际贸易局,民二二,411—39页。

《烟酒税史》,整理烟酒税务委员会编,财政部烟酒税处,民一八。

(二)杂志论文

《东三省烟草事业》,《中东半月刊》一卷十一号,27—34页,民19—12,16。

《满洲烟草之产销及其输出入概况》,《中东半月刊》三卷十二号,18,26页,民21,7,1。

《山东之烟叶》,《中外经济周刊》第九十七号,1—7页,民14,1,31。

《湖北省之烟草》,《中外经济周刊》一百十号,1—9页,民14,5,2。

《浙江烟叶调查》,《工商半月刊》一卷十五期,调查10—16页,民8,8,1。

《广东之土产烟叶》,《中外经济周刊》一百八十八号,1—12页,民15,11,13。

《上海华商卷烟工业现状》,《工商半月刊》五卷一期,调查79—97页,民22,1,1。

刘风五:《中国烟草业的危机及其将来的发展》,《社会杂志》二卷四期,1—22页,民20,10,15。

《英美烟公司在华事绩纪略》,《东省经济月刊》五卷十二号专载,41—55页,民18,12,15。

《南洋兄弟烟草公司调查录》,《工商半月刊》一卷一期,调查14—28页,民18,1,1。

《南洋兄弟烟草公司停业之原因》,《工商半月刊》二卷八期,调查43—47页,民19,4,15。

江问渔:《中国对外贸易中之烟类》,《人文月刊》二卷二号,1—18 页,民 20,3。

"Tobacco cultivation and industry in Manchuria", *China Weekly Review*, July 18, 1931, pp. 251-259.

"Tobacco cultivation and trade in Chekiang", *Chinese Economic Bulletin*, March 19, 1927 (Bibliography on tobacco at end of article,) pp. 145-147.

"Tobacco growing in Shantung", *Chinese Economic Journal*, Jan. 1932, pp. 37-44.

"Cigarettes in China", *Chinese Economic Bulletin*, Jan, 24, 1925, pp. 43-45 (On methods of distribution)

"Cigar manufacture in Shanghai", *Chinese Economic Journal*, June, 1933, pp. 626-634.

第十四讲　中国之精盐业

一、粗盐

　　甲，历史——神农时夙沙氏煮海为盐，是为我国制盐之始；唐虞南风之歌，咏及解池，是为池盐之起源。周秦之际，李冰凿井，井盐以兴。历代盐政，亦时有变迁，三代有盐贡，无盐禁。周代太宰，掌山泽之赋。春秋管子监盐铁之利，而国大富。秦商鞅主政，盐铁并税。汉桑弘羊置盐官。唐刘晏试行就场征税，宋代盐法大备，元行盐销法。明有引额，有销岸，举措不当，因以病民，清代多袭明制，然厘定盐法，国家总盐政，商买盐于灶，官取税于商，配销各有定地。民国初元，财部设司征税。民二善后借款，以盐税作担负，雇用洋员，盐税遂为外人所支配。新盐法主就场征税，自由贸易，然迄未见诸实行也。

　　乙，种类——海盐，井盐，池盐，石盐。

　　丙，制盐之法——晒与煎

　　丁，产盐区及产额——两淮，四川，山东，长芦，东三省，江浙，两广等。

　　戊，输出——民元以来输出增加十倍，多由胶州大连等处，输往日本及朝鲜。

　　己，税捐——历年来税率之变更，盐税在岁入所占之地位。

二、精盐

甲,历史——外侨以土盐不合卫生,输入精盐,政府为抵制洋盐计,乃颁布条例,提倡制炼精盐。久大公司于民国三年成立,继起者甚多,以引岸关系,与旧盐商时起争讼。日人在大连安东亦设有精盐公司。

乙,地理上之分布——辽宁(大连,牛庄,安东,复县),河北(塘沽,丰润),山东(烟台,青岛),江苏(上海),浙江(定海,余姚)。

丙,精盐公司之组织

1. 以久大为例:总公司(营业部,会计部),工厂(制造部,管理部,人事部),黄海工业化学研究社。
2. 全国精盐总会(南京)。
3. 精盐公司请求立案之必要条件。

丁,生产

1. 制造之方法
    a. 锅熬法,洗涤法,真空管制法。
    b. 锅熬法之程序——去泥沙,打卤,煎盐,冷却,烘干,包装。
    c. 精盐之制耗
2. 劳工——种类,职务,工资,工时。
3. 产量——可能产量与实有产量之比较。

三、交易

甲,精盐之种类——粉盐,粒盐,砖盐,洗涤盐。

乙,运销地带——通商口岸等。

丙,税捐——税率之高低,随销售地而异。

丁,输出

1. 历年来输出额之增加。

　　　2. 输出口岸：大连，牛庄，天津，烟台，胶州，上海。

　　　3. 输往国家：日本，期鲜。

　四、精盐业之将来

　　甲，粗盐与精盐之产量比较

　　乙，精盐之利益

　　　1. 为国家——有税捐收入之益，无私盐充斥之弊。

　　　2. 为人民——有益康健，减轻负担。

参考书

（一）书籍

贾士毅：《民国续财政史》上册，第二编，169—257，民一八。

《民国十八年盐务年刊》，财政部盐务署，民一九。

林颂和：《塘沽工人调查》，北平社会调查所，民一九。

《天津工商业》卷上，第四章第一节，天津特别市社会局，民一九。

《中国矿业纪要》

　　第二次（民七至一四），民一五，279—308。

　　第三次（民一四至一七），民一八，346—52。

　　第四次（民一八至二〇），民二一，180—188。

（二）杂志论文

徐乾一：《中国之盐产》，《时事月报》八卷二期，九卷二期及三期，民22，2，8及9月。

赵叔雍：《中国盐务之鸟瞰》，《申报月刊》一卷三期及四期，民22，9及10月。

《我国精盐事业概况》，《工商半月刊》五卷四期撰述 1—15，民 22，2，5。

徐尚：《西南制盐工业初步计划》，《建设》十三号 363—369，民 21，1。

Gale, E. M.: "Public administration of salt in China—a historical survey", in *Annals of American Academy of Political and Social Science* 152: 241-251, November, 1930.

第十五讲　中国之造纸业

一、纸之历史

甲，中国——古者书契，韦编竹简，自秦以后，乃用缣帛，后汉蔡伦（102 A. D.）以简重缣贵，不便于人，乃以树皮麻头，蔽布渔网造纸，名曰网纸，是为世界发明以纤维造纸第一人。魏晋之间，竹帛废而纸大行。自晋以来，纸有南北之分。唐宋以前蜀纸名满天下，自宋以降，江浙之纸业日盛。明清以来，闽，赣，川，浙，湘，鄂，粤，皆为产纸名区。

乙，西洋——我国造纸之法，751年传于阿剌伯，十二世纪，欧亚通商，纸先到希腊。造纸之术由阿剌伯传于埃及，由埃及传于摩洛哥，十二世纪中叶，由摩洛哥侵入西班牙，携造纸之术以俱来。然后由西班牙传之于法德诸国，意大利习得造纸之术，系起于阿剌伯人侵入西西里之时。英国造纸则始于十四世纪之初。

二、手工造纸

甲，简史——自后汉蔡伦发明造纸时起，至今日迄未停止。

乙，原料：

1. 北方：棉，麻，秋，秸，等。
2. 南方：竹，稻，草，桑，楮皮，破布等。

丙，种类——按原料分：竹纸，皮纸，藁纸，其他。

丁，产区——赣，浙，闽，川，为最发达；湘，粤，皖，次之；以鲁,甘,桂,为最少。

戊,造纸之方法

1. 做料——依原料不同而各异,大致为选择,蒸煮,洗净,漂白,用臼捣乱成纸料,加黏液配合。
2. 造纸——大致为漉抄,压榨,烘焙,切磨。

己,产量及输出量

庚,衰败之原因

1. 拘守旧法,不求改进。
2. 运输不便,原料之需供不济,且燃料运费太高。
3. 赋税过重。
4. 品逊价贵,销路减少。
5. 舶来品之竞争。

三、机器造纸

甲,简史

光绪十三年大成机器造纸公司设于香港。

光绪十七年李鸿章创纶章造纸厂于上海(此厂民七改为宝源西厂,复改天章造纸西厂)。

光绪二十四年中外合资华章造纸厂设于上海,浦东。

光绪三十一年重庆,商川纸厂,成立(专制火柴盒用纸)。

光绪三十二年龙章造纸厂设于龙华。

仝年滦源纸厂成立,复改成业,又改华兴。广东官纸局亦于是时成立。

宣统二年,张之洞创白沙洲造纸厂于湖北;财政部之造纸厂亦设于是焉。

民国元年至八年商办纸厂营业不振。

民国九年华盛纸板公司成立。

民国十年杭州武林造纸公司成立。

民国十三年上海有意成,天章二厂成立。

民国十四年江南纸厂成立于上海。

民国十八年福建造纸厂成立于福州。

乙,地理上之分布

江苏(上海,苏州,无锡,镇江),浙江(嘉兴,杭州),湖北(武汉),江西,四川(成都,重庆),河北(天津,北平),山东(济南),山西(太原),广东,东三省(安东,吉林),福建。

丙,组织

1. 分军营制(例:华丰纸厂)及分部制(例:江南纸厂)。
2. 各地有纸业公会。

丁,生产

1. 原料——稻草,芦苇,破布,纸脚,木浆(舶来品)等。
2. 制造方法

    a. 做料——依原料不同而异。大致为除尘,选别,蒸煮,洗濯,离解,漂白,配合等。

    b. 造纸,大致为抄纸,排水,烘干,榨压。

    c. 整理——轧光,切纸,包装。

3. 劳工——种类,职务,工资,工时。
4. 产量。

四、贸易

甲,纸之种类

乙,纸商之种类——槽户,纸厂,纸商,纸行,纸栈,纸铺等。
　　丙,运销地带——多销国内。
　　丁,洋纸之输入
　　　　1. 输入之种类——约五十余种。
　　　　2. 输入之趋势——与年俱增。
　　戊,捐税
五、我国机器制纸业衰败之原因,及今后振兴之方策
　　甲,衰败之原因
　　　　1. 资本不足。
　　　　2. 管理不善。
　　　　3. 成本太高——原因：
　　　　　　a. 原料不足——木浆须自外洋运来。
　　　　　　b. 运输不便,运费太高。
　　　　　　c. 化学药品缺少。
　　　　4. 水利不给。
　　　　　　a. 水力缺乏。
　　　　　　b. 水质不良。
　　　　5. 时局影响。
　　　　6. 捐税太重。
　　乙,振兴之方策
　　　　1. 增加造纸原料,并谋改进。
　　　　2. 利用水利制纸。
　　　　3. 培养人材,改进技术及组织。
　　　　4. 筹备设厂须规划周详。
六、造纸工业之辅助机关

甲,浙江工学院制纸实验部

乙,浙江省立改良手工造纸传习所

参考书:

(一)书籍

《浙江之纸业》,浙江省政府设计会,民一九。

许衍灼:《中国工业史略》,上海新学会社,民一二。

(二)杂志论文

周珌:《中国造纸工业概况》,《工商半月刊》四卷16—22期,民二一。

《中国之纸业》,《上海总商会月报》四卷四期,民一三。

《中国制纸法》,《农商公报》第六十五期,民八。

《全国纸业调查记》,《农商公报》第118,119,121期,民一三。

《我国市场上元洋纸》,《工商半月刊》一卷十二期,民十八。

《中国纸之需给状况》,《中东经济月刊》七卷五期,民二〇。

《上海机器制纸业之调查》,《经济半月刊》,第二卷第十一期,民一七。

《一九三一年之上海造纸工业》,《国际贸易导报》三卷一期,民二一。

《上海之纸业》,《社会月刊》二卷十号及十一号,上海市社会局,民20。

《上海之纸业》,《工商半月刊》三卷十期及十一期,民二〇。

《中日两国在鸭绿江下游制纸事业之概况》,《中东半月刊》一卷七期,民一九。

《鸭绿江造纸会社概况》,《中东经济月刊》四卷四期,民一七。

《福建造纸厂参观记》,《工商半月刊》,五卷十三期,民二二。

"Paper Manufacture in China", *Chinese Economic Monthly*, Vol. II, No. 4, 1925.

"Importance of Paper Industry", *Chinese Economic Journal*, Vol. IV, No. 5, 1929.

"Paper Manufacture in Shanghai", *Chinese Economic Journal*, Vol. II, No. 6, 1928.

第十六讲　中国之水泥工业

一、概论
　　甲,水泥之各种名称及种类——种类有天然,Portland 及火山灰 Puzzolanea 等,以 Portland 为最重要。
　　乙,水泥之用途
　　丙,水泥之优点
　　丁,水泥之发明简史
二、中国水泥工业之沿革
　　光绪二年开平矿务局就煤田附近创办水泥厂,是为我国水泥工业之发轫,光绪三十三年让归启新公司接办。
　　光绪十二年,英商青洲公司成立于香港。
　　光绪三十三年,官办士敏土工厂设于广州。
　　光绪三十四年,日商小野田水泥会社设立支社于大连。
　　宣统二年,湖北大冶水泥厂成立,后改名华记湖北水泥公司。
　　民国六年日人占青岛,设山东洋灰公司于青岛之沧口。
　　民国七年,刘鸿生设上海华商水泥公司于龙华。
　　民国十一年,中国水泥公司成立于龙潭。
　　民国十八年,广东西村士敏土厂成立。
三、华洋水泥厂之概况
　　甲,华商水泥厂:

1. 启新洋灰公司(唐山)
2. 致敬水泥公司(济南)
3. 华记湖北水泥公司(大冶)
4. 中国水泥公司(南京龙潭)
5. 上海华商水泥公司(龙华)
6. 广州士敏土厂(广州)
7. 西村士敏土厂(广州)
8. 其他

乙,洋商水泥公司:

1. 英商青洲水泥公司(澳门九龙)
2. 日商小野田支社(大连)
3. 日商满洲水泥会社(大连)
4. 日商山东兴业水泥公司(青岛)
5. 其他

四、水泥厂之组织

甲,内部之组织——以上海水泥公司为例。

乙,华商水泥公会:

1. 会员:启新,华记,上海等。
2. 宗旨:避免互相倾轧,厘定价格,推广销路。
3. 事业:研究,规定出品标准。

五、生产

甲,原料

1. 种类:石灰石,粘土,及石膏。
2. 产地:

   a. 石灰石——各省皆有。以辽,吉,冀,豫,鄂,晋,苏,浙,粤,湘为最富。

    b. 粘土——到处皆有。

    c. 石膏——鄂(应城),湘(湘潭),晋(平陆,介休,大同),苏(萧县),皖(贵池,休宁),粤(钦县)。

乙,水泥制造之方法

  1. 干制

  2. 湿制

丙,包装之种类

丁,产量之估计

六、贸易

甲,水泥交易之方法

乙,输入及输出之数量价值与趋势

丙,消费量之估计

丁,水泥统税

七、水泥工业不克发展之原因及挽救之方策

甲,不克发展之原因

  1. 规模小。

  2. 运销不当。

  3. 原料及燃料之供给问题。

  4. 外厂与外货之竞争。

  5. 事局影响。

乙,挽救之方法

  1. 提倡国产水泥。

  2. 加征外货倾销税。

  3. 扩充已有之厂,并添造新厂。

4. 开发国内之石膏矿。

5. 谋运输便利并减轻运费。

6. 设法减低成本。

参考书

(一) 书籍

《中国矿业纪要》,第二次,第三次,第四次,地质调查所,北平。

(二) 杂志论文

《中国水泥工业》,《工商半月刊》,三卷十七期,民二〇。

《我国之水泥工业》,《浙江建设月刊》,七卷一期,民二二。

《中国士敏土之需给状况》,《农商公报》,第一一四期,民一二。

《中国之水泥制造业》,《中外经济周刊》第82期,民一三。

《广州士敏土之销路》,《工商半月刊》,五卷八期,民二二。

《上海华商水泥厂》,《国际贸易导报》,四卷七期,民二一。

《启新洋灰公司》,《上海总商会月报》,二卷八期,民一八。

《参观上海龙华水泥厂报告》,《建设》,三期,民十八。

《东三省洋灰之供给与需求》,《中东经济月刊》,七卷二期,及四五期合刊,民二〇。

"Cement Industry in China", *Chinese Economic Journal*, Vol. X, No. 1, 1932.

"Cement Manufacture in China", *Chinese Economic Monthly*, Vol. II, No. 5, 1925.

"Growing popularity of Chinese cement in North Manchuria",

Chinese Economic Bulletin, Vol. XVII, No. 26, 1930.

"Cement Factory in Tayeh, Hupeh", *Chinese Economic Bulletin*, No. 248, 1925.

"Cement Industry of Lungtan", *Chinese Economic Bulletin*, Vol. XXII, No. 9, 1933.

第十七讲　中国之火柴工业

一、简史

甲，我国古时取火之法

燧人氏钻木取火。

周时以矢遂取火于日,实为火镜之滥觞。

后人发明镰石取火,取火之法尤便。

五季北宋之交,始有发烛之制,其法削木为片,其薄如纸,镕硫黄涂木片顶少许,遇火即燃,名曰发烛,又曰火寸。

乙，我国火柴工业之沿革

清同光年间即有火柴输入,然历史无可稽考,光绪二十二年始有日本火柴输入。

光绪十五年四川重庆聚昌火柴公司成立,此实为我国火柴工业之嚆矢,继起者有汉口之燮昌,长沙之和丰,及上海之燮昌。

民国四年,国人抵制日货,乃纷起设厂,以致供过于求销路停滞,乃跌价竞争,赔累过巨。复加瑞典火柴跌价倾销,致使我国之火柴工业,危机环生,日趋衰落。

二、地理上之分布

甲，分散各地之原因

1. 交通不便运费过钜。
2. 黄燐火柴,性易燃烧,远地运输,实有自焚之危险。

乙,华商火柴厂(1929)

东三省23,冀14,甘3,浙6,陕3,豫11,皖5,川13,鲁23,晋9,苏18,两广41,闽3,两湘6,滇7,共计185。

丙,日商火柴厂(大部分股票已入瑞典人之手)多在长春,大连,沈阳,天津,青岛等处。

丁,瑞典商收买上海日商燧昌火柴公司

三、组织

甲,例:大中华火柴股份有限公司

1. 事务所(即营业部)——分文牍,会计,采办,营业,总务五科。
2. 工厂(制造部)——分齐梗,排板,上油,上药,装盒,调燐,配药,杂药,白药,烘房,拆板,堆盘,装盒,刷燐,纸包,篾篓,盒清,招贴,栈房十八部。

乙,同业联合会之组织

1. 各地:江苏省,东三省等。
2. 全国:中华全国火柴同业联合会。

丙,制梗厂概况:

江苏(上海),浙江(富阳,诸暨,杭州,丽水),辽宁(安东,营口),山东(烟台)。

四、生产

甲,火柴名称:洋火,火柴,日人称之为燐寸。

乙,种类

1. 危险火柴——黄燐火柴,硫黄火柴,硫化燐火柴。
2. 安全火柴——赤燐火柴,一名瑞典火柴。

丙,原料

1. 木材——制梗盒用
2. 药品——计十余种

丁,劳工

1. 工资——分计件,计时二种,工资低微。
2. 工作情形
    a. 无导烟通气设施,致使厂内燐气弥漫,工人多中燐毒。
    b. 无洗濯设备,乏工人饭厅,工人两手涂燐,就餐于工作之所,中毒尤易。
3. 政府之救济方策——民十二年北京政府农商部通令于民国十四年一月起,禁用黄燐制造火柴。

戊,制造之方法

1. 梗子制造——剥,锯,蒸,刨,切,烘,扎。
2. 盒子制造——将已切好之木片交工人制成盒底,盒套。然后糊贴商标招纸,刷燐于盒壳之两边。
3. 火柴制造——排梗,齐梗,排板,上油,上药,烘干,拆板,装盒,打包,装销。

己,我国火柴之产量

五、贸易

甲,交易之方法——设分销处,或以佣金托商号代销。

乙,火柴输出入——输入方面,瑞典火柴起而夺日本火柴之地位;输出方面,多去南洋群岛一带。

丙,制造火柴原料之输入

戊,火柴之销费额

己,火柴之税捐

1. 关税
2. 统税

六、火柴业衰落原因及挽救方策

甲，衰落原因

1. 供过于求——厂多，产剩。
2. 同业竞争——互相倾轧，暗中跌价竞销。
3. 成本提高——工资加高，金价暴涨，税捐太重。
4. 外商侵略
5. 工潮迭起

乙，外商之侵略

1. 外商侵入时期之分析

   a. 光绪二十二年前欧洲火柴专利时期。

   b. 光绪二十二年至民国七年，日货畅销时期。

   c. 民国十六年后，瑞典火柴侵入时期。

丙，瑞典火柴之侵入

a. 瑞典火柴托辣斯之组织及势力。

b. 侵略之方法

利诱——以高价收买火柴公司股票。

威迫——跌价倾销。

丁，挽救方策

1. 合并已有工厂增厚势力。
2. 组织联合贩卖机关，取消无谓之竞争。
3. 谋管理，组织，及技术上之改良。
4. 提高火柴进口税，减免，原料进口税，施行倾销税。
5. 实行火柴专卖——《东北火柴专卖条例》。

参考书

（一）书籍

《火柴业调查报告》,天津市社会局,民二〇。

许衍灼:《中国工业史略》,新学会社,民一二。

（二）杂志论文

《中国之火柴工业》,《工商半月刊》,三卷十九期,民二〇,十,一。

《瑞典火柴托辣斯与我国之火柴工业》,《国际贸易导报》二卷三期,民二〇,三。

《中国火柴业之危机及其救济策》,《社会月刊》一卷九期,上海市社会局,民一八。

《上海之火柴业》,《社会月刊》二卷八及九期,上海社会局,民二〇。

《天津火柴工厂之调查》,《工商半月刊》一卷九期,民一八。

《山东全省火柴事业调查》,《工商半月刊》三卷三期,民二〇。

《浙江之火柴业》,《工商半月刊》一期二十二期,民一八。

"Match Industry in China", *Chinese Economic Journal*, Vol. X, No. 3, 1932.

"Match Making Industry", *Chinese Economic Journal*, Vol. IV, No. 4, 1929.

"Shanghai Match Industry", *Chinese Economic Journal*, Vol. III, No. 3, 1928.

图书在版编目(CIP)数据

方显廷文集. 第4卷/方显廷著. —北京：商务印书馆，2015
 ISBN 978-7-100-11658-9

Ⅰ.①方… Ⅱ.①方… Ⅲ.①方显廷—文集 ②工业发展—中国—近代—文集 Ⅳ.①C53 ②F429.05-53

中国版本图书馆 CIP 数据核字(2015)第 245745 号

所有权利保留。
未经许可，不得以任何方式使用。

方 显 廷 文 集
第 4 卷
方显廷 著

商 务 印 书 馆 出 版
(北京王府井大街36号 邮政编码 100710)
商 务 印 书 馆 发 行
北 京 冠 中 印 刷 厂 印 刷
ISBN 978-7-100-11658-9

2015 年 12 月第 1 版　　开本 880×1230　1/32
2015 年 12 月北京第 1 次印刷　　印张 20¼　插页 9
定价：65.00 元